Minority Ethnic Mobilization in the Russian Federation

This book seeks to explain how state institutions affect ethnic mobilization. It focuses on how ethno-nationalist movements emerge on the political scene, develop organizational structures, frame demands, and attract followers. It does so in the context of examining the widespread surge in nationalist sentiment that occurred throughout the Soviet Union and Eastern Europe during the late 1980s and early 1990s. It shows that even during this period of institutional upheaval, preexisting ethnic institutions affected the tactics of movement leaders.

This book challenges the widely held perception that governing elites can kindle latent ethnic grievances virtually at will in order to maintain power. It argues that nationalist leaders cannot always mobilize widespread popular support and that their success in doing so depends in turn on the extent to which ethnicity is institutionalized by state structures. It also shifts the study of ethnic mobilization from the *whys* of its emergence to the *hows* of its development as a political force.

Dmitry P. Gorenburg is a research analyst and Director of Russian and East European Studies at the Center for Strategic Studies of the CNA Corporation. He has published several articles on minority nationalism in the Russian Federation that have appeared in journals such as *World Politics*, *Ethnic and Racial Studies*, and *Europe-Asia Studies*. He has conducted extensive field research and is a native speaker of Russian.

Minority Ethnic Mobilization in the Russian Federation

DMITRY P. GORENBURG
Center for Strategic Studies,
CNA Corporation

CAMBRIDGE
UNIVERSITY PRESS

University Printing House, Cambridge CB2 8BS, United Kingdom

Cambridge University Press is part of the University of Cambridge.

It furthers the University's mission by disseminating knowledge in the pursuit of education, learning and research at the highest international levels of excellence.

www.cambridge.org
Information on this title: www.cambridge.org/9780521818070

© Dmitry P. Gorenburg 2003

This publication is in copyright. Subject to statutory exception and to the provisions of relevant collective licensing agreements, no reproduction of any part may take place without the written permission of Cambridge University Press.

First published 2003

A catalogue record for this publication is available from the British Library

Library of Congress Cataloguing in Publication data

Gorenburg, Dmitry P., 1970–
Minority ethnic mobilization in the Russian Federation / Dmitry P. Gorenburg.
 p. cm.
Description of the national movements in Tatarstan, Chuvashia, Bashkortostan and Khakassia during the 1980s and 1990s.
Includes bibliographical references and index.
ISBN 0-521-81807-9
1. Nationalism – Russia (Federation) – Case studies. 2. Nationalism – Soviet Union – Case studies. 3. Minorities – Government policy – Russia (Federation). 4. Minorities – Government policy – Soviet Union. 5. Russia (Federation) – History – Autonomy and independence movements – Case studies. 6. Soviet Union – History – Autonomy and independence movements – Case studies. I. Title.
DK 510.33 .G67 2003
320.54'0947'09049 – dc21   2002031584

ISBN 978-0-521-81807-0 Hardback
ISBN 978-0-521-03239-1 Paperback

Cambridge University Press has no responsibility for the persistence or accuracy of URLs for external or third-party internet websites referred to in this publication, and does not guarantee that any content on such websites is, or will remain, accurate or appropriate.

For Ida and Jacob

Contents

List of Figures and Tables		*page* viii
Preface		xi
1	Minority Ethnic Mobilization in Russia: An Introduction	1
2	Explaining Ethnic Mobilization: The Role of Ethnic Institutions	27
3	From Cultural Society to Popular Front: The Formation and Development of Nationalist Organizations	49
4	The Soviet Institutional Legacy and Ethno-Nationalist Ideology	77
5	Institutions Matter: Measuring Support for Nationalism	118
6	Intragroup Variation in Support for Nationalism: Not All Ethnics Are the Same	167
7	Outcomes: Did Regional Governments Adopt the Nationalist Agenda?	200
8	The Larger Picture: Support for Nationalism in Russia's Other Republics	234
9	Institutions and Nationalism	257
Appendix: Construction of Variables and Indices		272
References		279
Index		293

Figures and Tables

FIGURES

1.1	Selected regions of the Russian Federation	page 21
2.1	Structure of the Soviet federation	31
3.1	Political context and movement structure	69
5.1	Nationalist protest in Tatarstan	123
5.2	Nationalist protest in Bashkortostan	129
5.3	Support for Tatar separatism	149
5.4	Support for state language in Bashkortostan	153

TABLES

1.1	Characteristics of the four republics in 1989	23
2.1	Extent of native-language education, by ethnicity	40
2.2	Extent of scientific research, by region	42
2.3	Effects of administrative status and regional demographics on the publication of native-language newspapers	43
2.4	Cultural institutions, by region	45
2.5	Ethnic representation in regional government and industrial administration	47
5.1	Support for Tatar nationalist organizations among Tatars expressing a political preference	151
5.2	Sense of belonging to ethnic region	159
5.3	Awareness of nationalist activity	159
5.4	Should the titular language be the sole official language in ethnic republics?	161
5.5	Should all inhabitants of an ethnic republic know the titular language of that republic?	161

Figures and Tables

5.6	Should titular-language study be compulsory in all schools in ethnic republics?	162
5.7	How do you feel about the declarations of sovereignty by the former autonomous republics of the Russian Federation?	162
5.8	Should all republics have the right of self-determination, including the right of withdrawal from the Russian Federation?	164
5.9	Should control of the army, police, and security forces be transferred to the jurisdiction of the sovereign republics of the Russian Federation?	164
6.1	Factor matrix for indexes of support for nationalism: Colton/Hough survey	176
6.2	Factor matrix for indexes of support for nationalism: Laitin/Hough survey	177
6.3	Mean values of ethnic mobilization indexes	178
6.4	Ethnic mobilization in Tatarstan	179
6.5	Effect of language-use variables on support for nationalism in Tatarstan – Laitin data	181
6.6	Effect of language-use variables in Tatarstan – Laitin data	182
6.7	Ethnic mobilization in Bashkortostan	187
6.8	Effect of language-use variables on support for nationalism in Bashkortostan – Laitin data	188
6.9	Effect of language-use variables in Bashkortostan – Laitin Data	189
6.10	Ethnic mobilization in Chuvashia	192
7.1	Regional sovereignty declarations	202
7.2	Regional constitutions	206
7.3	Regional language laws	211
7.4	Regional ethnic revival policies	217
8.1	Should the titular language be the sole official language in ethnic republics?	236
8.2	Should all inhabitants of an ethnic republic know the titular language of that republic?	238
8.3	Should titular-language study be compulsory in all schools in ethnic republics?	239
8.4	How do you feel about the declarations of sovereignty by the former autonomous republics of the Russian Federation?	241
8.5	Should all republics have the right of self-determination, including the right of withdrawal from the Russian Federation?	242
8.6	Should control of the army, police, and security forces be transferred to the jurisdiction of the sovereign republics of the Russian Federation?	243
8.7	Factor matrix for indexes of support for nationalism: Colton/Hough survey	244

8.8	Mean values of ethnic mobilization indexes, by region	245
8.9	Support for increase in language status, by region	246
8.10	Support for regional separatism, by region	250
8.11	Pooled results	252
8.12	Intercepts for pooled results with ethnic dummies	253
8.13	Highest grade in which national language serves as medium of instruction, by year	255
A.1	Factor matrix for native-language education index	276
A.2	Factor matrix for language fluency index	277
A.3	Factor matrix for language-use homogeneity index	277

Preface

This book seeks to explain how state institutions affect ethnic mobilization. It does so in the context of examining the widespread surge in nationalist sentiment that occurred throughout the Soviet Union and Eastern Europe during the late 1980s and early 1990s. My analysis of the development of minority nationalist movements during this period in four republics of the Russian Federation shows that even during this period of institutional upheaval, preexisting ethnic institutions affected the preferences and tactics of movement leaders. These Soviet institutions shaped the messages that were used to appeal for popular support, the form that ethnic mobilization took, and the reaction of both the elites and the masses to the nationalist message.

The story of nationalist mobilization during the *perestroika* period presents both interesting similarities and interesting variations across cases. The institutional explanation is strengthened by the fact that members of virtually every ethnic minority in the Soviet Union organized nationalist movements that were initially similar in form and goals. These movements differed greatly, however, in their ability to attract popular support. Furthermore, their uniformity of message did not last long – some movements began to articulate radical demands, while others remained moderate. The burden of this study is thus to show that the institutional explanation can account not only for the similarities in nationalist mobilization throughout the Russian Federation, but also for the differences across cases.

In the course of discussing ethno-nationalist mobilization in Russia, this book pursues two other objectives. One is to challenge the widely held perception that governing elites can kindle latent ethnic grievances virtually at will in order to secure or maintain their hold on power. I argue that nationalist leaders are not always able to mobilize widespread popular support and that their success in doing so depends in turn on the extent to which ethnicity is institutionalized by state structures.

The other objective is to shift the study of ethnic mobilization from the *whys* of its emergence to the *hows* of its development as a political force.

Throughout this study, I focus less on whether ethnic mobilization occurs because of economic grievances, cultural differences, or the activities of ethnic entrepreneurs and more on showing how ethno-nationalist movements emerge on the political scene, develop organizational structures, frame demands, and attract followers. The nature of these processes, I argue, is determined by the ethnic and political institutions established by the state.

In the course of writing this book, I have incurred many profound debts, both intellectual and personal. The project began as a doctoral dissertation in the Department of Government at Harvard University. Many thanks go to my teachers and advisors there, and especially to the members of my dissertation committee, all of whom read multiple drafts of the manuscript. Timothy Colton has been unfailingly supportive of my work on ethnic politics in Russia while at the same time encouraging me by his example to understand the multifaceted nature of Russian politics. Without Grzegorz Ekiert's efforts to push me to understand the interaction between ethnic politics and social movements, this study would have taken a very different, and probably less interesting, form. Grzegorz has also been a model for me in my efforts to maintain a balance between academic pursuits and other interests. David Laitin has always pushed me toward greater scientific rigor, challenging me to clarify my initial puzzle and to select the right cases to test my theories. Finally, Mark Kramer, although not officially a member of my dissertation committee, took the time to read most of the chapters that make up the study and made numerous valuable suggestions for improvement.

The source of my interest in ethnic politics was an undergraduate seminar at Princeton University on reform in South Africa, led by Ambassador Donald Easum, who encouraged me to follow my instincts as I traced the causes of violence during that country's initial liberalization to political, rather than cultural, factors. I would also like to thank Ashutosh Varshney, who encouraged me to pursue my interest in ethnic politics and who served on the dissertation prospectus committee. Finally, I would like to acknowledge my debt to the late Myron Weiner, who taught me much of what I know about conducting fieldwork abroad.

I also want to thank the many people who read and commented on various portions of this manuscript. They include Kanchan Chandra, Elise Giuliano, Katherine Graney, Henry Hale, Pauline Jones Luong, Daniel Posner, Stephen Shenfield, Joshua Tucker, Edward Walker, the members of the Post-Communist Politics Workshop and of the Sawyer Seminar on the Performance of Democracies, and three anonymous reviewers. My gratitude also goes to Lewis Bateman of Cambridge University Press for believing in this project and moving it smoothly through the review process and into publication.

My fieldwork in Russia would have been impossible without the help of scholars at the Institute of Ethnology and Anthropology of the Russian Academy of Sciences in Moscow, particularly Mikhail Guboglo and Galina

Komarova. In Tatarstan, Damir Iskhakov, Guzel Stoliarova, and Roza Musina helped to arrange interviews, while Galiia Zakirova was an invaluable guide to the collections of the Tatarstan National Library. Ildar Gabdrafikov, Sergei Lee, and Altaf Galeev facilitated my fieldwork in Bashkortostan; Ivan Boiko performed a similar service in Chuvashia. My trip to Khakassia would have been impossible without the hospitality and assistance of Liubov Aeshina. I would also like to thank all of the scholars and political leaders who agreed to be interviewed for this study. Without them, my understanding of nationalism in Russia would have been much poorer. Among the many friends who helped to preserve my sanity during the months in Russia, I particularly want to thank Leyla Drovnikova, Kay Hope, Amy Randall, and Ed Vajda.

For financial support during the dissertation stage, I thank the National Science Foundation, IREX, the Institute for the Study of World Politics, the Mellon Foundation, and the Davis Center for Russian Studies. The Davis Center also provided crucial institutional support. I completed revisions of the manuscript with the assistance of a postdoctoral fellowship from the Social Science Research Council. Parts of the book have been published previously. An abbreviated version of Chapter 6 was published as "Not with One Voice: An Explanation of Intragroup Variation in Nationalist Sentiment," *World Politics* 53 (1): 115–142. Chapter 8 previously appeared as "Nationalism for the Masses: Popular Support for Nationalism in Russia's Ethnic Republics," *Europe-Asia Studies* 53 (1): 73–104. I thank the publishers of these journals for allowing me to include these materials here.

Finally, I would like to thank my family. My parents instilled in me a love of learning and were understanding when I chose to apply that love in unexpected ways. I dedicate this book to two people. My wife, Ida, not only read and reread numerous drafts, she also accompanied me to some of the more remote reaches of Russia, all the while displaying her usual good humor and helping me through the often difficult and lonely process of researching and writing a book. Without her encouragement, this book might never have come to fruition. Finally, since his arrival in 1999 on the day I completed my first round of manuscript revision, Jacob has always displayed his perfect sense of timing, even as he ensured that Daddy did not spend too much time in front of the computer that might have been better spent reciting Dr. Seuss or singing "Baby Beluga."

1

Minority Ethnic Mobilization in Russia

An Introduction

On 15 October 1991, the 449th anniversary of the conquest of Kazan by the Russian czar Ivan the Terrible, tens of thousands of Tatars gathered on Freedom Square, across from the Tatarstan Republic parliament. They were there to protest the government's refusal to issue a declaration of independence from the Russian Federation and the Soviet Union. The political situation in the republic had been tense for months, ever since a wave of nationalist demonstrations and hunger strikes in May had forced the government to disavow its support for allowing locals to vote in Russian presidential elections. Passions were further inflamed by the publication in the Tatar-language press of an article by the nationalist firebrand Fauzia Bairamova, which called for all real Tatars to show that they were not slaves to the Russians by demonstrating in the square. The October demonstration culminated in violence when protesters attempted to storm the parliament building and were rebuffed by police. Tensions were defused only when parliament agreed to adopt a declaration that confirmed the republic's sovereignty and to hold a referendum on the republic's independence.

Three months later and seemingly a world away, a few hundred Khakass nationalists gathered in front of the parliament in the newly created republic of Khakassia. They were protesting the election of an ethnic Russian as the chairman of the legislature as well as the legislature's reluctance to approve a sovereignty declaration. This was the first nationalist demonstration in Khakassia. The event shocked the republic's political elite and prompted the chairman's replacement by an ethnic Khakass. However, this turned out to be a pyrrhic victory, as the parliament proceeded to reject sovereignty and thereafter steadfastly opposed all Khakass demands. In the end, Khakassia became the only republic of the Russian Federation not to pass a sovereignty declaration. And the republic's first nationalist demonstration also became its last.

As these vignettes show, nationalist demands among minorities in the Russian Federation and the extent of public support for these demands were not uniform. This study aims to explain the emergence of ethno-nationalist movements and the variations in support for ethno-nationalism in Russia's ethnic republics by focusing on the ethno-federal institutions of the Soviet Union as a source of nationalist mobilization. It accomplishes this task by analyzing the development of nationalist movements in four ethnic regions: Tatarstan, Chuvashia, Bashkortostan, and Khakassia. The analysis is based on extensive fieldwork in these regions and utilizes multiple sources of data, including interviews, content analysis of the local press, protest event counts, election results, and survey data. The study examines the similarities and differences in the development of nationalist movements in these four regions during the period of democratic transition. In doing so, it goes beyond traditional debates about the sources of ethnic mobilization to focus on the mobilization *process*. By showing how this process was structured by the institutions of the Soviet regime even after the dissolution of the Soviet state in 1991, it emphasizes that even governments that were totally dedicated to political reform were limited in the scope of their actions by the structure of the pre-reform political system and the beliefs and expectations that it had created among the populace.

THE MANIPULATIVE POWER OF NATIONALIST ELITES VERSUS THE STRUCTURING INFLUENCE OF ETHNIC INSTITUTIONS

Many recent studies of nationalist mobilization emphasize the role of governing elites in the development of minority nationalist mobilization. According to the commonly held "ethnic entrepreneur" view of nationalist mobilization, the emergence of nationalist movements is a function of the interaction between central and regional governing elites in ethnically divided societies. Nationalist mobilization is portrayed as part of an effort by regional elites who belong to ethnic minority groups to increase their power vis-à-vis central elites by advocating ethnic claims. The mobilization of popular support for these efforts is viewed as a means of putting pressure on the central elites. In this scenario, the members of the minority ethnic group are portrayed as purely reactive players. They are essentially pawns in a power game played out by politicians.

In this study, I argue that mass nationalist mobilization can arise independently of elite power struggles. I argue that the formation of nationalist movements in the ethnic republics of the Russian Federation was spearheaded by intellectuals and students, not by local political elites, who at first opposed the emerging movements. Although local politicians did recognize later that they could use the nationalist threat to increase their power relative to the government in Moscow, they continued to attempt to suppress popular nationalist movements in their regions. Faced with hostility from local political leaders, advocates of ethnic revival turned to popular mobilization in order to pressure local governments into supporting the nationalist program.

State institutions[1] structured the interaction between political elites and the rest of the population, influencing the sources from which nationalist appeals emerged, the forms that nationalist mobilization took, and the reactions of both the elites and the masses to nationalism. Paradoxically, the ethnic institutions of the Soviet Union, created by the founders of the Soviet state during the 1920s and 1930s for the purpose of extinguishing nationalism as a political force, had the effect of promoting ethnic identity and nationalist ideas among the ethnic minorities found in the Soviet Union's constituent ethnic regions.[2] These institutions determined how members of minority groups viewed themselves and their homeland, what type of education they received, and which career paths they could pursue. In this way, Soviet ethnic institutions enshrined ethnicity as the dominant form of self-identification among non-Russians throughout the Soviet Union. All members of minority ethnic groups, including the political elites, were equally subject to the effects of these ethnic institutions (Brubaker 1996, Slezkine 1994b, Suny 1993).

Because of the importance of ethnic institutions, nationalism quickly became the dominant form of protest among the non-Russian population of the USSR when central political elites began to liberalize (Beissinger 1998). Throughout the *perestroika* and post-*perestroika* periods, existing Soviet ethnic institutions continued to structure the interactions between regional and central political elites and between regional political elites and the inhabitants of the regions they controlled.

The explanation that I propose shows how ethnic institutions shaped the preferences and tactics of the cultural elites who initiated the nationalist movements, the messages these elites used to appeal for popular support, and the ability of those messages to resonate with the values and beliefs of potential followers. Institutions, I argue, were also critical in creating the social ties and networks of communication through which the nationalist message was spread and new activists were recruited.

EXPLANATIONS OF ETHNIC MOBILIZATION

The most common theories currently being used to explain ethnic mobilization concentrate on explaining *why* ethnic mobilization occurs in general, why it occurs at certain times, and why it occurs in certain places. Apart

---

[1] I use a broad definition of 'institutions' taken from the historical institutionalist literature, which takes institutions to include "both formal organizations and informal rules and procedures that structure conduct" (Thelen and Steinmo 1992).
[2] I define 'ethnic institutions' as those institutions that are established to oversee a state's interactions with ethnic groups living on its territory. They include territorial administrative units for ethnic minorities, separate educational systems, language laws, official ethnic categories for censuses and identity papers, affirmative action programs for ethnic minorities, etc.

from institutionalism, these theories include explanations based on cultural differences, social psychology, and economic incentives.

Cultural explanations of ethnic mobilization treat ethnicity as an ascribed characteristic, not voluntarily chosen but largely determined by the accident of birth. Proponents of this view argue that ethnic ties are stronger than other types of group identification because they are based on kinship and therefore produce feelings of intense solidarity among group members, even giving an aura of sacredness to the ethnic group. Ethnic mobilization is seen by them either as a direct outgrowth of intergroup cultural differences or as part of an effort to avoid domination by a group with higher status. Because of the intense emotions produced by cultural solidarity and the unchangeable nature of ethnic identity, ethnic conflict is viewed as particularly intense and difficult to resolve.[3]

These cultural explanations have come under fire from the instrumentalist point of view. Instrumentalists argue that ethnic groups are essentially modern creations, formed for the purpose of securing economic benefits for their members. Ethnic mobilization is initiated by elites who seek to use the power of the group to acquire material benefits or political power. Elites persuade potential followers to join the mobilization effort by providing selective benefits to participants. Members of the group mobilize when the gains from a combination of these benefits and the potential benefits of victory outweigh the potential costs of losing (Bates 1983, Hardin 1995, Hechter 1992).

The institutionalist explanation of ethnic mobilization adopts many of the features of the instrumentalist explanation.[4] Like instrumentalists, institutionalists argue that ethnic identity is constructed and mutable. However, they disagree on the extent to which change is possible and about the speed at which it can occur. Institutionalists argue that identity is shaped by the institutions of the state, which establish the ethnic categories to which individuals can assign themselves and create incentive structures that induce these individuals to choose one or another ethnic identity. Identity shift thus occurs not because of the incentives of economic competition but as a result of institutional change, which is usually a slow and gradual process.

While institutionalist scholars agree with instrumentalists that differences in preferences explain whether individuals join ethnic mobilization efforts, they are more sensitive to the psychological dimension of these preferences. Although they argue that ethnic identity is constructed and can change

---

[3] See Geertz (1973), Smith (1974), Kuper (1969), Isaacs (1975), Huntington (1996), and Kaplan (1993). For applications of this view to the Soviet Union, see Carrere d'Encausse (1979), Rywkin (1990), Brzezinski (1989/90), and Horowitz (1992). For a critique, see Eller and Coughlin (1993).

[4] See Brubaker (1996), Suny (1993), Roeder (1991), Laitin (1991), and Laitin (1998).

over time, they recognize that most individuals see their ethnic identities as fixed and unchangeable. If individuals perceive their identities as fixed, then psychological factors such as relative status and self-esteem become important in determining individual behavior. Attitudes toward participation in ethnic mobilization are thus explained by a combination of economic incentives for participation and psychological attitudes toward other groups (Laitin 1998).

The main problem with existing institutional explanations is that they, like other explanations of ethnic mobilization, limit themselves to explaining the reasons for the emergence of ethnic mobilization in particular circumstances. Because they are not overly concerned with the process through which ethnic mobilization becomes a potent political force, they focus almost exclusively on the behavior of political elites as the key explanatory variable in determining the timing and location of ethno-nationalist mobilization. As I show in the next section, most institutionalist explanations simply assume that the important political decisions are made by the governing elites, who then induce the masses to follow their decisions.

This study is an effort to move beyond these elite-focused accounts of why ethnic mobilization occurs. The key question motivating the inquiry is not *why* but *how*. In the ensuing chapters, I show how ethno-nationalist movements emerge on the political scene as a result of government-sponsored liberalization, how they use institutionally provided resources to create organizational structures, how they frame their demands to resonate with their target audience, and how they recruit their supporters. The nature of these processes, I argue, is determined by the ethnic and political institutions established by the state.

A PROCESS-ORIENTED INSTITUTIONALIST EXPLANATION OF POST-SOVIET ETHNIC MOBILIZATION

Several scholars have pointed to Soviet ethnic institutions as the main explanation for ethnic mobilization during the 1980s and 1990s. Brubaker (1996, 41–42) elegantly describes the nature of Soviet ethno-federalism and argues that the structure of the Soviet state played a critical role in the breakup of the Soviet Union. Roeder (1991) points out that the extent of nationalist mobilization depended on a region's position in the four-tier Soviet ethnofederal hierarchy. He argues that the Soviet government sought to control ethno-politics by giving control of ethnic regions to indigenous elites, by punishing members of the elite who sought to use nationalism in order to gain popular support, and by allowing the elite to have a monopoly over mobilizational resources within the ethnic community. By controlling these resources, ethnic elites could determine "when the ethnic group would be mobilized to action" (199). Both the number of resources and the extent of elite control over them decreased with each step down in the administrative hierarchy. Laitin (1991) adds elite incentives to the institutionalist model, showing that regional political elites activated nationalist movements not whenever they had the resources to do so, but only in those situations when doing so would help to increase their power vis-à-vis the central government. Treisman (1997) builds on this work by spelling out how regional elites used the institutional resources provided by ethnic institutions to help in their competition for power with the center.

These studies have greatly increased our understanding of the role played by state institutions and by governing elites in fostering ethnic nationalism. This study continues their effort by extending the institutional explanation beyond the political elites. While the existing studies have concentrated on the role of political elites in mobilizing ethnic minorities, I show that the support of political elites is not a necessary component of a widely supported nationalist movement. In several of Russia's ethnic republics, cultural elites formed successful nationalist movements despite opposition from both local and central political elites. This study analyzes the process by which cultural elites mobilized their followers and shows which factors determined the extent of popular support for minority nationalism.

In focusing on elite bargaining, some of the existing studies treat ethnicity as largely epiphenomenal and blur the distinction between ethnic republics and administrative regions. Treisman, for example, argues that the demands and actions of the ethnic regions were similar to the tactics used by Russia's nonethnic regions to extract benefits from the center (1997, 247). I argue that the presence of mass separatist movements in the ethnic regions made the struggle for power between the ethnic regions and the center fundamentally different from the bargaining game between Moscow and Russia's nonethnic provinces.

Finally, while the existing studies have noted the connection between administrative status and resource allocation and the importance of these resources for the formation of nationalist movements, they have not explained the process by which differences in administrative status affect political mobilization. The following account of ethno-nationalist mobilization shows how institutional differences led to variations in resource availability, which in turn caused the wide regional differences in the ability of nationalist leaders to mobilize the population and achieve their goals.

A mass-based explanation of ethnic mobilization needs to explain three things. First, it must explain how and why the movement leaders choose to begin the mobilization process. Second, it must explain how the movement leaders convince others to support the movement. And third, it must explain how and why a significant proportion of the population joins the movement. In the rest of this chapter, I present a summary of the argument. Each of the points mentioned here is elaborated in subsequent chapters.

Movement Formation

The emergence of a protest movement requires a change in the political opportunity structure,[5] sufficient organizational resources among prospective challengers, a common identity among prospective founders of the protest movement, and incentives for these prospective founders to actually take part in the organization of protest activities (McAdam 1982).

Protest movements tend to form during periods when the political structure begins to show signs of change that serve to modify the calculations on which the balance of power in the political establishment is based (Kriesi et al. 1995). There are many possible sources of such change, including war, demographic change, economic decline, changes in the international balance of power, industrialization, and many others (McAdam 1982, 41). Regardless of its origin, the change in the political structure leads to expanded political opportunities for actors who were previously excluded from the political system.

Openings in the political opportunity structure can occur either as part of a systemwide political crisis, which affects all potential insurgent groups, or through smaller changes in the balance of power, which often result from long-term socioeconomic changes and usually affect only one or two potential protest constituencies (McAdam 1982, 42). In the Soviet Union, Gorbachev's liberalization program led to a systemic crisis of the political system, allowing the emergence of many kinds of protest movements.[6] Gorbachev's reforms encouraged the emergence of protest movements in three ways. First, his stated policies of *glasnost* (openness) and *demokratizatsia* (democratization) emboldened protesters by making it clear that the expression of opinions opposed to official policy would no longer result in repression. As some pioneering dissidents began to state their opinions openly and even held public demonstrations for greater liberalization without negative consequences to their liberty, other potential activists emerged and sought to capitalize on the new openness in order to publicize their demands. In Tatarstan, for example, initially groups of fewer than 100 prodemocracy activists gathered in public squares and parks to discuss liberalization. Seeing that these meetings were not broken up by police, environmentalists and nationalists began to hold their own meetings and, eventually, demonstrations.

Second, the central government's prohibition on repression reduced the power discrepancy between governing elites and potential protesters at the

---

[5] The concept of political opportunity structure refers to those aspects of the political environment that act to encourage or discourage popular mobilization (Tarrow 1994, 18).

[6] Most notably, these included the pro-democracy movement (Zdravomyslova 1996, Fish 1995), the environmentalist/antinuclear movement (Dawson 1996), and the women's movement (Sperling 1997), as well as the nationalist movement discussed in this study.

local level. Local administrators who were perceived as "hard-liners" or holdovers from the old regime were threatened with removal from their positions. Thus, protest in Bashkortostan began in earnest after the Moscow government persuaded the relatively liberal party leadership of the republic's capital city (*gorkom*) to declare that it had no confidence in the conservative Bashkortostan Communist Party *obkom*, forcing the collective resignation of the latter. Such examples made surviving leaders in other regions more reluctant to use repressive tactics against protesters for fear of likewise being punished by central elites.[7] This point is related to the first point, but with an important difference. The first point addresses the effect of central government policy on protesters, whereas the second addresses its effect on local governing elites.

Third, as the Soviet political crisis continued to deepen and spread, regional elites who had managed to forestall the emergence of significant protest by preventing the emergence of a free press and continuing to repress activists found themselves under increasing pressure from the center to "get in line" with the rest of the country on liberalization, at the same time that they were becoming increasingly subject to the weakening of government authority that resulted from the breakdown of chains of command across the country. As a result of these processes, the power discrepancy between local governing elites and their potential challengers was significantly reduced, making the formation of social movements more attractive for potential activists.

Most studies of social movement emergence examine how changes in political opportunity structure affect protest movements exclusively on a national level (Kriesi et al. 1995, Rucht 1996, Urban 1997). In the Russian Federation, the political opportunities available to potential protesters varied dramatically from region to region. Some regional governments exhibited a greater willingness to liberalize and were less likely to use repressive methods. In other regions, elites were divided and therefore more likely to form alliances with challenging groups. In yet other regions, the governing elites remained united and opposed to liberalization (Fish 1995). Furthermore, different protest movements were faced with different political opportunity structures. In some regions, governing elites who were willing to form alliances with pro-democracy or environmentalist groups continued to use repressive measures against any sign of nationalist activity. In other regions, the situation was precisely the reverse, with nationalist groups being favored as partners over pro-democracy activists. This regional and sector-based variation in the political opportunity structure largely determined the timing

---

[7] Repressive tactics were, of course, still used against protesters by both the regional and central governments. However, the frequency of repression was significantly reduced, and the threshold after which protest was answered with repression became much higher during this period.

of the emergence of protest movements in each region and the sequence in which different types of protest movements emerged.

In describing the emergence of social movements, McAdam writes, "A conducive political environment only affords the aggrieved population the opportunity for successful insurgent action. It is the resources of the minority community that enable insurgent groups to exploit these opportunities." (1982, 43) Research has shown that the emergence of new protest movements is strongly assisted by the presence of significant stocks of social capital among the aggrieved community[8] (McAdam 1986). Protest movements are able to form when the aggrieved community possesses a strong network of already-existing associations and organizations that can help provide the material resources needed by the newly forming movement, supply the initial leaders of the movement, and simplify communication between members. The presence of existing organizational networks also helps in the recruitment of new members by increasing the number of links between potential recruits and by allowing emerging movements to use the existing organizations' structures of selective incentives (McAdam 1982, 44–8).

The importance of existing organizations to the emergence of social movements provides one of the key links between the political process model and historical institutionalism. The types of organizations that exist among the population are frequently determined by state institutions, particularly in an authoritarian political system such as the Soviet Union. Minority nationalist movements in the Russian Federation benefited especially from the institutionalization of the study and development of minority culture. Ethnonationalist organizations were formed in the universities, social science institutes, and writers' unions located in each ethnic region. These organizations, often headed by sympathetic administrators, provided a safe haven for the nationalist movements, insulating activists from reprisals by employers. These organizations also provided activists with scarce material resources, including meeting space and photocopying and printing facilities. Although the republic's political leadership opposed the movement's formation, sympathetic university administrators allowed the Tatar nationalist movement to hold initial organizational meetings and its first convention at the university meeting hall. The ability to tap into preexisting social networks within the workplace simplified the task of recruiting core activists for emerging nationalist organizations.[9] Once the Tatar nationalist activists decided to establish a

---

[8] Social capital is defined as "[t]hose aspects of social organization, such as trust, norms, and networks, that can improve the efficiency of society by facilitating coordinated actions" (Putnam 1993, 167).

[9] The workplace played a critical role in the lives of Soviet citizens. It was a source not only of employment, but frequently also of housing, childcare services, and even social activities. Furthermore, for most Soviet citizens workplace Communist Party cells provided the only legitimate locale for political activity. Considering this structural legacy, it is not surprising that the initial formation of nationalist movements took place in the workplace.

nationalist organization, they easily recruited hundreds of fellow academics, who made up the bulk of the attendees at the first movement convention. Finally, membership in government-supported academic institutes gave nationalist leaders a forum to express their ideas, lending them an air of legitimacy as scholars and making their statements appear more authoritative. At a time when access to the media was still sharply restricted, scholars were able to use their academic credentials to obtain permission to make public statements about the nationalities question in newspapers and on the radio.

Who were the initial activists? And why did they choose to participate in the nationalist movement? In the early stages of movement formation, movement leaders were comprised almost entirely of scholars from the social science institutes and universities. In Tatarstan, nine of the eleven movement founders were scholars based at the republic's Academy of Sciences branch or at Kazan State University. The academy fostered the development of a common identity among scholars who had devoted their careers to the study of the culture, literature, language, or history of their ethnic group. They perceived themselves not simply as part of the Soviet intellectual elite, but as the intellectual elite of their ethnic group, a position that for them carried with it a duty to press for the continued cultural development of their ethnic group. In essence, they saw the task of leading the nationalist movement as part of their position in society and their identity as *ethnic* scholars.

These scholars were at the forefront of nationalist organization because for them, activism brought greater benefits and lower costs than it did for members of other social groups. In addition to the psychological rewards of taking a position as leaders of the ethnic group, scholars also were likely to receive material rewards for their participation. These scholars' jobs were closely linked to the cultural development of their ethnic group. If nationalist activism resulted in greater funding and opportunities for cultural development, these scholars would be first in line to head new programs, conduct new studies, write new textbooks, and instruct new language and history teachers. In other words, cultural development would increase these activists' chances for career advancement and make their chosen careers more central to government policy and therefore more prestigious. But if existing cultural policies were maintained, the likelihood was high that trends toward increasing assimilation and language loss among members of the ethnic group would continue. In that case, ethnic scholars would become increasingly irrelevant as demand for new texts and instructors declined. These scholars' calculations proved correct. In the ethnic revival that was spearheaded by the nationalist movements, new universities, academies of science, and institutes were established in every republic, increasing career opportunities and prestige for ethnic academics.[10] Members of other social groups, by contrast,

---

[10] A new university was established in Khakassia. Republic academies of science were created in Tatarstan, Bashkortostan, and Chuvashia. New academic institutes focusing on social science and history were opened in Tatarstan and Bashkortostan.

did not stand to gain materially from the success of nationalist movements and were correspondingly less likely to participate in the early stages, when success seemed unlikely.

Although the political liberalization of the mid-1980s resulted in the expansion of opportunities for all types of protest movements, the institutionalization of ethnicity ensured that ethno-nationalist movements would become the most important source of protest activity during the ensuing protest cycle. Academic institutions focused on the study of ethnic groups played a particularly crucial role in this process, in effect acting as an incubator for nationalist leaders and then providing them with the material and organizational resources necessary to successfully launch a protest movement.

Convincing Followers

For a protest movement to be successful, it is not enough for it to acquire organizational resources and a cadre of dedicated activists. It also needs to formulate an appeal that will strike a chord among potential supporters and ensure that its message is widely disseminated. The movement needs to convince people that its demands are legitimate and that now is an opportune time to press these demands. It will be successful if it is able to create a perception among the target population that they have been the victim of an injustice, that this injustice is correctable, and that the present circumstances increase their likelihood of success while keeping the costs of participating to a minimum (McAdam 1982).

The process through which movement activists seek to influence potential supporters is known as *framing*. Frames are defined as interpretive schemes that condense and simplify a person's experience by selectively highlighting and encoding certain situations, objects, events, and experiences. Frames serve to "either underscore and embellish the seriousness and injustice of a social condition or redefine as unjust and immoral what was previously seen as unfortunate but perhaps tolerable" (Snow and Benford 1992, 137). In this manner, frames "organize experience and guide action" (Snow et al. 1986, 464). In order to persuade potential followers to join the movement, movement organizers formulate their demands in a way that resonates with the grievances of the target population. If they are to achieve this end, grievances must be described using language and symbols that are congruent with the target population's beliefs and values, while at the same time being compatible with the goals of movement activists (Tarrow 1994, 123).

Framing is used not only to convince potential followers that their situation is intolerable, but also to convince them that political action can change the situation for the better, that participation in the movement is the most effective way of bringing about such a change, and that success is particularly likely at the present time. During this "cognitive liberation" process, movement activists first must convince the target population that their plight is the result of systemic rather than individual factors (McAdam 1982, 49–50).

Second, activists have to assign blame for the injustice and propose a "line of action for ameliorating the problem" (Snow and Benford 1992, 137). Finally, activists need to show potential supporters that the political system is becoming increasingly vulnerable to challenge, increasing the probability of achieving the goals of the movement.

Framing processes played a crucial role in popularizing the appeal of nationalist movements. To be successful, nationalist leaders had to frame their demands in language and imagery that could resonate with the population. Seventy years of Soviet ethnic policy had decisively molded the perceptions, beliefs, and identities of minority ethnic group members. The nationalist leaders who were successful were those who crafted their messages to correspond to the political ideas of the population. These ideas were shaped by the four ethnic institutions of territorialized ethnicity, republic boundaries, ethnic hierarchy, and passport identity.

The establishment of ethnic administrative units that were considered to "belong" to the members of an ethnic group produced a series of demands related to a perceived discrepancy between the theoretical titular ownership of the region and the actual domination of many aspects of local affairs by members of other ethnic groups, particularly Russians. Nationalist leaders advocated a dramatic expansion of the use of the titular language in administration, education, and other spheres of public life. Some leaders argued that lack of knowledge of the titular language among the Russian population was a mark of their disrespect for the titular ethnic group and its culture. This demand reflected the importance attached by Soviet ethnic policy to the development of native languages and the direct link between language and ethnic identity in the Soviet definition of nationality. Nationalists also argued that the governments of ethnic regions were responsible for the cultural development of their ethnic groups, that members of the titular ethnic group had a right to play a dominant role in local administration, and that quotas in hiring should be instituted in order to rectify the economic imbalance faced by indigenous groups. All of these arguments were based on the assumption that members of the titular ethnic group, by virtue of their indigenous status, should have special rights within their homeland.

The boundaries of most ethnic regions did not fully correspond to the areas inhabited by members of the titular ethnic group. Most ethnic groups had sizeable and compact diaspora populations living in areas adjacent to the ethnic region. While in many cases around the world such a situation has led to irredentist claims against neighboring regions (Horowitz 1985), the importance and legitimacy attached to boundaries ensured that irredentist appeals were virtually nonexistent in most ethnic regions of the Soviet Union.[11]

---

[11] Several exceptions to this rule led to violent interethnic conflict, most notably in North Ossetia/Ingushetia and Nagorno Karabakh. These cases, however, involved calls for either a return to earlier Soviet-era boundaries (North Ossetia) or the transfer of entire subordinate

Because irredentist appeals were precluded, nationalist leaders could express their concern about the future of the diaspora population only in terms of cultural and linguistic issues. Calls for the republic government to provide books and teachers for co-ethnics living outside the republic were legitimate; territorial claims were not.

Nationalist demands for sovereignty and self-determination were based on the perceived unfairness of the hierarchy of regions within the federal administrative system. Nationalist leaders pointed to the differences in economic development between their regions and regions at the next-highest level of the federal hierarchy. They claimed that the best way to improve the regional economy was to increase local control of budgets and state enterprises at the expense of the union republic to which the region was subject. Similarly, they argued that regions with higher status had better cultural facilities and better opportunities for cultural development. Yet even though nationalist leaders perceived the inequality created by the asymmetric federal system, they did not argue for its replacement by a symmetric federation where all ethnic regions would have equal status.[12] Their views had been shaped by the long-term institutionalization of asymmetric federalism, and they did not question this institution's legitimacy. They argued only that the Soviet government had unjustly prevented *their* region from claiming its legitimate place at a higher level in the hierarchy. Other, supposedly less developed regions could remain at their previous position in the hierarchy.

Finally, passport ethnicity reified the existing ethnic categories, made preferential hiring policies feasible, and made individual attempts at assimilation highly visible to co-ethnics. Because all Soviet citizens were required to belong to an ethnic group, had this identity inscribed in their passports, and were not allowed to change the passport inscription, passing as a member of another ethnic group was virtually impossible. Individuals had to state their ethnic identities in filling out paperwork whenever they came into contact with the state bureaucracy, increasing the salience of ethnic identity for the individual. Because of the importance of passport ethnic identity in hindering assimilation, nationalist leaders argued vehemently against issuing new passports that did not include such labels. Passport ethnic identity also increased the legitimacy of preferential hiring policies by removing any uncertainty about individual ethnic identity. Each individual could quickly and definitively judge the effect of such policies on him- or herself. The lack of ambiguity increased the support for such policies among the titular ethnic group, whose members stood to benefit materially.

---

administrative regions to a different union republic (Nagorno Karabakh). To my knowledge, there were no cases of irredentism involving areas inhabited by co-ethnics that were not previously part of an ethnic administrative unit.

[12] Andrei Sakharov, an ethnic Russian, was the most visible proponent of a fully symmetric federation.

Even if nationalist leaders were able to convince the population of the validity of their claims, participation in protest would remain unlikely if people believed that the campaign was unlikely to succeed or that they were likely to suffer high costs for participating. Unauthorized public demonstrations had been illegal in the Soviet Union for many decades and were usually met with swift police action and lengthy prison terms for the participants. If the protest campaign were to generate mass appeal, it would need to assure the population that dissent was no longer being repressed and that the movement was strong enough to achieve its objectives. To achieve these goals, nationalist leaders acted publicly to demonstrate their strength and publicized protest activities in other regions in order to show that a wave of protest was sweeping the country. To show that nationalism was becoming increasingly widespread throughout the country, nationalist leaders wrote and spoke publicly about the example of the Baltic republics, where nationalist rhetoric was being combined with peaceful protest. At the same time, they underplayed violent events in the Caucasus, which could have scared potential participants away from the movement. The experience of peaceful protest and nationalist mobilization in other parts of the country served to create an atmosphere in which public dissent was increasingly seen as a normal part of the political process. This acculturation to new modes of behavior put pressure on recalcitrant local elites to allow peaceful protest in their regions as well.

To show their local strength, nationalists organized outdoor public rallies. As these rallies were allowed to take place by regional governments, more and more people came to believe that participants were safe from repression. As a result, participation in these rallies grew over time. As the rallies grew, the appearance of movement strength further increased, leading to even more participation. Similarly, the publishing of articles by nationalist leaders in official newspapers gradually convinced the population that the long-forbidden nationalist discourse that had become widespread in other parts of the country was now considered acceptable by the local authorities as well. This belief also encouraged participation in the movement. Finally, the election of many nationalist leaders to local Supreme Soviets was a further indication of their strength.

Nationalist leaders were able to influence public opinion because of their level of access to the media. The policy of *glasnost*, enforced from above, ensured that previously banned opinions could be expressed on the pages of newspapers and magazines and on local radio and television programs. Nationalist leaders were able to use these media particularly effectively. Their status as respected scholars and writers, who had often contributed to these media in the past on less controversial topics, gave them greater access to the media and their opinions greater weight in the community than would have been the case had they come from a different social group with lower status.

Why Masses Join

Now that I have summarized the argument on the formation of nationalist movements and the appeals used by movement founders in their efforts to mobilize the population, it remains to be explained why members of an ethnic group heed the call to mobilization. As already discussed, many accounts of nationalist mobilization assume that members of an ethnic minority are willing to mobilize whenever called upon to do so by the elites. This perspective tells us little about the motivations and decision-making processes of potential movement supporters among the population. An alternative perspective begins with the importance of social networks and information exchange mechanisms for generating links between masses and elites (Fearon and Laitin 1996, 718–19). These links are then used to inform potential supporters of the existence of selective material and psychological incentives for joining. The extent to which the mobilizing effort proves successful depends on the density of social networks, the ability of elites to provide selective benefits, and the usefulness of these benefits to members of the target population. The extent of popular support for mobilization is reflected in the attendance at protest events and the extent to which nationalist candidates are supported in local elections.

Popular support of mass movements was promoted by factors such as a strong sense of common identity among the target population, the strength of social ties between individuals within the target population, and the existence of social networks linking movement leaders and potential followers. A strong sense of common identity is as important for mobilization among followers as it is among movement organizers. People for whom ethnicity was not a crucial component of their identity tended to be less responsive to nationalist appeals. To join the nationalist movement, these people had not only to have a strong sense of ethnic identity, but also to view ethnicity as a category that could be the basis for political action. As shown earlier, the sense of common identity among the members of an ethnic group was fostered through native-language schools, passport ethnic identification, and the other Soviet ethnic institutions. The perception that political action could be based on ethnic identity was also fostered in the schools, where students learned about Soviet nationalities policy and the government's use of political means to influence ethnic identities. Schoolchildren in titular-language schools were taught about the role of the Soviet state in promoting education and modernization among the non-Russian population and, most importantly, about the creation of national homelands for minority groups. This education provided examples of the use of ethnic identity for political ends under Soviet rule. Ethnic identity was therefore particularly strong in rural areas, where native-language education predominated, and among those inhabitants of urban areas, particularly migrants from rural areas and the older population, who had had experience with native-language education before it was largely eliminated from the cities during the 1960s. Survey data shows that members of these groups were significantly more likely than other members of their ethnic group to support nationalist movements.

Political process scholars have emphasized the importance of social networks for the recruitment of new movement activists. The likelihood of recruitment has been shown to be almost entirely a function of the existence of interpersonal links between potential recruits and movement members (Snow et al. 1980). The founders of nationalist movements in the ethnic republics were connected to potential recruits largely through university students and recent migrants from rural areas. University students became involved in the nationalist movement after taking classes and participating in discussion groups led by the scholars who had founded the movement. These students were, however, divided into two groups. Students from urban areas had without exception attended Russian-language schools, usually had poor knowledge of their native language, and had little exposure to their ethnic group's traditions and culture. They were thus frequently apathetic about ethnic revival and tended to avoid the nationalist movements in their republics. Most of the students who were involved in the movement thus came from rural areas, where they had received a native-language education and been taught about the culture of their ethnic group. These rural students spread the movement's message when they returned home for vacations. After graduating, some of the students who returned home helped to found local movement branches. Similarly, recent migrants from rural areas who took jobs in universities, academic institutes, and other places where nationalist movement ideas were commonplace retained contacts with their home regions and fostered the spread of movement activism there.

The denser the social networks and the closer the social ties linking members of a particular community, the faster and easier it was for movement activism to spread among the group. When a trusted member of a local group or association joins a movement or political party, other members of the group are subsequently far more likely to join the movement.[13] In the Soviet Union, the absence of independent associations prior to the late 1980s meant that the strongest groups were those that had been supported by the state. In urban areas, the strongest links were forged among students, who were linked not only through classes and dormitories but also through the Komsomol, the official organization for university-age youth. When the Komsomol broke up in the late 1980s, nationalist youth organizations were among its most prominent successors in virtually every ethnic region. Groups such as the Union of Bashkir Youth and Azatlyk, the Tatar youth organization, maintained a strong presence on university campuses and encouraged links between students studying at different institutions.

---

[13] For a fascinating account of how this process led to the dominance of the Nazi party in a small German town in the 1930s, see Allen (1984).

Recent migrants from rural areas maintained strong ties with people from the same district, although these ties rarely led to the establishment of formal associations. Instead, migrants maintained informal links both with other migrants from the same rural district and with relatives and friends who remained behind. In addition, these migrants were more likely to retain a strong sense of their ethnic identity, developed through native-language education in the village and maintained because of their exposure to members of other ethnic groups upon arrival in the city. In the rural areas themselves, close associational ties were enforced by the structure of the collective farm, which ensured that the peasants remained in close contact with each other both through their work on common property and through formal associations such as the village council (*selsovet*). Furthermore, the importance of collective farm and village council chairmen in rural life ensured that the sympathy of either figure for the nationalist view would persuade the majority of the villagers to join as well.[14]

A sense of common identity, networks connecting movement leaders and potential followers, and dense social networks among the potential followers make it easier for individuals to overcome their suspicion of new groups and become willing to join a movement. But in order to become active participants, potential followers also need to have some specific incentives to join. These incentives can be either material or psychological. In the case of nationalist movements in the Soviet Union, both types of incentives were present. The material incentives included the desire to preserve preferences in hiring and education and the possibility of using the movement for personal advancement. The possibility that a new political system for the Soviet Union would eliminate hiring preferences encouraged members of the groups that benefited from such preferences to mobilize for their preservation. The possibility of using movement participation for personal advancement and enrichment encouraged some individuals to start local chapters of existing nationalist organizations or even to found entirely new movement organizations. In one case, Khakass villagers created a local branch of the Khakass nationalist movement because they wanted to increase the number of ethnic Khakass villagers in leadership positions at the local state farm.[15]

Psychological incentives for mobilization included the desire to preserve the common ethnic identity and the desire to end discrimination by Russians against members of the ethnic group. The same group of Khakass villagers lamented the decline of the Khakass language among children, with the branch leader noting that "if the child does not absorb the native language with his mother's milk ... he will be a Khakass only in his passport entry on ethnicity." They also blamed the village leaders for discriminating against

---

[14] At the same time, if these village leaders made it clear that they opposed the nationalist movement, farm workers would often oppose the movement as well.

[15] V. Ivanchenko, "I rodilsia v Sonskom 'Tun'," *Sovetskaia Khakassia*, 28 February 1991.

Khakass villagers in housing distribution.[16] The desire to preserve the common ethnic identity emerged from the sense that the culture and values of the ethnic group were a unique public good that was worth preserving for its own sake. In addition, increased use of the native language in the public sphere would increase the demand for speakers of the language to fill administrative and other public sector jobs – contributing to the material welfare of members of the ethnic group. The psychological benefits of ending discrimination against members of the titular ethnic group are obvious. The most common forms of this discrimination outside the economic sphere included the use of ethnic slurs against people speaking non-Russian languages in public and the presence of a hostile atmosphere in the workplace and in school.

The extent to which members of titular ethnic groups supported nationalist movements thus depended on a combination of facilitating conditions, such as a common identity and social networks, and the presence of material and psychological incentives. In regions where ties between movement leaders and potential followers were particularly weak, the popularity of the nationalist movement was correspondingly lower. Similarly, in areas where movement leaders were unable to provide selective benefits for joining the movement, participation was also not as great.

RESEARCH DESIGN

This study explores the role of state institutions in the wave of nationalism that spread throughout the Soviet Union during the *perestroika* period. The goal is to examine whether the number and density of ethnic institutions in a region determines the strength of nationalist sentiment in that region. The study covers the period from the formation of the nationalist movements in 1987 through 1994, by which time they had largely faded from the scene.

The research is based on extensive fieldwork conducted in Tatarstan, Chuvashia, Bashkortostan, Khakassia, and in Moscow during the course of four research trips that took place between April 1995 and March 1998, including a total of twelve months in the field. The extent of popular support for nationalism is measured in several ways, including electoral support for nationalist candidates, the size and frequency of public protests,[17] and responses to public opinion polls and surveys conducted by social scientists.[18] Analysis of the nationalist movements' emergence is based primarily on

---

[16] Ibid.
[17] In addition to a protest event database compiled during my fieldwork on the basis of local newspaper accounts, this study has benefited from a protest event database using national sources that was generously provided by Mark Beissinger. For more details on the protest event databases used in this study, see Chapter 5.
[18] I have used two sets of survey data on attitudes toward ethnic and political issues in the regions, generously provided by Timothy Colton, David Laitin, Jerry Hough, and Susan Lehmann. For more details on these surveys, see Chapters 5, 6, and 8.

interviews with nationalist activists, government officials, and local scholars; on archival materials detailing the development of ethnic institutions in the regions; and on a content analysis of the local press in the four regions.

Because of the impracticability of learning four separate languages in order to conduct the study on which this book is based, the primary sources used are almost exclusively in the Russian language. The lack of primary sources in the languages of the groups being studied does not bias the results of the study. All scholars and political figures, including nationalist activists, in the regions under study used Russian at least as frequently as they used their native language. At no time during my fieldwork did I feel that I was unable to access information because of my lack of knowledge of the local language. Nationalist leaders in all of the regions published their programs and ideas in local Russian-language newspapers. While it is true that additional nationalist writings were available in the native-language press, I do not believe, based on reading several translated articles from these sources, that this additional material would have changed my findings in any way.

I focus on the ethnic republics of the Russian Federation because of the variation in institutional development found among them. The former union republics are excluded because their independence, achieved in 1991, sent the nationalist movements in these countries on an entirely different trajectory that cannot be compared to that of movements in territories that remained within Russia. Nonethnic regions within Russia are also excluded, for the simple reason that such regions lacked indigenous ethnic groups and therefore lacked indigenous ethno-nationalist movements. Because the analysis in this study focuses exclusively on the mobilization of non-Russian minority groups, rather than separatist efforts purely at the elite level, such as occurred in the Sverdlovsk province, it was impossible to include regions where such groups do not live. Finally, the study also excludes minority ethnic groups that lacked their own homelands. Such groups are generally either too small in size or too dispersed in settlement area to provide a valid comparison.[19]

The four cases were selected because they differ along institutional, economic, and cultural lines. Since it is impossible to provide a representative sample of a population that varies on so many potentially significant variables using only four cases, I develop the theory by using the critical-case comparison method. This method is useful in small-N studies because it identifies the cases for which the theory is least likely to hold true. If one can show that it does hold true for these cases, it is quite likely that it would also hold true for other cases where conditions are not as adverse for the theory in question. In this study, Khakassia and Chuvashia serve as critical cases for

---

[19] The one other possible alternative, Tatars living in Bashkortostan, cannot serve as a valid comparative case because of the additional variation introduced by their location in an area adjoining their territorial homeland (Tatarstan).

comparing the institutional and economic instrumentalist theories, since the first has a strong economy but few ethnic institutions, while the latter has the opposite. Should ethnic mobilization be widespread in Khakassia despite the lack of ethnic institutions, the economic theory would be confirmed. On the other hand, if mobilization were widespread in Chuvashia despite the lack of economic development, the economic theory would be disconfirmed in favor of the institutionalist theory. Tatarstan and Bashkortostan play similar roles for the cultural versus institutionalist explanations. A brief history and description of each of the four regions and their titular ethnic groups follows. The most important characteristics of each region are summarized in Table 1.1 (page 23), and their geographic locations within the Russian Federation are shown in Figure 1.1.

Tatarstan

Tatarstan is located on the Volga River in central Russia, about 450 miles east of Moscow. The region has about 3.6 million inhabitants, approximately half of whom are of Tatar ethnicity. Tatarstan is highly urbanized and economically well developed, with two-thirds of the population living in cities and a 1992 per capita income of 28,300 rubles, double the Russian average for that year. The main industries in the region include machine building and chemical and petrochemical production. Before the industrial collapse of the 1990s, the KamAZ automobile factory in Naberezhnye Chelny was one of the largest factories in the Soviet Union, producing 50% of the country's trucks. During the 1970s, the republic was the largest producer of oil in the Soviet Union. Although production has fallen by about two-thirds since the 1975 peak, there still exist significant reserves, and the republic contributes approximately 7% of the Russian Federation's total oil production, making it the second-largest oil-producing region.

Tatars claim to be the inheritors of a rich political and cultural history. Their ancestors, the Bulgars, established a powerful state that controlled the middle Volga region for over 400 years, until the Mongol-Tatar conquest of the thirteenth century. In 922, the local leaders converted to Islam, which over time became a key part of the Tatar identity. At present, Tatarstan is known as the northernmost outpost of Islam in the world. Following the collapse of the Mongol state, the Tatars established the Kazan Khanate, which was the main political rival of the emerging Muscovite Russian state until the capture of Kazan by Ivan the Terrible in 1552. Despite suffering persecution during four centuries of Russian rule, Tatars were able to maintain a vigorous intellectual and cultural life that made them the best-educated nation in the Russian empire on the eve of the revolution.

Chuvashia

Chuvashia is located on the Volga River, northwest of Tatarstan and 377 miles east of Moscow. With an area of only 18,000 square kilometers

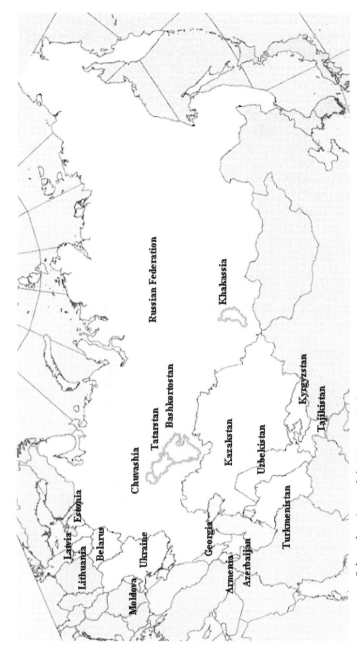

FIGURE 1.1. Selected regions of the Russian Federation.

and a population of 1.3 million, the republic is one of the most densely populated regions in the Russian Federation. The Chuvash people are Turkic but predominantly Christian. They have no history of independent statehood and have been ruled by Moscow since the 1400s. They represent a clear majority of the republic's population (68%), with Russians comprising only 26%.

The republic's economy is predominantly agricultural, with little industry and no significant natural resources. Furthermore, the republic is heavily subsidized by the central government. Per capita income in 1992 was only 7,900 rubles. Grain, potatoes, milk, and vegetables are all produced here, as well as 80% of the Russian Federation's total production of hops. Industry is limited to the construction of heavy tractors, diesel engines, and appliances, as well as a few chemical factories in the capital. In addition, the republic is a significant producer of hydroelectric energy.

Bashkortostan

Bashkortostan is located between the Volga River and the Ural Mountains, immediately southeast of Tatarstan. It is inhabited by 3.9 million people, making it one of the most populous regions in Russia. The capital, Ufa, is 726 miles east of Moscow. Bashkirs make up only 22% of the population, a smaller fraction than either Tatars (28%) or Russians (39%). In addition, one-fifth of all Bashkirs speak Tatar as their native language, so that only 16% of the republic's population actually speaks its titular language. The Bashkir people are closely related to the Tatars and share a common religion. Also, their languages are mutually intelligible. After witnessing the consequences of the conquest of Kazan, the Bashkir people joined the Russian empire voluntarily on favorable terms in 1557 rather than face an extended war.

Bashkortostan is highly economically developed, in terms of both industrial enterprises and natural resource extraction. Per capita revenue in 1992 was 35,500 rubles, the fifth-highest figure in the country. Petroleum is the most important natural resource. Oil drilling began in Bashkortostan in the 1930s, and the republic was the country's largest oil producer in the 1950s, before the full development of production in Tatarstan. Currently, the republic produces 6% of the Russian Federation's oil, just less than Tatarstan (Wallich 1994, 190). However, unlike Tatarstan, the republic not only extracts oil but is also one of the leading oil-refining and petrochemical centers in the country. Other natural resources found in the republic include natural gas, coal, gold, copper, manganese, and iron ore.

Khakassia

Khakassia is located far away from the other three republics examined in this study, in southern Siberia. It is 2,100 miles east of Moscow. Yet despite

TABLE 1.1. *Characteristics of the four republics in 1989*

	Tatarstan	Bashkortostan	Chuvashia	Khakassia
Area (sq. km)	68,000	144,000	18,000	62,000
Population (millions)	3.6	3.9	1.3	0.6
% titular population	49	22	68	11
% urban population	66	49	50	42
Distance and direction from Moscow	451 miles east	726 miles east	377 miles east	2100 miles northeast
Form and date of incorporation into Russia	Conquest 1552	Treaty 1557	Petition 1400s	Treaty 1727
Dominant religion	Muslim	Muslim	Orthodox	Shamanist
Per capita income[a]	28,300	35,500	7,900	13,000

[a] Wallich 1994, 277–80.
Source: Demographic information is from 1989 census data published in Goskomstat 1992.

this distance, a common Turkic heritage has engendered significant similarities between its cultural traditions and language and those of the other republics.[20] Islam did not spread to this part of Siberia – most Khakass are shamanists, although a small minority is Orthodox Christian. The Khakass were conquered by Russia during the early eighteenth century. The discovery of coal in the 1950s led to a rapid increase in Russian in-migration. Russians made up 80% of the 570,000 inhabitants in 1989, while only 11% were Khakass. However, the presence of coal, as well as the later discovery of gold and the construction of the largest hydroelectric power station in Russia during the 1970s, led to significant economic development and made the republic largely independent of central subsidies at the beginning of the transition period. Khakassia's 1992 per capita revenue of 13,000 rubles was near the average for Russia's regions.

OVERVIEW OF THE BOOK

The next three chapters address the formation of nationalist movements and the role of state institutions in this process. Chapter 2 describes the formation of the Soviet ethno-federal state, which assigned homelands to non-Russian minorities and created ethnic institutions such as cultural development programs, native-language education, and affirmative action programs for each minority group. I compare the formation of these institutions in Tatarstan, Chuvashia, Bashkortostan, and Khakassia and show that the number and strength of ethnic institutions in an ethnic region depended on the region's position in the Soviet ethno-federal hierarchy.

[20] The territory of Khakassia is, in fact, the place of origin for all Turkic peoples.

Chapter 3 begins by analyzing movement formation, which depends both on institutional and structural factors and on conscious crafting by activists. I describe the influence of preexisting social networks on the types and methods of movement organization. Bounded ethnic communities, urban-rural connections, and interaction among members of the intellectual ethnic elite facilitated the emergence of ethno-nationalist movements. In addition, and despite the government's repression of nationalism, the institutions of the Soviet state provided spaces and resources for nationalists to organize, both immediately preceding and during the period of political liberalization.

Chapter 4 describes the ideologies and grievances that framed movement demands. I start by describing the basic demands and ideologies of nationalist movements in the four republics. I show how Soviet-era institutions – such as republic hierarchical status, boundary definitions, passport nationality, and titular "ownership" of the republic – determined the repertoire of demands used by nationalist movement leaders. Nationalist ideologies adopted the familiar forms provided by Soviet institutions and filled them with new content, as exemplified by the nationalist challenge to autonomous republic status, which argued for turning autonomous republics into union republics rather than abolishing the hierarchy altogether. In this manner, the legacy of Soviet institutions determined the form and extent of nationalist demands in the ethnic republics.

The second part of the book examines the extent to which popular support for nationalism was correlated with the density and number of ethnic institutions in each region. In Chapter 5, with the help of survey data, election results, and protest event analysis, I describe the interregional variation in popular support for nationalism. The results show that the institutionalist theory correctly predicts the extent of nationalist mobilization across regions. Areas where ethnic institutions play a significant role in structuring people's lives are home to the strongest and most popular ethno-nationalist movements. At the same time, these results contradict the frequently made argument that a region's economic wealth is most important in determining support for separatism, showing that economically poor regions with extensive ethnic institutions can have much stronger nationalist movements than wealthy regions with few ethnic institutions. Institutions are thus shown to be crucial in determining the popularity of nationalist movements and their programs.

Chapter 6 discusses variation in support for nationalism across social groups within each region. I show how movement founders used preexisting social networks and group identities to disseminate the nationalist message and increase the breadth of support for their movement. I use statistical analysis of survey data to show which social groups were particularly likely to support nationalism. The evidence presented in this chapter confirms that the form of state institutions plays a key role in determining the extent of popular support for nationalist movements.

The final three chapters deal with the impact of minority nationalism in Russia on Russian politics and on political science. In Chapter 7, I analyze the effect of mass mobilization and protest on governmental decisions and policies. I find that in regions where ethnic institutions had been more developed during the Soviet period, government leaders were more likely to implement the ethno-cultural and political demands of the ethno-nationalist movements. Support of nationalism by government leaders appeared to be much more important than other factors, such as a movement's popularity among the population, in determining whether an ethnic movement's demands were deflected or adopted by the government.

Chapter 8 tests the theory developed in this study by showing how it explains support for nationalism in an additional thirteen ethnic republics of the Russian Federation. Statistical analysis of survey results is used to show that my thesis about the role of ethnic institutions in increasing support for nationalism holds true in this larger set of cases.

Chapter 9 concludes by exploring further the relationship between the structure of state institutions and mass mobilization in support of nationalist movements. I argue that the post-Soviet experience shows that ethnic mobilization is most likely to occur in countries that combine an ethnically based federal state structure with efforts to assimilate minority groups. The ethnic strife that has plagued the former Soviet region and the Balkans in the aftermath of the collapse of communism must serve to caution constitutional designers who believe that establishing an ethno-federal state or creating ethnic institutions for minority groups will put an end to minority nationalism. This study shows that such measures can frequently have exactly the opposite effect.

CONCLUSIONS

This study seeks to shift the emphasis in studies of ethnic nationalism from attempts to explain why ethnic mobilization occurs to an effort to explain the process through which nationalist movements emerge and develop. In doing so, it focuses on the role of the institutional structure of the state in promoting the development of an ethnic elite and in strengthening ethnic identities. This study seeks to extend the institutionalist analysis of ethnic mobilization beyond elite-focused explanations by focusing on the mass-based nature of most nationalist movements. Analysis of ethnic institutions can explain not only the behavior and motivations of nationalist leaders, politicians, and government officials, but also how these actors attempt to persuade potential followers to join nationalist movements and why these followers accept or reject these efforts. In moving beyond elite-focused accounts of ethnic mobilization, I emphasize the importance of collective identities and social networks in spreading the nationalist message beyond its initial core supporters. In doing so, I argue that ethnic groups are not herds of sheep that ethnic entrepreneurs are able to mobilize at will in order to achieve their political ends. In order for members of an ethnic group to join a nationalist mobilization effort, they must become convinced that they would gain either materially or psychologically from their participation.

2

Explaining Ethnic Mobilization
The Role of Ethnic Institutions

Institutions are often considered the most important force in shaping ethnic identities. This is so because they are seen as defining not just the options available to political actors or the actors' preferences, but also the actors' self-definitions. Institutions are defined as "the formal or informal procedures, routines, norms and conventions embedded in the organizational structure of the polity" (Hall and Taylor 1996, 938). Institutions affect politics in two crucial ways. First, institutions create enforcement mechanisms for agreements, assess penalties for violating the agreements, and control the flow of information, thus constraining the strategies pursued by actors in the political arena. By limiting the realm of the possible in politics, institutions force political actors to choose from a limited menu of options. Second, the institutional context shapes not only the strategies, but also the preferences and goals of political actors. Institutions influence preferences by providing cognitive and moral templates that actors can use to interpret and analyze a situation and possible courses of action. They have great power over political activity because they not only shape the ability of individuals to pursue their interests, but also structure the nature of the interests themselves (Hall and Taylor 1996, Thelen and Steinmo 1992).

The effects of institutions are not limited to shaping preferences. Through their control of information and their ability to set the rules of political competition, institutions also influence how political actors perceive themselves. Although many scholars discuss institutional effects on identity together with their effects on preferences (Hall and Taylor 1996, 939; Krasner 1988, 72), the two need to be carefully distinguished from each other. While preferences are the choices individuals make given a certain menu of options, identities come prior to these choices and reflect the groups to which individuals see themselves as belonging. Institutions influence these identities either explicitly, by assigning people to particular groups,[1] or implicitly, by structuring political competition in such a way that association along certain lines brings benefits, while association along certain other lines becomes in some way damaging.[2] Soviet ethnic institutions became one of the primary causal factors in the emergence of separatism in the Soviet Union under Gorbachev precisely because they manipulated ethnic identities in ways that promoted ethno-nationalism (Slezkine 1994b). Soviet ethnic institutions were critical for ethnic mobilization because they not only constrained the actions of members of minority ethnic groups, but also shaped their goals and preferences. Furthermore, through mechanisms such as passport ethnicity and territorial delimitation, these institutions largely determined individuals' sense of belonging to particular ethnic groups.

The Soviet effort to shape ethnic identities through the power of state institutions was certainly not unique in the history of the world. Benedict Anderson points out that the origin of such practices was firmly rooted in the practices of nineteenth-century colonial powers. He shows that the three colonial institutional innovations that played the greatest role in creating a sense of national identity among the colonized peoples were the census, the map, and the museum (Anderson 1991, 163). As I will show in this chapter, these three institutions, with the addition of the school and the passport, played the most important role in establishing a firm sense of national identity among the Soviet Union's minority populations. The Soviet Union thus essentially adopted and honed the colonialist policies it had inherited from the Russian Empire. Not surprisingly, its ethnic institution building resulted in the same increase in nationalist sentiment as had occurred in Asia and Africa as the result of similar colonialist policies on the part of Britain and France.

The discussion of Soviet ethnic institutions as a source of nationalist sentiment points to a possible explanation of variation in the level of ethnic mobilization. If ethnic institutions play such an important role in shaping and promoting ethnic identity, then regions where ethnic institutions under Soviet rule were stronger and more numerous should have stronger ethno-nationalist movements than regions with few and weak ethnic institutions. Since the extent to which ethnicity was institutionalized in the Soviet Union depended largely on a region's position in the administrative hierarchy (see the following discussion), the strength of ethno-nationalism in an ethnic region would largely depend on that region's position in the hierarchy.[3]

---

[1] Examples of such groupings include occupations lists, officially recognized religions, and, most importantly for the purposes of this study, ethnic categories.

[2] On this latter point, see Luong (2002).

[3] This position, in turn, was based largely on the size of each ethnic group's population and territory, not on factors such as cultural and economic development. Furthermore, the ethno-federal hierarchy was set by the mid-1930s. For these reasons, the argument that status in the administrative hierarchy is merely a reflection of cultural and economic factors does not hold. At most, this status may be a function of cultural and economic development in the 1920s,

Ethnic mobilization should therefore be most pronounced in union republics, followed by autonomous republics, and so forth, with the lowest levels of mobilization found among ethnic groups who lack an ethnic homeland of their own.

This chapter describes the types of ethnic institutions that existed in the Soviet Union and examines the extent to which ethnicity was institutionalized in each region. It provides the necessary baseline for our examination of the extent to which the breadth and depth of ethnic institutionalization during the Soviet period influenced the extent of nationalist mobilization in Russia's ethnic republics during and after the *perestroika* period.

THE FORMATION OF AN ETHNO-FEDERAL STATE

Soviet ethnic institutions, established in the 1920s and 1930s and largely unchanged since that time, were based on a dual conception of ethnicity as both personal and territorial.[4] Soviet ideology and scholarship followed Stalin in defining an ethnic group in a primordialist manner, as a "historically evolved, stable community based on a common language, territory, economic life and psychological makeup manifested in a community of culture" (Stalin 1950 [1913], 31). The personal conception of ethnicity was based on the idea that each individual belonged to a specific ethnic group and to that group alone. During the formative period of Soviet ethnic policy, ethnographers were instructed to determine the distinctive cultural features, language, and physical characteristics of each ethnic group, eliminating overlapping definitions and establishing criteria that would allow individuals to place themselves unerringly in a single ethnic category (Hirsch 1997).

Once individual ethnic groups had been distinguished, the next step in the institutionalization process involved ensuring that each individual was assigned to a particular ethnic group. This process began in 1932 with the introduction of the internal passport as the main identity document for Soviet citizens. Initially, ethnic identity was recorded according to the self-identification of the individual to whom the passport was being issued. This procedure mirrored the criteria used for ethnic identification of individuals in the 1926 census. Once the passport was issued, however, individuals were prohibited from changing their passport ethnicity.[5] Furthermore, children

---

disregarding changes in both factors during 70 years of Soviet rule. Furthermore, Daniel Treisman has determined by statistical methods that administrative status is significant in determining the extent of ethnic mobilization even when controlling for other factors that may be correlated with such status (Treisman 1997, 230–1).

[4] See Slezkine (1994b), Suny (1993), and Connor (1984). The discussion of the institutional forms of ethnicity in the Soviet Union, including the distinction between personal and territorial conceptions of ethnicity, is largely based on Brubaker (1996).

[5] The criterion of self-identification continued to be followed by the censuses, leading to occasional discrepancies between individual passport and census ethnic identity. Recent surveys have measured this discrepancy at approximately 2% of the population. (Data from a 1993

were required to select the same ethnicity as their parents. Children of mixed marriages were allowed to select the ethnicity of either parent at the age of sixteen, but had to choose one and were not allowed to alter this decision after that time[6] (Zaslavsky and Luryi 1979). By the end of the 1930s, most transactions between individuals and the state required the individual to publicly declare his or her ethnic identity – which was recorded in employment records, student files, and army documents in addition to the aforementioned internal passport (Hirsch 1997, 268). It is not surprising that the constant declaration of one's ethnic identity had the effect of reinforcing the strength of that identity.[7] By requiring that individuals be "marked" with their ethnic identity in this manner, the Soviet state ensured that ethnicity became a highly relevant identity marker and tied the individual to his or her ethnic group.[8]

The second side of the Soviet conception of ethnicity connected each ethnic group with a piece of land that was considered to belong to that group. As its name indicates, and unlike the highly centralized Russian Empire, the Soviet Union was from its creation designed to be, at least formally, a federal state. The crucial innovation of its federalism was that each constituent region was supposed to represent a particular ethnic group. This connection of ethnicity to territory, which followed from Stalin's definition of nation, had a decisive impact on the development of ethnic relations in subsequent decades (Suny 1993, 110). By establishing and institutionalizing the connection between each ethnic group and a particular piece of land, the Soviet government planted the seeds of secessionist ethno-nationalism – seeds that were to sprout sixty years later.

The territorial conception of ethnicity was consolidated through two related institutions: the division of the country into a federation of ethnically based administrative units, and the establishment of a hierarchy among these units. The creation of ethnically based administrative units had two important effects.[9] First, by granting ethnic regions a certain degree of autonomy

---

Laitin/Hough survey entitled "Nationality and Politics: The Dismemberment of the Soviet Union.")

[6] What I am describing here are the formal rules according to which personal ethnic identity was regulated. Occasionally, individuals were able to have their ethnic identity changed for career purposes. For more on this, see Gorenburg (1999).

[7] This effect was less pronounced among ethnic Russians because of the government campaign to link Russian ethnic identity and Soviet national identity. Nevertheless, the reification of ethnic categories prevented a wholesale re-identification of Russians as Soviets.

[8] Much has been written on why the avowedly internationalist and antinationalist Soviet state created an institution that had the effect of separating people according to ethnicity. I find Slezkine's account to be the most convincing; he argues that Communist leaders decided that they could succeed in preaching socialism to ethnic minorities only through the medium of the minority culture – hence the slogan, "National in form, Socialist in content" (Slezkine 1994b).

[9] There is a large literature on the creation of the Soviet federal system. For good historical accounts, see Pipes (1964) and Nahaylo and Swoboda (1990). For a more analytical account that focuses on the effects of this policy on ethnic identity, see Slezkine (1994b).

Explaining Ethnic Mobilization 31

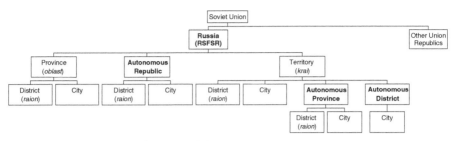

FIGURE 2.1. Structure of the Soviet federation.

in the name of the right to self-determination, the Soviet state contributed to the development of a belief among these minorities that sovereignty was their right and that the purely formal sovereignty of the Soviet period should be replaced by actual sovereignty and even independence[10] (Sheehy 1991, 84). Second, by endowing each ethnic region with its own governing institutions, the Soviet state created a "durable institutional frame" for the development of national political and cultural elites and the promotion of national cultures and languages (Brubaker 1996, 30). This institutional frame depended on a combination of personal and territorial conceptions of ethnicity.

The second part of the territorial conception of ethnicity consisted of a division of the ethnically based administrative units (and the ethnic groups associated with them) into a four-tier hierarchy (see Figure 2.1). The level of both formal and actual autonomy possessed by a region increased with each level of the hierarchy. At the top of this hierarchy were the *union republics*, which were formally declared fully sovereign, had their own constitutions, and were given the theoretical right to secede and to conduct foreign relations. More practical advantages of union republic status included republic academies of science, greater representation in the federal legislative body,[11] greater linguistic autonomy, a complete native-language educational system including universities, and a significant degree of self-rule by local elites. During periods of liberalization, union republic governments also controlled economic and budgetary decision making for the territory (Gleason 1990, 82–83; Simon 1991, 4).

One level lower were the *autonomous republics*, each of which was subordinated to a union republic and roughly equivalent to a nonethnic province (*oblast*) in status. Autonomous republics were considered partially sovereign and also had their own constitutions and governmental organs, which did not need to be approved by the government of the union republic. They also

---

[10] The development of this ideology is dealt with in detail in Chapter 4.
[11] The Nationalities Chamber of the Supreme Soviet included 32 members from each union republic, 11 deputies from each autonomous republic, 5 deputies from each autonomous province, and 1 deputy from each autonomous district (Connor 1984, 222).

had the right to initiate legislation in the union republic Supreme Soviets. Unlike union republics, they did not have the right to secede or to conduct foreign policy. Instead of their own academies of science, they had branches of the union republic academies of science or simply institutes for the study of local culture. Education in autonomous republics was conducted in the native language either until the upper grades or through the end of high school. Autonomous republics printed fewer native-language publications, and their universities taught only in Russian. These regions had some self-rule, particularly in cultural decisions and spending, although most economic and budgetary decisions were made at the union republic level (Lapidoth 1997, 89–90).

Autonomous provinces were not sovereign and did not have their own constitutions. Instead, the provincial council had the right to recommend a law for the autonomous region, which was then adopted by the Supreme Soviet of the union republic (Lapidoth 1997, 89). The autonomy of these provinces was largely limited to cultural matters, and they were subject to three levels of bureaucracy – the union, the union republic, and the administrative territory (*krai*) of which each was a part[12] (Schwartz 1990, 128). These provinces generally lacked native-language education beyond the third or fourth grade and had no universities on their territory. The promotion of local culture was conducted by small institutes of ethnic culture. Local ethnic elites sometimes did not control the provincial government, which had only administrative powers in any case. The provincial budget allocation, for example, was entirely determined by the *krai* administration.

At the bottom of the hierarchy stood the *autonomous districts*, which had been created largely to provide ethnic homelands for the indigenous population of the Soviet far north.[13] These districts were similar in status to autonomous provinces, although they often had no native-language education whatsoever, and their local governments were rarely controlled by the indigenous population. Like the autonomous provinces, each district was part of a *krai* (Lapidoth 1997, 88).

Outside of this hierarchy, and below all of the other ethnic groups in status, stood those ethnic groups that were not provided with their own ethnic territories. These groups had no ethnic institutions except for passport identification. They had no native-language schools, no culture-producing institutions, and no preferential quotas in employment (Slezkine 1994b, 445). As a result, these groups were highly vulnerable to assimilation; the total population of many of these groups has remained at a constant level for several decades (Anderson and Silver 1990, 128–30).

---

[12] *Krai* was the designation for a territorially large *oblast*-level administrative unit that contained an autonomous *oblast* or *okrug* within it. Otherwise, the terms *krai* and *oblast* are identical designations.

[13] For more detail on the northern peoples, see Slezkine (1994a).

This hierarchy thus played a role in fostering ethno-nationalism for both symbolic and practical reasons. The rank ordering of ethnic groups on the basis of their positions in the hierarchy led to resentment among members of many lower-ranked groups, who believed that their groups were equally worthy of having union republics. The differences in autonomy, local self-government, and cultural development affected the strength and unity of the national intelligentsia and the extent to which the members of the group as a whole were able to avoid Russification.

I will now briefly describe the establishment of ethno-territorial federalism in each of the four republics under study. These accounts demonstrate the differences among the regions in the extent to which ethnicity was institutionalized, including differences among regions at the same level of the ethno-federal hierarchy.

Tatarstan. In the aftermath of the overthrow of the Russian monarchy in February 1917, Tatar leaders joined the leaders of other Muslim ethnic groups in pressing for greater cultural autonomy for non-Russian peoples. Although most Tatar leaders supported extraterritorial cultural autonomy, they were outvoted at the First All-Russian Muslim Congress, held in Moscow in May 1917, by supporters of territorial autonomy within a federal state. This event marked the beginning of a division among Muslim ethnic groups in Russia, a division that culminated in the Bashkir leaders' refusal to participate in a Tatar-Bashkir republic and the creation of a separate Bashkir Autonomous Soviet Socialist Republic (ASSR) in 1919 (Rorlich 1986, 128, 137). A separate Tatar ASSR was established in May 1920. Because Lenin rejected a proposal to include the entire Ufa province in the republic, only one-third of the Tatars living in the Volga region were included within its boundaries (Batyev and Fatkullin 1982, 91).

The Tatar ASSR was given more control over its own affairs and more influence on the central government than other autonomous republics. The chairman of the Tatarstan Supreme Soviet's Presidium was usually appointed the deputy chairman of the Presidium of the Russian Federative Republic's Supreme Soviet (Batyev and Fatkullin 1982, 167). Tatarstan was one of the few autonomous republics whose 1937 Constitution enshrined the publication of all official documents in the titular language in addition to Russian. The republic government was responsible for determining the republic budget and economic plan and for allocating funds to cities and districts within the republic. The republic's Supreme Soviet was given the authority to amend the republic Constitution and to formulate legislation for the republic. The 1977 Constitution gave the republic Supreme Soviet the right to propose legislation in the Supreme Soviets of the Russian Federal Republic and the Soviet Union (Batyev and Fatkullin 1982, 123–7, 161). Of course, many of the powers assigned to the republic government by the Constitution were purely formal. But these formal rules created expectations and norms that enabled the republic leadership to wrest a significant amount of control away from Moscow during the *perestroika* period.

Bashkortostan. Bashkir historians consider Bashkortostan to be the first autonomous republic created by the Communist government. Its establishment in March 1919 was the culmination of a drive by Bashkir nationalist forces to prevent the creation of a Tatar-dominated Turkic republic in the Volga-Ural region. This republic was significantly smaller than present-day Bashkortostan. For the first few years of its existence, the republic was governed on the basis of a treaty between the Bashkir nationalist forces and the Bolshevik government. This agreement gave the Bashkir government broad powers, including the right to maintain its own army (Kasimov 1991, 11). By 1922, the Soviet government had ceased to accept the treaty as binding and had removed the original Bashkir nationalist leadership in favor of a new, mostly non-Bashkir group of leaders (Iuldashbaev 1995a, 107–8). Soon thereafter, most of the Ufa province was joined to the republic, and the capital was moved to the city of Ufa. Since the newly added territory was populated mainly by Russians and Tatars, this territorial change significantly altered the demographic balance. From then on, Bashkirs were outnumbered in the republic by both Tatars and Russians.

The authority of the Bashkir government, which at first saw itself as an equal partner to the Russian government, was gradually reduced during the 1920s and 1930s. The 1925 draft constitution of the republic declared Bashkortostan to be a state that had freely joined the Russian Federated Republic. Under this constitution, the Bashkir government had sole control over several ministries, including those of agriculture, industry, health, education, and culture. During the discussion of the 1936 constitution, Bashkir and Tatar leaders unsuccessfully proposed making their regions union republics. Instead, the powers of the Bashkortostan government were significantly reduced, so that it no longer had sole control of any ministries, instead sharing authority over them with the government of the Russian republic (Iuldashbaev 1995a, 146). At the same time, Bashkortostan retained formal authority over the budget and other aspects of local government, in roughly the same dimensions as Tatarstan.

Chuvashia. Because of their Orthodox Christian religion, the Chuvash did not become part of the Tatar-led pan-Islamic movement. Nevertheless, they petitioned Tatar leaders to include their territory in the autonomous Volga-Ural state proposed by the Tatar Communist Mullanur Vakhitov in 1918 (Pipes 1964, 159). After this idea was scuttled by Bashkir nationalists, the Soviet government decided to create an autonomous Chuvash province. The province was officially established in June 1920. This territory, although populated almost entirely by Chuvash, was small and lacked the industrial centers to make it viable in the eyes of Soviet officials. For this reason, the following five years were spent in negotiations on expanding the region's territory. At the conclusion of these negotiations in 1925, three Russian-majority districts, including the industrial center of Alatyr, were added to Chuvashia. At the same time, the region was upgraded to the status of an autonomous republic (Ivanov 1992, 18–20).

The republic's first Constitution, adopted in 1926, formally imbued Chuvashia with broad powers of self-government. The republic government had complete control over internal affairs, justice, education, health, agriculture, and social welfare, while sharing jurisdiction over finances, labor, and trade with the Russian Federative Republic. Jurisdiction over military affairs, transport, and foreign policy was ceded to the government of the Soviet Union (Akhazov 1979, 22–3). Like other autonomous republics, Chuvashia had the right to pass its own legislation and to propose legislation in the Supreme Soviets of the Russian Republic and the Soviet Union. The 1926 Constitution officially enshrined Russian and Chuvash as the official languages of the republic (Konstitutsiia 1930, 6). Later republic constitutions did not discuss language status, although the 1936 constitution did state that the courts in Chuvash-majority areas must conduct their affairs using the Chuvash language (Konstitutsiia 1961, 20). Although Chuvashia remained an autonomous republic, its effective status was lower than that of the Tatar and Bashkir republics. From 1929 to 1936, the republic was under the jurisdiction of the Nizhegorod territory (*krai*), effectively giving it the same status as an autonomous province. The republic government and Communist Party branch were both subject to decisions made in Nizhni Novgorod, the capital of the territory (Kuznetsov 1967, 68).

Khakassia. Like members of other ethnic groups, the Khakass saw the collapse of the Russian monarchy as an opportunity to achieve self-government. Toward this end, they convened several congresses from May 1917 to May 1918, culminating in the adoption of a declaration of Khakass self-government (Tuguzhekova 1993, 9–10). For the first six months of 1918, the group practiced a form of self-government, with Khakass councils governing Khakass villages, while Bolshevik councils governed Russian villages. The Council of the Steppe was considered the supreme governing body of the Khakass people and had jurisdiction over agriculture, trade, education, and social services in the areas under its control. The Council also began to establish a system of Khakass courts. This first attempt at Khakass self-government was terminated by the conquest of the area by Admiral Kolchak's White Army in 1918 (Mitiukov 1973, 40–1).

After the reconquest of the area by the Red Army in 1920, Communist leaders decided to establish an ethnic administrative unit in the Khakass region. The Khakass district (*uezd*) of the Enisei province was established in 1923. In 1925, the new Russian Constitution delineated the status of national districts (renamed *okrugs*). The Khakass district government was given the authority to implement the decisions of the provincial government and to oversee the political, cultural, and economic development of the region, as well as the right to send representatives to the provincial soviet.

The district was not considered a self-governing unit of the Russian republic (Mitiukov 1973, 42–6). In 1930, the central government established the Khakass autonomous province (*oblast*) as part of the West Siberian territory (*krai*), which was later renamed the Krasnoyarsk territory (Tuguzhekova 1993, 24).

As an autonomous province, Khakassia remained essentially a district of West Siberia, but a district with some powers of self-government and with direct representation in Moscow. During the first several years of its existence, Khakassia had direct control over education, health and social services, land issues, courts, and local budgets. The autonomous province also sent a delegate to the Russian Republic Supreme Soviet and had a representative in Moscow for direct contacts with the executive branch (Mitiukov 1973, 49–50). At the same time, it did not have many of the formal attributes of sovereignty possessed by autonomous republics. These missing attributes were both symbolic – for example, the lack of a flag and coat of arms – and substantive – the lack of a constitution, Supreme Soviet, and government ministries. The constitutional reform of 1936 left Khakassia's position in the federal structure largely unchanged, with the exception of its representation in Moscow. According to the new rules, Khakassia sent five delegates to the Supreme Soviet, instead of just one. But at the same time, the position of representative to the executive branch was eliminated, leaving the region highly dependent on the Krasnoyarsk administration (Tuguzhekova 1993, 30; Mitiukov 1973, 54).

The creation of ethno-federal regions in the Soviet Union helped to solidify ethnic identities among minority ethnic groups. A region's administrative status determined the extent to which members of the native ethnic group controlled the government. When ethnic regions were being established, their initial status depended primarily on the size of the area inhabited by the region's titular ethnic group and the size of that group's population. The largest ethnic groups were granted the highest status, particularly if they inhabited large contiguous regions, while small and widely scattered ethnic groups received regions with lower status.[14] Cultural and economic factors were largely ignored in this process. For example, Bashkortostan was established as the first autonomous republic in Russia despite its economic backwardness. Chuvashia, by contrast, was not initially granted this status despite a relatively high level of cultural development. In-depth analysis of the establishment of ethno-federalism confirms Daniel Treisman's statistical finding that administrative status is not significantly correlated with cultural and economic factors in determining the ethno-territorial status of a region (Treisman 1997, 230–1).

---

[14] Although the ethnic groups of the far north inhabited very large areas, these areas were sparsely populated.

THE DEVELOPMENT OF ETHNIC INSTITUTIONS

Differences in ethno-federal status determined the extent to which other ethnic institutions were developed in each region. These institutions included systems of native-language education, academic institutes for the study of local culture, cultural institutions, and ethnic preferences in government employment. The spread and penetration of these institutions largely determined the ability of nationalist movements to foster ethnic mobilization in each region.

Native-language Education

Most scholars of nationalism focus on the importance of native-language education for the consolidation of national or ethnic identity (Anderson 1991, Gellner 1983, Horowitz 1985). Soviet ideology considered the promotion of the native language as particularly crucial to the consolidation of ethnic identity because in the Soviet Union, language was considered the most important characteristic that distinguished ethnic groups from each other (Slezkine 1994b, 428). To ensure the continued vitality of the language, the governments of all Soviet ethnic regions developed programs of native-language promotion and native-language education. Before the 1959 school reform made titular-language classes optional, all students irrespective of nationality were required to study the language of the region in which they lived. Furthermore, most students who belonged to the titular ethnic group attended schools where all subjects were taught in the native language (Silver 1974, 31). After the reform, the native-language educational systems began to decline in most ethnic regions, although the rate of decline varied depending on the region's place in the administrative hierarchy. Beginning in the 1960s, most non-titular schoolchildren no longer attended titular-language classes. In many regions below union republic level, native-language education gradually became unavailable in urban areas and at higher grade levels. Nevertheless, throughout the ethnic regions, education in the native language continued to be dominant in rural areas, which increasingly provided the bulk of the administrators and creative intelligentsia in ethnic republics. Even in urban areas, where native-language education declined dramatically during the 1960s, study of the native language as a subject continued to be universally available (Silver 1978, 261).

Even in its post-1959 weakened form, native language education ensured that a large proportion of each ethnic group maintained a link with the culture and traditions of the group. Since language was the most important aspect of ethnic identity, people who spoke the ethnic group's language were relatively unlikely to change their ethnic self-identification. Various studies have shown that Russification was negatively correlated with the extent of native-language education – ethnic groups with more developed native-language educational systems counted fewer Russian-speakers among their members (Silver 1978; Anderson and Silver 1990, 109) In combination with the passport registration of ethnicity, knowledge of one's native language was a strong deterrent to assimilation.

By the 1980s, the extent of native-language education in ethnic regions varied in accordance with the region's status in the ethno-federal hierarchy. Tatarstan and Bashkortostan, which had a higher functional status than other autonomous republics, had the most extensive programs of native-language education. Chuvashia, despite having the highest titular proportion of the population, was well behind. Khakassia, as an autonomous province, by 1989 had no education in the native language and only limited teaching of the Khakass language as a subject.

In *Tatarstan*, native-language education was always available in all ten grades. However, the percentage of Tatar students in Tatar-language schools gradually declined. Until the mid-1950s, all Tatar schoolchildren were taught in the Tatar language. By 1959, this figure had dropped to approximately 60% (138,000). Ten years later, these numbers were only slightly lower, but by 1980 the percentage of Tatar students taught in Tatar had dropped to approximately 40%. These numbers continued to decline steadily during the 1980s. In 1990, of the approximately 245,000 Tatar students, only 27% were being educated in the Tatar language. The vast majority – over 70% – of the remaining 180,000 Tatar schoolchildren studied Tatar as a subject. The overwhelming majority of Tatar-language schools were located in rural areas. While approximately two-thirds of rural Tatar schoolchildren were educated in Tatar, only 2% of urban Tatar children attended Tatar schools.[15]

Bashkortostan, like Tatarstan, has always made a full ten-year education in Bashkir available to its students. Data on native-language education in the republic prior to the 1970s is not available. The 1972 data shows that approximately 50% of Bashkir students (98,000) were educated in the Bashkir language. Since 30% of the Bashkir population declared Tatar to be their native language in the 1970 census, the extent of Bashkir education may be more accurately portrayed as a percentage of the total Bashkir-speaking student population. If the Tatar-speaking Bashkir population is excluded, 78% of the remaining Bashkir-speaking Bashkir schoolchildren were receiving a Bashkir-language education in 1972. By 1981, this figure had dropped slightly, to 73% (65,000) of the Bashkir-speaking Bashkir student population. During the 1980s, the decline was more significant, so that by 1989 only 50% (44,000) of the Bashkir-speaking Bashkir students were receiving a Bashkir-language education. Another 40% of the Bashkir-speaking Bashkir students studied Bashkir as a subject.[16]

---

[15] Data from Terentieva and Alishev (1993), Iskhakov and Musina (1992, 135) and the Tatarstan Ministry of Education.

[16] Data drawn from Iuldashbaev (1995b, 25, 33), Murzabulatov (1995, 128), and the Bashkortostan Ministry of Education and its archive.

In *Chuvashia*, the 1959 reform resulted in a gradual reduction of the maximum available number of years of Chuvash-language education from seven to four. In 1961, 61% (82,000) of all Chuvash students were being educated in the Chuvash language. Of this number, most were in primary school. Overall, native-language education covered 90% of children in primary school, 40% of children in grades five through seven, and none of the children in the upper grades. By 1980, the percentage of children being educated in Chuvash had fallen to 32%, all in grades one through four. During the 1980s, the percentage of Chuvash students educated in Chuvash continued to fall, reaching its lowest level of 22% in 1990. An additional 32% of students studied Chuvash as a subject.[17]

As an autonomous province, *Khakassia* never had as much native-language education as the autonomous republics. Prior to 1959, Khakass schoolchildren were educated in their native language through the fourth grade. After the school reform, most Khakass schools gradually began to teach entirely in Russian, beginning with the first grade. In 1960, 37% (3,300) of all Khakass schoolchildren were being educated in Khakass, including 53% of the children in primary school. An additional 21% (1,900), or 70% of all children in grades five through ten, studied Khakass as a subject. After 1966, instruction in the Khakass language was gradually eliminated, so that by 1989 there were no schools in Khakassia where classes were conducted in Khakass. In addition, of the 11,300 Khakass students in the region, only 7,722 (68%) attended classes where Khakass was taught as a subject. In urban areas, only 26% of Khakass students were taught Khakass in school.[18]

None of the four regions discussed in this study had any universities where classes were taught entirely in the titular language. In the Soviet system of ethnic institutions, such universities were allowed to exist only in union republics. The three autonomous republics had small titular-language departments in the universities, as well as departments dedicated to producing titular-language teachers in the pedagogical institutes. Khakassia had only the latter.

Academic Institutions

A native-language educational system required an ethnic intelligentsia to create curricula, write literature, and interpret the traditional culture of the ethnic group for a modern audience in a socialist state. To this end, each ethnic region established institutes and academies whose primary task was

---

[17] Data from Goskomostat (1995, 90–4), the Chuvashia Ministry of Education, and the Chuvash Republic State Archive, f. 221, op. 31, d. 265; and f. 221, op. 31, d. 144.
[18] Data from Khakassia Ministry of Education; the Republic of Khakassia State Archive, f.229 op. 1 d. 62a; and the Republic of Khakassia Supreme Soviet, *Gosudarstvennaia Programma Sokhraneniia i Razvitiia Iazykov Narodov Respubliki Khakassia na 1994–2000 gg.* (Abakan: Khakassia Supreme Soviet, 1994).

TABLE 2.1. *Extent of native-language education, by ethnicity*

	Education with Native Language of Instruction			Native Language as Subject 1989–90: % of Total Titular Students
	Highest Grade Available 1989	% of Total Titular Students 1980	% of Total Titular Students 1989/90	
Tatar	10	40	27	52
Bashkir	10	73	50	40
Chuvash	4	12	22	32
Khakass	0	0	0	68

Sources: As cited in text.

to study and produce the culture of that region's titular ethnic group. Most regions had no secular academic institutions prior to the Communist revolution. The earliest steps to establish such institutions were taken during the 1920s and 1930s, the period when minority cultural development was most strongly encouraged by the Soviet state. During this period, most ethnic regions established academic institutes dedicated to studying the history, culture, and language of the titular ethnic group. Although these institutes were initially under the direct authority of the region's government, many were later integrated into regional scientific centers that were part of the unionwide Academy of Sciences. In one form or another, these institutes remained the institutional base for the academic study of titular ethnic groups throughout the Soviet and post-Soviet periods. In most regions, the earliest institutions of higher education were also established during this period. These consisted primarily of teachers' colleges and agricultural institutes. During the 1950s and 1960s, universities were established throughout the autonomous republics, further expanding the academic networks in these regions. Autonomous provinces were not allowed to establish universities until the 1990s, when their status became equal to that of the autonomous republics in the wake of the Soviet Union's collapse.

The establishment of these academic institutes and universities led to the emergence of an intellectual elite whose members were often viewed as the leaders of the nation. This elite was also only tangentially connected to the Communist Party and the rest of the governing elite. Once in place, members of the cultural elite had strong incentives to ensure that ethnic cultural development was maintained and expanded, as this would ensure their job security and the maintenance of their status in the community. For these reasons, members of this elite were both well positioned to emerge as an alternative political elite during the liberalization of the 1980s and highly interested in getting involved in politics. As I discuss in Chapter 4, this group formed the core of most ethnic movements during the *perestroika* period.

In addition to encouraging the emergence of an intellectual elite, academic institutions in ethnic republics promoted ethnic mobilization by providing material resources, meeting places, and a source of potential recruits for movement activists. The extent to which academic institutions could play this role depended largely on their size and power. Some regions had their own branches of the Soviet Academy of Sciences, often with several institutes dedicated to the study of the titular ethnic group, while others were limited to a single Institute of Culture. Autonomous republics tended to have their own state universities, while autonomous provinces and districts did not. Finally, while all ethnic regions had at least one pedagogical institute, the number and location of these educational institutions influenced the availability of ethnic teachers, particularly in rural areas.[19]

Tatarstan's academic institutions were among the most developed in the country. Kazan State University had been founded in 1804 and was considered one of the five most prestigious universities in Russia throughout the nineteenth and early twentieth centuries. Under Soviet rule, an additional fourteen institutions of higher education were founded in the republic, including three technical institutes in Kazan, one in Naberezhnye Chelny, three pedagogical institutes (in Kazan, Naberezhnye Chelny, and Elabuga), a medical school, and a conservatory, as well as several other institutions. These institutions had a total of 66,000 students and 5,800 faculty members. The Tatar language and culture were studied at several departments of the university, at the pedagogical institutes, and at the Kazan Institute of Art and Culture. In addition to the educational institutions, Tatarstan boasted the largest branch of the Soviet Academy of Sciences among the autonomous republics. The Kazan branch, opened in 1945, included five institutes, including one focused on the Tatar language, literature, and culture. Because it was part of a branch of the Academy, the Tatar Institute of Language, Literature, and Culture had the authority and resources to publish its own monographs. In addition to the Academy, more than 25 scientific institutes were based in the republic (Mustafin and Khuzeev 1994, 65–7; Zakiev 1995, 151).

As of 1990, *Bashkortostan* had nine institutions of higher education, including the Bashkir State University, three pedagogical institutes, two technical institutes, a medical school, and institutes of agriculture and the arts. The university, founded in 1957, enrolled 8,600 students taught by 590 faculty members. Departments conducting research on Bashkir culture included those of history, geography, law, economics, and Bashkir philology. The

---

[19] The collapse of the Soviet Union led to a sharp drop in state financing of scientific research and education, leading to substantial changes in the structures of the academic environment in all of the regions. I have attempted to describe each republic's academic institutions as they existed in the late 1980s, when their influence on the formation of nationalist movements was at its peak.

TABLE 2.2. *Extent of scientific research, by region*

	Tatarstan	Bashkortostan	Chuvashia	Khakassia
Academy of Science branch	Yes	Yes	No	No
University	Yes	Yes	Yes	No
VUZy (total)	15	9	3	2
Research institutes (total)	30	14	8	1

Sources: As cited in text.

university shared responsibility for academic research and publishing on this subject with the Ufa Scientific Center of the Urals Branch of the Soviet Academy of Sciences, established in 1951. The Ufa Scientific Center included institutes of history, language, and literature (founded in 1930), of the peoples of the Urals, and of economics and sociology – all of which focused on the study of the Bashkir nation – that collectively employed over 200 researchers. There were eleven other academic institutes in the republic, primarily concerned with technology and the natural sciences (Shakurov 1996).

Chuvashia's academic institutions were significantly less developed than Tatarstan's. The first institution of higher education in the republic, a pedagogical institute, opened in 1930, followed by an agricultural institute in 1931. The republic did not have its own university until 1967, when the Chuvash State University opened. As of 1995, the university enrolled 11,000 students and had 864 faculty members. In addition to the university, academic research on Chuvash culture was conducted at the Chuvash Institute of Language, Literature, History, and Economics, which had been run by the republic government since 1930. Although this institute was the center of academic research on the Chuvash ethnic group, because it was not a part of the Soviet Academy of Sciences its works were published by the university. In addition to this institute, there were seven other research institutes in the republic, mostly involved in technical and agricultural research (Sergeev and Zaitsev 1995, 51–6).

As an autonomous province, *Khakassia* was not allowed to establish a university, although an effort to this end was made in the 1970s.[20] Scientific research in the republic was carried out by the Department of Culture at the Abakan Pedagogical Institute, which had been established in 1939, and by the Khakass Institute of Language, Literature, and History, established in 1944. Both institutes were limited in their ability to publish research by a

---

[20] Mikhail Mitiukov, "Khakassii nuzhen gosuniversitet," *Abakan*, 10 March 1993.

TABLE 2.3. *Effects of administrative status and regional demographics on the publication of native-language newspapers*

Explanatory Variable	% Titular Papers
Administrative status	10.319 (2.479)*
% titular population	.712 (.112)*

Note: Entries are multiple regression coefficients; standard errors are in parentheses. N = 49
* $p < .0001$

lack of facilities and their lack of juridical status. Other than the pedagogical institute, the only institution of higher education in the republic was a branch of the Krasnoyarsk Polytechnic Institute.

Cultural Development

Ethnic institutions played a key role in determining the extent of cultural development in each republic. The strength of these institutions, as indicated by the number and circulation of titular-language newspapers, the existence of professional unions of cultural workers, and the status of titular-language theaters obviously depended on the proportion of the region's population made up by the titular ethnic group. The administrative status of the ethnic region, however, also correlated strongly with the extent of these institutions, even when controlling for demographic factors. For example, these two variables together explained 76% of the variation in the extent of native-language newspaper publishing. While each additional percentage point of titular population increased the balance of native-language newspapers by .71%, a one-step increase in level within the ethno-federal administrative hierarchy increased the percentage of native language newspapers by an additional 10.3%.[21]

The media played an important role in spreading the nationalist message. Although all ethnic regions had their own native-language television and radio stations, in the early years of *perestroika* television and radio tended to be subject to strict controls that prohibited the broadcast of nationalist messages. For this reason, native-language newspapers, which were usually more willing than Russian-language papers to print articles with a nationalist

---

[21] Other variables, such as the total population of the region and the total titular population of the region, were not significant. Data includes all ethnic regions of the Soviet Union and is drawn from the 1979 census and the catalog of Soviet periodical publications entitled *Letopis Periodicheskikh i Prodolzhaiushchikhsia Izdanii*, 1980 edition.

tone, were particularly crucial in spreading the nationalist message during the early stages of the movement. The reach of these newspapers helped to determine the ability of nationalist activists to spread their ideas outside urban centers, to areas where public protest actions did not occur. Tatarstan had the most highly developed network of native-language newspapers. Fifty-one newspapers had a combined circulation of 537 copies per 1,000 titular inhabitants, which translated into 54% of the total newspaper circulation in the republic. Tatarstan also had 10 Tatar-language magazines, with a total circulation of 571 copies per 1,000 titular inhabitants. Bashkortostan had two Bashkir-language republic newspapers and 24 local newspapers with a combined circulation of 294 copies per 1,000 titular inhabitants. Since Bashkirs made up only a small percentage of the republic's total population, Bashkir-language newspapers constituted only 16% of the total newspaper circulation in the republic. There were also seven Bashkir-language magazines, with a total circulation of 232 copies per 1,000 titular inhabitants. Chuvashia, despite its majority Chuvash population, had a less extensive network of Chuvash-language newspapers, which included the republic newspaper *Khypar* and 23 local newspapers. These newspapers had a total daily circulation of 191 copies per 1,000 titular inhabitants, which was only 35% of the total newspaper circulation in the republic. In addition, there were six Chuvash-language magazines, with a total circulation of 155 copies per 1,000 titular inhabitants. Khakassia had only one Khakass-language newspaper, with a circulation of 95 copies per 1,000 titular inhabitants, which made up only 5% of the total republic newspaper circulation. There were no Khakass-language magazines and no local Khakass newspapers (Pechat' 1991).

Professional unions of cultural workers were second only to academic institutes as a source of nationalist leaders. The types of unions included under this category included unions of writers, journalists, composers, cinematographers, theater workers, architects, and artists. Of these, the unions of writers, artists, and composers were the most likely to serve as a base for ethno-nationalist recruiting. As with other cultural institutions, the strength and number of such unions depended on the administrative status of the region. Autonomous republics tended to have their own unions of writers, artists, and musicians, while autonomous districts' unions were considered merely sections of the union republic's relevant union. Tatarstan, Bashkortostan, and Chuvashia all had strong unions of writers, artists, and composers that by 1990 had been in existence for at least 50 years. By contrast, Khakassia had only a Union of Composers and a section of the Union of Soviet Writers. In all cases, members of these unions, and particularly members of writers' unions, were overwhelmingly members of the titular ethnic group. For example, in Bashkortostan, 74% of the writers and 53% of the composers were Bashkir, although only 19% of the artists belonged

TABLE 2.4. *Cultural institutions by region*

	Tatarstan	Bashkortostan	Chuvashia	Khakassia
Number of titular newspapers	51	25	24	1
Titular newspaper circulation per 1,000 titular inhabitants	537	294	191	95
Number of titular magazines	10	7	6	0
Titular magazine circulation per 1,000 titular inhabitants	571	232	155	0
Number of cultural unions	3	3	3	1.5
Number of titular theaters	8	6	4	1.5

Sources: As cited in text.

to the titular ethnic group. Similarly, in Chuvashia, 90% of the writers and 84% of the composers were Chuvash, as well as 48% of the artists.[22]

Finally, national culture was spread by a web of titular-language theaters and performing groups, which were based in the major cities of each ethnic region but frequently traveled to rural areas to stage plays and performances that emphasized the history and culture of the titular ethnic group. In Tatarstan, there were eight Tatar theaters, including three outside the capital (Mustafin and Khuzeev 1993, 24). In Bashkortostan, there were six Bashkir theaters, including four in Ufa and one each in the southern cities of Salavat and Sibai (Bashkortostan 1996, 72–3). In Chuvashia, there were four Chuvash theaters in Cheboksary, but none outside the capital city (Sergiev and Zaitsev 1995, 67–70). Finally, in Khakassia, there was no official independent Khakass dramatic theater. Instead, Khakass and Russian troupes shared the State Drama Theater in Abakan. In addition, also in Abakan, there was a small traditional Khakass theater (Tuguzhekova 1993, 76–7).

The development of cultural institutions thus shows a pattern similar to that of academic institutions. Tatarstan had the best developed system of cultural institutions, followed in order by Bashkortostan, Chuvashia, and Khakassia. Strong and numerous cultural unions and theaters provided an additional source of nationalist activists, while the number and circulation

[22] For information on these unions, see Pimenov and Ivanov (1991, 173), Mustafin and Khuzeev (1993, 67), Shakurov (1996, 537–8), Sergeev and Zaitsev (1995, 63–70), and Giliazetdinov (1993, 38–9).

of titular language newspapers and magazines reflected the ability of these activists to spread their message to members of the titular ethnic group who did not belong to social groups which constituted their initial base of support.

Ethnic Preferences and Quotas

Since each ethnic region "belonged" to its titular ethnic group, it seemed natural that local government was run by members of the group. The policy of indigenization of governing elites was called *korenizatsiia* and extended not only to administrative jobs, but also to jobs in the Communist Party, trade unions, the judiciary, and industry, and to admissions to universities and prestigious schools (Simon 1991, 20–70). "Most official positions and school admissions in the Soviet Union were subject to complex ethnic quotas" (Slezkine 1994b, 439). During the peak of indigenization in the 1920s, Tatar representation in local councils increased dramatically, as did the use of the Tatar language in the conduct of government business in Tatarstan. Bashkirs were significantly overrepresented in the republic government, making up 30% of the Supreme Soviet and executive during the 1930s, when their percentage of the total population hovered around 25%. In Chuvashia, titulars made up 68% of the republic government and 59% of the republic Communist Party. In Khakassia, titulars comprised about 40% of the provincial council's membership and almost half of the membership of local councils in the province, despite comprising only 16% of the population.

Although the concept of *korenizatsiia* was officially dropped from Soviet ideology in the 1930s, the quota system remained in use throughout the postwar period, leading to occasional charges of reverse discrimination against Russians and other non-titulars (Karklins 1986, 96). Throughout this period, Tatars usually comprised 50–55% of the total number of deputies in both the Tatarstan Supreme Soviet and the republic's local councils (Batyev and Fatkullin 1982, 130, 144). Bashkir representation in local councils increased from 24% in 1939 to 35% in 1980, while their share of top positions in the government and the republic's Communist Party remained at approximately 28% (Iuldashbaev 1995a, 250). Although Bashkirs never controlled a majority of positions in government, the first secretary of the republic's Communist Party was invariably a Bashkir. His position at the top of the regional government ensured that Bashkir interests were taken into account in local policy making. In Chuvashia, titular representation in government actually rose during the 1950s, so that by 1963, 76% of the members of local councils and 61% of government ministers were Chuvash. These numbers remained relatively constant until the political reform of the late 1980s (Akhazov 1977, 24; Prokopev et al. 1974). During the postwar period, Khakass representation in government began to decline, although it remained significantly higher than the group's share of the region's population, which remained at

Explaining Ethnic Mobilization 47

TABLE 2.5. *Ethnic representation in regional government and industrial administration*

	Tatarstan	Bashkortostan	Chuvashia	Khakassia
Indigenous administrators[a]	115	126	96	109
Indigenous directors[b]	88	82	81	61

[a] The figures in this row represent the percentage of titular administrators in the regional government divided by the percentage of titulars in the republic population, multiplied by 100.
[b] The figures in this row represent the percentage of titular industrial directors in the region divided by the percentage of titulars in the republic population, multiplied by 100.
Source: Unpublished 1989 census data provided by L. V. Ostapenko.

approximately 12% throughout the period. Thus, in 1957, Khakass members comprised 27% of the provincial council (Meshalkin 1963, 264). Similarly, in 1971, 23% of the region's senior Communist Party officials were ethnic Khakass (Mitiukov 1973, 56).

The continuation of affirmative action policies through the *perestroika* period ensured that minorities remained overrepresented in the administrations of virtually all ethnic territories, although position in the administrative hierarchy influenced the extent of titular control of local government. This was true for 14 of the 20 autonomous republics and provinces in the Russian Federation. It was also true for three of the four ethnic regions in our sample. In Tatarstan, Tatars comprised 56% of the administration but only 49% of the population; Bashkirs in Bashkortostan made up 28% of the administration but only 22% of the population; and the administration in Khakassia was 12% Khakass, while only 11% of the population was Khakass. In Chuvashia, on the other hand, although members of the titular ethnic group made up the overwhelming majority of the administration (65%), their high proportion of the total population (68%) meant that the Chuvash were actually underrepresented.[23]

Evidence on the makeup of the local legislatures in Tatarstan and Bashkortostan confirms the tendency to titular overrepresentation in the administration. In 1990, the Tatarstan Supreme Soviet was 58% Tatar. Similarly, in 1990, the Bashkortostan Supreme Soviet was 34% Bashkir (Iuldashbaev 1995b, 69). Unfortunately, similar data is not available for the Khakass and Chuvash Supreme Soviets. The disproportionate representation of titulars in administrative positions was particularly noteworthy because members of titular ethnic groups were universally underrepresented in the broader category of white-collar employment (see Table 2.5). Preferences for members of the titular ethnic group in staffing the administrations of ethnic republics represent the extent to which titular ethnic groups were

[23] Calculated from unpublished 1989 census data provided by L. V. Ostapenko.

perceived as having the right to control the political life of "their" regions. The presence of such preferences in virtually all ethnic regions of the Russian Federation shows that this belief existed at all levels of the ethno-federal hierarchy, including the autonomous provinces.

Affirmative action policies gave ethnic elites significant control over the administration of "their" republics. While during the Soviet period this control usually had a moderating effect on ethno-nationalism (Roeder 1991), affirmative action also created expectations of continued and gradually expanding indigenous control of the political and economic life of the regions. When such control was threatened, ethnic elites usually responded by encouraging protests and violence, as was the case during the 1978 demonstrations over language status in the Caucasian republics (Simon 1991, 331) and the 1986 Alma-Ata riots over the appointment of a Russian as first secretary of the Kazakhstan Communist Party (Olcott 1997, 552). By the time of *perestroika*, the belief that ownership of a particular territory by an ethnic group entitled that group to exercise control over regional politics and preferential access to jobs and education had become firmly ingrained among the populations of the ethnic territories.[24] It was to become a cornerstone of the nationalist movements' ideologies.

CONCLUSIONS

Administrative status was thus a key factor in determining the extent to which other ethnic institutions were developed in a particular region. It affected the extent of native-language education, the number of academic institutes dedicated to the study of the titular group's culture, the number and size of cultural organizations, and the extent of titular control over local administrations. Ethnic institutions were most developed in Tatarstan and Bashkortostan and least developed in Khakassia, with Chuvashia occupying an intermediate position. These institutions played a crucial role in strengthening ethnic identities and creating dense social networks among the titular population. As I show in subsequent chapters, these institutions played a key role in determining the ability of nationalist movements to get organized and to win popular support among the population.

[24] Including many members of the Russian population. Fifty-three percent of the Russian inhabitants of the autonomous republics of the Russian Federation believed that all schoolchildren, irrespective of nationality, should be required to learn their republic's titular language. Twenty-two percent went further, agreeing with the proposition that all inhabitants of ethnic regions need to learn to speak the titular language fluently. (Data from a 1993 survey project entitled "Pre-election Situation in Russia," conducted by Timothy Colton and Jerry Hough.)

3

From Cultural Society to Popular Front[*]

The Formation and Development of Nationalist Organizations

How did it come about that a regime that had experienced virtually no political opposition suddenly was faced with powerful protest movements that threatened the country's integrity? How did nationalist organizations appear, gain strength, and spread throughout each republic in societies with no history of independent political associational life, and where nationalism was condemned? Even in states that have strong civil societies and do not suppress nationalism, political organizers face formidable obstacles. Since Mancur Olson first described the free-rider problem in *The Logic of Collective Action* (1965), the formation of groups for the purpose of achieving political goals has been seen as a puzzle that needs to be solved. Proposed solutions have included the provision of selective benefits to movement activists (Olson 1965, Hardin 1995), the presence of interpersonal or civic trust and other psychological factors (Ferree 1992, Putnam 1993), and the presence of social networks in the community or workplace (Snow et al. 1980)

Minority nationalist mobilization in the Soviet Union during the late *perestroika* period was characterized by its rapid spread throughout the region and by the organizational similarities shared by the nationalist movements of a wide variety of minority groups. In this chapter, I show that the existence of a common set of ethnic institutions among all the ethnic regions of the Soviet Union ensured that the newly formed nationalist movements in the various regions were initially organized along similar lines and had roughly similar agendas. This finding demonstrates the importance of ethnic institutions for determining the form and goals of nationalist movements. I also demonstrate how state institutions provided the founders of nationalist movements with the resources that allowed them to take advantage of the opportunities created by Gorbachev's political liberalization. By

---

[*] The term "popular front" (*narodnyi front*) was used by activists during the *perestroika* period to refer to a social movement organization that sought to unite all sectors of society behind the reform effort.

taking advantage of the resources and connections provided by state-run academic institutions, which were frequently sympathetic to the nationalist cause, movement founders were able to create powerful nationalist movements in a society that seemed to lack the organizational resources necessary for the establishment of movement organizations.

SOVIET INSTITUTIONS AND MOVEMENT ORGANIZATION

Nationalist movements, like other kinds of social movements, emerge when political opportunities for those opposed to ruling elites expand rapidly. The opportunities most relevant to the emergence of social movements include "the opening up of access to power, shifting alignments, the availability of influential allies, and [divisions] within and among the elites" (Tarrow 1996, 54). These kinds of opportunities usually emerge in the context of a crisis of the old regime, often resulting in an effort by the governing elites to remain in power by attempting to reform the system (Hroch 2000, xiv).

When Gorbachev's liberalization made mass protest possible, nationalist movements were not the first to appear on the Soviet political scene. Initially, pro-democracy movements benefited from these changes in Soviet politics to a much greater extent than nationalist movements did. The increased openness on the part of reformers in government applied primarily to pro-democracy activists. Nationalist protest was still met with repression by the central government, as evinced by the use of Soviet troops against nationalist protesters in Georgia, Uzbekistan, Estonia, and Latvia in April 1989 (Fisher 1993, 540). Furthermore, despite some disagreements over the extent of liberalization, all political leaders at the union level were in agreement in opposing nationalist mobilization. There were no elite divisions fostering the growth of nationalist movements. While nationalist protest was encouraged to some extent by local politicians who had abandoned the Communist Party in order to support the nationalist agenda, most of these alignment shifts occurred after nationalist movements had already become powerful actors on the local political scene. For this reason, nationalist movements emerged later than pro-democracy movements and in many cases used other types of demands as a cover for their nationalist agendas. In fact, nationalist movements were able to become a powerful social force largely as a result of changes in the Soviet political structure created by the pioneering pro-democracy movement.

Although pro-democracy movements blazed the trail in opening up provincial political systems to political protest and opposition, they soon faded from the scene, victims of internal conflicts and a limited support base. In their place, nationalist movements emerged as the dominant source of political opposition to the entrenched Communist elites. In the language of social movement theory, the pro-democracy movements had functioned as initiator movements, opening the political opportunity structure and thereby creating a space for social movements in each region's political life. In this context, the nationalist movements were spin-off movements, using this new opening to establish themselves and drawing on the experience and knowhow of the initiator movement. However, the nationalist movements could not have succeeded without independent sources of support. Their success was rooted in their ties to institutions created by the Soviet government and in their collective ethnic identity, which that government had promoted. Despite the opportunity provided by the initiator pro-democracy movements, the nationalist movements could not have taken root without these connections.

In the early stages of formation, social movement organizations can greatly benefit from support provided by powerful sympathetic organizations. Such organizations may include government bureaus, local nongovernmental organizations (NGOs), private employers, and even locally influential social clubs. These organizations can provide places to meet and facilities that can be used to disseminate movement propaganda. They also provide a setting in which people with similar ideas can meet and establish social ties, eventually forming the core of a new social movement organization. Finally, these influential organizations can shield movement activists associated with them from reprisals from opponents or the state (Lofland 1996, 186–7, 193–5). In post-totalitarian states such as the Soviet Union, the absence of civil society means that these organizations are most likely to be tied to the state.

In the cases discussed in this study, state organizations that dealt with cultural and ideological issues became the locus for the formation of ethnonationalist social movement organizations (SMOs). Primarily, these were republic institutes and university departments dedicated to studying the culture, history, and language of titular ethnic groups. These organizations encouraged the "half-forgotten poets and lonely philologists" (Laitin 1988) who are frequently in the vanguard of ethnic mobilization, by providing them with resources that were indispensable for forming a movement organization, especially in a society where such resources were largely unavailable to the general public. In many cases, the directors of these organizations were favorably disposed, or at least neutral, toward nationalist activity, which allowed nationalists working in these institutes to join nationalist organizations without having to face the risk that they would lose the benefits provided by employers in the Soviet system. These academic institutes thus became a sort of safe haven for nationalist organizations, a place from which they drew their core activists, one that gave them a forum to air their ideas at a time when nationalist ideology was still deemed unacceptable by the central government, and one that provided them with publicly unavailable resources that were necessary for the organizations to function. A few of the nationalist leaders were also connected with the ideological departments of local branches of the Communist Party. In these cases, additional resources were made available to nationalist organizations. Most importantly, nationalists with ties to the party organization had access to its formidable propaganda machinery, including the ability to publish statements and interviews in its publications.

Not only did academic institutes and universities provide resources and space that greatly assisted in the creation of ethno-nationalist SMOs, they also facilitated the development of a common identity among a core group of scholars and intellectuals with nationalist ideas. The existence of a common *collective identity* among a group of activists is crucial for the creation of an SMO. Collective identity is defined as "the shared definition of a group that derives from members' common interests, experiences, and solidarity" (Taylor and Whittier 1992, 105). Collective identities are formed through the creation of boundaries that separate and differentiate a group of people from the rest of society, the development of an awareness of reasons for the group's position, and the celebration of the group's "essential differences" (Taylor and Whittier 1992, 122). These identities can be used to encourage involvement in the movement by activists, who make participation one of the markers of group identity. The creation of this identity marker is usually carried out by movement organizers who are widely recognized as leaders within the community. Once this marker is created, participation allows community members to confirm their collective identity through their behavior. The appearance of control mechanisms that tie identity to participation in the movement eliminates the free-rider problem. Members of the community must participate or face the loss of their collective identity in the public eye. In this way, collective identity becomes an important organizational resource for the nascent SMO (Friedman and McAdam 1992).

All of the activists in the newly forming nationalist organizations saw themselves not simply as intellectuals but as Chuvash intellectuals or Tatar intellectuals – in other words, as the intellectuals of their ethnic group. Consistent with the high value placed on intellectual activity in Soviet society (Hosking 1992, 2), this self-view included the idea that these people were the leaders of their nation. As national leaders, these intellectuals believed that it was their duty to their nation to lead a drive for its spiritual and cultural rebirth. The academic institutes promoted this identity and sense of mission by fostering the study of the ethnic group's culture, history, and literature, in effect creating a cadre of people who had devoted their lives to their ethnic group. The titular intellectual identity, however, did not simply originate in the institutes. It was also a product of the Soviet institutional legacy described in Chapter 2. The interaction of what Rogers Brubaker calls personal nationality, ascribed by birth and recorded in virtually every bureaucratic transaction, and territorial nationality served to consolidate national intellectuals into a single group by giving members of the titular ethnic group preferences in college admissions and job prospects (Brubaker 1996, 30).

Furthermore, virtually all social scientists and members of the creative intelligentsia in a particular republic belonged to that republic's titular ethnicity. As a result, they shared not only a Soviet education and a disciplinary outlook based on their profession, but also a common attitude toward the problems faced by their ethnic group. This common outlook was critical in leading ethnic intellectuals to focus their energies on ethno-politics.

The academic institutes and universities also provided nationalist movement founders with preexisting workplace-based social networks that greatly facilitated the recruitment of new members. Social networks are a critical resource for recruiting activists, particularly in the early stages of an SMO's development. Interpersonal ties encourage participation by reinforcing activists' sense of collective identity, by acting as a means of exerting social influence, and, at the macro level, by acting as conduits for transmitting information between activists (McAdam and Paulsen 1993). As movement organizations continue to develop, social networks among activists and their relatives, friends, and colleagues working in other organizations and even in other towns allow the organization to expand to areas previously untouched by movement organizers. In Russia's ethnic regions, social networks among ethnic intellectuals served as conduits for the transmission of nationalist ideas and for the recruitment of new movement members.

By comparison, pro-democracy movements tended to lack an institutional home base, which meant that the social ties connecting potential activists were not as strong, limiting these movements' potential for expansion. The lack of an institutional home base also meant that pro-democracy activists had few organizational resources, making it difficult for them to meet and to spread their message. In particular, the pro-democracy movements had virtually no access to the press until late in the liberalization process and did not have the financial resources to establish their own newspapers; the nationalist activists, by contrast, published articles in university and Academy of Science newspapers and received financial assistance that enabled them to start their own publications. Finally, pro-democracy activists lacked a collective identity that went beyond their opposition to the Communist regime. As a result, they failed to formulate an alternative to the system they were criticizing and had a difficult time attracting new supporters.

During their formative period, and despite differences in the timing of their emergence, nationalist movements exhibited striking similarities in organizational development. From their beginnings in academic institutes and universities, to their initial close ties with pro-democracy movements, and finally to their successfully gaining new followers outside their initial base by using social networks, the movements shared an institutional background that quickly helped them to join the ranks of the most powerful political organizations in their republics.

THE CREATION OF MOVEMENT ORGANIZATIONS IN THE FOUR ETHNIC REGIONS

Tatarstan

The Tatar nationalist movement began to form comparatively early in the liberalization process. The first meeting of the activist core who would go on to form the Tatar Public Center (TPC) was held on 27 June 1988. This meeting was attended by 200 people, most of them scholars at the Institute of Language, Literature, and History of the Kazan branch of the Soviet Academy of Sciences,[1] although several scholars and students from the Kazan State University across the street also participated (Iskhakov 1992, 6). This initial meeting of the first Tatar nationalist organization illustrates most of the key factors that shaped the emerging Tatar movement: its origin in academic institutions, its use of existing social networks for the recruitment of new activists, and the importance of a sense of common identity among those who joined.

The existence of an academic institute dedicated to the study of Tatar culture, language, and history was the critical factor in the establishment of the TPC. The Institute not only brought together like-minded individuals who were concerned about the future of Tatar culture, but also provided these people with funding, office space, and even a newspaper in which to voice their concerns. Scholars at the Institute had begun to discuss possible remedies for the decline of Tatar culture as early as 1982. The Communist Party inadvertently provided these scholars with an opportunity to act on some of these discussions by asking them to contribute suggestions on the topic of ethnic relations for discussion at the Nineteenth Communist Party of the Soviet Union (CPSU) Party Conference, which was to be held in June 1988 (Iskhakov 1993, 27). In compiling these suggestions, the scholars saw that their shared ideas had a broad constituency among the scholarly community and decided to organize their own meeting to discuss ethnic issues. During this initial meeting, the group decided to elect an initiative group to write an action program. This group wrote the first TPC platform, organized two citywide discussion meetings, and organized the first TPC congress, which was held in February 1989.[2]

In the context of a provincial city that in 1988 had barely begun to feel the impact of *glasnost*, it may seem surprising that such large numbers of workers from a single organization were willing to join an informal political organization that was critical of the government. However, if we consider the role of organizational incentives, social networks, and a common identity,

---

[1] Hereinafter referred to as the Institute.
[2] Damir Iskhakov, a cofounder of TPC and a staff researcher at the institute, interview, 26 October 1995.

their participation becomes far less puzzling. The scholars' heavy personal investment in the study of Tatar culture had led to the creation of a common identity among this group. During the course of their work, they had come to believe that the policies of the Soviet government had led to a decline in their culture, particularly with respect to language knowledge among the Tatar population.[3] Furthermore, the scholars saw themselves as the intellectual elite of the Tatar nation, with a responsibility for the nation's cultural development. Once *glasnost* and liberalization provided the opportunity to reverse the decline of Tatar culture, members of this intellectual elite quickly came to believe that they had a responsibility to act.

Social networks provided an additional boost to activist recruitment. Here, common identity interacted with geographical proximity to create conditions in which close social ties between scholars were the norm. Not only did these scholars share a vocation, they all worked within a two-block area in the center of Kazan, further contributing to social interaction.

Finally, the directors of the Institute and of several departments at Kazan University came from the same milieu and were sympathetic to the movement, providing facilities for group meetings, allowing TPC organizers to use their organizations' printing and photocopying facilities, and, perhaps most importantly, not threatening movement leaders with dismissal from their jobs, a tactic commonly used against regime opponents in other organizations. Furthermore, by allowing TPC activists to publish their views in the academic newspaper *Nauka* at a time when all other newspapers prohibited the publication of articles on "nationalist" themes, the directors allowed activists to spread their message beyond the walls of their academic institutes.

Immediately after the nationalist movement's founding, it began to look for allies from all parts of the political spectrum. On the one hand, the TPC soon began to cooperate with the local Communist Party apparatus. One of the movement's cofounders, Rafael Khakimov, joined the CPSU *obkom*'s[4] ideological department in order to prevent direct conflict between the two organizations.[5] Another leader, Marat Muliukov, who later became president of the TPC, was a professor of Communist Party history at the university and remained a member of the party until August 1991 (McAuley 1997, 55). In fact, the TPC maintained good relations with the party *obkom* for the first six months of its existence, even having its platform published in the party's propaganda journal.[6] Forty percent of the delegates to the first TPC congress

---

[3] For example, see Damir Iskhakov, "Nigilisty ponevole," *Komsomolets Tatarii*, 26 November 1988; and Rafael Khakimov, "Tatarii – status soiuznoi respubliki," *Vecherniia Kazan*, 2 February 1989.

[4] The term *obkom* refers to the central committee of a regional branch of the Communist Party in either a province or a autonomous republic of the Soviet Union.

[5] Rafael Khakimov, interview, 27 October 1995.

[6] Tezisy Platformy Tatarskogo Obshchestvennogo Tsentra, *Slovo Agitatora*, no. 23–24 (1988).

were Communists (Tatar Public Centre 1990, 155). By having, albeit temporarily, the favor of the local Communist Party *obkom*, the TPC was able to spread its message to, and to gain a measure of legitimacy with, that part of the public that still trusted the Party. Some of this support remained even after relations between the TPC and the *obkom* became hostile in January 1989, following the TPC's efforts to make contact with Tatar organizations outside the republic (Iskhakov 1992, 6–7).

At the same time, the movement also cooperated with the local pro-democracy movement. Several nationalist activists were also active in the Popular Front of Tataria, an umbrella group for pro-democracy activists, which supported the sovereignty drive in its initial stages (Iskhakov 1994, 67). Members of the TPC published articles describing their agenda in Popular Front publications,[7] and the two groups cooperated in selecting candidates for the 1989 elections to the Soviet Congress of People's Deputies. In fact, Fauzia Bairamova, later the chair of the radical Tatar political party Ittifaq, began her political career by running against a friend of the *obkom* first secretary as a Popular Front candidate.[8]

The experience of cooperation proved useful for the nationalist movement in the long run. Nationalist activists adopted forms of activity pioneered in the Soviet Union by the pro-democracy movement, including political discussion clubs and public meetings and demonstrations. While both movements were being organized in the republic practically simultaneously, the democrats drew on the experience of already-existing pro-democracy organizations in Moscow, St. Petersburg, and the Baltic republics. The information about protest organizations received through these channels was also adopted by the nationalist movement and had a profound effect on how the TPC carried out its protests long after its alliance with the democrats had ended.

During the first six months of its existence, the TPC sought to expand its social composition and its geographic scope. Beginning in September 1988, the organization sought to organize Tatars in other cities within Tatarstan. As preparation for the first TPC congress got under way, these contacts were expanded to include Tatar communities in areas outside of the republic. This effort was quite successful, as shown by the presence of 149 representatives from 32 cities outside of Tatarstan at the February 1989 congress (Iskhakov 1992, 6–7). By 1994, the TPC had established 130 chapters, including 93 outside of Tatarstan (Iskhakov 1994, 64).

The movement's efforts to extend its core of activists beyond the intelligentsia were less successful. Intellectuals made up over 50% of the delegates to each of the first two TPC congresses, and 25% of the delegates to the first congress were academics. Furthermore, 17 out of 21 members of the

---

[7] See Fauziia Bairamova, *Vestnik NF*, no. 13 (1989).
[8] For a description of the Popular Front's 1989 election campaign, see Pribylovskii (1993).

TPC coordinating council were academics. In fact, members of only two other professions joined the movement in significant numbers during this period. These included the creative intelligentsia and teachers, who made up 18% and 7% respectively of the first congress delegates (Iskhakov 1992, 7-9). The writers and other cultural workers who made up the creative intelligentsia had similar incentive structures for joining the movement, as did the academics. They were intimately concerned with the fate of Tatar culture, were closely connected to each other through professional unions (the writers' union, the artists' union, etc.), and were based almost exclusively in Kazan. The support of this segment of the intelligentsia was cemented at the republic conference of the writers' union, held in May 1989, which gave its full support to the TPC (Tatar Public Centre 1990, 155). Starting in 1989, the creative intelligentsia formed a separate, but equally active, network of nationalist activists, eventually launching their own nationalist organization called the Sovereignty Committee (Iskhakov 1994, 65).

In line with the interests of its founders, the TPC focused primarily on cultural demands during the early period of the movement's existence. In particular, activists focused on raising the status of the Tatar language and on improving access to Tatar culture for Tatars living outside the republic. This focus on cultural issues ensured that the TPC was at first perceived as a cultural organization, dedicated to ensuring the preservation of Tatar culture. However, once preparations for the first TPC congress commenced, and particularly after the publication of the TPC platform in October 1989, the movement became identified as primarily a political organization, dedicated to improving the status of Tatars in Tatarstan and of Tatarstan in the Soviet Union.

During this period of organizational development, the Tatar nationalist movement was united in a single organization that was seen as representative of all Tatars who sought equality with the dominant Russian population. For this reason, the Tatar Public Center allowed both individual and group membership. In fact, several Tatar cultural organizations and even a Jewish cultural group obtained group membership.[9] The TPC held on to this coordinating role for a time even after rifts began to appear among the nationalist activists. For example, the radical Tatar organization Ittifaq held group membership in the TPC during its first year of existence[10] (Iskhakov 1992, 8).

The Tatar nationalist movement came into existence in institutional spaces created by the Communist government. It quickly used the social ties, collective identities, and organizational resources provided by these institutions to establish itself as a viable political movement in the republic. But it also

[9] Marat Muliukov, interview, November 1995.
[10] For a discussion of the establishment of Ittifaq, see Gorenburg (1997).

made sure to separate itself from the ruling elite by working together with pro-democracy activists and Tatars living outside the republic.

Bashkortostan

The early history of the Bashkir nationalist movement is twofold. First, a cultural organization was established for the purpose of promoting a Bashkir cultural revival. Second, several political organizations were established to counter the Tatar nationalist movement in the republic. The two branches remained separate thereafter, pursuing different goals with different strategies.

The Bashkir cultural center, Ak Tirme, was founded in March 1988 for the purpose of creating local clubs for lovers of Bashkir culture.[11] Its members organized language classes, founded folklore ensembles, and generally worked to strengthen Bashkir cultural and linguistic traditions. The CPSU *obkom* at first reacted negatively to the creation of ethnic cultural centers, but soon came to support them, giving them space to meet and perform in the so-called Palaces of Culture (Khusainova 1991, 143–44). In exchange, the cultural centers of various ethnic groups agreed to cooperate, culminating in the opening of the Friendship Center for Ethnic Cultures in January 1989.[12] In ensuing years, these centers continued to cooperate and to focus exclusively on cultural matters.

As the country's political liberalization progressed, several more politically oriented ethnic organizations came into existence, beginning with the Tatar Public Center of Bashkortostan, which was founded in January 1989 (Guboglo 1992b, 218). This organization was created with the assistance of activists from Tatarstan. Unlike most other nationalist movements, its core activists were members of the scientific scholarly community, including some mathematicians and engineering professors.[13] This movement sought equal rights for Tatars within Bashkortostan – advocating, in particular, official status for the Tatar language, the opening of more Tatar schools, and an increase in Tatar representation in government (Guboglo 1993, 59–62).

This agenda directly threatened the status of Bashkirs in the republic, who feared that Tatar schools would replace existing Bashkir schools, that Tatars would take the place of Bashkir officials in government, and that Bashkir-speakers would be in danger of assimilation by Tatars. In the winter of 1989, in response to this perceived threat, Bashkir intellectuals began to create a political organization that would work to counter the Tatar

---

[11] Vasil Babenko, a researcher at the Bashkortostan State Assembly, interview, November 1995.
[12] E. Polevin, "Obshchii sbor," *Vecherniia Ufa*, 13 February 1989.
[13] Marat Ramazanov, chairman of the Bashkortostan TPC, interview, December 1995. In the four republics described in this study, there is a pattern in which the leaders of titular movements are drawn primarily from the creative intelligentsia and the social scientific community, while the leaders of antisovereignty movements are drawn primarily from the hard sciences.

agenda. To this end, they held a meeting in May 1989 at which the Republic Club for Bashkir Culture (RCBC) was created. The aims of this club were more political than those of the already-existing Ak Tirme (Guboglo 1992b, 177–84). As it turned out, the RCBC was a transitional organization and was replaced in August 1989 by the Bashkir National Center (BNC), which held its founding congress in December of that year (Khusainova 1991, 146). The BNC expanded rapidly, opening chapters in virtually every district of Bashkortostan.

Most of the BNC's leaders came from the older creative intelligentsia, and several, including the chairman and the chief ideologist, were professors at Bashkir State University. Like educational institutions in other republics, the university was generally sympathetic to the nationalist movement, providing it with meeting space and allowing activists to publish articles in its newspaper, *Kafedra*.

Also, the students of the Bashkir State University provided an initial activist base and proved to be vital in linking movement organizers with their supporters in the rural areas of the republic (Kulchik 1992, 10, 21). This connection was particularly important because most of the founders and activists in the movement were first-generation city dwellers who had grown up in predominantly Bashkir villages. The students, most of whom also came from rural Bashkortostan, carried nationalist ideas to their home villages on their trips home. The movement drew most of its support from rural Bashkirs and first-generation migrants, feeding on the problems faced by both groups during the *perestroika* period. Recent migrants not only faced a new and unfamiliar environment, they also were likely to be found in the least-skilled, lowest-paying jobs and often had inadequate housing. At the same time, Bashkir villages were facing a crisis caused by poor infrastructure and difficult working conditions (Sattarova 1990, 48–49). These conditions encouraged members of these groups to become active in the Bashkir nationalist movement.

Clan ties also played an important role in encouraging participation in the BNC. Most Bashkirs took pride in being able to trace their descent from a particular clan.[14] While clan affiliation did not play a direct role in the republic's political life, it did have an impact on the recruitment of activists by the nationalist movement. The need to avoid infiltration by movement opponents and security forces made trustworthiness critical in recruiting new activists, especially during the movement's early stages, when liberalization was only beginning. A common clan affiliation, which usually denoted a common ancestral home, meant the existence of social ties and a common identity, both critical to increasing trust among activists. Recruitment through clan connections meant that the movement largely excluded

---

[14] Zufar Enikeev, chairman of the Parliamentary Committee on Local Government, Civic and Religious Organizations, and Ethnic Issues, interview, November 1995.

Bashkirs from northwestern clans because of the significant cultural and linguistic differences between them and the southern and eastern Bashkirs who had founded the movement.[15]

Unlike the other movements described in this study, the Bashkir nationalist movement had few ties to the pro-democracy movement in the republic, which was more closely tied to Tatar movement activists. In fact, most of the Bashkir movement leaders were conservative and connected to the republic's political elite. Even those nationalist activists who had the democrats' support also maintained close contacts with the authorities.[16] Help from the republic government was particularly crucial in the movement's organizational development. While the Khabibullin government, which was in power until the spring of 1990, was suspicious of all nationalist activity and did not support the formation of the BNC, the Rakhimov government that succeeded it traded material resources for the nationalist movement's political support. In this way, nationalist organizations obtained offices in a Communist Party–owned building and were allowed to hold their meetings in Communist Party–owned conference halls. In addition, rumors circulated that the government helped the BNC to finance the printing of its newspaper and that it had provided the organization with cars and even computers. While there is no direct proof that the government was the source of these material benefits, multiple sources indicate that the BNC had many sympathizers among government officials.[17]

The Bashkir nationalist movement, like nationalist movements in other republics, was formed by members of the intellectual elite at an educational institution. Unlike the others, it never had close ties with a pro-democracy movement organization; instead, it was formed as a response to the threat posed by the emerging Tatar nationalist movement in the republic, which in turn was connected to the pro-democracy movement. The Bashkir National Center was also unusual in the closeness of its ties with the republic authorities and its dependence on rural support.

Chuvashia

Of the four movements discussed in this study, the Chuvash nationalist movement had the closest connection to its republic's pro-democracy movement. From its beginning, the pro-democracy movement in Chuvashia was at the same time focused on ethnic concerns, closely resembling the Baltic

---

[15] For a discussion of these cultural differences, particularly as they relate to identity choice, see Gorenburg (1999).
[16] Zufar Enikeev, interview, November 1995.
[17] Sergei Fufaev, interview, December 1995; Vasil Babenko, interview, November 1995; Zufar Enikeev, interview, November 1995.

popular fronts in its advocacy of ethnic revival by democratic means and with democratic rhetoric. Most of the nationalist movement's leaders began their political careers in the democratic movement. The first democratic organization was the semiofficial Coordinating Center for Creative Youth (CCCY), sponsored by the Chuvash Communist Youth League (Komsomol) and founded in April 1987. This organization was headed by Atner Khuzangai, a philologist at the Chuvash State University and the son of the most famous Chuvash poet of the twentieth century, who later became the leader of the Chuvash nationalist movement. Although it was established for the purpose of restructuring (*perestroika*) arts and literature in Chuvashia, the CCCY soon began to develop close relations with the Baltic popular fronts. Its annual Creative Youth Forums became known as places for pro-reform intellectuals from different ethnic regions to meet and share ideas. Although the center ceased to exist in the spring of 1990, its forty members went on to become key figures in both Democratic Alternative and the Chuvash Rebirth Party, respectively the leading pro-democracy and nationalist organizations.[18]

The CCCY was not only the first public organization to advocate ethnic revival, it also served as a center for members of different branches of the intelligentsia to interact. Because the Komsomol sponsored the group and selected its members, its membership was not limited by members' social and organizational ties. Academics, writers, artists, composers, and journalists all belonged to the organization.[19] By bringing together all of these people, the CCCY ensured that nationalist activists in Chuvashia came from a broader cross section of society than nationalists in other republics. Komsomol sponsorship also gave the CCCY a public forum – the Komsomol newspaper, *Molodoi Kommunist*.

In 1988, several members of the CCCY decided to create an independent organization for the development of Chuvash culture. The Iakovlev society, named after a nineteenth-century educator and spiritual leader of the Chuvash people, was formed at a meeting held in April 1988 at the Chuvash State University. Of the five members of the organizing group, three were members of the CCCY. Other sponsors of the society included the literature department at the university, the Institute for the Study of Chuvash Language, Literature, History, and Economy (the Institute), and the Writers' Union of Chuvashia.[20] Nevertheless, the establishment of the

---

[18] Based on Atner Khuzangai, "My khotim otkrytogo dialoga...," *Molodoi Kommunist*, 14 April 1988; Vladimir Aktashev, "Byt li KtsTM?," *Molodoi Kommunist*, 1 March 1990; and Petr Krasnov, "CHAP: vchera, segodnia, zavtra," *Sovetskaia Chuvashia*, 31 October 1991.
[19] Atner Khuzangai, "My khotim otkrytogo dialoga...," *Molodoi Kommunist*, 14 April 1988.
[20] Ustav Obshchestva I. Ia. Iakovleva, *Molodoi Kommunist*, 29 September 1988; Vitalii Stanial, "Obshchestvo I. Ia. Iakovleva: chto, kak i pochemu," *Molodoi Kommunist*, 20 October 1988.

Iakovlev society was forbidden by the Communist Party *obkom*, which feared the creation of an organization that could oppose the republic's Communist Party.[21]

A year later, a second attempt to create a Chuvash cultural center proved more successful. The creation of the Chuvash Public Cultural Center (CPCC) was undertaken by members of the Writers' Union, with help from the Institute.[22] The establishment of this center was supported by the authorities, who were represented at the CPCC founding congress in December 1989 by the chairman of the republic's Supreme Soviet and the second secretary of the *obkum*.[23] The presence of the *nomenklatura* led some of the leading members of the Chuvash nationalist movement to stay away from the CPCC, which Khuzangai described as a showpiece for the authorities.[24]

Because of the closing of the CCCY and the rejection of the Iakovlev Society by the republic authorities, the pro-democracy nationalists were without a formal organization of their own during much of 1990. For a time, they united with non-Chuvash democrats in the Democratic Alternative umbrella organization.[25] By the fall of 1990, conflicts within Democratic Alternative over whether to support a sovereignty declaration and a language law split the organization and led Chuvash activists to organize a Chuvash nationalist organization, the Chuvash Rebirth Party (CRP). The majority of Democratic Alternative activists joined the new organization, and Democratic Alternative faded from the political scene.[26]

With the establishment of the CRP, the Chuvash nationalist movement finally had its "own" organization. While the CPCC was the organizational home of the older creative intelligentsia, the CRP was dominated by scholars and those members of the creative intelligentsia who had previously participated in the CCCY. Its influence in the republic's political life was assured by the presence of several republic Supreme Soviet deputies among its founders.[27]

While the procession of organizations representing the Chuvash nationalist movement during a four-year period may give the appearance of instability within the movement, in reality all of these organizations were run by the same core group of activists. This group included Khuzangai, the sociologist Petr Krasnov, the philologist Vitalii Stanial, the writer Valerii Turgai, and

---

[21] Petr Krasnov, "CHAP: vchera, segodnia, zavtra," *Sovetskaia Chuvashia*, 31 October 1991.
[22] A. Alekseev, "Sobranie Uchreditelei," *Sovetskaia Chuvashia*, 30 September 1989; interview with Mikhail Iukhma, *Sovetskaia Chuvashia*, 16 December 1989.
[23] A. Soloviev, "Odna sudba," *Sovetskaia Chuvashia*, 23 December 1989.
[24] Atner Khuzangai, "Podniat Status Avtonomii," *Molodoi Kommunist*, 15 February 1990.
[25] Atner Khuzangai, interview, February 1996.
[26] The decline of Democratic Alternative can be illustrated by the number of people present at its demonstrations, which declined from 10,000 in February 1990 to only 400 in October of that year. A. M., "Chvashen-Ekspress," *Avani*, 20 October 1990.
[27] Vladimir Aktashev, "Uchreditelnyi sezd CHAP," *Molodoi Kommunist*, 28 March 1991.

the sculptor Fedor Madurov. These activists first came into close contact with each other after being selected to participate in the Cultural Center for Creative Youth. The Center not only helped to cement social ties between activists from different backgrounds, it also helped to create a common identity among these activists. The activists saw themselves as *Chuvash* intellectuals, who had been chosen by society to work on improving Chuvash culture.[28] They differed from nationalist leaders in other republics in that none of them had any involvement with the Communist Party, a fact that helped them attract to the movement supporters of democratization for whom ethnic revival was a secondary concern.[29]

As this core group gradually came to believe that cultural revival required political changes, its agenda began to diverge from that of the Komsomol, leading to the end of Komsomol support in 1989.[30] The activists turned first to the university and then to the Institute for organizational support. While the university was at first sympathetic to nationalist concerns, providing meeting space and allowing its faculty to participate in the movement, its directors turned against the movement in later years, forcing some of the nationalist leaders to leave its employment.[31] With the appointment of a sympathetic director in 1989, the Institute became the center for nationalist meetings, providing organizational resources throughout the period of movement activity.

Even greater resources for nationalist mobilization became available after Khuzangai, Krasnov, and Madurov were elected to the republic Supreme Soviet in 1990, with Khuzangai heading the Commission on Culture, Language, and Ethnic Relations. Parliamentary activity also brought several new allies, most significantly Arkadii Aidak, a highly respected collective farm chairman who had previously been elected to the USSR Congress of People's Deputies and led the Peasant Union faction in the Supreme Soviet.[32] The support of the Peasant Union proved crucial in spreading the nationalist message to the Chuvash countryside, where Aidak was by far the most popular political figure (Tafaev 1991a, 23).

Publicity for the movement came from both the Komsomol's *Molodoi Kommunist* newspaper and from the Chuvash-language *Khypar* newspaper, whose editor joined the CRP executive committee. Several local radio and television programs also aired programs with nationalist participants.[33]

---

[28] Atner Khuzangai, "My khotim otkrytogo dialoga ...," *Molodoi Kommunist*, 14 April 1988.
[29] "Suverenizatsiia i Mezhantsionalnye Otnosheniia" (Moscow: Institut Gumanitarno-Politicheskikh Issledovanii, 1993), 11.
[30] Vladimir Aktashev, "Byt li KtsTM?," *Molodoi Kommunist*, 1 March 1990.
[31] Ivan Boiko, deputy director of the Institute, interview, February 1996.
[32] Vladimir Aktashev, "Uchreditelnyi sezd CHAP," *Molodoi Kommunist*, 28 March 1991.
[33] Atner Khuzangai, "My khotim otkrytogo dialoga...," *Molodoi Kommunist*, 14 April 1988; Aleksei Leontiev, editor of *Khypar*, interview, February 1996.

It is notable that while the Writers' Union supported Chuvash cultural revival, it limited its support to the largely cultural Chuvash Public Cultural Center, refraining from giving any support to the more politically oriented Chuvash Rebirth Party and its leaders. Thus, despite a broader base and wider membership than nationalist movements in other republics, the main Chuvash nationalist movement organizations still depended primarily on educational institutions for their organizational needs.

Of the four movements analyzed in this study, the Chuvash nationalist movement shows the clearest progression from its origins as a cultural revival organization to a popular front and then to an organization focused on nationalist political goals. During this gradual evolution, the activist core of the movement remained in command even as the movement's organizational structure and goals changed. Throughout its early development, the Chuvash movement benefited from the institutional support provided by academic institutes and the region's Komsomol organization.

Khakassia

The Khakass national movement is unique in that for the first year of its existence it was based outside of Khakassia. The movement got its start in 1988, when several Khakass students at Leningrad State University, home for the summer, found that the celebration of a traditional Khakass holiday, Tun Bairam, had been canceled. In response, these students initiated a public campaign to overturn the cancellation, collecting 1,500 signatures for a letter of protest to the *obkom* Communist Party first secretary. The protest campaign succeeded in convincing the authorities to reinstate the holiday celebration. However, the end of the campaign meant a temporary halt to nationalist activity in Khakassia, as the students had to return to Leningrad to resume their studies.[34]

Upon their return to the university, these students founded a Khakass political organization called Tun. As Tun was one of the first ethnic organizations in Leningrad,[35] its members were in demand for speaking engagements at political discussion clubs, where they described to democratic activists the plight of small Siberian ethnic groups. During the fall of 1988, the initial seven organizers expanded the group's membership and began to publish a monthly magazine. The peak of Tun's activity in Leningrad occurred during the spring of 1989, when its members spearheaded the formation of a Siberian cultural center in Leningrad and organized the First All-Union Conference of the Indigenous Peoples of Siberia. Having pioneered the creation of ethnic cultural centers in the cradle of Russian democracy,

---

[34] The founding of the Khakass nationalist movement is described in Kostiakov (1990).
[35] *Tun* means "first" in Khakass.

the members of Tun returned to Khakassia upon their graduation in June 1989 (Kostiakov 1990, 12).

In the meantime, the republic had been shaken by interethnic clashes between Russian and Khakass youth in October 1988.[36] These events led older members of the Khakass intelligentsia in the republic, who had not participated in the 1988 protest, to begin to engage in political activity for the first time. During the fall and winter of 1988–89, prominent Khakass intellectuals met with local party leaders in an effort to ensure that such clashes would not recur.[37] The leaders of Tun sought the support of these intellectuals, who were widely respected among the Khakass population. In order to gain additional public support, they sought to publicize their concerns about the dangers of assimilation and language loss by holding a public meeting in the capital city, Abakan, in early July 1989. Tun leaders were able to use the city party committee's refusal to permit such a meeting to persuade the established intelligentsia that they needed to become actively involved in the republic's political life. In the end, the Khakass groups and the authorities were able to reach a compromise in which they established a discussion forum on ethnic issues at the Komsomol *obkom*.[38]

The discussion forum, which met monthly for over a year and received significant coverage in the local press, brought together activists from Tun, other members of the Khakass intelligentsia, and representatives of Khakassia's Communist Party to raise concerns and attempt to influence government policy on ethnic issues.[39] Leaders of the just-forming pro-democracy movement also participated in these meetings, and generally spoke in support of Khakass concerns. As a result of these actions, the fall of 1989 saw nationalists, democrats, intellectuals, and local government leaders all cooperating in an effort to persuade the public of the need to separate Khakassia from Krasnoyarsk territory (*krai*), while raising its status from autonomous province (*oblast*) to autonomous republic.

What can we learn from the empirical description just presented? First, although the Khakass national movement emerged from the pro-democracy movement, its formation took place not in Khakassia – where pro-democracy activism had not commenced until 1989, but in Leningrad – where such activism was already in full swing by the fall of 1988. The more liberal attitude toward informal organizations found in Leningrad allowed Tun activists to surmount the initial organizational hurdle. By the time they had returned

---

[36] Alexander Kostiakov, Tun chairman, interview, June 1996; see also *Tos*, no. 2 (1989).
[37] *Tos*, no. 2 (1989).
[38] V. Kokova, "Chtoby vsem v Khakassii zhilos luchshe," *Sovetskaia Khakassia*, 16 July 1989.
[39] For coverage of the forum, see T. Shapovalova, "Vo ves golos," *Sovetskaia Khakassia*, 27 July 1989; A. Baidosheva, "Pritiazhenie zemli Khakasskoi," *Sovetskaia Khakassia*, 1 October 1989; *Tos*, no. 7 (December 1989).

to Khakassia a year later, they had formed a cadre of several committed activists, formulated an action program, and learned a great deal about organizing discussion forums and petition drives.

Once in Khakassia, the young nationalists found a base of support at the Abakan State Pedagogical Institute and the Khakass Institute for the Study of Language, History, and Literature, which provided the majority of the discussion club's membership. Many of these activists quickly joined Tun, expanding its ranks to over 100 members within a year.[40] The support of leading Khakass historians and ethnographers from these academic institutions, as well as other prominent local intellectuals, gave Tun legitimacy among the largely rural Khakass population, who otherwise might not have trusted a group of recent university graduates. Because the director of the Institute was far less supportive of nationalist ideas, it did not serve as the center of nationalist activity, as did its counterparts in other republics.[41] Instead, the nationalist movement based itself at the pedagogical institute and the Khakass-language newspaper and radio station, all of which assisted the nationalist movement organizationally. In addition to providing material resources, the newspaper and radio station – one headed by a sympathetic editor, the other employing the Tun chairman as one of its editors – were also crucial in allowing Tun to disseminate its views to the Khakass population.

The local branch of the Communist Party also provided organizational assistance – although this was clearly not their intent – when they provided the discussion club with meeting space. The club's status was further enhanced by the attendance of high party officials, especially as their presence at the meetings was reported in the newspapers. While these reports were designed to show that the authorities were taking the public's concerns seriously, they also showed that Tun was an organization that could get things done in the realm of ethnic and cultural affairs.

The small size of the Khakass intelligentsia and of the Khakass nation as a whole encouraged the formation of close social ties and a sense of common identity that played a role in persuading people to join the nationalist movement. Social ties among the Khakass elite were developed from an early age, as the brightest Khakass children from the entire region were sent to the Katanov boarding school in Abakan. Unlike elite schools in other regions, the Katanov school was not designed exclusively for children of the governing and cultural elite of the capital city. While the children of this cohort made up part of the student body, the majority were accepted on a competitive basis and came primarily from rural areas. The Katanov school helped to create close ties between the children of the elite and high-achieving children from

---

[40] Valerii Ivandaev, Chon Chobi chairman, interview, June 1996.
[41] Gavriil Kotozhekov, former editor of *Khakas Chiri* and subsequently director of the Institute, interview, June 1996.

rural areas, who tended to remain in Abakan and constituted Khakassia's intellectual elite. The school also encouraged upward mobility by concluding an agreement with Leningrad State University that allotted five guaranteed university spaces each year to graduates of the Katanov school.[42] Thus, the school assisted the formation of the nationalist movement by enabling some of its graduates to study in Leningrad, where they organized the movement. Upon their return, ties between school graduates helped to make dialogue between members of the intelligentsia and the Khakass Communist Party leaders possible.

Since most graduates of the school came directly from rural areas, they provided a critical link between the movement leadership in Abakan and its supporters in the predominantly Khakass rural districts. The importance of this connection is made clear by the emphasis placed by Tun activists on holding meetings in Khakass villages to discuss their efforts to correct the inequalities faced by the Khakass nation (Kostiakov 1990, 10).

The school not only encouraged the formation of close social ties between future movement activists, but also instilled in its graduates a sense of Khakass identity. Students were taught that as the national elite, they were responsible for preserving the Khakass culture and language. This sense of duty led many students to focus on studying Khakass history, including the many episodes of Russian repression of the Khakass people.[43] By studying these episodes, Khakass students learned to separate themselves from the majority Russian population, establishing a distinct identity for themselves. In the aftermath of the violent clashes between Khakass and Russian students in the fall of 1988, this separate identity became politicized. Members of the intelligentsia came to believe that they could safeguard the future of the Khakass nation only by expanding its political rights, and that such an expansion of political rights could come about only as a result of concerted action on their part.

Like nationalist movements in the other republics, the Khakass nationalist movement came into being as a result of the concentration of ethnic intellectuals in organizations that provided the incentive structure, social ties, and organizational resources that made the creation of a nationalist movement possible. The Khakass nationalist movement was unique in having spun off from Leningrad's pro-democracy movement. The lack of a pro-democracy movement in Khakassia meant that the initial impetus for movement formation had to come from elsewhere. However, once formed, the movement quickly found a home within the institutional structure of Khakassia and gained adherents from the local intelligentsia. Despite being formed thousands of kilometers away, the Khakass nationalist movement showed that it

---

[42] Liubov Aeshina, State Assembly deputy and former director of music at the Katanov School, interview, June 1996.
[43] See Chistanov (1989); Alexander Kostiakov, interview, June 1996.

was subject to the same institutional effects as locally initiated movements in other republics.

INTEREST GROUPS, GRASSROOTS MOVEMENTS, AND POLITICAL PARTIES[44]

Although newly formed ethno-nationalist movement organizations initially assumed relatively similar organizational structures in all of the republics, within a short period of time differences in political opportunity structure (POS) among the regions had caused their nationalist movements to follow quite different paths of development. Two of the movements formed Western-style interest groups; another began to resemble a political party; while a fourth focused on achieving grassroots support. Later, two of the movements splintered into several competing organizations, while the others became institutionalized within government structures. This divergence in organization and goals among the movements had little to do with ethnic institutions. Instead, the movements sought to adapt in ways that would maximize their effectiveness in the political conditions prevalent in their regions. Such adaptations were based on the extent of the movements' access to the electoral system and ability to influence regional ruling elites, as well as on the relative strength or weakness of the executive branch vis-à-vis the other branches of government in the region.

Depending on the particular combination of these factors in each region, nationalist movements tended toward one of three models. The *grassroots model* was characterized by a relatively loose, informal, and decentralized structure, an emphasis on unruly, radical protest politics, and a reliance on committed adherents. The *interest-group model* relied on a more formal organizational structure and was focused on influencing policies through actions such as lobbying. The *party-oriented model* also relied on formal organization but emphasized participation in the electoral process through engagement in party politics.

How did these factors translate into movement types? The model consists of four propositions, which are summarized in Figure 3.1. First, relatively free electoral competition encourages the formation of party-oriented movement organizations. If movement leaders recognize that the possibility of coming to power through elections exists, they tend to organize their movements to take advantage of this opportunity. Such movements tend to act like political parties in order to be most effective in winning elections. Second, if movement activists have access to policy makers and influence over government decision making, their organizations tend to act like

---

[44] This section is a greatly condensed version of one part of Gorenburg (1997), which also addresses the development of nationalist movements during the period of their decline in popularity (1993–95).

From Cultural Society to Popular Front

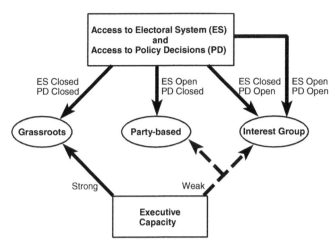

FIGURE 3.1. Political context and movement structure.

interest groups in order to take advantage of these opportunities. Third, if the electoral system is closed and movement activists have no access to policy makers, they try to cultivate popular support from below, creating informal grassroots-style organizations. Fourth, grassroots-style organizations are more likely to emerge in states where the government has a strong executive and an extensive repressive capacity.

Despite the outward appearance of democratization, politics in *Tatarstan* remained under the firm control of the republic's former Communist Party first secretary, Mintimer Shaimiev. Shaimiev limited electoral competition in the republic and maintained strict controls on access to policy makers for nationalist activists. At the same time, the government was less affected by the Russia-wide weakening of executive power, retaining almost complete control over political affairs in the republic.

The limits on electoral competition in the republic were initially more evident in presidential than in parliamentary elections. Although the 1990 elections to the republic legislature were subject to manipulation by local Communist leaders, several supporters of the nationalist movement were nonetheless elected to the republic Supreme Soviet.[45] However, because the electoral laws of the time forbade the establishment of opposition political parties, opponents of the regime ran as part of a broad coalition or as individuals. Although opposition candidates were relatively successful in the 1990 elections, their success did not lead to the formation of opposition political parties in the republic. Even this limited freedom to participate in electoral

---

[45] The most frequent form of government interference in this election consisted of refusing to register opposition candidates.

politics soon vanished. The 1991 presidential elections demonstrated that the *nomenklatura* was not going to give its opponents any opportunity to take power. By promulgating a restrictive electoral law and calling snap elections before nationalists had time to organize, the governing elite ensured that the Tatarstan presidential election would be a single-candidate affair and prevented opposition forces from engaging in electoral politics.

The strength and unity of the governing elite limited nationalist activists' access to and influence on policy makers. The leaders of the Communist Party in Tatarstan were able to maintain power during the transition period. Mintimer Shaimiev, the first secretary of the Tatarstan *obkom*, became first the chairman of the Supreme Soviet and then president of the republic, thus leaving the Communist Party leadership just before the party collapsed. The government's executive capacity was strong not only because of the continuity in its administration, but also because the republic Constitution made the executive branch far stronger than the legislature. The president was given the power to introduce legislation, appoint the prime minister and local heads of administration, and reject ministerial decisions (Constitution of the Republic of Tatarstan 1995, Article 111).

How did these factors influence the organizational development of the Tatar nationalist movement? Tatar nationalist organizations adapted to their environment. They avoided electoral politics, boycotting all federal elections held after 1990. Unable to gain influence in the corridors of power – and having no opportunity to win an office on one of these corridors through electoral means – the movement had no choice but to focus on attracting individual supporters at the local level. These adherents expressed their support primarily by engaging in demonstrations and other forms of protest. Even those SMOs that were formally organized as political parties, such as Ittifaq, spent more resources on organizing protests than on fielding candidates. For example, Ittifaq fielded only 22 candidates in the 1995 local parliamentary elections – all of whom were defeated.[46]

The emphasis on local protest action affected the internal organization of nationalist SMOs. Successful grassroots organizing required greater autonomy for local branches in order that the organizations could adjust to local conditions. Decentralization and internal democracy were also encouraged as a response to the hierarchy and the rigid control of the Communist Party; the nationalists wanted to resemble the CPSU as little as possible. The TPC leaders avoided any semblance of hierarchy within the organization, rejecting the familiar "director–deputies–assistants" structure in favor of a more egalitarian model led by seven coordinators of equal status.[47] Faced with harsh limits on access to political power, the Tatar nationalist movement

---

[46] There were 130 seats being contested in this election. The list of candidates was published in Ittifaq (1995), 20–2.
[47] Ustav Tatarskogo Obshchestvennogo Tsentra, *Sovetskaia Tatariia*, 10 October 1989.

was left with little choice but to follow the grassroots model of organizational development.

Bashkortostani politics during the Gorbachev period were unusually unstable for an autonomous republic. The entire leadership of the republic Communist Party was reprimanded and replaced on two occasions, first in 1987 and again in February 1990. These replacements of the governing elite, as well as the way in which the transfer of power took place, had a decisive impact on the development of the Bashkortostani political system during the post-Soviet period. During this period, the system was characterized by a weak but gradually strengthening government, relatively little electoral competition, a strong alliance between the government and Bashkir nationalist forces, and powerful opposition to this alliance from Russian and Tatar groups.

The removal of the last Communist Party chief in February 1990 led to the transfer of power to Murtaza Rakhimov, the chairman of the newly elected republic Supreme Soviet. However, Rakhimov was elected to this position in a very close vote, forcing him to depend on alliances with other leaders, and especially with Bashkir nationalist groups, in order to remain in power.[48] Over the next several years, Rakhimov was able to consolidate his authority and to prevent open access to the electoral system by his opponents. However, he was not able to establish a strong executive system until the end of 1993. Thus, during the peak years of nationalist mobilization, Bashkir nationalists were faced with a closed electoral system and open access to a relatively weak executive.

In this environment, the Bashkir nationalist movement needed a strong organizational base in order to engage on multiple levels with a decentralized government. A party-oriented form of organization was precluded because of the lack of access to electoral politics. An interest-group-based form of organization, on the other hand, could take advantage of the connections between nationalist leaders and top government officials in order to set up a successful lobby in the government. Because of this orientation, the Bashkir National Center did not devote much energy to fielding candidates in republic elections. It also largely avoided mass protest actions. Instead, the bulk of the Center's resources were devoted to increasing the organization's influence with the government. To this end, it maintained an office in the parliament building and cultivated contacts with prominent legislators and members of the presidential staff. Because of these efforts, at the nationalist movement's peak of popularity in early 1992 government policy was being determined through "a symbiosis of nomenklatura and nationalism" (Safin 1997, 128).

---

[48] Sergei Fufaev, an independent local journalist, interview, December 1995.

The one exception to this form of organization among Bashkir nationalist groups was the Union of Bashkir Youth (UBY), which frequently staged mass protest actions, including demonstrations, hunger strikes, and symbolic acts such as desecrating the Russian flag.[49] The youth union was organized informally, based on the grassroots support of students in the republic capital. Unlike its "parent" organization, the UBY could not organize as an interest group because it had no access to the government, which avoided dealing with youth organizations except in the immediate aftermath of their protest actions.[50] This exceptional case thus turns out to prove the rule, as it functioned within a different political opportunity structure than the other Bashkir nationalist organizations.

The political situation in *Chuvashia* was profoundly influenced by the removal of the Soviet-era governing elite in the wake of the August 1991 coup. This event both weakened the government's executive capacity and established the conditions for relatively open electoral competition in the republic. Chuvashia's electoral system remained open to competition for two reasons. First, the 1990 elections to the republic Supreme Soviet were more free than similar elections in other regions. Representatives of the Communist *nomenklatura* controlled only 101 of the parliament's 200 seats. They were opposed by approximately 30 nationalist deputies and several more non-nationalist members of the pro-democracy movement. The remainder of the parliament consisted of unaligned deputies, primarily representing professional associations (Filippov 1994, 11).

Second, the republic's Soviet-era governing elite was replaced in the wake of the 1991 coup, giving pro-democracy activists control of local government. These activists ensured that the Chuvash presidential elections of December 1991 were entirely free and fair. The inability of any candidate to gain a majority in this contest caused the elections to be declared invalid.[51] Although the pro-democracy activists remained in power, their candidate's poor showing seriously weakened their authority and prevented them from limiting access to the electoral system or increasing the powers of the executive branch.

While it had free elections, the Chuvash political system was only partially open to nationalist lobbying activity. The Soviet governing elite was opposed

---

[49] A. Kochkin, "Strasti na teletsentre," *Sovetskaia Bashkiriia*, 15 November 1991; Ural Suleimanov, "Khunveibiny Bashkortostana," *Leninets*, 16 November 1991; "Intsident u pamiatnika," *Leninets*, 16 April 1992.

[50] See, for example, the declaration made by the Supreme Soviet and the Council of Ministers in the wake of the April 1992 UBY hunger strike. Published in *Sovetskaia Bashkiria*, 21 April 1992.

[51] The pro-democracy head of the government fared particularly poorly, finishing third out of four candidates. V. Dimov, "Kruglyi stol dlia vyrabotki delovykh reshenii – ili diskussionnyi politklub?," *Chavash'en*, 1 February 1992.

From Cultural Society to Popular Front 73

to establishing ties with nationalist organizations. After it was removed from power in 1991, the democratic leadership was open to an alliance with nationalist forces but was rebuffed by the nationalist leadership. These leaders opposed entering into alliances with either the Communists or the democrats because they were convinced that they had sufficient popular support and organizational resources to win popular elections and take power in the republic on their own.[52] Because of this lack of connection between the nationalists and the government, the relative openness of the Chuvash political system did not translate into significant nationalist influence on government decision making.

The nationalist movement in Chuvashia tended toward the political party form of organization because of the openness of the republic's electoral system and the widespread perception that nationalists were sufficiently popular to be able to take power through elections. This perception was validated when the nationalist candidate finished first in the annulled 1991 presidential elections, receiving the support of 46% of the electorate in the final round. Because of their focus on replacing the government, nationalists deemphasized efforts to increase their influence with that government. They also refrained from orchestrating mass demonstrations, recognizing that their supporters came predominantly from rural areas and were unlikely to participate in such actions. The passivity of these supporters made them perfect candidates for an election-focused approach, in which a cadre of committed full-time activists carried out most of the organization's affairs, requiring mass participation only to the extent of voting in the elections themselves.

Khakass nationalists faced a more open political system than nationalists in the other three republics. The transition from autonomous province to republic led to numerous elections and a shake-up among the ruling elite. It also ensured that the government would remain weak while the new republic's governing institutions were in the process of development. A strong opposition further encouraged the creation of strong formal organizations in the nationalist movement.

Khakassia had one of the most open electoral systems of any of Russia's ethnic republics. No leader was able to "capture the state" and its electoral machinery until Aleksei Lebed's closely contested victory in the 1996 gubernatorial elections. Throughout the early 1990s, electoral laws were fairer and more democratic than the laws governing most provinces and republics.[53] As a result, members of the opposition had relatively unhindered access to

---

[52] Atner Khuzangai, interview, February 1996.
[53] Law of the Russian Soviet Federated Socialist Republic (RSFSR) on the transformation of the Khakass Autonomous Province into the Khakass Soviet Socialist Republic within the RSFSR, 3 July 1991. Published in *Sovetskaia Khakassia*, 24 July 1991.

the media, and many of them ran for seats in the new republic Supreme Soviet.[54] Autonomous province status also prevented the local Communist *nomenklatura* from having complete control over politics in the republic. Until 1991, all government policies had to be approved by the territory administration in Krasnoyarsk, leaving local leaders with little authority even over purely local affairs.[55] After separation, the new republic's transitional political system retained the weak executive / strong legislature system that was characteristic of local government throughout the Russian Federation under Soviet rule. A strong executive was instituted only with the adoption of a new Constitution in May 1995.[56]

During its initial months of activity in Khakassia (June 1989 to March 1990), the nationalist organization Tun sought to become an alternative political party in the region, opposed to the Communist Party and supportive of both democracy and ethnic revival. At this time, Tun showed its influence with the Khakass population by collecting 4,000 signatures on a petition to create a Khakass republic.[57] It also successfully negotiated with the government to establish a political discussion center at the *obkom*. This discussion club gave Khakass nationalists access to policy makers, which made possible a gradual change of focus for the nationalist organization.[58]

This change began to occur gradually once nationalist activists gained access to government policy makers. With the election of an ethnic Khakass as chairman of the Provincial Soviet in March 1990, the government and Tun began to coordinate their efforts to separate Khakassia from Krasnoyarsk territory and to turn it into an autonomous republic. This cooperation between nationalists and the government gradually led Tun to deemphasize its electoral aspirations in favor of a focus on maintaining a close relationship with sympathetic policy makers.

As a result of this alliance, the parliament approved the establishment of a permanent elected consultative body representing the interests of the Khakass people before the government. This body, the Popular Council (Chon Chobi), was proposed by the Fourth Khakass Congress in 1992 and approved by parliament in April 1994. Chon Chobi was given the right to propose laws for consideration by the Supreme Soviet and to be consulted by the government on matters concerning the Khakass people.[59] The creation of Chon Chobi formalized the access given to Khakass nationalists by government leaders in the republic.

---

[54] A. Kostiakov, "Vozrozhdenie," *Sovetskaia Khakassia*, 19 November 1991.
[55] V. Shtygashev, "Radost byla i pechal est," *Sovetskaia Khakassia*, 27 July 1991.
[56] Constitution of the Khakass Republic, published in *Khakassia*, 22 June 1995.
[57] K. Sokolova, "Poisk putei obreteniia samostoiatelnosti," *Sovetskaia Khakassia*, 4 April 1990.
[58] T. Shapovalova, "Vo ves golos," *Sovetskaia Khakassia*, 27 July 1989.
[59] L. Gorodetskii, "Protivostoiianie – put v tupik," *Khakassia*, 2 April 1992; Law on the Congress of the Khakass People, published in *Khakassia*, 7 May 1994

Because of changes in its political opportunity structure, the Khakass nationalist movement passed through two phases during its early development. Initially, because it was denied access to policy makers during a period when electoral competition was relatively open, the nationalists focused on efforts to gain enough popular support in the republic to come to power through elections. For this purpose, they sought to establish Tun as a political organization that could organize local chapters for the purpose of contesting republic elections.[60] When sympathetic leaders came to power after the 1990 Supreme Soviet elections, the emphasis of their organizing efforts shifted. Tun began to deemphasize its electoral program and local chapters, focusing instead on establishing a single central organization that would be consulted by the government and legislature on issues of concern to the Khakass people. These efforts culminated in the creation of Chon Chobi in 1994.

CONCLUSIONS

This chapter has shown that the emergence of nationalist movements was structured by a combination of the institutional legacy of the Soviet period and the opening of political opportunities for protest movements in the context of unionwide political liberalization. In explaining the emergence of ethnic mobilization, I have emphasized an institutionalist approach. I have shown how the organizational support provided by Soviet academic institutions was crucial for minority nationalists in Russia, providing organizational assistance in establishing movement organizations and fostering social ties and common identities that encouraged affiliates of the organizations to become involved in the new movements. I have also shown how institutional similarities among the four republics led the emerging social movement organizations to develop similar organizational structures. The first nationalist organizations to emerge were cultural clubs dedicated to reversing the gradual decline of ethnic culture in the regions. From this base, nationalists began to shift their focus to political demands, changing their organizational structures to fit this new mission. From their beginnings as cultural clubs to their transformation into broad popular fronts fighting for sovereignty, nationalist organizations in the early years of their existence followed a common path of organizational development. But that was where the similarities ended. In the next stage of their organizational development, nationalist movement organizations began to diverge in line with differences in the political contexts in the republics.

The institutionalist approach shows how institutions not only affect ethnic mobilization directly, but also modify the cultural, psychological, and economic factors that are usually believed to explain the emergence of

---

[60] See V. Ivanchenko, "I rodilsia v Sonskom 'Tun,'" *Sovetskaia Khakassia*, 28 February 1991 for a description of the creation of a local Tun chapter.

nationalism. In the Soviet Union, ethnic institutions designed to promote a group's culture and language changed existing cultural identities in ways that encouraged ethnic mobilization, enabling movement leaders to recruit co-ethnics and to promote their cause as the cause of the entire ethnic group. These institutions also contributed to the formation of dense social networks among co-ethnics, promoting a sense of kinship that also made recruitment easier. Finally, these institutions created material incentives that encouraged activists to focus on ethnic concerns as a means of improving their personal welfare. The institutionalist approach thus nullifies the debate between cultural and materialist explanations of nationalism by showing that both cultural and economic incentives for mobilization are created and modified by a society's political institutions.

4

The Soviet Institutional Legacy and Ethno-Nationalist Ideology

When the Communist Party created the Soviet Union's ethno-federal state structure in the 1920s, its goal was to persuade minority ethnic groups to accept communism by packaging it with the end of oppressive tsarist policies directed against the country's non-Russian population. For this reason, immediately after the October revolution, Lenin's government issued a "Declaration of the Rights of the Peoples of Russia," which guaranteed minorities sovereignty, self-determination, equality, and the right to cultural development. During the formative years of the Soviet state, government policy toward ethnic minorities established formal autonomy while ensuring that this autonomy would be used to establish socialist governments (Nahaylo and Swoboda 1990, 18–19). "Language and other manifestations of national uniqueness . . . were merely forms. It was the party, acting through the state, which would give them content." (Connor 1984, 202) This policy was characterized by the slogan, "national in form, socialist in content." The government sought to institutionalize ethnicity in order to promote and institutionalize communism among the non-Russian population.

The longevity of the Soviet state gave its ethnic institutions a high level of legitimacy among the population. At the same time, the lack of ethnic content in the ethnic regions of the country served as a major source of dissatisfaction with Soviet rule among the regions' titular inhabitants. The nationalist movements that emerged during *perestroika* thus had to work within the framework of these institutions in order to create a new nationalist ideology based on increasing the level of ethnic content within the existing ethnic forms. By staying within the confines of the Soviet ethno-federal structure while seeking to restore ethnic self-rule and cultural development, the nationalists sought to create a state that was *socialist in form, but nationalist in content*, turning the old Soviet slogan on its head. The importance of the ethno-federal structure in framing minority nationalist ideology shows that the strongest effects of the Soviet institutional legacy can be found in Russia's ethnic republics. These republics became, in a way, the repositories of Soviet primordialist ideas on ethnicity after the union's collapse. This situation was used by movement activists to formulate a message that would resonate with each republic's titular ethnic population.

NATIONALIST FRAME REPERTOIRES

In order to successfully mobilize their supporters, movement activists need to formulate demands and select symbols and slogans that will resonate with their target audience. To accomplish this, activists develop mobilizing frames, which are defined as interpretive schemes that simplify and condense a person's experience by selectively highlighting and encoding situations, objects, events, and experiences within his or her environment. Each movement develops a repertoire of possible frames that it can use to generate support among its target audience.[1]

The frames that nationalist leaders used to mobilize their supporters included greater regional economic autonomy, political independence, and cultural revival.[2] Movement leaders in all four republics began their campaigns for popular support by focusing on the decline of native languages and cultures in the face of official neglect and gradual Russification. Rafael Mukhametdinov, the first chairman of Ittifaq, described the ethnic intelligentsia as lasting only one generation. Tatar intellectuals, he said, come out of rural Tatar schools and settle in cities. They send their children to Russian-language schools because they perceive the limits on career opportunities set by limited Russian-language knowledge and because the cities lack Tatar schools. These children grow up as Russified Tatars and cannot contribute to the cultural development of their ethnic group.[3] Nationalist leaders in the other republics shared similar concerns. Reviving the native language was seen as especially important, because language was considered not just a means of communication but a direct expression of national culture and a repository of everything unique about the nation. Chuvash leaders, for example, argued that language is the symbol of the nation, the most important source of national unity, and the foundation of national culture.[4]

Nationalist leaders presented a wealth of statistical data to support their claim that native languages and cultures were unjustly neglected by the Soviet regime, including census data showing the gradual decline of native-language

---

[1] The notion of a repertoire of frames is based on the concept of repertoires of collective action. As elaborated by Charles Tilly (1992) and Sidney Tarrow (1994), repertoires of collective action represent the range of possible forms of protest available to a particular movement. Similarly, the repertoire of frames represents the range of mobilizing frames available to a protest movement.
[2] This list of frames is based on Henry Huttenbach's (1990) analysis of nationalist movements in the Soviet Union.
[3] Rafael Mukhametdinov, "Davaite Dumat' Vmeste," *Vecherniia Kazan*, 23 May 1988.
[4] "O nashem gosudarstvennom iazyke," *Sovetskaia Chuvashia*, 12 August 1989.

knowledge among members of titular ethnic groups and especially among urban youth.[5] Nationalists also noted the decline in the number and quality of native-language schools since the 1960s and the reduction of native-language use in government and public life. Nationalist leaders feared that their languages were quickly becoming no more than "kitchen languages," rarely used outside the home, even when only titulars were present. To highlight the injustice of their situation, activists compared the cultural development of their regions to that of the union republics. They found that the union republics spent more on culture, published more books in the native language, and provided more extensive educational systems for the non-Russian population. Furthermore, these republics had cultural institutions that were completely lacking in autonomous republics, including separate academies of science and native-language universities. The nationalists pointed out that autonomous republic status had not just retarded rates of cultural development, but at times had actually reversed development altogether. One Tatar nationalist, for example, published a chart comparing Tatar-language publishing with publishing in four union-republic languages. While the number of titles published in Georgian, Ukrainian, Azeri, and Uzbek increased by an average of thirteen times between 1913 and 1956, the number of Tatar titles declined by one-third. "If Tatarstan had been a union republic and not a part of Russia, could such a regression have occurred?" he asked.[6]

Nationalists saw similar problems with their republics' economic and environmental situations. They blamed the hierarchical structure of the Soviet Union for slowing the economic development of autonomous republics by subjugating their interests to the interests of the Russian republic of which they were a part. Nationalists in those republics that possessed natural resources declared that Moscow was exploiting the republic by extracting resources without fair compensation. In republics without such resources, nationalists pointed out that profitable local factories were under Russian or Soviet jurisdiction and therefore did not contribute to the republic government's budget. In either case, the activists explicitly compared local economic conditions to the situation in the union republics, finding that the union republics had greater control over local industry and received more income from the natural resources extracted from their territory. Similarly, local environmental degradation was seen as the result of a lack of concern in Moscow for the effects of Russia-wide industrial policies on local conditions. The building of environmentally hazardous power

---

[5] See, for example, R. Baimov, "Bilinguizm," *Leninets*, 17 December 1988; F. Iumaguzin, "Kakimi voidem v XXI vek?," *Leninets*, 21 February 1989; Damir Iskhakov, "Nigilisty ponevole," *Komsomolets Tatarii*, 26 November 1988; T. Shapovalova, "Vo ves' golos," *Sovetskaia Khakassia*, 27 July 1989.
[6] E. Mingazov, "Mozhet li Tatarin byt' natsionalistom?," *Vecherniia Kazan*, 7 February 1991.

stations, both nuclear and hydroelectric, was seen as symbolic of this lack of concern.[7]

According to the autonomy frame, the economic and cultural decline of the regions was due to excessive centralization. Leaders in Moscow did not understand local conditions and had no compunctions about exploiting the regions. Nationalists in a region believed that if their territory received greater control over its own affairs, the local government would be more responsive to local needs and would act to curtail exploitation by the center. The easiest way to achieve this increase in autonomy was through upgrading the region's status in the federal administrative hierarchy. Thus, most of the nationalists' early campaigning sought to establish union republics in place of autonomous ones and to create autonomous republics in place of autonomous provinces, both in the name of removing a layer of bureaucracy between the central government and the region.

Some nationalist leaders were not satisfied with increasing local autonomy. They believed that Soviet development policies had been biased in favor of Russians and against titulars. These nationalists argued that large industrial projects were built mainly by Russian migrants, who stayed on and took the best jobs and housing once the construction was completed. Members of the titular ethnic groups received only low-paying, unskilled jobs in these enterprises. In addition, titular-majority areas within the republics were avoided when such projects were built. They therefore could not benefit from these projects and remained seriously underdeveloped, with poor housing, little infrastructure, and few jobs. To reinforce this point, nationalists pointed to statistics that showed that their regions produced more than the national average, while consumption and living conditions were shown to be significantly below the national average, especially in areas populated by members of the titular group. Using this argument, nationalist leaders were able to describe federal assistance in local economic development as exploitation designed to wring labor and resources from the region while providing nothing in return.

These nationalists constructed the cultural revival frame, which sought to ensure that once the regions won political autonomy, members of the titular ethnic group would control the governments of the newly sovereign republics in order to direct most benefits to the titular group. Proposals for assuring this control varied depending on the percentage of the republic's total population that was titular. Where titulars were a clear majority, majority rule through contested elections was considered sufficient. Where

---

[7] Nuclear power stations were under construction in Tatarstan and Bashkortostan during the late 1980s. Khakass and Chuvash nationalist leaders were concerned about changes in the local environment and climate caused by recently completed hydroelectric dams and their reservoirs. For more on the use of environmental concerns to frame nationalist demands, see Dawson (1996).

the population was evenly divided or where titulars constituted a minority, mechanisms such as parliamentary quotas and upper chambers with members elected separately within each ethnic group were proposed. Regardless of the demographic balance, nationalists in all republics demanded that republic presidents speak the titular nationality's language and that the ministries of culture and education be headed by members of the titular group.

In order to cement titular control over the ethnic regions, nationalist leaders called for a broad program of national cultural revival. The most important element of this program in all ethnic republics was the adoption of a state language law that would, at a minimum, ensure equal status for the titular language in public life and government activity. A policy of this type was seen as a necessary precondition for improving the status of native languages. The opening of schools that either provided education in the native language, or at the very least taught the language as a subject, was required in order to reverse the accelerating assimilation and Russification of ethnic youth. Finally, nationalists called for a state-led cultural renaissance that would increase the number of books and newspapers published in the native language, the number and status of ethnic theaters and performance groups, and the level of funding given for the study of ethnic culture and history.

The most radical nationalists went beyond political autonomy and cultural revival by calling for national independence. They saw the Soviet state not just as an empire, but as a Russian empire. If the Soviet Union was, in essence, a Russian empire, then mere union republic status within the USSR could not be sufficient to restore the nation to its former glory. Only complete independence backed by the force of international law would allow the nation to withstand Russian political, cultural, and economic domination.

The pro-independence nationalists sought to justify their claims through appeals to history and the right of national self-determination. In describing their ethnic group's history, they frequently referred to it as indigenous to the land that it currently occupied, having lived there since time immemorial. In doing so, nationalist framers contrasted their own group to others, especially Russians, who could be portrayed as relatively recent migrants, even if some had lived on this territory for several centuries. By arguing that their group had "been there first," nationalists sought to persuade potential supporters that they had greater claim to the territory than any other ethnic group that might lay a claim to it. They further argued that this was not merely the land that their group had occupied first, it was the only land they could claim as their own and on which they could fulfill their aspirations to national statehood. They contrasted their ethnic group to the Russians in their republic, who possessed a state of their own in Russia proper.

To further the legitimacy of their claims to statehood, nationalists emphasized previous periods of independence in their history, even if this independence dated back to the twelfth or thirteenth century. Inevitably, the earlier independent state was described as not just a run-of-the-mill state, but as the most powerful, economically well-developed, and culturally dominant state in the region at the time. This proud history was then contrasted to the period following Russian colonization of their territory. This time was portrayed as a time of cultural decline for the ethnic group, as Russian governors betrayed agreements made with local leaders, forced natives to pay onerous amounts of tribute, and replaced native education with a system designed to promote Russification.

While independence-seeking radicals were present in all four regions, the extent to which they shaped nationalist frames depended on institutional and demographic factors. Nationalists saw Soviet state policy as the major cause of their ethnic groups' cultural and economic decline. The solution to this decline was cast primarily in political terms and involved a thorough rejection of the basic norms of the Soviet state. Movement leaders believed that widespread disillusionment with Soviet ideology, combined with equally widespread resentment among titulars against the supposedly advantaged Russians, would make the nationalist frames they had constructed resonate strongly with their intended audience.

SOVIET INSTITUTIONAL LEGACIES

The extent to which a frame resonates with a target audience depends primarily on the social mentalities of the population. Sidney Tarrow defines social mentalities as "popularly held values and practices about private life and behavior" (1992, 177). Tarrow argues that mentalities are too diffuse to be affected by the mobilizing frames of movement activists. At the same time, these mentalities play an important role in determining the extent to which particular frames make sense to the people they are designed to influence. Furthermore, these mentalities affect movement activists as much as they affect their potential supporters. For these reasons, the mobilizing frames designed by these activists are shaped by the social mentalities of the population. These mentalities are in turn shaped by the institutional structures in which movement activists and their potential supporters live their political lives. These institutions shape mentalities by affecting people's perceptions of what is politically possible and what is considered just. Frames that don't mesh with the institutional framework are dismissed as foreign, old-fashioned, or simply unsuited to the place and time.

The institutionalization of ethnicity in the Soviet Union proceeded in two directions: personal and territorial. Soviet leaders institutionalized ethnicity territorially by constructing an explicitly supra-national federal state made up of national republics and regions. They then institutionalized it on a personal level by requiring all citizens to select an ethnic category for themselves, enshrining this selection in identity documents, and pegging opportunities for education, promotion, and political power to this identity. Finally, the

Soviet system brought together the territorial and personal aspects of institutionalized ethnicity through the concept of the titular nationality. The titular nationality of an ethnic unit of the federation was defined as the ethnic group for which the territory was named. The territory in effect was described as the semiautonomous state of the titular nationality. Members of this ethnic group were given privileges in the territory, including quotas in top government positions, preferences in hiring and university admission, and the fulfillment of their cultural needs exclusively in this territory (Brubaker 1996). By institutionalizing ethnicity in this way, Soviet leaders not only planted the seeds for the future disintegration of the country, but also created expectations of what the proper position of an ethnic group in society should be.

In formulating mobilizing frames, nationalist leaders followed the norms created by the Soviet institutionalization of ethnicity. They accepted as a given the norm that each ethnic group deserved to have its own state, questioning only the lack of autonomy and sovereignty possessed by the preexisting national states (autonomous republics and provinces). In seeking to raise their republics' administrative status within the ethno-federal hierarchy, they accepted the legitimacy of the hierarchy itself. They likewise accepted the norm that each ethno-territorial unit of the federation was created for the benefit of its titular ethnic group, which should therefore have priority in cultural and educational funding, as well as precedence in filling top posts in government and industry. Finally, nationalist leaders accepted the territorial institutionalization of ethnicity by viewing the boundaries of ethnic units, for the most part artificially created, as the legitimate boundaries of their national states. Regardless of how many co-ethnics lived outside the ethnic unit, nationalist leaders refused to pursue irredentist demands to include them in a "greater" national state. At the same time, the personal institutionalization of ethnicity allowed these leaders to call on the ethnic units to act as national states and fulfill the cultural needs of the diaspora. By placing personal and territorial conceptions of ethnicity at the heart of the state's institutional system, the Soviet government not only reinforced the significance of ethnicity in organizing political life, it strongly affected how the demands for changing this political life would be framed.

Titular "Ownership" of Ethnic Territories

As described in Chapter 2, the Soviet state had created ethnic administrative units in order to convince each ethnic group that it had its own self-governed political unit. In order to persuade members of titular ethnic groups that their autonomous republic or region belonged to them, the government promoted the use of the titular language in education, staffed the local power structure with members of the titular ethnic group, provided titulars with preferences in hiring and university admissions, and advertised these policies as proof of the Soviet state's success in "solving the nationalities question." These policies were more successful than their designers wanted them to be. They not only succeeded in convincing the Soviet people that the ethnic forms were authentic, they also fostered the belief that these ethnic forms should be imbued with ethnic content.

Most importantly, the state convinced both titular and Russian inhabitants of the ethnic regions that these regions belonged to the titular ethnic group. This allowed nationalists to argue that all inhabitants of the republic, regardless of nationality, had a responsibility to learn the titular group's language. The arguments used to advance this claim stemmed from the idea that in the international community, states are allowed to require their citizens to learn the language of the dominant ethnic group.

As the homeland of a particular ethnic group, the ethnic region was also held to be responsible for promoting and financing the titular ethnic group's cultural and linguistic development and for developing programs that would rectify any economic underdevelopment among the titular ethnic group. Furthermore, nationalists argued that the existing level of titular preferences in hiring for government positions was insufficient. A republic that was designed to be the homeland for a particular ethnic group had to be governed by members of that ethnic group. Members of other ethnic groups had their own homelands, where they could develop their culture and have the opportunity to become part of the government. Finally, nationalists argued for directly enhancing the ethnic content of the homeland by creating an ethnic "feel," through the use of ethnic place names, street signs in the titular language, and aspects of the national architectural style in new construction.

Although these institutions had been designed during the 1920s with the goal of ensuring that ethnic minorities supported the new Soviet state, their long-term effect was to create a perception of titular ownership of ethnic regions. In practice, during the Soviet period titulars shared this ownership with the Russian population, who considered the entire Soviet Union their homeland and were allowed to remain largely unaffected by local ethnic institutions. During the liberalization period of the late 1980s, however, this feeling of titular ownership legitimized calls by nationalist movement leaders for giving members of the titular ethnic group preferential treatment over all other groups, including the Russian population.

Position in the Ethno-Federal Hierarchy

By creating four kinds of ethnic administrative unit within the Soviet Union, the Soviet government sought to give each ethnic group a level of formal self-government that was appropriate to its size, level of development, and geographical location. In theory, larger and more developed ethnic groups were granted autonomous or union republic status, while smaller, economically underdeveloped groups were granted autonomous province or district status. But regardless of size or level of economic development, ethnic groups whose territories did not touch the Soviet Union's international borders were not granted union republic status. These differences in status had consequences far beyond the psychological value of higher status. They affected the extent of cultural development, the development of local political institutions, representation in the Soviet Congress of Peoples' Deputies, and many other aspects of political life in each region. For this reason, nationalists in the lower-status regions attached great importance to revising this hierarchy in order to correct perceived injustices to their ethnic groups.

Yet in seeking to change the hierarchy, titular nationalists implicitly reaffirmed its power to structure their demands. They sought higher status for their regions within the hierarchy, rather than demanding the abolition of the hierarchy altogether, as was proposed by Andrei Sakharov and other *Russian* liberal democrats.[8] By following this course, the nationalists showed that they were unable to renounce the institutional legacy of Soviet ethnofederalism.[9] This tendency hindered the formation of alliances among nationalist movements of different ethnic groups by ensuring that they would compete against each other for higher status, rather than uniting to work together against the central government. The Soviet government's policy of "divide and rule" thus continued to work, even as the state was collapsing.

Inviolability of Boundaries

The boundaries of the ethnic regions were created by the Soviet state during the 1920s in such a way that they deviated from the contours of the territories in which ethnic groups predominated – either by including significant pockets of non-titular populations within the republic boundaries, as occurred in Chuvashia, or by excluding a segment of the titular group outside these boundaries, as happened to the Tatars. In either case, the end result was an increase in the likelihood of assimilation among minority ethnic populations (Schwartz 1990). Despite their arbitrary nature, these boundaries became critically important for titular ethnic groups. They functioned as markers between areas where ethnic culture was promoted and areas where it was suppressed. The areas they enclosed became identified as national homelands, whereas areas outside these boundaries "belonged" to other ethnic groups, even if co-ethnics happened to live there.

---

[8] Andrei Sakharov, "Konstitutsiia Soiuza Sovetskikh Respublik Evropy i Azii: Proekt," *Vecherniia Kazan*, 21 December 1989.
[9] Support for a federation of equal republics did eventually begin to spread among titular nationalists, but only after the government of the Russian Federation unilaterally instituted this idea in the summer of 1991 by raising the status of autonomous provinces to that of autonomous republics.

Over time, these boundaries became such a part of the ethnic groups' national identities that the national movements of the *perestroika* period did not seek to alter them in order to annex contiguous territories with sizeable co-ethnic populations. Demands for territorial adjustments occurred only in those areas where territorial boundaries had been changed later in the Soviet period. For example, Tatars in Bashkortostan refrained from demanding that their territory be joined to neighboring Tatarstan, instead calling for the reinstatement of the Ufa province, which had existed as a separate administrative unit of the USSR during the 1920s. Similarly, despite the existence of large Bashkir enclaves in several neighboring provinces, Bashkir nationalists supported boundary adjustment in only one instance – the noncontiguous Argaiash canton, which had been part of Bashkortostan until 1934. The possibility of adjusting borders to include Bashkirs living in territories directly bordering Bashkortostan that had never been a part of the Soviet republic was not considered.

By becoming a part of each ethnic group's identity, Soviet-era boundaries gained a permanence that could not have been predicted at the time of their creation. They influenced the ideologies of nationalist movements by largely removing territorial demands from the political arena.[10] Lacking this dimension, nationalist movements expressed their concern for diaspora populations exclusively in cultural and linguistic terms.

Identity and Passports

The ethnicity of each Soviet citizen was listed on his or her passport. Unlike ethnic identity as reported to census administrators, this ethnic label was determined by descent rather than by self-identification. Individuals whose parents were members of the same ethnic group were required to declare that nationality as their own. Those whose parents belonged to different groups could choose either (Anderson and Silver 1990, 112). This institution prevented assimilation except in cases of mixed marriages. Even the most Russified member of a titular ethnic group – one who neither identified with that group's culture nor spoke that group's language – was still identified publicly as a member of that group. In addition, by creating a public and immutable record of individual ethnic identity, the internal passport ethnic label made possible the assignment of jobs, positions in government, and places in universities through an ethnic quota system. All of these factors

---

[10] As indicated earlier, territorial demands were not entirely absent from the political arena. They occurred wherever boundaries had been adjusted during the Soviet period. The most widely known examples of the emergence of such demands include the Nagorno-Karabakh conflict in the Caucasus and the dispute over Crimea between Ukraine and the Russian Federation.

strengthened ethnic identity, ensuring that individuals retained a psychological link to their ethnic group that could be activated by nationalist leaders during a period of upheaval.

Nationalist ideology reflected the ease of determining individual ethnic identity. Instead of seeking to end discrimination against minorities by ensuring equal rights for all, regardless of ethnicity, nationalist leaders focused on the preservation and expansion of quotas for members of their own ethnic groups, confident that these policies could easily be implemented and that the beneficiaries could easily be determined. They rejected claims by liberal democrats that passport identity should be eliminated as undemocratic and discriminatory by arguing that these demands were merely cleverly camouflaged attempts at encouraging Russification.

A NOTE ON VARIATION OVER TIME

Nationalist ideology was not constant in any of these republics. Ideologies changed as the result of events such as the breakup of the Soviet Union and, in some cases, because of the changing attitudes of local governing elites. Adjustments were also made on the basis of experience – some messages worked in mobilizing followers, while others failed to resonate. Nevertheless, the basic outlines remained largely the same as they were at the movements' creation. For this reason, and in keeping with the emphasis in the rest of the study, most of the following analysis is focused on the period from the movements' emergence in 1988–89 through their peak in late 1991 and 1992.[11] This was the period during which the frames through which movement leaders sought to mobilize their potential followers were first formulated and then elaborated, and the time when nationalist influence in the regions was at its peak. In subsequent years, some of the movements (Khakassia, Tatarstan) pursued increasingly radical agendas, while others (Bashkortostan, Chuvashia) gradually moderated their ideologies.[12]

TATARSTAN: AN INDEPENDENT REPUBLIC?

The ideology of the Tatar nationalist movement was based on opposition to Communism and the rejection of the inequalities created by Soviet ethnic institutions. These ideas were expressed using mobilizing frames that focused on cultural revival, democratization, and the creation of a multiethnic Tatar union republic within the Soviet Union. The radical wing of the movement went further, calling for special political rights for the titular Tatar nation and

---

[11] However, information from as late as 1995 is cited when relevant.
[12] For a more detailed and theoretically grounded discussion of the later development of nationalist ideologies, see Gorenburg (1997).

advocating the establishment of a fully independent Tatar state that would function as a homeland for all Tatars. These demands brought the radicals into confrontation with both the Russian population of the republic and the moderate wing of their own movement.

Political Sovereignty for the People of Tatarstan

From the time of the movement's founding, Tatar nationalists made attaining union republic status the cornerstone of their political program. The founding congress of the Tatar Public Center (TPC), held in February 1989, declared that the federal structure of the Soviet Union and the Russian republic violated the Communist principle that all nations are equal by providing them with homelands that differed in status and rights. They argued that as an autonomous republic, Tatarstan lacked the opportunities for political, economic, and cultural development that were provided to all union republics.[13] Furthermore, autonomous republic status was an affront to the dignity of the titular ethnic group, since the idea that ASSRs were second-rate compared to union republics was firmly embedded in the subconscious of all Soviet citizens.[14]

The solution to the problem of status was straightforward. Nationalists advocated the establishment of a Tatar union republic, equal in status and rights to the fifteen older union republics. Nationalists also advocated republic sovereignty and clearly spelled out what they meant by this idea – the republic was to have full authority on its territory, except for those functions that it freely transferred to the federal government. Furthermore, the republic was to have a legal mechanism for suspending those actions of the central government that contradicted the interests of the population. Finally, Tatarstan was to have equal representation in all federal legislative bodies, as well as a representative in the executive branch.[15]

Nationalists pointed to the history and demographic status of the Tatar people to justify their claims that retaining ASSR status for the Tatar republic would be unjust. They argued that the Tatars, as the heirs of the ancient Bulgar state and the Kazan khanate, had a 1,000-year history of statehood.[16] Seeking to justify the legitimacy of union republic status for Tatarstan, nationalists also noted that the Tatars were the sixth-most-numerous ethnic group in the union, far larger than the Latvians, Armenians, or Kyrgyz, all of whom had long had union republics. Furthermore, the economic

---

[13] TPC Founding Congress, Resolution No. 2, "On the Status of the Tatar Republic," in *Materialy* (1989, 49); TPC platform, published in *Panorama*, no. 5 (1990).
[14] Talgat Bareev, "Zarozhdaetsia dvizhenie," *Vecherniia Kazan*, 7 November 1988.
[15] TPC Founding Congress, Resolution No. 2.
[16] Suggestions for CPSU plenum, TPC Founding Congress, (in *Materialy* 1989, 58–65); Marat Muliukov, "Ravny liubomu narodu," *Komsomolets Tatarii*, 18 November 1990.

development of Tatarstan significantly exceeded that of the Central Asian republics (Materialy 1989, 58). Nationalist leaders initially avoided purely ethnic appeals, arguing that union republic status would benefit all citizens of Tatarstan, as non-Tatars would share in the benefits of greater economic self-government, increased funding for culture, and improvements in environmental conditions.[17] Thus, according to the nationalists, economic, demographic, and historical reasons all pointed to the justice of the Tatar claim for union republic status.

By the summer of 1990, Tatar nationalists, following the example of Russia and the other union republics, decided to press for the adoption of a sovereignty declaration. The TPC argued that sovereignty should be proclaimed in the name of the multinational people of Tatarstan, reaffirming its contention that political sovereignty would benefit all citizens. It argued further that only as a sovereign republic could Tatarstan become a law-based state that could guarantee human rights to all of its inhabitants.[18] The adoption of the sovereignty declaration was portrayed by movement leaders as the successful outcome of a struggle by all democratic forces, not just the national movement.[19]

The movement became substantially more radical in its demands in the wake of the August 1991 coup and the subsequent breakup of the Soviet Union. These events strengthened the power of the Russian government vis-à-vis the ethnic territories within its boundaries. Whereas on the eve of the coup Russia had been willing to allow Tatarstani leaders to sign the union treaty independently, afterward Russian leaders renewed their insistence that Tatarstan and all other autonomous republics were an integral part of the Russian Federation and would not be allowed to secede.[20] In response, even moderate nationalists such as Rafael Khakimov began to argue in favor of independence, noting that a union treaty was no longer sufficient to guarantee equality for all nations.[21] As the fight for sovereignty intensified, with violent clashes in October 1991 and the sovereignty referendum of March 1992, TPC activists began to advocate the establishment of Tatarstan as an independent multiethnic state.

The TPC's multiethnic vision of Tatarstan was opposed by the nationalist political party Ittifaq, which from the time of its founding in 1990 had advocated the creation of an ethnic Tatar state. It argued that every nation had an inalienable right to its own independent state and that the disappearance of any nation was a crime against humanity.[22] Ittifaq argued that the

---

[17] Rafael Khakimov, "Tatarii – status soiuznoi respubliki," *Vecherniia Kazan*, 2 February 1989.
[18] TPC declaration, "Interesy respubliki prevyshe vsego," *Sovetskaia Tataria*, 18 August 1990.
[19] TPC declaration, 10 September 1990, in Tafaev (1991b, 59–61).
[20] Ruslan Khasbulatov, *Izvestiia Tatarstana*, 5 November 1991.
[21] Rafael Khakimov, "Net vozvrata k proshlomu," *Sovetskaia Tataria*, 4 September 1991.
[22] Ittifaq declaration of principles, published in *Respublika*, no. 3 (1990).

Tatar nation had lost its statehood in 1918, with the defeat of the Tatar-led Volga-Ural Confederation by the Red Army, and that it was Ittifaq's task to bring about the restoration of Tatar statehood. Toward this end, Ittifaq called for an end to the Russian occupation of Tatarstan and called on the Russian people to reject their state's civilizing mission toward the so-called backward peoples. In its vision of the Tatar state, Ittifaq saw the state as the protector of the national language and culture, while at the same time rejecting any privileges for Tatars and guaranteeing equal rights for members of other ethnic groups as long as they remained loyal to the state and recognized its language. The Tatar republic would be democratic but would adapt this democracy to the unique features of the Tatar people. It also would recognize dual citizenship for Tatars living outside of the republic, who would be eligible to vote in Tatarstan elections.[23] Ittifaq's conception of a Tatar state contrasted sharply with the TPC's vision of a multiethnic state based on the territory of Tatarstan. These two contrasting visions of statehood were at the core of the division of the Tatar nationalist movement into moderate and radical branches.

Political Sovereignty for the Tatar Nation

Although the TPC called for a multiethnic state, it based its case for sovereignty on the norm of national self-determination. This argument led TPC activists first to concern themselves with the fate of Tatars living outside the republic, then to explore mechanisms for increasing Tatar political representation, and finally to support the establishment of a separate legislative assembly for ethnic Tatars.

The first TPC platform argued that national sovereignty trumped state sovereignty – "the free development of nations cannot be limited by existing administrative-territorial divisions. Only the combination of the territorial and extra-territorial principles of national existence can ensure [the nation's] harmonious development."[24] Therefore, the government of Tatarstan had a responsibility to help Tatars living outside the republic to preserve their culture and to create institutions for local self-government and cultural autonomy. In their first open break with Lenin's ideas on ethnic relations, TPC activists called for the creation of a system of self-governing nonterritorial cultural autonomies for minorities living outside their republics.[25] In addition to self-government, the Tatar diaspora was to receive language and history teachers from Tatarstan. The Tatarstan government was also charged with ensuring the delivery of Tatar books and periodicals to Tatar settlements

---

[23] Ittifaq program, published in *Panorama*, no. 6 (1991).
[24] TPC platform, published in *Panorama*, no. 5 (1990).
[25] For more on Communist ideas on ethnic relations, see Connor (1984).

outside the republic and with the establishment of a shortwave radio station that could be heard in these areas.[26]

At the same time, Tatar activists were becoming concerned with the fate of Tatars within the republic. They argued that the socialist system had been responsible for the creation of a deformed occupational structure among the republic's Tatar population, with Tatars overrepresented in agriculture and underrepresented in industry and the service sector, particularly in skilled positions. To ameliorate this problem, the TPC called for regulating settlement in new urban areas in order to ensure that the percentage of Tatars settling there was no lower than their overall percentage of the population in the republic. Furthermore, it called for giving Tatars priority in some areas of employment and for increasing the number of Tatars admitted to universities and vocational schools. Finally, the TPC called for the adoption of limits on the immigration of non-Tatar workers, measures to encourage members of the Tatar diaspora to return to the republic, and regulations requiring students from outside the republic to leave Tatarstan after completing their education.[27]

An idea of how these resolutions were to be implemented on the local level is provided by a document entitled "Primary Goals of National Reform in Naberezhnye Chelny," published in 1990 by the Chelny branch of the TPC.[28] The Chelny TPC called for all local soviet deputies, government employees, and enterprise directors to learn Tatar. It advocated the annulment of agreements to bring Ukrainian workers into local auto manufacturing plants, preferring that these factories be staffed by members of the returning Tatar diaspora. Major enterprises would be forbidden to hire non-Tatar directors from outside the republic. Special zones for Tatar business development would be created, and Tatar-only shops and brigades would be organized in factories. Finally, major streets would be given new Tatar names, and a monument to Tatar statehood would be built. All of these goals show that even before the official split between moderates and radicals, two distinct ideas about the nature of the new state were present among TPC activists. The radicals, who were especially strong in Chelny, supported the establishment of an ethnic Tatar state from the very beginning.

After the March 1989 elections to the Soviet Congress of People's Deputies, the first democratic elections in the country, Tatar activists became concerned with Tatar underrepresentation in legislative bodies. They complained that only two of Tatarstan's eleven national-territorial districts were represented by Tatars, especially as five Russians had run unopposed. The TPC co-chairman Talgat Bareev argued that the nomination of non-titular

---

[26] TPC Founding Congress, Resolution No. 6, "Tatar National Consolidation," in Materialy (1989, 51–2).
[27] TPC Founding Congress, Resolutions No. 7 and No. 8, in Materialy (1989, 52–4).
[28] *Azatlyk*, no. 5 (1990).

candidates to run in national-territorial districts distorted their purpose, since these candidates knew nothing about the problems of ethnic minorities. He believed that a consensus should have been reached allowing only Tatars to run in these districts, while non-titulars could run for seats in the other chamber.[29] Tatar activists called on the titular population to vote for Tatars in subsequent elections and were rewarded with a republic Supreme Soviet whose deputies were 56% Tatar.

Following their success in assuring Tatar representation in the republic legislature, Tatar nationalist leaders sought to establish a representative legislative body for the Tatar nation. They noted that because 75% of Tatars lived outside Tatarstan, Tatar national sovereignty could be fully expressed only by a legislature that would include representatives of the diaspora's self-governing institutions. This proposed institution, the Milli Mejlis, would work in cooperation with the republic legislature and have jurisdiction over Tatar culture, education, and media.[30] The Milli Mejlis idea was never implemented by the TPC, but it was adopted for their own purposes by the radicals, led by Ittifaq's chair, Fauzia Bairamova.

The leaders of Ittifaq recognized the Milli Mejlis as a useful tool in their quest for an ethnic Tatar state. In convening the Mejlis in February 1992, radical nationalists sought to create a legislative body that would serve as an alternative to the existing Supreme Soviet. The purpose of the Mejlis was to adopt laws that would affect the Tatar nation wherever it was located. This fit perfectly with the radicals' ideology – they could in effect create an extraterritorial national state. Yet this conception of the Mejlis conflicted with the radicals' desire to take power in the territorial republic. Thus they disagreed on whether to consider the Mejlis as primarily a national legislature or to seek to turn it into an alternative to the Supreme Soviet, which was often hostile to nationalist interests. In the end, the national parliament idea won out, thus avoiding the possibility of a Chechnya-style violent attack on the Supreme Soviet.[31]

By adopting the creation of a Tatar national state as their goal, the radical nationalists represented by Ittifaq divided the movement and alienated the non-Tatar supporters of sovereignty. However, they made a concerted effort to unite Tatars in the republic with the Tatar diaspora. In doing so, they had to argue against the Soviet and international tradition of placing territorial boundaries ahead of ethnic identity in determining political loyalty.

[29] Talgat Bareev, "Paradoksy nashego doma," *Komsomolets Tatarii*, 10 December 1989.
[30] TPC second platform, published in *Panorama*, no. 2 (1991).
[31] Draft law of the Tatar nation on the Milli Mejlis, photocopy in author's possession. The debate on the status of the Milli Mejlis is reflected in the Tatarstan press throughout early 1992. See, for example, I. Durmanov, "Na poroge dvoevlastiia," *Vecherniia Kazan*, 27 January 1992; "Strasti protiv mudrosti," *Sovetskaia Tatariia*, 4 February 1992; interview with Fauziia Bairamova, *Izvestiia Tatarstana*, 22 May 1992; interview with Talgat Abdullin, *Izvestiia Tatarstana*, 19 June 1992.

Cultural Revival

Tatar nationalists saw official language status for Tatar as the cornerstone of an ambitious cultural revival program. The movement was divided on whether Russian should also be a state language or merely a language of interethnic communication. The disagreement was mainly over status, since both sides agreed on the steps necessary to revive the Tatar language. According to Tatar Public Center documents, as a state language Tatar would be used alongside Russian in government business, would be required for some categories of state officials, and would be a language of higher education in the republic. Parliamentary speeches could be made in either language, with synchronous translation provided. All street signs and public announcements would be bilingual. All citizens of the republic would be given the opportunity to study the language in schools and special courses. Most importantly for the future of the Tatar nation, all Tatar children would be educated in Tatar-language schools or at least have the opportunity to attend Tatar-language classes. Other aspects of the cultural revival program set out at the first TPC congress included expanding Tatar publishing, opening a shortwave Tatar radio station and a national film studio, and restoring Tatar architectural monuments. The nationalists also sought to improve Tatarstan's place in the Soviet scientific community, calling for the establishment of an independent academy of sciences; the opening of new history, economics, and language institutes; and the creation of a theater department at the Kazan Institute of Culture. All of these innovations were designed to place Tatarstan on an equal footing with the union republics.[32]

In its 1991 platform, the TPC retained many cultural demands from the 1989 platform, while switching its primary focus from language to education. It argued for a unified Tatar educational system, with Tatar-language instruction that would encompass all schools and classes where Tatar children were being educated. This system would feed into Tatar sections at major universities and into a new Tatar National University. Particular importance was also placed on giving the republic a Tatar "feel," by giving toponymic features new Tatar names, replacing Russian signs with bilingual ones, and designing buildings in a Tatar style. The new platform also focused on the role of Islam as one of the foundations of Tatar culture. While calling for respect toward all faiths, the TPC sought to popularize Islamic history, to create a Muslim council of elders, and to open an Islamic university and several new *medresses*.[33] The cultural demands in this platform were virtually identical to those made by Ittifaq during this period.

---

[32] TPC platform, published in *Panorama*, no. 5 (1990); TPC Founding Congress, Resolutions No. 4, 9, 11, in Materialy (1989, 50–1, 54–6); Rafael Khakimov, "Argumenty bez emotsii," *Vecherniia Kazan*, 2 August 1989.

[33] A *medresse* is a traditional Islamic school. TPC second platform, Parts 3 and 7, published in *Panorama*, no. 2 (1991).

Although radical and moderate nationalists disagreed on the political goals of sovereignty, the two wings of the movement were in agreement on the steps that were needed to bring about a revival of Tatar culture. These steps consisted primarily of the extension of Tatar-language education to urban areas and the use of the language in official government business, on a par with Russian. Differences between the two groups were based primarily on intent, with radicals seeking cultural revival measures as the first step toward an ethnic Tatar state, while moderates saw cultural revival as an end in itself.

Economic Sovereignty

Compared to their ideas on culture and politics, the nationalists' economic programs can only be described as perfunctory. Nevertheless, economic claims were vital in justifying sovereignization and primarily consisted of calls for the republic government to take control of local state-owned enterprises. These ideas were set out in the first TPC platform, which declared that a sovereign republic should have the freedom to control all of its natural resources, to create its own strategy for economic development, to establish direct economic ties with other regions, to have free access to the world market, and to levy its own taxes.[34] Nationalists argued that the profits gained from selling oil at world market prices, if given to the republic government, could improve the standard of living of all inhabitants of Tatarstan. They also noted that enterprises under union or Russian jurisdiction were the worst polluters, damaging the local environment without paying any local taxes or sharing any revenue with Tatarstan. By transferring these enterprises to Tatarstan's jurisdiction or by winning the right to tax these enterprises, the government could improve environmental conditions and the social infrastructure in ways that would benefit members of all nationalities.[35] After the collapse of the Soviet Union, the TPC economic program remained largely unchanged, focusing on the establishment of a Tatarstan national bank and a state currency as a way to secure full sovereignty and prevent Russian interference in the republic's economy.[36] Throughout this period, the TPC discussed economic reform only as a means of increasing state sovereignty.

Although it was also designed to promote the movement's political goals, Ittifaq's economic reform strategy was developed in greater detail than that of the TPC. The Ittifaq program declared that Tatarstan's economic system

---

[34] TPC platform, Part 3, published in *Panorama*, no. 5 (1990).
[35] Rafael Khakimov, "Malenkaia lozh'," *Komsomolets Tatarii*, 6 May 1990; TPC platform, published in *Panorama*, no. 5 (1990).
[36] A. Makhmutov and G Murtazin, "Kontseptsiia k programme zakrepleniia gosudarstvennogo suvereniteta respubliki Tatarstan," *Suverenitet*, April 1993.

must reflect the characteristics of the Tatar nation. It called for leaving large enterprises and oil production in state hands, while privatizing small and medium-sized enterprises. Ittifaq also supported private ownership of land, but wanted only citizens of the republic to have this right. According to the Ittifaq plan, economic growth would be achieved through the export of agricultural goods and petroleum products, as well as through the development of the tourist industry. The program called for a special relationship with Turkey and the Arab world, which would be encouraged to invest in the region and would also provide revenue from tourism.[37] The Ittifaq economic plan is notable for its attempt to connect economic reform to the creation of a national state, with the dominant religion playing a part in the choice of economic partners.

Ethnic Institutions and the Construction of Nationalist Mobilizing Frames in Tatarstan

As this discussion of nationalist mobilizing frames in Tatarstan shows, Tatar nationalist leaders accepted the constraints placed on them by the legacy of Soviet ethnic institutions. Their earliest appeals focused on turning Tatarstan into a union republic. In pressing this demand, they accepted the validity of the ethnic hierarchy established by the Soviet government during the 1920s. Rather than declaring, à la Sakharov, that all ethnic groups in the Soviet Union should have equal rights, they focused on proving that Tatarstan deserved union republic status because of its size, its level of economic development, and the size of its titular ethnic group. Similarly, the nationalist leaders accepted the idea that Tatars deserved special rights and privileges in Tatarstan because of their status as the titular ethnic group. This titular ownership norm led to nationalist demands that the Tatar language be used in all government activity and be required for government and service-sector employees. The titular ownership norm also legitimized demands for the establishment of preferential quotas for Tatars in employment and education. Movement radicals went even further, calling for the establishment of an ethnic Tatar state. Finally, despite their concern that the diaspora that made up 75% of the total Tatar population lacked access to Tatar culture and was in danger of assimilation, nationalist leaders refused to challenge the legitimacy of republic boundaries that had been established by the Soviet government with little attention to including all areas of compact Tatar settlement. Thus, Tatar nationalists refused to support demands that Tatarstan annex the contiguous area of northwestern Bashkortostan, which was home to 1.2 million Tatars. Over a 70-year period, the ethnic institutions established by the Soviet government during the 1920s had shaped the mentality

---

[37] Ittifaq program, published in *Panorama*, no. 6 (1991).

of the Tatar population, limiting the range of mobilizing frames used by nationalist leaders.

BASHKORTOSTAN: NATION BUILDING

Although it was formed relatively late, the Bashkir national movement became one of the most radical in the Russian Federation. Bashkir nationalists, unlike their Tatar counterparts, saw the advancement of the Bashkir nation, both culturally and politically, as their primary goal. They considered republic sovereignty and autonomy to be subordinate to this goal. The program of the Bashkir National Party (BNP) declared that only Bashkirs had the right to determine the form of its state, which would be based on Bashkir historical, national, and cultural traditions (Guboglo 1993, 143). While the state had many responsibilities, nationalists felt that its most important obligation was the preservation of the Bashkir nation.[38] The Bashkir nation-building program was based on the idea that the Bashkir nation should have preeminence in the republic and included cultural, political, and economic aspects.

The Right to National Self-Determination and Political Nation Building

Bashkir nationalists justified their fight for a national state by pointing to Bashkir history and relations with neighboring ethnic groups. They described the Bashkirs as an ancient nation that had for centuries been caught between the dangers of Tatar assimilation and Russian conquest. They claimed that their ethnic group had been living on the same territory since the sixth century, long before the Tatars or the Russians had formed as ethnic groups, which gave them claim to the title of indigenous nation.[39] After becoming subject to the Russian empire, the Bashkirs conducted a series of rebellions against Russian rule over a 200-year period, proving their commitment to their land and to independence.[40] Their fight for autonomy during the Russian Civil War culminated in a treaty creating a Bashkir autonomous republic, the first autonomous ethnic territory in the Soviet Union. Modern Bashkir nationalists regarded this treaty as the starting point for negotiations on republic status (Kulsharipov 1992). According to nationalist leaders, Bashkir history justified their claim to indigenous status, their commitment to independence, and their right to national autonomy in the modern age.

In addition, Bashkir nationalists feared that unless Bashkortostan was declared a Bashkir nation-state, Bashkirs would continue to be subject to

---

[38] "Vtoroi Kurultai," *Volia*, no. 5 (1991).
[39] R. Akkildin, "Razreshite vas popravit', Aidar Khalim," *Oran*, no. 1 (1991).
[40] A. Biishev, "Put' k konsolidatsii," *Volia*, no. 2 (1991); B. Akramov, "Chto takoe korennoi narod," *Zamandash*, 31 January 1991.

Russian and Tatar assimilation. They noted that the Bashkir percentage of the population had declined from 30% in 1920 to 22% in 1989, while the Tatar and Russian proportions had grown by 7% and 5% respectively. They noted that Russian-language schooling and Bashkir migration out of the republic were responsible for a rapid rise in Russification among the Bashkir population. Nationalists also claimed that the existence of 200,000 Tatar-speaking Bashkirs showed the success of a deliberate program of Tatar assimilation carried out during the 1930s and 1940s.[41] They feared that if these trends were left unchecked, Bashkortostan would be left without any Bashkirs.[42] To counteract this threat, nationalists called on the government to give extra funding for Bashkir cultural and educational needs and demanded that Bashkirs play a dominant role in governing the republic.

Prior to political reform, their titular status had given Bashkirs control of the republic government. Nationalists feared that democratization would not only end this control but also result in a decline in Bashkir representation in parliament that would leave Bashkirs unable to influence political decision making in their own republic. They argued for the establishment of Bashkortostan as a union republic, not out of a belief in the need for independence, but in order to increase the status of the Bashkir nation and to ensure their control over the state.

Bashkir nationalists argued that since Bashkirs constituted the only indigenous nation in the republic, they should have the sole right to determine the republic's status. When their opponents called for referendums on sovereignty or language status, the nationalists declared that because Bashkirs could never win such referendums, as they were outnumbered by non-titular ethnic groups, the votes were merely tactics designed to deny Bashkirs their right to national self-determination.[43] Unlike Tatar nationalists, most Bashkir nationalists did not call for independence after the collapse of the Soviet Union, limiting themselves to demands for complete autonomy in internal affairs.[44] They believed that while independence was precluded by the republic's demographic balance, complete internal autonomy would be a less controversial way for Bashkirs to establish their own state and to ensure the survival and development of their nation.

To secure their control of the state, Bashkir leaders sought to create a system of quotas and privileges for members of the indigenous nation in all areas of political life. By 1990, nationalist leaders were arguing that Bashkirs

---

[41] A. Aznabaev, "Kak eto proiskhodilo," *Zamandash*, 28 December 1990.
[42] "Obrashchenie 1 s'ezda Bashkirskogo narodnogo tsentra 'Ural'," 18 December 1989, in Guboglo (1992b, 108–17).
[43] Marat Kulsharipov, "Ili edinaia i nedelimaia?," *Vecherniia Ufa*, 4 October 1990; Z. Mufteev, "Ne opazdat' by," *Sovetskaia Bashkiriia*, 19 November 1991.
[44] Z. Mufteev, "Ne opazdat' by," *Sovetskaia Bashkiriia*, 19 November 1991.

should comprise 50% of the party and government bureaucracies.[45] Later statements included calls for 50% quotas for Bashkirs in local and republic legislatures, a consociational electoral system with separate voting lists for each ethnic group, and guarantees that only Bashkirs would be allowed to represent the republic in the nationalities chambers of the Soviet and Russian legislatures.[46] Furthermore, the president of the republic was to be required to know Bashkir.[47] When the Russian parliament was debating the possibility of removing ethnic identity from the Russian Federation's internal passport, Bashkir leaders argued that such an act would lead to imbalances in ethnic representation in republic parliaments, leaving no legal basis for quotas and *denying nations the right to have an ethnic identity*.[48] Outside of government, Bashkir leaders called for quotas for administrative positions in industry, agriculture, science, and medicine.[49] Bashkir leaders also called for quotas and separate admissions for Bashkirs in higher education, hoping to create a cohort of well-educated Bashkirs qualified to run the government and industry.[50] Finally, they sought to replace several prominent Tatar administrators with Bashkirs, including the directors of the republic library and museum.[51]

All of these demands had one common aim – preserving Bashkir control of the state apparatus despite democratization and the end of the central government mandate for titular preferences in the ethnic republics. Bashkir nationalists saw this control as essential for the continued development and security of the Bashkir nation.

Cultural Nation Building

Worried about the decline of Bashkir culture and the assimilation of Bashkirs by other ethnic groups, Bashkir nationalists sought to spur cultural and linguistic development through government programs. They were particularly

---

[45] "Rezoliutsiia sobraniia obshchestvennosti Ufy i respubliki, sozvannogo Bashkirskim narodnym tsentrom 'Ural' i klubom Bashkirskoi kultury 'Ak Tirma'," 10 May 1990, in Guboglo (1992b, 117–20).

[46] Rinat Shakur, "Otkrytoe pismo B. N. Yeltsinu," *Volia*, no. 1 (1990); "Manifest o sovremmenom polozhenii Bashkirskogo naroda i problemakh ego vozrozhdeniia," 23 February 1991, in Guboglo (1992b, 133–7).

[47] "Rezoliutsiia VI Vsesoiuznogo Vsebashkirskogo s'ezda po dokladu Predsedatelia BNTs 'Ural' M.M. Kulsharipova 'Obshchestvenno-politicheskaia i sotsialno-ekonomicheskaia situatsiia v Bashkortostane'," 25 December 1991, in Guboglo (1992b, 157–9).

[48] S. Gainanov, "Piatyi punkt," *Zamandash*, 14 December 1991.

[49] Fanil Faizullin, Damir Valeev, and Fagim Sadykov, "Natsionalnye otnosheniia v sovremmenom Bashkortostane," *Izvestiia Bashkortostana*, 29 December 1992.

[50] Raisa Sorina, "Budem znakomy," *Izvestiia Bashkortostana*, 1 May 1991.

[51] "Rezoliutsiia V Vsesoiuznogo Bashkirskogo narodnogo s'ezda o Bashkirskom gosudarstvennom ob'edinennom muzee," 22 February 1991, in Guboglo (1992b, 129); author's field notes.

concerned about the status of the Bashkir language, which was spoken by only three-quarters of the Bashkir population (i.e., by only 16% of the republic's total population). The first Bashkir Congress, held in December 1989, declared that Bashkir had to become the republic's sole state language because it was the language of the indigenous nation that gave the republic its name. With this status, the language could be preserved and its usage in society extended.[52] Official status would lead to the use of Bashkir in parliamentary debates and government documents, a greater emphasis on Bashkir-language publishing and broadcasting, and the teaching of Bashkir to all Bashkir schoolchildren.[53] In order to create a Bashkir educational system, nationalists argued, the government should build separate Bashkir high schools in each city in the republic, triple the number of Bashkir teachers, and create a separate oversight structure for Bashkir education in the education ministry.[54] These measures would reverse the trend toward Russification among Bashkir youth.

The BNC later moderated its stand on the language law, accepting Russian as a second state language, but it continued to reject the possibility of declaring Tatar as a third state language. Tatar nationalists argued that Tatar should be a state language because Tatars made up 28% of the republic's population, outnumbering the Bashkirs by 250,000. Bashkir leaders rejected this argument because they believed that only those nations that were indigenous to a particular territory had the right to national self-determination and that only their languages could receive official status. Russian could be an official language in the republic because Bashkortostan was a part of the Russian Federation. Giving official status to Tatar would mean a rejection of Bashkir self-determination, "giving Tatars 1.5 states, while Bashkirs would be limited to half a state."[55] If Tatar became a state language, they worried, its status would encourage an increase in Tatar assimilation that would spell the end of the Bashkir nation.[56]

The nationalists' cultural nation-building program was not limited to language issues. They called on the republic government to institute a special

---

[52] "Rezoliutsiia I s'ezda Bashkirskogo narodnogo tsentra 'Ural'," 18 December 1989, in Guboglo (1992b, 103–7).

[53] "Manifest o sovremmenom polozhenii Bashkirskogo naroda i problemakh ego vozrozhdeniia," 23 February 1991, in Guboglo (1992b, 133–7); "Obrashchenie I s'ezda Bashkirskogo narodnogo tsentra 'Ural'," 18 December 1989, in Guboglo (1992b, 108–17); "Rezoliutsiia I s'ezda Bashkirskogo narodnogo tsentra 'Ural'," 18 December 1989, in Guboglo (1992b, 103–7).

[54] "Rezoliutsiia VI Vsesoiuznogo Vsebashkirskogo s'ezda po narodnomu obrazovaniiu," 25 December 1991, in Guboglo (1992b, 162–4).

[55] "Byt' ravnymi s drugimi," *Zamandash*, 17 August 1991; Rinat Baimov, "Po povodu odnoi 'utki'," *Volia*, no. 3 (1990).

[56] "Obrashchenie I s'ezda Bashkirskogo narodnogo tsentra 'Ural'," 18 December 1989, in Guboglo (1992b, 108–17).

program for the preservation, consolidation, and further development of the Bashkir nation.[57] Suggested measures to strengthen Bashkir culture included the creation of a Bashkir film studio, the expansion of the republic museum – whose main goal was to describe the history of the Bashkir people – and the creation of a Bashkortostan Academy of Sciences separate from the Russian Academy. Local museums and libraries were likewise to be transformed into "areas for the study and propagation of Bashkir history and their spiritual heritage." Bashkir culture was to be given priority in determining the government's cultural budget.[58] All of these measures were to be instituted in order to enable Bashkir culture to withstand the assault of the "stronger" Tatar and Russian cultures.

Economic Nation Building

Economic sovereignty had two uses for Bashkir nationalists. It would help to justify the benefits of sovereignty to non-Bashkirs, and its benefits could be used to help develop the Bashkir nation. In justifying the sovereignty campaign to the wider public, Bashkir nationalists described the exploitation of the republic by the Soviet and Russian governments in terms very similar to those used by Tatar nationalists. They focused on statistics that showed that Bashkortostan was one of the leading producers in the Russian Federation, while lagging far below the average in fulfilling its inhabitants' socioeconomic needs.[59] They argued that the sovereignty that would come with union republic status would allow Bashkortostan to become economically independent of the central ministries, reduce the amount of republic revenue sent to Moscow, and thus allow the local government to improve the well-being of all of its citizens.[60] Nationalists also argued that the republic should follow in Tatarstan's footsteps and take control of a portion of its oil reserves for the purpose of selling it on the world market. By withdrawing from the Russian Federation, the republic would have to share revenues only with the union government, leaving more for the region. This money would benefit all inhabitants of the republic, nationalist leaders argued.[61]

Nationalists also blamed the central government for making Bashkortostan a center for the petrochemical industry and thus turning the republic into an ecological disaster area. This was cited as an example of Soviet

---

[57] "Rezoliutsiia 1 s'ezda Bashkirskogo narodnogo tsentra 'Ural'," 18 December 1989, in Guboglo (1992b, 103–7).
[58] "Manifest o sovremmenom polozhenii Bashkirskogo naroda i problemakh ego vozrozhdeniia," 23 February 1991, in Guboglo (1992b, 133–7); "Rezoliutsii V Vsesoiuznogo Bashkirskogo narodnogo s'ezda," 22–3 February 1991, in Guboglo (1992b, 128–30).
[59] "Eto nuzhno vsem," *Vecherniia Ufa*, 25 September 1990.
[60] D. Valeev, "Dlia chego nuzhen status soiuznoi respubliki," *Vecherniia Ufa*, 3 October 1990.
[61] Irek Mukhametov and Bulat Khamidullin, "S'ezd nadezhdy," *Izvestiia Bashkortostana*, 28 February 1991.

colonialist policy toward its ethnic minorities – each ethnic republic was required to concentrate on the production of something harmful to the environment: cotton in Uzbekistan, petrochemicals in Bashkortostan, and nuclear power in several other regions. The resulting environmental disaster did not concern officials at the center.[62] Nationalists argued that sovereignty would allow the republic government to take control of polluting enterprises previously under central jurisdiction, forcing them to clean up and to pay local taxes – thus improving the lives of everyone in the republic.[63]

Although during the struggle for sovereignty Bashkir nationalists argued that it would bring economic benefits to all of the republic's inhabitants, once sovereignty was achieved they sought to make sure that Bashkirs were the primary recipients of these benefits. BNC statements on economic policy usually called on the republic government to take special measures to improve the infrastructure and industrial base in the backward southern, eastern, and northeastern regions of the republic, where most of the Bashkir population lived. These measures were to include the restoration of villages, the opening of cultural and educational centers, improvements in social services, and the construction of new factories.[64] Nationalist leaders hoped that improvements in infrastructure and services in Bashkir-populated areas would slow the flow of migrants out of these areas and prevent the demographic decline of the Bashkir nation.

Similarly, Bashkir nationalists sought to use the republic's political sovereignty to avoid implementing Russian Federation laws on land reform. They fervently opposed private ownership of land, fearing that poor Bashkir villagers would sell their land to outsiders and migrate to the cities or even to areas outside the republic – leaving the nation both weakened demographically and without the land that the nation had owned collectively from time immemorial. They argued that forcing the Bashkir population to accept private land ownership would be an attempt to force an indigenous nation out of its homeland and would lead to interethnic clashes. Furthermore, they argued that the only people who could afford to buy land would be profiteers who would institute tenant farming and thus reintroduce serfdom for the Bashkir people.[65]

---

[62] Irek Agishev, "Byt' ili ne byt'," *Zamandash*, 28 December 1990.
[63] "Oktrytoe pismo o ekologicheskoi katastrofe v Bashkortostane," *Zamandash*, 29 March 1991.
[64] "Obrashchenie I s'ezda Bashkirskogo narodnogo tsentra 'Ural'," 18 December 1989, in Guboglo (1992b, 108–17); "Rezoliutsiia I s'ezda Bashkirskogo narodnogo tsentra 'Ural'," 18 December 1989, in Guboglo (1992b, 103–7); "Rezoliutsiia V Vsesoiuznogo Bashkirskogo narodnogo s'ezda ob ekonomicheskom polozhenii Bashkortostana i programma vykhoda iz ekonomicheskogo krizisa," 22 February 1991, in Guboglo (1992b, 127–8).
[65] Marat Kulsharipov, "Obshchestvenno-politicheskaia i sotsialno-ekonomicheskaia situatsiia v Bashkortostane," *Zamandash*, 21 December 1991; Z. Mufteev, "Otkrytoe pismo o zemlevladenii," *Zamandash*, 29 February 1992.

Bashkir nationalists saw economic sovereignty as a way to generate extra revenue and to avoid those aspects of economic reform that ran counter to their interests. The prospect of extra revenue was used to persuade non-Bashkirs that sovereignty would help them. After sovereignty was declared, the same nationalist leaders argued that the financial gains from economic self-rule should primarily go toward the development of Bashkir-populated regions. Economic sovereignty thus became another aspect of the nationalists' struggle to increase the rights of the Bashkir nation.

Ethnic Institutions and the Construction of Nationalist Mobilizing Frames in Bashkortostan

Whereas in Tatarstan, only radical nationalists called for the establishment of an ethnic Tatar state, the right of ethnic Bashkirs to have such a state was a fundamental aspect of the mobilizing frames that were formulated by the mainstream Bashkir nationalist movement. The movement sought to establish a Bashkir ethno-national republic, with privileges for members of the Bashkir ethnic group and government assurances of continued Bashkir cultural development. Like Tatar nationalists, Bashkir leaders at first sought to establish such a state in the form of a union republic within the Soviet Union, accepting the Soviet ethno-federal hierarchy. After the union's collapse, nationalist leaders rejected independence as unfeasible and continued to call on the Russian government to grant the republic the equivalent of union republic status within the Russian Federation.

Because of identity conflicts with the Tatar population of Bashkortostan, the issues of passport ethnicity and republic boundaries proved to be particularly important to Bashkir nationalist frame construction. Nationalist leaders saw ethnic identification through the internal passport as the only sure way to distinguish between culturally and linguistically similar Tatars and Bashkirs in the republic's northwest. They feared that if ethnic identification ceased to be listed in passports, many Bashkirs would gradually come to identify as Tatars, endangering the cultural survival of the Bashkir nation.[66] As a result of this fear, Bashkir nationalists sought to ensure the maintenance of cultural and institutional boundaries between the two ethnic groups. This fear of assimilation also shaped Bashkir nationalist attitudes toward the geographical boundaries between regions. Nationalist leaders feared that the republic's Tatar population would seek to separate the northwestern regions from the rest of the republic in order to join them to Tatarstan. To prevent this outcome, they sought to promote the legitimacy of the 1922 republic boundary. At the same time, nationalist leaders refrained from calling for the annexation to the republic of Bashkir-populated border regions in Orenburg

---

[66] S. Gainanov, "Piatyi Punkt," *Zamandash*, 14 December 1991.

and Perm provinces.[67] Bashkir nationalists thus sought to use Soviet ethnic institutions to forestall Bashkir assimilation and to bring about the establishment of an ethnic Bashkir state.

CHUVASHIA: SOVEREIGNTY WITHIN RUSSIA

Chuvash nationalists framed their movement's goals primarily in terms of Chuvash cultural revival. Most of their statements dealt with reversing the decline of the Chuvash language and culture through the adoption of new laws and government programs. Political issues, such as republic sovereignty, were placed in the cultural revival frame by focusing on the role played by autonomous republic status in causing Chuvash cultural decline. Unlike the more radical movements in Tatarstan and Bashkortostan, Chuvash nationalists sought to portray their movement as anti-Communist and anti-Soviet but not as anti-Russian, and to preserve Chuvashia's links with the Russian state.

Political Sovereignty

Chuvash nationalist activists began to advocate political sovereignty in late 1989, over a year after the movement began to work for Chuvash cultural revival. This delay was caused in part by the activists' gradual radicalization, but mostly was a result of the greater freedom granted to opposition activists as *glasnost* began to penetrate into the provinces. From the beginning, advocates of political sovereignty framed the issue in terms of a natural desire for statehood among all nations of the world. The Chuvash people were just following the course already charted by the Turks, the Czechs, the Algerians, and many others. As one author put it, "The Chuvash people had dreamed of sovereignty for centuries, but historical conditions prevented its establishment."[68]

Movement activists believed that by showing that the Chuvash people had a long history of independent statehood stretching back to the eleventh-century Volga Bulgar state, they could refute their opponents' claim that Chuvashia did not need greater sovereignty because it owed its existence as a distinct nation to Russian assistance (Dmitriev 1994). The importance attached to this connection was shown by the state-sponsored celebrations of the eleven hundredth anniversary of the founding of the Volga Bulgar state.[69] Beyond the difficult task of showing the value of a claim to independent

---

[67] Although they did explicitly declare that they retained the right to call for such changes in the future (Guboglo 1992a, 126–8).
[68] S. Maliutin, "Za suverennuiu avtonomiiu," *Sovetskaia Chuvashia*, 6 September 1989.
[69] "Vystuplenie Prezidenta N. Fedorova na torzhestvennom sobranii v chest' 75-letiia Chuvashskoi avtonomii i 1100-letiia Chuvashskoi gosudarstvennosti," *Sovetskaia Chuvashia*, 24 June 1995. For a description of the Bulgar state, see Rorlich (1986, 10–16).

statehood 750 years before, activists had to prove that the modern Chuvash people were descended from the Bulgars. Because official Soviet historical texts portrayed the Bulgars as the ancestors of the Tatars, proving such a claim had the added benefit of showing that the Soviet state (and its Russian rulers) had stolen from the Chuvash people not only their opportunity for statehood, but even their own history. The sovereignty struggle could then be portrayed not just as a fight for political power, but as an indigenous battle to reclaim the nation's past. By portraying the Chuvash people as the inheritors of the Bulgar legacy, nationalist leaders sought to create a sense of continuity between a thousand-year-old state and the sovereign territory they were trying to create.[70]

These activists sought political sovereignty for its symbolic meaning and its consequences for cultural development rather than for its potential economic or political benefits. They argued that Chuvashia's status as an autonomous republic was insulting to a nation that had a long history of struggle for sovereignty and previous experience as an independent state. Union republic status, with its symbolic attributes of statehood, was for them the appropriate expression of this quest for symbolic sovereignty in the Soviet context. Symbolic attributes such as a constitution, a flag, and a state language were seen as the most important benefits of sovereignty. Only if Chuvashia became a union republic would the Chuvash nation be respected by members of other ethnic groups.[71]

This attitude toward sovereignty persisted among nationalist leaders until the disintegration of the Soviet Union in 1991. This event made the push for union republic status meaningless and led activists to begin seriously to consider which areas of policy making they wanted to control locally. Not until the first Chuvash National Congress (CNC) was held in October 1992 did the movement issue a resolution on Chuvash state sovereignty that went beyond cultural matters. Resolutions adopted at the CNC called for land reform, the transfer of federal property to local ownership, and measures to forbid federal interference in local budgeting.[72] These new demands brought the movement's ideology closer to statements made by republic officials, who had focused on the political and economic benefits of sovereignty since adopting a sovereignty declaration in 1990.

Unlike activists in Tatarstan, most Chuvash nationalists did not equate sovereignty with outright independence from the Russian Federation. Demands for independence were made in only 3% of the publications concerning the nationalist movement, and no such demands were made until 1992,

---

[70] For a detailed description of the conflict between the Tatars and the Chuvash over their ancestry, see Shnirelman (1996).
[71] Atner Khuzangai, "Podniat' status avtonomii," *MK*, 15 February 1990.
[72] "Rezoliutsiia o gosudarstvennom suverenitete Chuvashskoi respubliki," *Chavash'en Express-Vypusk*, 7 October 1992.

when the movement was already weakening. Most nationalist activists rejected the idea of independence, arguing that Chuvashia needed to be a part of Russia because of the two states' long history of association and economic interconnectedness and because of Chuvashia's geographic position in the center of Russia. As long as Chuvashia was given the symbols of statehood and partial autonomy in determining its own policies, most ethnic movement activists stated that they would be satisfied.[73]

This reluctance to call for Chuvash independence stemmed in large part from the traditionally friendly and close ties between the Chuvash and Russian peoples. The Chuvash were the first Turkic people to be added to the Russian empire and the only ones to convert en masse to the Russian Orthodox religion. Furthermore, Ivan Iakovlev, the nineteenth-century educator and spiritual leader of the Chuvash nation, had called on the Chuvash people to "honor and love the good and wise Russian people.... May their joys be your joys, and their sorrows your sorrows." At the same time, Iakovlev cautioned the Chuvash people never to forget their own language and culture. He was explicit in arguing that "in focusing on your native language, you are not betraying Russia: you can serve the Russian motherland without forgetting your native language" (Iakovlev 1992). Nationalist leaders frequently referred to Iakovlev's statement as a model for their agenda, assuring potential supporters that they sought Chuvash cultural revival while opposing separation from the Russian Federation.

This history of good relations strongly affected the nationalist discourse in the republic. Unlike activists in Tatarstan and Bashkortostan, Chuvash elites emphasized the history of good relations between Russians and Chuvash. While Tatar and Bashkir activists called for the separation of their republics from Russia, the vast majority of Chuvash leaders argued that Chuvashia could not exist outside the Russian Federation. Similarly, Chuvash nationalists never advocated the creation of a Chuvash national state, describing Chuvashia as a multiethnic republic with responsibility for Chuvash national development. Chuvash leaders also opposed preferences for titulars in employment, education, and political office, a policy made easier to advocate by Chuvash numerical dominance in the republic. Unlike the other three republics, Chuvashia was in no danger of being controlled by non-titular leaders, even without special safeguards.

Linguistic and Cultural Revival

While government officials wanted sovereignty in order to increase their autonomy in economic policy making and the design of state institutions,

---

[73] Georgii Ivanov, "V gosudarstvennoi ideologii Chuvashskoi Respubliki proiskhodiat izmeneniia," *Chavash'en*, no. 40 (1993); A. Sidorov, "Gosudarstvennost' – eto, v tom chisle, i simvolika," *Chavash'en*, no. 23 (1994).

movement activists believed that political sovereignty was most useful as a means for bringing about a cultural renaissance. For example, nationalist candidates in the elections to the Russian and Chuvash Supreme Soviets, held in March 1990, published a joint resolution that began with a call for national self-determination, followed by a list of reasons for making this demand. All of these reasons concerned the need to remedy the cultural and linguistic backwardness of the Chuvash people.[74]

Although Chuvash intellectuals recognized that cultural revival was composed of several factors, they clearly considered language to be the most important of them. In 1988, the first year that articles on ethnic issues were allowed to be published in the Chuvash press, almost two-thirds of all such articles concerned language issues. This issue retained the highest salience until the passage of the language law in 1990. Nationalist leaders gave pre-eminence to language revival because they were worried about the gradual assimilation of their ethnic group into the surrounding Russian community. The Chuvash language was seen as being much more than simply a means of communication. It was the direct expression of national culture and, as such, the repository of everything unique about the Chuvash people.[75] The importance attached to linguistic revival makes sense, considering that most national leaders believed that the disappearance of the Chuvash language would spell the imminent demise of the Chuvash ethnic group.

Initially, leaders refrained from making openly political demands. Instead, they called for reversing the long-term decline of Chuvash-language use through increasing native-language instruction in schools, improving the quantity and quality of Chuvash publishing, and expanding Chuvash use among government officials.[76] These proposals were framed by the parameters set out by Soviet institutional guidelines. Readers were reminded that the Constitution of the Soviet Union guaranteed the Chuvash language a certain status and many specific rights.[77] The injustice of the hierarchical ethno-federal system was particularly prominent in early critiques. Union republic language institutes published their own manuscripts and journals and were allowed to acquire foreign publications dealing with their subject matter. Most ASSR language institutes had no such rights.[78] Commentators in the republic press decried the decrease in the percentage of Chuvash

[74] Petr Krasnov, "Pochemu ia ne vstupil v partiiu," *Molodoi Kommunist*, 1 March 1990.
[75] "O nashem gosudarstvennom iazyke," *Sovetskaia Chuvashia*, 12 August 1989.
[76] Mikhail Fedotov, "V zashchitu rodnogo iazyka," *Molodoi Kommunist*, 7 January 1988; Mikhail Fedotov, "Snova o rodnom iazyke i eshche koe o chem," *Molodoi Kommunist*, 7 July 1988; Atner Khuzangai, "Kak vazhno pomnit o korniakh," *Molodoi Kommunist*, 22 September 1988.
[77] Mikhail Fedotov, "V zashchitu rodnogo iazyka," *Molodoi Kommunist*, 7 January 1988.
[78] With the exception of the Tatar and Bashkir language institutes, whose rights were similar to those of the union republic institutes. Mikhail Fedotov, "V zashchitu rodnogo iazyka," *Molodoi Kommunist*, 7 January 1988.

speakers among the Chuvash population, brought about, in their opinion, by the decline in Chuvash-language schooling throughout the republic since the 1960s. Furthermore, many writers complained that Russian migrants to the republic refused to learn Chuvash and discriminated against local residents whose command of Russian was less than perfect.

At first, movement activists argued for administrative solutions to these problems. They called for increasing the number of Chuvash-language schools and improving their quality. The inadequacy of Chuvash-language study in the schools was to be addressed by increasing the number of years in which Chuvash-language education was available. They also argued for increasing the number of Chuvash-speakers in government employment, especially in those positions where they were likely to come in frequent contact with Chuvash-speakers who knew Russian poorly, such as in the court system.[79] The charter of the first Chuvash nationalist organization, the Iakovlev Society, declared that the society's main goal was to foster Chuvash cultural and linguistic development.[80] As the political climate in the USSR became increasingly free, movement leaders began to link their demands for cultural revival to political issues. By 1989, the need for a state language was explicitly linked to the issue of state sovereignty. As one analyst noted, "The Chuvash ASSR even today is formally considered a sovereign national republic.... And every sovereign state must have its own state language."[81] Nationalists believed that if Chuvash were a state language, it would be given equal rights with Russian in the public sphere, the government would assist in its development, and schools would open classes where adults who did not speak Chuvash could learn the language. For nationalist leaders, neglect of the Chuvash language in public life came to symbolize the inferior status of the Chuvash ASSR.

When they focused on nonlinguistic cultural issues, nationalist leaders were primarily concerned with ensuring the cultural survival of the Chuvash population living outside the republic and ensuring this diaspora's link with the Chuvash republic. The Chuvash Public Cultural Center (CPCC) dedicated most of its resources to establishing Chuvash cultural organizations among the diaspora. It also sent Chuvash books and newspapers to these regions.[82] Similarly, the Chuvash National Congress adopted several resolutions calling for the establishment of Chuvash film and shortwave radio studios, an increase in Chuvash television broadcasting to seven hours daily, the creation of a republic information agency, an increase in government financing of Chuvash book publishing, and the expansion of Chuvash

---

[79] For example, see V. Stepanov, "Iazyk i sudoproizvodstvo," *Molodoi Kommunist*, 10 August 1989.
[80] Iakovlev Society charter, *Molodoi Kommunist*, 29 September 1988.
[81] "O nashem gosudarstvennom iazyke," *Sovetskaia Chuvashia*, 12 August 1989.
[82] Mikhail Iukhma, CPCC chairman, interview, February 1996.

education.[83] The main goal of these policies was to ensure the consolidation of the Chuvash diaspora with the Chuvash population in the republic by creating a single community of information for all Chuvash, regardless of their place of residence. Nationalists feared that unless they established strong cultural ties between the diaspora and the republic, the diaspora would become Russified. With 50% of ethnic Chuvash living outside the republic, they saw such an outcome as a potential blow to the vitality of the Chuvash nation.

Ethnic Institutions and the Construction of Nationalist Mobilizing Frames in Chuvashia

Like nationalist leaders in all of the other republics, Chuvash nationalists sought to correct the perceived injustice done to their ethnic group by the Soviet government by increasing the status of the group's territorial homeland. Nationalist leaders argued that, unlike the existing Chuvash autonomous republic, a Chuvash union republic would have the authority to institute the policies of cultural revival that were their chief concern. Chuvash nationalists were not hostile to the Russian population and rejected the idea of independence for the republic. These leaders were also less concerned than nationalist leaders in the other republics about securing titular dominance in the republic through emphasizing titular ownership. Because of Chuvash demographic dominance in the region, titular dominance was secure before the mobilization drive began. On the other hand, Chuvash leaders were concerned about the assimilation of the sizeable Chuvash diaspora population. Nevertheless, they limited their proposals for helping the diaspora to efforts to establish a single information community and to provide Chuvash-language printed matter to Chuvash settlements. Like the other nationalist groups, they refused to advocate the revision of Soviet-era republic borders.

KHAKASSIA: THE STRUGGLE FOR CULTURAL SURVIVAL

The ideology of the Khakass nationalist movement was decisively influenced by the ethnic group's small numbers and the region's status in the federation. Since their ethnic group numbered only 80,000, according to the 1989 census, and comprised only 11% of the territory's population, Khakass leaders made Khakass ethno-cultural survival their primary goal. At the same time, the region's low status in the Soviet federal hierarchy made their task more difficult by making the local government subject to three levels of superior authority and by giving ethnic Khakass fewer privileges than were given to the titular nations of autonomous and union republics. These factors precluded demands for independence, limiting the movement to arguments in favor of greater political and economic autonomy.

---

[83] The CNC resolutions are found in *Chavash'en Express-Vypusk*, 7 October 1992.

Battle for a Republic

The struggle for increasing Khakassia's autonomy was not limited to Khakass nationalist organizations. It was carried out by an alliance of Khakass nationalists and pro-democracy activists that survived much longer than similar alliances in the other republics, where democrats and nationalists parted ways over sovereignty. This campaign began in the summer of 1989 and included two related but separate demands. First, activists sought to withdraw Khakassia from Krasnoyarsk *krai*, making it directly subject to the Russian Federation government. Second, they sought to raise Khakassia's status from autonomous province to autonomous republic.[84]

In calling for the establishment of a Khakass republic, Khakass nationalists justified their demands by referring to the ancient history of statehood among local Turkic groups, the struggle for national statehood around the 1917 revolution, and the damage done to the nation by Soviet nationality policy and Stalinist repression. Khakass leaders portrayed the states that existed in the region from the sixth to the thirteenth century, and again from the fifteenth to the seventeenth century, as ancient Khakass states, using their existence to claim that Khakass statehood and civilization had a proud past but had declined as a result of external conquest and colonization, first by the Mongols and then by the Russians. Using this view of local history, Khakass nationalists sought to portray the reestablishment of Khakass statehood as the restoration of historical justice.

Khakass readiness for statehood was further underlined by descriptions of the movement for Khakass self-government in 1917 as the immediate forerunner of the modern independence movement, sharing a similar agenda.[85] Soviet nationalities policy was blamed for the repression of the Khakass elite during the 1920s and 1930s, the construction of environmentally damaging industrial projects, such as the Saiano-Shushenskaia hydroelectric dam, and the mass Russian in-migration that accompanied them (Chistanov 1989). Since the vast majority of Russians in the republic had arrived during the previous 40 years, they could easily be portrayed as settlers with no local roots who did not care for the inhabitants of the region or its environment. Nationalists argued that the establishment of a Khakass republic would halt the cultural decline of the Khakass ethnic group by placing it on an equal footing with the other minority ethnic groups living in the Russian Federation.

Arguing from the point of view of national self-determination, these nationalists advocated a simultaneous withdrawal from the *krai* and transformation of Khakassia into a republic. Valerii Ivandaev, one of the leaders

---

[84] That is, to the status that the other three republics in this study already had.
[85] A. Gladyshevskii, "Ot inorodcheskikh uprav – do uezda," *Sovetskaia Khakassia*, 28 March 1991 and 3 April 1991.

of Tun, argued that only the titular nation had the right to determine their region's form of statehood – that this was not a matter to be decided by a majority of the total population in a referendum.[86] The First Khakass Congress, meeting in August 1990, reaffirmed that Khakassia should become a republic, citing in its decision both economic reasons and the Khakass right to national self-determination.[87] Throughout the battle for republic status, which reached a successful conclusion in July 1991, the predominantly Russian pro-democracy organizations supported the idea of a Khakass republic based on Khakass national self-determination.

The nationalists' arguments contrasted with the republic government's goal of separation from Krasnoyarsk without transformation into a republic. This position was based on the economic and political benefits of separation for the entire population of the region and ignored demands for Khakass self-determination and cultural revival. Supporters of this view claimed that Khakassia's current status made it no better than a district (*raion*) of the *krai*, as it had no right to supervise its own territory or develop its own legislation. Furthermore, its budget was part of the *krai*'s and therefore could be changed by the *krai* administration at will, usually to take money away from Khakassia in favor of one of Krasnoyarsk's central regions.[88] The *krai* was blamed for treating Khakassia as a colony by taking away its agricultural produce, construction materials, and natural resources without paying for them.[89] Separation from the *krai* would allow Khakassia to fully exploit its economic potential, which was greater than that of most Russian provinces and autonomous republics. Economic development, according to local government officials, thus appeared to be the primary rationale for increasing sovereignty and separating Khakassia from Krasnoyarsk.

Cultural Survival

While nationalist activists in other regions focused on their nation's political status, Khakass leaders were primarily concerned with their nation's survival as a distinct culture. The movement's early activities focused on reinstating a Khakass ethnic holiday and investigating the social conditions in which rural Khakass lived.[90] In the summer of 1989, Khakass intellectuals began to express worries about the fate of their nation at public meetings. The biggest threats included rapid linguistic assimilation of Khakass youth, a high rate of intermarriage with Russians, inadequate government spending on culture,

[86] Valerii Ivandaev, "O natsionalno-gosudarstvennom ustroistve Khakassii," *Tos*, no. 7 (1989).
[87] "Rezolutsii s'ezda Khakasskogo naroda," *Sovetskaia Khakassia*, 18 August 1990.
[88] V. Shtygashev, "Doverie, iskrennost, velikodushie dolzhny napolniat nashi mezhnatsionalnye otnosheniia," *Sovetskaia Khakassia*, 29 October 1989.
[89] V. Torosov (first deputy chairman of the republic executive committee), "Khakassii nuzhna realnaia samostoiatelnost," *Sovetskaia Khakassia*, 11 April 1991.
[90] Aleksandr Kostiakov, "Tun znachit pervyi," *Tuur*, no. 1 (1990).

environmental degradation and the destruction of archeological monuments, and underrepresentation of ethnic Khakass in the government.[91]

Khakass leaders connected lack of language knowledge with loss of ethnic identity. Only 60% of Khakass children studied their native language in schools, leading to high rates of Russification among the younger generations. Nationalist leaders also provided statistics showing that even in rural areas, 30–50% of Khakass married Russians, with 70% of their children choosing Russian as their ethnic identity. This trend showed, they argued, that the entire Khakass ethnic group was disappearing and that urgent measures were needed to counteract this trend.[92] They blamed this trend on Soviet nationalities policy, which ignored the interests of small nations. In order to stop this "cultural genocide," nationalists called for the expansion of Khakass-language use in education and the media, the establishment of facilities for language study, and improvements in Khakass cultural facilities. In August 1990, the First Khakass Congress adopted a resolution on the problems of the Khakass nation and methods for solving them that called on the government to open ethnic schools in all Khakass settlements. These schools would feature Khakass-language instruction in the early grades, switching to instruction in Russian in the upper grades while preserving Khakass as a subject. The Congress also called for the establishment of Khakass-language newspapers in each county. In the area of culture, it called for training more specialists to study and teach traditional Khakass music and the establishment of a new state-run Khakass theater. Unlike nationalist congresses in other republics, the congress did not press for the use of Khakass in government activity, perhaps believing that such a demand would be unrealistic considering the low percentage of Khakass speakers in the region.[93]

Nationalist fears of Khakass extinction extended beyond the realms of language and culture. Nationalists also decried the migration of many Khakass to areas outside the region, a diaspora that comprised 25% of the total Khakass population by 1989. The Khakass diaspora was created almost entirely through migration, since, unlike the ethnic groups discussed earlier, Khakass had not traditionally lived outside their region. Nationalists sought to improve economic and cultural conditions in the region in order to reduce this migration rate and to establish mechanisms for the return of earlier generations of Khakass migrants. High rates of alcoholism among the Khakass population were also seen as a step on the path to national extinction.[94] In order to counteract this tendency, Tun repeatedly launched propaganda campaigns aimed at persuading Khakass villagers to refrain from drinking

---

[91] T. Shapovalova, "Vo ves' golos," *Sovetskaia Khakassia*, 27 July 1989.
[92] Iuliia Kostiakova, "Glasno o proshlom, nastoiashchem i budushchem," *Tos*, no. 7 (1989).
[93] Resolution of the First Khakass Congress: "O sovremennykh problemakh Khakasskogo naroda i o putiakh ikh resheniia," *Sovetskaia Khakassia*, 18 August 1990.
[94] Ibid.

alcohol. By 1993, they considered this their most important goal – connecting the introduction of alcohol into the Khakass population with Russian colonialist policies aimed at taking away Khakass land.[95]

The revival of traditional religious practices was an integral part of Tun's effort to counteract Khakass apathy toward their culture – which was seen as the enabling condition for all of the problems already discussed. As a way to revive interest in traditional cultural practices, Tun conducted mass celebrations of Khakass holidays and included modern interpretations of shamanistic religious rituals in these ceremonies. The celebrations also included traditional performances and arts and crafts competitions. They became very popular, attracting thousands of participants and spectators on a yearly basis and eventually receiving government sponsorship.[96]

Khakass nationalists also called for economic measures to prevent the continued decline of their ethnic group. They called on the government to establish a foundation for Khakass development, which would raise money to improve the cultural facilities and social infrastructure in Khakass settlements. They argued that the government should also finance the education of gifted Khakass youth abroad – where they could learn the basics of business and management. To end the flood of Russian migrants into the region, the First Khakass Congress declared that the future construction of large industrial projects should require the approval of the Khakass Supreme Soviet, which in turn could give its approval only after consultation with representatives of the indigenous ethnic group.[97]

Khakass nationalists were most concerned about the dangers of land privatization. Mirroring the arguments of Bashkir nationalists, they argued that the history of their nation had always been tied to the land. Private ownership of this land would go against Khakass tradition. Permitting the sale of land would gradually allow wealthy outsiders to dispossess the Khakass nation of its most important resource – and thus hasten its extinction. In light of this situation, Khakass nationalists argued that the Khakass people should have exclusive rights to the land and resources that had traditionally belonged to them. Non-Khakass individuals and organizations were to be allowed only to lease land in the region. These arguments were presented as being in accordance with international legal documents regulating indigenous land use, such as the International Labor Organization's Conventions on Indigenous

---

[95] "V sovete assotsiatsii Khakasskogo naroda 'Tun'," *Tuur*, no. 1 (1990); A. Sulberekov, "Ochnis' brat!" *Abakan*, 25 May 1993.
[96] For descriptions of some of these celebrations, see A. Baidosheva, "Tun Pairam: Utolenie zhazhdy," *Sovetskaia Khakassia*, 21 June 1991; V. Kokova, "Prislushat'sia k slovu stareishin," *Sovetskaia Khakassia*, 8 August 1991; Iu. Kostiakova, "Voskhozhdenie na Uitag," *Sovetskaia Khakassia*, 24 July 1992; A. Kostiakov, "Den' pamiati predkov," *Abakan*, 29 June 1993; author's field notes from the 1996 celebration of the Tun Pairam festival.
[97] Resolution of the First Khakass Congress: "O sovremennykh problemakh Khakasskogo naroda i o putiakh ikh resheniia," *Sovetskaia Khakassia*, 18 August 1990.

and Tribal Nations and on the Protection of Indigenous Populations, which had recently become the basis of Soviet and Russian policies on the protection of small ethnic groups.[98] The land ownership issue continued to be a source of conflict between Khakass and Russian leaders in the republic, culminating in heated nationalist protests against the adoption by the Supreme Soviet of a law on land reform that permitted the sale of land into private hands.[99]

The most controversial aspects of Tun's program for averting Khakass extinction concerned the political institutions of the new republic. Tun was concerned that, as a by-product of competitive elections, Khakass representation in various legislative bodies would decline. This concern was shown to be justified by the results of the 1990 regional legislative elections. In response, the First Khakass Congress called for the creation of a bicameral legislature, with 50% of the seats in one chamber given to members of the titular ethnic group.[100] Various proposals to guarantee Khakass overrepresentation in parliament were proposed as the new republic's institutions were being created, but in the end none of them was approved, causing great consternation among Khakass nationalists.[101] When only 13 Khakass deputies were elected to the new 100-member republic parliament in December 1991, Tun demanded that its chairman be of Khakass ethnicity. While this demand was satisfied, after several days of public protest and stormy parliamentary debate, the victory came at the cost of Tun's alliance with Democratic Russia. In the wake of this event, the parliament rejected a sovereignty declaration, making Khakassia the only republic in the Russian Federation that did not declare its sovereignty during the early 1990s.[102] These events led to Tun's radicalization. Its leaders became even more committed to winning special privileges for their ethnic group and soon began to make hostile comments about the Russian "occupiers" of Khakass lands. At the Fourth Khakass Congress, which met in March 1992, Tun leaders attempted to pass a resolution giving the congress the power to rescind decisions of the republic legislature and Council of Ministers that violated Khakass interests.[103] These statements alienated both the majority of the Khakass population and

---

[98] Ibid.; "Deklaratsiia o prave sobstvennosti Khakasskogo naroda na zemliu i ee bogatstva," *Sovetskaia Khakassia*, 21 December 1990; A. Kostiakov, "O prave naroda," *Sovetskaia Khakassia*, 1 February 1991.
[99] Sergei Sipkin, "Zhestokoe bezvremenn'e," *Iuzhno-Sibirskii Vestnik*, 18 December 1992.
[100] Resolution of the First Khakass Congress: "O sovremennykh problemakh Khakasskogo naroda i o putiakh ikh resheniia," *Sovetskaia Khakassia*, 18 August 1990.
[101] Valery Ivandaev, interview, June 1996.
[102] A. Borisova, "Parad suverenitetov. Komu on nuzhen?," *Sovetskaia Khakassia*, 18 February 1992; Iuriy Ugolkov, "Passions for Sovereign Power," *Rossiiskaia Gazeta*, 22 May 1992, cited in FBIS-USR-92-065, 3 June 1992; Sergei Sipkin, "Zhestokoe bezvremenn'e," *Iuzhno-Sibirskii Vestnik*, 18 December 1992.
[103] L. Gorodetskii, "Protivostoianie – Put' v tupik," *Sovetskaia Khakassia*, 2 April 1992.

previously sympathetic ethnic Russian liberals, leading to Tun's marginalization from the republic's political life.

The failure of its effort to control the legislature led Tun to propose the establishment of protective reservations in areas where the Khakass were concentrated. This idea had first been proposed at the First Khakass Congress, but had been rejected at the time.[104] Tun continued to argue in support of this idea – noting that it was the only way for a minority nation such as the Khakass to achieve self-government. By December 1992, Khakass nationalists were arguing that the creation of ethnic reservations was the only way to preserve the Khakass language and culture. They even advocated the creation of ethnic neighborhoods in urban areas as a means toward ethnic self-government and the establishment of Khakass schools.[105]

Ethnic Institutions and the Construction of Nationalist Mobilizing Frames in Khakassia

Compared to nationalist movements in other republics, the Khakass nationalist movement started with few institutional advantages. Whereas movements in the other three republics sought to transform existing autonomous republics into union republics, Khakass nationalists had to fight for the establishment of an autonomous republic. Whereas in the other republics titular nationalists were concerned about maintaining titular control of the republic government in the aftermath of democratization, in Khakassia the titular group lacked such control in the first place. Although Khakass nationalists sought to institute cultural revival policies that were very similar to those advocated in the other republics, they started with fewer and weaker existing cultural institutions than did nationalists in the other republics.

Nevertheless, the mobilizing frames constructed by Khakass leaders proved to be very similar to those developed by nationalist movements in the other regions. Like the others, Khakass nationalists argued that their ethnic group deserved an increase in the status of its administrative unit. The political and economic arguments used in constructing this frame were virtually identical to the arguments used by nationalists in the other regions in calling for union republics. Khakass nationalists believed that as the titular ethnic group, the Khakass had a right to control the republic government and to institute affirmative action programs in employment and education for the titular population. Like the others, Khakass leaders did not discuss boundary revision, although this was made easier by the lack of compactly settled Khakass diaspora groups in adjoining regions. Thus, the differences between

---

[104] Valery Ivandaev, "Politicheskie problemy v zhizni Khakasskogo naroda," *Sovetskaia Khakassia*, 16 August 1990.
[105] Chon Chobi proposal for a state program on language development in the Khakass republic, 19 December 1992.

INSTITUTIONS AND FRAMES

As shown in the case studies, nationalist leaders framed their demands around the institutional legacies of the Soviet Union. Both territorial and personal institutionalization of ethnicity structured nationalist demands. The influence of territorial institutions can be seen in the acceptance of artificially created boundaries as given, even when they did not correspond to the geographic distribution of the titular ethnic group, and in the nationalist movements' focus on campaigning for higher administrative status for their territories. In all of the regions except Bashkortostan, territorial institutions succeeded in channeling nationalist demands toward a "civic" conception of sovereignty and away from pure ethno-nationalism. Finally, the institutionalization of ethnicity on a personal level allowed nationalists to demand control of the government and the enactment of affirmative action programs for titular ethnic groups in their "own" republics.

The territorial boundaries of Russia's ethnic republics were created during the 1920s by the Soviet state. These boundaries frequently ignored the boundaries of the ethnic communities that they were supposedly enclosing, sometimes including vast areas populated by other ethnic groups while excluding adjoining areas compactly settled by the republic's titular ethnic group. All of the republics discussed in this study were constructed in this way. Bashkortostan included Tatar and Russian-majority areas in the northwest while excluding Bashkir areas to the south. Chuvashia excluded one Chuvash area because Lenin's birthplace was located there, while including purely Russian areas in order to increase the republic's industrial capacity. The other two republics were created with similar inconsistencies. Yet once these boundaries were delimited, they were seen as sacrosanct, and demands for boundary adjustment were considered off-limits. Chuvash leaders did not attempt to resurrect the Greater Chuvashia movement that had existed during the 1920s, nor did they countenance the possibility of creating a monoethnic republic by ceding the two Russian counties to a neighboring province. Radical Khakass nationalists' calls for ethnic reservations were designed to leave republic boundaries untouched while granting privileges to Khakass in certain parts of the republic. Bashkir leaders campaigned for the acceptance of current republic boundaries as reflecting the historical extent of Bashkir lands, going so far as to invent a history of Tatar assimilation to explain the lack of Bashkirs in the republic's northwestern areas. The Tatar response to this campaign is the exception that proves the rule. While Tatars in their own republic rejected the possibility of expanding Tatarstan to include adjoining

Tatar-populated parts of Bashkortostan, Tatars in Bashkortostan did advocate boundary change in order to leave the Bashkir-dominated republic. Yet these Tatars did not demand that their lands become a part of Tatarstan. Instead, they advocated the restoration of the Ufa province, an area that had been added to Bashkortostan in 1922 and that had previously existed as a separate administrative unit within Russia. By structuring their demands in this manner, Tatar leaders recognized the legitimacy of Soviet boundary lines, seeking to restore a previously existing boundary rather than undertaking a wholesale territorial revision.

The hierarchical four-tier federal structure of the Soviet Union influenced nationalist demands more than any other single factor. Nationalists in each region perceived the advantages of the greater autonomy given to higher-order republics and sought to achieve higher status for their own lands. Nationalists in the autonomous republics argued that their republics should rise to union republic status, noting that union republics had greater autonomy in all spheres of decision making. Nationalists in Khakassia wanted to advance one level as well, from autonomous province to autonomous republic, also claiming that such a status would allow for local decision making on local problems. However, status was the primary factor in nationalists' demands for increasing the administrative level of their regions in the federation hierarchy. Nationalists saw no reason why their territories, which were as populous and economically well developed as many higher-status regions, could not be equal to these regions in status. Thus Tatar nationalists argued that Tatarstan, with a population of 3.5 million, including 1.7 million Tatars, could be a union republic like Latvia, which had a population of 2.7 million, including 1.4 million Latvians. Similar arguments were made about Tatarstan's economic development relative to the other republics. The same arguments were also made in Bashkortostan and Chuvashia. Khakass nationalists compared their republic to the autonomous republics, noting that Khakassia was better developed economically than all but five of the ASSRs and several of the union republics as well. All of these arguments boiled down to relative status: the idea that there was no reason that ethnic group X should have a lower level of autonomy than ethnic group Y.

The existence of an ethno-federal system of territorial division, even if only as a cover for a unitary state, led nationalists to frame their demands in terms of republic sovereignty and self-determination. In three of the four republics, nationalist leaders focused on establishing territorial sovereignty for the region as a whole, rather than on seeking to create an ethnic state. Ethnic administrative units functioned as targets for nationalist mobilizing activities. Had the Soviet federal system been purely territorial, without regard for ethnicity, ethno-nationalist movements would have been far more likely to seek to create ethnic states. Even in Bashkortostan, the one region where the nationalist movement called for an ethnic state, their demands were cloaked in the rhetoric of republic self-determination. Soviet ethnic institutions thus both provided nationalist movements with the resources to become a potent political force and created mentalities that moderated these movements' demands.

The institutionalization of ethnicity on a personal level was carried out by forcing each individual to decide on a single ethnic identity, which was then inscribed in his or her internal passport. The ability to determine any individual's ethnic identity, together with the norm of titular ownership of the homeland, led nationalist leaders to argue for the preservation of Soviet-era ethnic quotas and the introduction of new quotas in areas of life previously untouched by them. These quotas were to be applied to representation in parliament, admission to institutions of higher education, and promotion to administrative positions in industrial enterprises. The importance of the passport as an identifying tool for ethnic preferences was illustrated by a Bashkir nationalist's statement that if personal identity papers did not identify the bearer's ethnicity, many members of minority groups would lose their strongest link to their ethnic group and be in danger of Russification.[106]

Soviet ethnic institutions were crucial in creating the social mentalities that influenced the repertoire of mobilizing frames adopted by nationalist leaders. The extent of these institutions' influence can be seen in the use of similar repertoires by nationalists in the Soviet Union's union republics (Hosking et al. 1992). In this chapter, I have shown how these institutional limits were translated into mobilizing frames that could resonate with the movements' potential supporters. In the next chapter, I discuss the extent to which the movements were successful in gaining popular support.

[106] S. Gainanov, "Piatyi Punkt," *Zamandash*, 14 December 1991.

5

Institutions Matter

Measuring Support for Nationalism

Support for social movements can be expressed in several different ways. Active supporters join movement organizations and participate in protest activities. More passive forms of participation include voting for the movement's candidates in elections and voicing support for movement goals in polls and surveys. This chapter measures the extent of popular support for nationalist movements by analyzing the full range of these activities. The highest levels of both passive and active support for ethno-nationalist mobilization are found in Tatarstan and Bashkortostan, with somewhat lower levels of support in Chuvashia. Nationalism finds the fewest adherents in Khakassia, the former autonomous province.

Protest activity is the most demanding way of demonstrating support for a political cause. Unlike voting and responding to surveys conducted by social scientists, public protest runs the risk of repression by an unsympathetic government or injury in clashes with movement opponents. Therefore, this form of movement activity attracts the smallest number of supporters and is most easily influenced by government and opposition actions. In examining protest activity, I focus on demonstrations, hunger strikes, and violent clashes as the most visible and galvanizing forms of protest.

Because of their novelty and their importance as an immediate and authoritative measure of public support, nationalist movements saw electoral politics as a central arena for testing their strength against other political forces in the regions. I use the results of several local and national elections and referenda during the 1989–93 period to measure the extent of public support for the nationalist movement and its candidates. Because of the sheer number of participants and their importance in shaping the course of local political life, electoral data are an important indicator of popular political sentiments. However, the infrequency of elections means that such data can provide only snapshots of voter sentiments and are unable to capture the dynamics of changes in support for nationalism. In addition, the electoral systems used in the Soviet Union and the Russian Federation tend to blur the extent of support for nationalism. During the transition period, when the country lacked a stable party system, the use of two-round or plurality electoral systems with single-member districts led to the predominance of independent, nonparty candidates. This creates some difficulties in identifying nationalist candidates and in distinguishing whether voters supported particular candidates because of their nationalism or because of other factors, such as their stands on economic reform or their personal qualities. For these reasons, I supplement electoral data with polling data, which measure public support for specific nationalist demands and are able to show the dynamics of support for nationalism.

Finally, I use data from Western and Russian social science surveys conducted in 1993. These studies used identical questionnaires and similar methodologies to assess the extent of nationalist sentiment in the four regions considered in this study. Although conducted during a period when support for nationalism was in decline, these surveys are helpful because they allow for direct comparisons of the extent of support for several types of nationalist demands among the regions.

Together, these four measures provide a multifaceted view of the extent to which the nationalist movements – founded by intellectual elites in academic settings – were able to spread beyond their initial social base and attract the support of a large proportion of the population.

NATIONALIST PROTEST ACTIVITY

Unlike more passive forms of movement support, public protest requires a substantial personal investment. While voting and responding to surveys are essentially anonymous activities that rarely lead to substantial negative consequences for the individual, participating in a protest is a very public act. People who participate in public protests risk being subjected to various forms of repression, including violence, arrest, and job loss. These risks are particularly great in the early stages of a protest campaign, when the number of participants is small. Furthermore, protest participation usually requires a large investment of time and energy, as participants need to travel to the protest location and spend a significant part of their day there. By contrast, voting is a relatively quick process that takes place at a location near the voter's home. While participation in a survey may take an hour or two, the survey participant can choose a convenient time and place for completing the survey. Because participation in public protest entails greater risks and greater costs than other ways of expressing support for a movement, protest actions usually involve a much smaller number of people than the total number of movement supporters.

The cost-benefit ratio of protest participation can be reduced through the actions of protest organizers, who can promote participation by providing selective incentives to participants or by linking participation to higher status in the community. By promoting a large turnout, such actions simultaneously reduce the risks of participation and increase its benefits to potential participants.

The government also has a decisive effect on the size of protests. If initial protest activity is met with police repression, potential participants are likely to stay away because of the increased sense of risk. On the other hand, if the early protests are allowed to proceed with impunity, and especially if some members of the ruling elite express sympathy for the protesters' goals, then the risks for participation in future protests become much lower and participation is likely to increase rapidly.

Demonstrations were the most common form of protest activity during the *perestroika* and post-*perestroika* periods. This marked a dramatic change from the dominant forms of protest before Gorbachev's liberalization, when less confrontational forms, such as petitions and hunger strikes, were the most common, and when protest demonstrations rarely attracted over 100 people (Beissinger 2002, 464; Kowalewski 1980, 187). During the Soviet period, demonstrations were usually state-sponsored rituals designed to show popular support for the Communist government on major holidays. With the advent of *glasnost* during the late 1980s, the demonstration was rapidly adopted by the pro-democracy movement in Leningrad and Moscow as a tool for mobilizing supporters (Zdravomyslova 1996, 129–30). It then quickly spread to the provinces and to other opposition movements, including nationalist groups in ethnic regions.

I define a demonstration as a voluntary, nonviolent gathering of persons for the purpose of engaging in a collective display of sentiment for or against a public policy. Violent confrontations, with opponents or with the government, are treated separately as mass violent events. Following Beissinger, I have chosen to examine only protests that involved a minimum of 100 persons and whose number of participants was not restricted by event organizers (Beissinger 2002, 464). Smaller demonstrations were not systematically covered in the newspaper sources. I include only those demonstrations that presented nationalist demands or were organized by nationalist organizations, thus excluding protests aimed primarily at promoting democracy or economic reform. Finally, ritual government-sponsored demonstrations on public holidays are largely excluded, except in cases where unapproved participants joined the demonstration and publicly demonstrated their opposition to the sponsoring government during its course (for example, by holding placards or chanting slogans).

I also follow Beissinger in excluding strikes and petitions from the analysis. This is done for two reasons. First, few strikes during this period were motivated by nationalist concerns. Although most strikes were politically motivated, they were organized primarily in support of rapid democratization or in opposition to the economic reforms being carried out by the Yeltsin government. Second, strikes and petition drives were not systematically covered by the regional newspapers that were the primary sources used in compiling the database of protest activity.

Unlike Beissinger, I include hunger strikes in the analysis, primarily because I found that they were systematically covered in the local press.[1] Hunger strikes are also theoretically important, as they tended to take place during periods of peak mobilization and had high symbolic value for both the population and the authorities. The authorities, in fact, were more likely to respond to hunger strikes than to demonstrations. In all of the hunger strikes described in this study, the hunger strikers placed themselves in public view throughout the strike, usually by living in a tent on the main square of the capital city. This was done to maximize the psychological impact of the hunger strike on opponents and bystanders. The psychological impact was further heightened by frequent, sometimes daily, demonstrations by movement sympathizers in support of the hunger strike.

Unlike events in some other ethnic regions of the Soviet Union, mass violent events in the four regions discussed in this study remained rare and caused few casualties and no deaths during the 1988–93 period. I define a mass violent event as "a mass political action whose primary purpose [is] to inflict violence, either in the form of an attack on people or on property" (Beissinger 2002, 464–5). Mass violent events require a minimum of fifteen participants. I include only those events that have a marked political and ethnic or nationalist character, excluding fights between youth gangs and economically motivated violence. In many cases, mass violence occurs as a consequence of a nonviolent demonstration. In this case, the event is counted as both a demonstration and a mass violent event.

My information on protest events in these regions comes primarily from three sources: a database of protest events described in the local newspapers, a chronology of "ethnic events" compiled by Galina Komarova of the Institute of Ethnology and Anthropology of the Russian Academy of Sciences, and the relevant parts of a national database of protest events compiled by Mark Beissinger. In compiling the newspaper database, I depended primarily on one newspaper from each region. In each case, this newspaper needed to be available during the entire 1988–93 period, to include coverage of political events in the region, and to be roughly similar in focus to the newspapers used in the other regions. In practical terms, this meant that youth newspapers, which were not available in all regions and which generally ceased to cover political issues after 1992, and "new" regional newspapers, which appeared primarily in 1991 or 1992, could not be considered. In all cases, the newspaper of the regional Communist party branch and Supreme Soviet was finally chosen.[2] Data from these newspapers were

---

[1] Hunger strikes are defined as the public refusal to accept nourishment for political reasons.
[2] The list includes *Sovetskaia Tataria* (renamed *Respublika Tatarstan*), *Sovetskaia Chuvashia*, *Sovetskaia Bashkiria*, and *Sovetsksaia Khakassia* (renamed *Khakassia*).

supplemented, where possible, by data from city and youth newspapers, as well as from new regional newspapers.[3] These newspapers were used to find additional information on the number of participants and their demands, rather than as a source of data on other protest events not covered in the main newspapers.

In an effort to make the coverage of protest activity more complete, I have used two sources in addition to the newspaper database. The chronology of ethnic events in Russia and the Soviet Union compiled by Galina Komarova includes information on important political events, including protests, in all of the former Soviet Union's ethnic regions during the 1989–91 period (Komarova 1994, Komarova 1996, Komarova 1997). Mark Beissinger's database covers demonstrations that took place in the Soviet Union during the 1988–92 period. Its sources are based in the United States and Moscow, thus complementing the other two main sources (Beissinger 2002). In comparing the three sources, I found that major events tend to be covered in all three sources, whereas smaller protests tend to be found only in the regional newspaper database. Except where otherwise cited, the discussion in the rest of this section is based on these sources.

Protest in Tatarstan

Tatarstan experienced more protest activity than any ethnic republic in the Russian Federation outside of the Caucasus. Although initially some of this protest activity focused on democratization and environmentalism, over time these issues faded and virtually all of the protest came to revolve around nationalist demands. Altogether, of the 173 protests that took place in Tatarstan between 1987 and 1993, 142 focused on nationalist demands. The level of participation in these protests was highly variable, with tens of thousands protesting during periods of peak mobilization, while only hundreds turned out at other times (Figure 5.1). Peaks of mobilization invariably occurred when key decisions on political sovereignty were about to be made by the republic's government or legislature. Tatarstan was also the only republic where protest actions outside the capital city were commonplace. A quarter of the total protests occurred in seven smaller cities throughout the republic. Tatarstan also had the most numerous and widespread occurrences of violent conflict over ethnic issues, both between nationalists and the government and between supporters and opponents of sovereignty.

Nationalist protest activity began during the fall of 1988. It became the main form of protest during the region in the summer of 1990, when the

---

[3] These include *Vecherniia Kazan, Kazanskie Vedomosti, Komsomolets Tatarii/Molodezh Tatarstana*, and *Izvestiia Tatarstana* in Tatarstan; *Molodoi Kommunist/MK* and *Chavash'en* in Chuvashia; *Vecherniia Ufa, Leninets*, and *Izvestiia Bashkortostana* in Bashkortostan; and *Abakan, Respublika*, and *Yuzhno-Sibirskii Vestnik* in Khakassia.

Institutions Matter

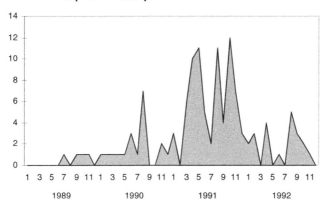

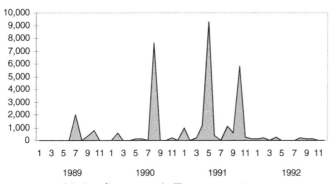

FIGURE 5.1. Nationalist protest in Tatarstan, 1989–92.

democracy movement split, and continued virtually without pause until the end of 1992.[4] Peak periods of mobilization, which occurred in August 1990, May 1991, and October 1991, coincided with important debates in parliament on issues related to the republic's political status. As the political situation in the region changed, the movement's demands gradually became more radical. While early protests called for increases in cultural autonomy, later protests focused on political demands – first for union republic status and later, after the August 1991 coup, for complete independence for the republic. Keeping in mind these general features of nationalist protest in the republic, let us now look at these events in greater detail.

---

[4] Occasional protests took place in later years, but participation rarely exceeded 100 people, and the mainstream press for the most part did not report these events.

Soon after its formation at a well-attended public meeting in October 1988, the Tatar Public Center (TPC) began to stage protests calling for greater cultural rights for the Tatar population. At first, the TPC was allied with the pro-democracy Tatarstan Popular Front, with the two groups holding occasional joint demonstrations and campaigning together in the run-up to the 1989 election. In 1989 and the beginning of 1990, the TPC campaigned for democracy and against the construction of a nuclear power station as actively as it campaigned for cultural rights. During this period, nine TPC demonstrations were held, attracting an average of 750 participants. Only half of these demonstrations focused primarily on cultural demands.

After the decline of the ecology and pro-democracy movements, Tatar nationalist activists came to focus more exclusively on cultural rights and greater political autonomy. Throughout the summer of 1990, participation at their protests gradually increased as the campaign for the adoption of a sovereignty declaration gained steam. This period of mobilization peaked in August, when over 7,000 protesters gathered in front of the Supreme Soviet in Kazan on five consecutive days to press for the adoption of a sovereignty declaration. After securing the adoption of the declaration in their preferred text, nationalists continued to hold occasional small protests throughout the fall and winter months to press for the official recognition of Tatarstan as a union republic within the Soviet Union and separate from Russia.

The first months of 1991 represented a lull in the mobilizing efforts of nationalist activists. Although they staged several demonstrations to protest against intervention by the Soviet army in Lithuania and to call on their supporters to vote against the preservation of the Soviet Union in the March 1991 referendum, these demonstrations were relatively sporadic and attracted an average of only 1,000 participants.

The next significant wave of nationalist mobilization began in April, as the republic's Supreme Soviet began to discuss whether Tatarstan should participate in the Russian presidential election. The nationalist movement called for a boycott and sought to institute a Tatarstan presidency instead. Between April and June 12, the date of the elections, Tatar nationalists held 25 protests in Kazan, Naberezhnye Chelny, and Almetevsk, with an average attendance of 5,000. The peak of the protest came in late May, after the Supreme Soviet decided to hold simultaneous elections for both the Tatarstan and Russian presidencies. During this period, tens of thousands of protesters gathered in front of the Supreme Soviet on successive weekends to call for a boycott of the Russian election in the republic. In addition to the demonstrations, sixteen nationalist activists began a hunger strike in mid-May. The hunger strike lasted for two weeks and was led by Fauzia Bairamova, a Supreme Soviet deputy and the chairperson of the radical Ittifaq Party. The presence of a woman hunger striker served as a powerful mobilizing symbol for the protest participants. The first violent confrontations between protesters and their opponents were recorded during this period, first in Almetevsk, where protesters attempting to take control of an oil pipeline were repelled by police, and later in Kazan, where one of the hunger strikers was beaten by unknown assailants. The nationalist protest had an effect on the local government, leading to a compromise solution in which the government allowed the Russian election to take place while refraining from officially endorsing it.

After several public events during the summer designed to publicize the movement's recent accomplishments, the nationalists returned to the streets in force in the aftermath of the August coup. Nationalists and antisovereignty democrats held daily joint protests during the coup, attracting some hundred people despite some arrests and the use of force by police to break up one of the demonstrations. As it became clear that the coup was failing, Ittifaq maintained its alliance with the pro-Moscow Democratic Party of Russia (DPR), arguing that recently elected president Shaimiev should resign because of his support for the coup. They were opposed by the TPC and the Sovereignty Committee, who saw a threat to Tatarstan's sovereignty in the possibility of Shaimiev's resignation. The Ittifaq/DPR alliance lasted only a few days and was followed by renewed disagreement over the relationship between Tatarstan and Russia. For the next several weeks, the DPR continued to hold large protests calling for the government's resignation, attracting as many as 5,000 supporters on several occasions. This period proved to be the peak of its popularity.

Within a week of the coup, Tatar nationalists, led by Ittifaq, for the first time began to call for the complete independence of Tatarstan. During the period between the coup and the end of October, they held 21 protests calling for independence, the establishment of a Tatar national guard, and even armed struggle against the Moscow government. These protests proved to be highly popular, with an average attendance of over 4,000 people. The wave of mobilization built gradually through September, culminating in daily demonstrations during the mid-October session of the Tatarstan Supreme Soviet. As many as 20,000 protesters sought to pressure the legislature to adopt a declaration of independence. The tensions crested on October 15, when violent clashes broke out between supporters and opponents of independence, followed by an attempt by nationalist radicals to storm the Supreme Soviet building. Clashes between protesters and police continued for the next several days, resulting in over 50 injuries. In an effort to defuse tensions, the Supreme Soviet adopted a statement about independence without actually declaring it outright.

Although nationalists continued to organize demonstrations throughout the rest of 1991 and 1992, these events quickly lost popular appeal, as movement leaders became increasingly radical, while the population became increasingly preoccupied with economic problems. Full independence and the establishment of a national guard remained the nationalists' primary demands. Economic problems were treated superficially, with calls for trade barriers against Russia and the establishment of a national currency. As a result of the gulf between nationalist demands and the concerns of their potential supporters, the average participation at the 32 protests held from November 1991 to December 1992 was only 200 people. In 1993, participation declined even further, as the media ceased to pay attention to the nationalist movement, while the movement itself became increasingly preoccupied with internal conflicts.

Protest in Bashkortostan

Public protest in Bashkortostan, although neither as frequent nor as popular as protest in Tatarstan, was nevertheless a fairly common event during the peak years of ethnic mobilization – from 1990 to 1992. Unlike events in Tatarstan, where protest occurred throughout the republic, almost all of the protest events in Bashkortostan took place in the capital city. Although ecological issues predominated in early protests and drew the largest crowds, by the fall of 1990 sovereignty and cultural rights had come to the forefront. Ethnic rights remained the dominant protest issue until the summer of 1992, when the countrywide economic collapse led to the eclipse of nationalist protests by protests against wage arrears.

During the spring and summer of 1990, newly established nationalist organizations took the lead in organizing numerous highly successful demonstrations to protest ecological conditions in the region. During this period, Bashkir, Tatar, and pro-democracy movement organizations worked in concert to blame the republic government for its conservatism and inaction in the face of environmental disasters. These groups held a total of twelve joint protests with an average turnout of 8,000 people, including two protests that mobilized in excess of 20,000 supporters. This period represented the peak in these groups' drawing power for public protest. The first of these protests, held in February 1990, successfully called for the resignation of the Bashkortostan Communist Party *obkom*. Following the contamination of Ufa's drinking water with phenol from an upstream chemical plant on March 30, activists held four protests against government inaction on a cleanup during a ten-day period, drawing 7,500 supporters at each of the two largest protests. After the cleanup was concluded, activists organized monthly protests calling on the government to close the chemical plant responsible for the spill and to establish close monitoring of ecological safety throughout the republic. These protests were even more successful, drawing as many as 30,000 participants on one occasion. During this period, nationalist organizations attempted to take advantage of the public's focus on ecological issues. By playing a leading role in environmental protests, they sought to create a positive image for their organization, an image that they hoped would carry over to support for their nationalist demands.

However, when their switch to explicitly nationalist demands occurred in September 1990, the nationalists' calculations proved false. Even at their peak, protests over nationalist demands attracted a much smaller group of participants than protests over ecological issues. To some extent, this was the inevitable outcome of the ethnic divide in the otherwise united environmentalist front. Although all groups could mobilize in favor of clean water, Bashkir and Tatar groups found themselves at odds when it came to nationalist demands. While Bashkirs advocated greater sovereignty and Bashkir cultural development, Tatars worried that these measures would lead to discrimination against their ethnic group and sought to enshrine the Tatar language in the republic constitution – along with Bashkir and Russian – as an official state language. Bashkir nationalists, in turn, feared Tatar cultural domination as much as they feared Russian political domination and sought to have Bashkir declared the sole state language. Inevitably, the Bashkir and Tatar nationalist movements became engaged in a confrontation that took their energies away from the fight for greater independence from Moscow.

Unlike events in Tatarstan, where nationalist organizations protested without pause for several years, nationalist protest in Bashkortostan tended to occur only during periods of peak tension. Between September 1990 and the summer of 1992, there were four such periods. The first occurred in October 1990, when Bashkir nationalist organizations held three public demonstrations to press for the approval of a sovereignty declaration by the republic's Supreme Soviet. Although participation figures are not available for these protests, we can estimate, based on similar protests, that approximately 2,000 people turned out in support of sovereignty. The Tatar nationalist movement organized a small protest in opposition to sovereignty. Furthermore, Tatar leaders led a hunger strike for Tatar cultural rights during this period. Following the parliament's approval of a sovereignty declaration on October 11, both sides quieted down.

Although a few protests took place during the ensuing months, these events were infrequent and sparsely attended. The next peak of mobilization in Bashkortostan occurred in the aftermath of the August 1991 coup. While Tatar, Bashkir, and pro-democracy groups came together in support of the Yeltsin government during the coup, bringing 1,500 people into the streets while the coup was still in progress, they split again immediately after the coup, as Tatar and pro-democracy activists sought to remove the ethnic Bashkir leadership of the republic for supporting the coup plotters, while the Bashkir nationalist movement came out in its support. Although each side mobilized thousands of people in support of its position, the Bashkirs prevailed in this confrontation, and the republic's leaders kept their jobs.

Only a month after this series of protests, tensions again began to rise over the impending election of the republic president. As Tatar activists renewed their push to make Tatar an official state language, Bashkirs mobilized to ensure that the newly elected republic president would be an ethnic Bashkir.

Altogether, five protests were held during October and November 1991 to influence the presidential election. Although they received extensive coverage in the local media, these protests were poorly attended, drawing no more than a few hundred supporters. Much of the media coverage centered on the actions of a Bashkir student who tore down the flag of the Russian Federation during one of the protests. After the Supreme Soviet canceled the presidential election in order to avoid instability in the region, 30 Bashkir students belonging to the Union of Bashkir Youth occupied the republic television center, refusing to leave until they were allowed to broadcast a message to the population. The political tension generated by the aborted election campaign led to a moratorium on elections in the republic that was not lifted until the countrywide parliamentary election of December 1993.

After mid-November, the nationalist movements refrained from public protest actions for several months. The final episode of nationalist mobilization took place in the spring of 1992, as nationalists mobilized first in support of the Tatarstan referendum on sovereignty and then in opposition to the signing of the Federation Treaty, a proposed pact between the Russian government and its constituent regions, by the leaders of Bashkortostan. In mid-March, Bashkir and Tatar nationalists joined together to express their support for Tatarstan's efforts to secure its sovereignty through a popular referendum. These demonstrations showed that popular support for the nationalist organizations had steeply declined since the previous year. Despite the cooperation between Tatar and Bashkir leaders, the demonstrations drew no more than 200 supporters. As the focus of political life in the region shifted from support for neighboring Tatarstan to internal conflict over whether Bashkortostan should sign the Federation Treaty, local Tatar organizations faded from the scene.

After the Rakhimov government signed the treaty in late March, Bashkir nationalists experienced a last brief period of popular support. Although a small protest was held in late March on this issue, tensions began to increase after the Union of Bashkir Youth declared a hunger strike on April 9. Its demands included the treaty's annulment and the resignation of the Rakhimov government that had signed it. On the night of April 13, the hunger strikers were attacked by unknown assailants, who were later assumed by most participants to have been members of the government's special forces unit (OMON). This attack led to a series of large protests in support of the republic's secession from Russia. The April 15 protest drew 4,000 people. Although the hunger strike continued for over three weeks, and further protests were held until the end of April, the Bashkir nationalists were unable to achieve their goals through protest. After April 1992, Bashkir nationalist organizations largely abandoned public demonstrations in favor of developing closer links with the republic government.

Bashkortostan was the scene of large-scale protest during the early part of the mobilization cycle, with massive and numerous

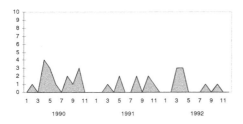
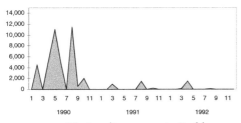

FIGURE 5.2. Nationalist protest in Bashkortostan, 1990–92.

nationalist-sponsored demonstrations throughout 1990 in support of environmental issues. Protests over ethnic issues, however, were relatively infrequent, occurring primarily during periods of high political tension in the region (Figure 5.2). As public protests declined in popularity, nationalist leaders increasingly drifted toward an interest, group form of political activity. The main Bashkir nationalist organization, the BNC, largely faded from the protest scene after the summer of 1991. Two-thirds of the Bashkir-organized protest actions held during the last two periods of peak mobilization were organized by the Union of Bashkir Youth. This was the only Bashkir nationalist organization that was not given access to the republic government during this period and therefore continued to use confrontational strategies.

Protest in Chuvashia

Chuvash nationalist organizations held infrequent demonstrations that were able to attract relatively large crowds during the early period of the movement, when it was still constituted as a pro-democracy movement. After the split between the Russian democrats and the Chuvash nationalist democrats during the fall of 1990, protest turnout decreased for both groups, although the nationalists continued to hold relatively frequent, if poorly attended, rallies.

The earliest protests in Chuvashia, held in February and May 1990, were organized by the Democratic Alternative movement. These rallies were aimed primarily against the Communist leadership of the region. The February rally, which attracted 10,000 participants, sought to persuade voters to support anti-Communist candidates in the March elections to the regional and Russian parliaments. The May rally, aimed at securing the resignation of the antireform local government, attracted 70,000 participants. These two large rallies represented the peak of popular protest mobilization in Chuvashia.

Following the split between nationalists and democrats, public demonstrations became more frequent but less well attended. During the period from October 1990 to October 1991, nationalists led by the Chuvash Rebirth Party (CRP) held seven rallies, none of which attracted more than 500 participants, and two hunger strikes. Four of the rallies and one of the hunger strikes were held in late August 1991 to protest the anti-Gorbachev coup. The rest mixed support for democracy and Boris Yeltsin with calls for the restoration of Chuvash national symbols and the promotion of Chuvash culture.

Nationalist public protest in Chuvashia declined even further after 1991, with only two major protest demonstration held in 1992 and none in 1993. The February and October 1992 demonstrations, although co-organized by the CRP, focused primarily on economic concerns such as the payment of wages and pensions. The small turnouts for protests during the previous year had shown the CRP that purely nationalist demands could not mobilize the public. By uniting with labor unions and focusing on economic demands, the CRP was able to mobilize thousands of protesters, who might thus have become more sympathetic to a nationalist party also concerned about their economic problems. During this period, in addition to the demonstrations, the CRP also staged two hunger strikes over economic demands.

Protest in Chuvashia was entirely nonviolent, with no clashes between protesters and authorities or between Chuvash and Russians recorded during the period. Demonstrations began relatively late, with no public protest recorded until 1990, and, with the exception of the two early pro-democracy rallies, were relatively sparsely attended. Unlike the Tatar activists, the Chuvash nationalist movement, focused on electoral politics and perhaps recognizing the passivity of its constituents, did not make public protest actions a priority in its political activity.

Protest in Khakassia

Khakassia experienced the fewest nationalist protests of the four regions discussed in this study. Almost all of the protest actions that did take place in the region were nondisruptive and had received prior approval from the local government.

The first nationalist activity in Khakassia occurred during the summer of 1988, when a group of Khakass students home on holiday from Leningrad State University organized a series of public meetings in Abakan and in

14 villages in the predominantly Khakass Askiz district to protest the cancellation of an annual Khakass holiday by the republic government.[5] This campaign set the tone for nationalist protest in the region. The meetings were held only with the prior approval of local authorities, and activists confined themselves to advocating procedural means of changing the situation, including meetings with republic leaders and petition drives.

Over the next several years, the Khakass nationalist movement rarely engaged in public protest, preferring instead to press its agenda in the media and through discussions with members of the government. During this period, it used occasional congresses and public meetings, rather than public protest, to maintain its links with the Khakass population. As a consequence of its defeat in the December 1991 local elections, the nationalist movement decided to change its strategy. When the newly elected Supreme Soviet met for the first time in January 1992, its members sought to replace the ethnic Khakass chairman of the body with an ethnic Russian. Tun responded with protest demonstrations in the capital, Abakan, and in Askiz, the central Khakass village. These demonstrations attracted an estimated 1,000 participants in each location and featured a single demand – the reinstatement of the previous, ethnically Khakass, Supreme Soviet chairman.[6] Most of the participants in the capital city had traveled there from rural regions (Kasimov n.d., 131). Although their demand was satisfied on the third day of protest, this outcome proved to be a pyrrhic victory for the Khakass nationalist forces, who lost most of their allies in both the pro-democracy and former *nomenklatura* camps as a result of these events. The isolation led to the movement's decline in influence, and such unsanctioned protests were not repeated in the republic.

Protest in Khakassia was without exception of a nonviolent nature. In fact, the only violent incident involved attacks by Russians on Khakass inhabitants of Abakan. On 30 October 1988, a gang of approximately 200 ethnic Russian youths gathered on the main street of Abakan and, chanting anti-Khakass slogans, proceeded to attack Khakass passers-by and throw stones at police. Information about these clashes was kept out of the news media, although rumors about the events led to the first meeting between the Khakass intelligentsia and members of the local government.[7] However, no further violent clashes between Russians and Khakass occurred, and interethnic relations gradually resumed their previous peaceful character. Perhaps because it occurred early in the liberalization period, when the local authorities still had full control over local political life and the press, this clash came to be

---

[5] *Tuur*, no. 1 (1990).
[6] Note that the ethnic Khakass population in the region totaled less than 70,000 people. The movement was drawing on a smaller population base than nationalist movements in the other regions.
[7] *Tos*, no. 2 (1989).

seen as an isolated incident, and its memory played little role in the region's political life.

Protest Participation as Popular Support

The extent of participation in public protest serves as an excellent indicator of the level of popular support for the movement organizing the protests. Greater participation and more frequent protests show both the extent to which a movement's agenda is supported by its potential supporters and the ability of the movement to organize and mobilize its supporters. Among our four cases, by far the highest levels of participation in protest activity were found in Tatarstan. Bashkortostan also experienced a fairly significant level of nationalist protest, occasionally with large numbers of participants. Although there were some very large pro-democracy protests in Chuvashia, nationalists in the republic turned to protest only sporadically and with rather limited success. Finally, nationalists in Khakassia organized only a single protest event with relatively moderate attendance. In all regions, protest activity reached its peak when the regional government or legislative body was debating issues related to national sovereignty. Similar increases in protest activity did not occur during election campaigns or during periods of high tension between the local government and Moscow.

ELECTORAL SUPPORT FOR NATIONALISTS

Protest participation is not the only indicator of social movement strength. Some movements eschew disruptive public protest in favor of strategies that emphasize electoral competition. For this reason, the ability of movement candidates to attract votes in elections serves as another indicator of the extent of popular support for nationalist movements. To measure the ability of nationalists to win votes, I look at both nationwide and local elections.

Four nationwide elections took place in the Russian Federation between 1989 and 1993. These included the March 1989 election to the USSR Congress of People's Deputies, the March 1990 election to the Russian Federation Congress of People's Deputies, the December 1993 election to the Russian State Duma, and the referendum on the proposed Russian constitution, which took place concurrently with the Duma election. Two other nationwide votes, including the Russian presidential election of 1991 and the 1993 referendum on support for the president and early elections, are not relevant for measuring support for nationalism in the regions and are therefore excluded from the analysis. The March 1991 referendum on the preservation of the Soviet Union is also excluded, because nationalist organizations did not take definite positions on its outcome.

In addition to the nationwide elections, numerous local elections were held during this period. In March 1990, regional legislatures were elected in all of the ethnic regions of Russia. Furthermore, between 1991 and 1993 most regions elected a head of the local government. Tatarstan was the first, holding a presidential election in June 1991. Chuvashia held two presidential elections, the first in December 1991 and the second two years later. Bashkortostan held a presidential election in December 1993. No presidential elections were held in Khakassia during this period. Other important local elections analyzed in this study include referendums on sovereignty held in Tatarstan in March 1992 and in Bashkortostan in December 1993, and Khakassia's election of a new republic legislature in December 1991.

Because these elections are scattered throughout the mobilization period, they can give a good portrait of the shifting fortunes of the nationalist movement over time. However, the picture is complicated by the instability of the political situation throughout the country during this period and by the type of electoral system used in the legislative elections. The "triple transition" from Communist dictatorship to multiparty democracy, from planned to market economy, and from centralized to federal state structure meant that elections were contested on a multitude of issues simultaneously (Offe 1991). In these circumstances, it was often hard to determine whether particular candidates were receiving support because of their views on nationalism, on democracy, or on the economic transition. This problem is made even more complicated by the electoral rules, which initially allowed only the Communist Party to contest the election as a party. Even when other parties were legalized, the single-member district / plurality electoral system served to weaken party identification among both candidates and voters. Because of these complications, in most of the legislative elections nationalist candidates could be determined only case by case on the basis of their electoral platforms. Only in a few cases were candidates officially endorsed by nationalist organizations. These factors make determining the absolute level of support for nationalist candidates in local elections almost impossible. However, since the problems are identical for all regions, we can compare relative levels of support for nationalist candidates.

Electoral Support in Tatarstan

The Tatar nationalist movement relied primarily on public protest to achieve its goals, treating electoral politics as secondary. Furthermore, beginning in 1990 it refused to field candidates in Russia-wide elections and called on supporters to boycott these votes. Nevertheless, electoral support for nationalists in the 1989 elections to the USSR Congress and the 1990 elections to the Tatarstan Supreme Soviet serve as important indicators of the level of popular support for nationalists during the early years of the movement. Furthermore, the results of the 1992 referendum on Tatarstan's sovereignty strongly reflect the extent of support for the nationalist agenda. Finally, the success of nationalist efforts to boycott Russian elections can be measured by comparing the region's turnout in each election with turnout in that election for Russia as a whole.

Because of restrictions and obstacles created by the republic government, the Tatar movement was unable to nominate candidates for the 1989 election to the USSR Congress of People's Deputies (Akhmetov 1993). Nonetheless, several candidates who held positions sympathetic to the nationalist agenda were nominated. These candidates distinguished themselves from the rest of the field by advocating either union republic status for Tatarstan or an increase in the use of the Tatar language in the region. Notably, half of the candidates advocating the nationalist agenda were ethnic Russians. This shows that in its early form, the nationalist campaign had an appeal that reached beyond the ethnic Tatar community. Altogether, candidates sympathetic to the nationalist agenda ran in 9 of the 21 districts, winning in five races and coming in a close second in multicandidate races in two others.[8] Prominent candidates who made nationalist appeals included two well-known writers, the editor of the most popular pro-reform newspaper, and the head of the Communist Party *obkom*.

The limits of support for nationalism were demonstrated, however, by a repeat election held in July 1989 in a predominantly Tatar rural district. Here, the candidates included Marat Muliukov, one of the co-chairmen of the Tatar Public Center; Mintimer Shaimiev, the head of the republic's Council of Ministers; and a prominent factory director who did not support the nationalist agenda. Both Shaimiev and Muliukov called for declaring Tatar the republic's official language, although only Muliukov advocated making Tatarstan a union republic. Only 11% of the voters supported the TPC candidate, and Shaimiev won with 77% of the vote.[9] This result shows that although the nationalist agenda was popular with voters, this support did not necessarily translate into electoral support for nationalist movement candidates.

By 1990, the Tatar Public Center had formulated its strategy calling for a boycott of all Russia-wide elections. Unlike its actions in later elections, in 1990 the TPC limited its opposition to a single public statement and a refusal to nominate candidates for the Russian Congress races. For this reason, the boycott had little effect on participation, and, as in 1989, candidates considered sympathetic to the nationalist agenda ran in several districts. Altogether, a total of nine pro-nationalist candidates ran in 7 of the 25 districts.[10] Unlike the previous year's candidates, nationalist sympathizers were almost entirely Tatar, with only one Russian advocating the nationalist agenda in his campaign. These candidates proved quite successful, winning in five districts and

---

[8] The results of the Tatarstan elections to the USSR Congress of People's Deputies may be found in *Sovetskaia Tataria*, 29 March 1989 and 11 April 1989.
[9] *Sovetskaia Tataria*, 11 July 1989.
[10] The list of Russian Congress candidates may be found in *Sovetskaia Tataria*, 28 January 1990. The results were published in *Sovetskaia Tataria*, 10 March 1990 and 22 March 1990.

placing second in a sixth. Support for them in the first round was quite variable, ranging from 5% to 33% and averaging 20%. Like the USSR Congress elections a year earlier, these elections demonstrated the strength of popular support for nationalist goals in the early years of the movement.

Popular support for nationalist candidates in the simultaneously held election to the republic Supreme Soviet was very strong. The main problem for the Tatar Public Center was finding candidates to run for the legislature. The Communist Party still had the power to intimidate potential opponents, and few people were brave enough to openly oppose the ruling elite. As it turned out, the lack of suitable candidates had a significant negative impact on the nationalists' strength in the Supreme Soviet. Nationalist candidates ran in only 13 districts out of a total of 250. Ten of those districts were in Kazan, and only one was in a rural area, showing the movement's urban recruiting bias. The nationalist candidates included eight scholars, the head of the pedagogical institute, two editors, a prosecutor, and the director of the Tatar Drama Theater. The nationalists won in ten of the thirteen races, including all three outside Kazan. Ittifaq's Fauzia Bairamova won in a rural constituency, taking more than 50% of the vote in the first round against the head of that district's Communist Party and another candidate. Three of the TPC's leaders also won in Kazan and Nabereznye Chelny. By comparison, the pro-democracy movement won only 11 out of the 39 districts in which it fielded candidates.[11]

Nationalist candidates did less well in repeat elections held in April in districts where no candidate was able to win a majority of the votes or turnout had been below 50%. Nationalist candidates ran in 5 of the 36 elections held at this time, winning only one.[12] It is not clear why there was such a significant difference between two elections held only one month apart. Perhaps the movement had a limited supply of strong candidates, and the best had already been elected in the first round. Regardless of the reasons for this failure, in the two elections combined the nationalists still managed to win 60% of the districts in which they fielded candidates. The democrats, by comparison, won only 30% of their races. Over time, the nationalists' strength in the Supreme Soviet increased, as many Tatar members of the *nomenklatura* joined their "Tatarstan" parliamentary bloc. At its peak in 1991 and 1992, the "Tatarstan" bloc could count on about 120 votes out of 250 and could usually achieve a majority for its less radical proposals (Mukhametshin 1993, 96).

The March 1992 sovereignty referendum proved to be a crucial moment in Tatarstan's political life. In the aftermath of the adoption of a parliamentary

---

[11] The list of local candidates may be found in *Sovetskaia Tataria*, 2 February 1990. The results are published in *Sovetskaia Tataria*, 13 March 1990 and 22 March 1990.

[12] The list of candidates may be found in *Sovetskaia Tataria*, 19 April 1990. The results are published in *Sovetskaia Tataria*, 24 April 1990.

resolution on independence in October 1991, the government decided to ease tensions by holding a referendum on the question of Tatarstan's status vis-à-vis the Russian Federation. The question put to voters stated: "Do you agree that the republic of Tatarstan is a sovereign state, a subject of international law, building its relations with the Russian Federation and other states on the basis of treaties between equal parties?" Although the wording of the question implied that an affirmative vote would lead to full independence, the Tatarstan government issued a statement of clarification shortly before the vote, noting that a positive result would not necessarily lead to full independence and that relations between Tatarstan and Russia would be determined through negotiations. Prior to the vote, the contesting sides appeared evenly matched, with the nationalist movement and the local governing elite calling for a "yes" vote, while the pro-democracy movement and the central government in Moscow argued for a "no" vote. As it turned out, the nationalists prevailed, winning with 61% of the vote in a turnout of 82% of the eligible voters. As might be expected, the vote was divided along ethnic lines, with most Tatars voting in favor of the referendum. Although most Russians opposed sovereignty, enough voted "yes" to give the nationalists a victory. Interestingly, controlling for ethnic balance, there was no difference in support for sovereignty between urban and rural inhabitants of the republic.[13] Nationalists won all rural districts and cities with Tatar majorities, most districts and cities with Tatar pluralities, and several districts and cities with Russian pluralities. As political events developed, the referendum victory turned out to be primarily symbolic, but it nevertheless created a substantial air of legitimacy for the nationalist movement's program and allowed the republic government to insist that the Russian government negotiate with it as an equal.

The strength of the nationalist movement in Tatarstan can be gauged not only by its ability to win electoral contests, but also by its ability to persuade potential voters to boycott nationwide elections. The nationalist movement organized boycotts of the June 1991 Russian presidential election, the April 1993 referendum on support for the president, and the December 1993 Duma elections and referendum on the proposed Russian constitution. After significant nationalist pressure led the Tatarstan government to declare voting in the 1991 Russian presidential election to be optional, only 35% of the population cast a ballot, compared to a nationwide turnout of 75%. This is especially striking given that 60% of the population voted in the Tatarstan presidential election being held simultaneously in the same precincts. The 25% of the population who took part in one but not the other

---

[13] Analysis based on linear regression of percent voting "yes" on percent Tatar and percent urban in each administrative district. "Yes" vote and percent Tatar had a 90 percent correlation level. Based on results published by the Central Election Commission and compiled by Dmitri Toropov. I would like to thank Pauline Jones Luong for providing these results.

went to the polls and refused to accept one of the two ballots they were given. Turnout was even lower for the 1993 referendum and elections. Only 23% of the population voted in the April referendum on confidence in the Russian president. In the December elections, the combined pressure of the republic government, the nationalist movement, and the Communist Party led to participation rates of only 14% in the republic as a whole. Turnout exceeded 30% in only one region. In the republic, the pattern was strikingly similar to the voting in the 1992 sovereignty referendum. Turnout was lowest in areas where most of the population was Tatar and highest in predominantly Russian areas. Surprisingly, considering the extent to which the rural electorate was thought to be controlled by the administration, there was no difference between rural and urban turnout after controlling for ethnic composition.[14]

Yet we should not overestimate the influence of the nationalist movement on electoral participation, particularly in the 1993 elections. Its calls for election boycotts were successful primarily when seconded by the republic government. When nationalists called for boycotts and the government urged people to vote, the boycotts failed (Luong 1998, 648). This outcome is illustrated by the March 1994 repeat election to the Russian Duma. Although it took place only three months after the boycotted 1993 election, the political situation had changed radically in the interim. Following the signing of a bilateral treaty between Tatarstan and Moscow in February, the republic government called for the population to participate in the elections, and the voters responded. Although the nationalists again called for a boycott, 58% of the voters participated. Even more significantly, turnout was higher in regions with predominantly Tatar populations and in rural regions. This outcome implies that the Tatar boycott of the preceding election was influenced more by the position of the government than by the position of the nationalist movement.

Electoral results from elections held in 1989 and 1990 show that support among the population for Tatar nationalism was very high. Although nationalist movement organizations did not run their own candidates in elections to federal bodies, candidates sympathetic to the nationalist viewpoint won a majority of the races in which they ran. Movement candidates did run in elections to the Tatarstan Supreme Soviet, again winning in a majority of their contests. The ability of the nationalist movement to influence their constituents is also evident in the willingness of the electorate to respond to calls for boycotting federal elections between 1991 and 1993. Similarly, the movement's gradual weakening can be seen in its inability to persuade voters to boycott the March 1994 repeat elections to the Russian State Duma and its poor performance in the 1995 elections to the republic parliament. While

---

[14] McAuley (1997, 107), for one, emphasizes the manipulable nature of the rural electorate in Tatarstan.

in 1990 Tatar nationalists could count on the support of a majority of Tatar voters in many urban districts, by 1993 their popular support was below the 10% level.

Electoral Support in Bashkortostan

Demographic factors were critical in determining the role of electoral politics for the Bashkir nationalist movement. After an early setback, Bashkir nationalists recognized that they could not achieve their goals by winning elections, as Bashkirs were significantly outnumbered by Russians and Tatars in the region. For this reason, they ceased to focus on winning elections and turned their attention to cementing their alliance with the Bashkir-dominated republic administration.

At the time of the March 1989 election to the USSR Congress of People's Deputies, the Bashkir nationalist movement had not yet emerged as a political force in the region. Unlike the situation in Tatarstan and Chuvashia at this time, neither cultural demands nor the status of the republic in the federal hierarchy had yet become an issue in the republic's political life. The first meeting of Bashkir intellectuals, which would result in the establishment of the Bashkir Cultural Center, was still two months away. So it is not surprising that none of the candidates running for seats in the USSR Congress, regardless of their ethnicity, advocated any goals that could be described as nationalist. In fact, aside from the presence of multiple candidates in most districts, the 1989 elections in Bashkortostan closely resembled the Soviet elections of the pre-democratization era. Most of the seats went to representatives of the *nomenklatura* or to token workers and peasants. Only 1 of the 21 seats was won by a pro-democracy candidate.[15]

A year later, the situation was very different. The Bashkir National Center had been established in the fall of 1989, and although most of its leaders did not run for seats in the Russian Congress or the Bashkortostan Supreme Soviet, its influence could be seen in the platforms of several candidates. In the Russian Congress election, supporters of Bashkir nationalist goals ran in 8 of the 27 districts, including those districts with the largest Bashkir populations. They were not very successful, garnering on average only 10% of the vote in each district and losing in every race. Three of the eight candidates finished in the top two positions in their districts in the first round. But these three all lost by wide margins in the runoffs, with none receiving more than 40% of the vote. The other five candidates received between 3% and 8% of the first-round vote.[16]

Supporters of nationalism were somewhat more successful in the elections to the 280-member Bashkortostan Supreme Soviet. Nationalist candidates

---

[15] *Sovetskaia Bashkiria*, 29 March, 16 May, and 23 May 1989.
[16] *Sovetskaia Bashkiria*, 10 March, 21 March, 25 April, and 11 May 1990.

ran in 35 districts, located primarily in the southern and northeastern parts of the republic, where the Bashkir population was concentrated. In these areas, nationalist candidates had the greatest success in rural settings, winning in 8 of the 23 rural districts in which they ran. Nationalists won in only two urban districts, both in cities with small Bashkir populations. Altogether, Bashkir nationalists ran in only a small percentage of the districts but were able to win in more than a quarter of the districts in which they did run.[17] With only ten seats in a legislature dominated by the *nomenklatura*, they soon found that they had little influence.

The next series of elections in Bashkortostan occurred in 1993. First, the republic government held a referendum on sovereignty concurrently with the April referendum on Yeltsin's rule. The referendum question asked whether voters agreed that "The Republic of Bashkortostan, in the interests of its peoples, should have economic self-rule (*samostoiatel'nost*) and treaty-based relations with the Russian Federation on the basis of the Federation Treaty and the appendix to it from the Republic of Bashkortostan." This was clearly a much less radical formulation of sovereignty than the one that had been put to voters a year earlier in neighboring Tatarstan. It generated little conflict with the central government in Moscow and was approved by 76% of the voters. Although this result shows that support for some measure of local autonomy extended to members of non-titular ethnic groups, a "yes" vote on this referendum did not necessarily translate to support for the Bashkir nationalist movement, whose demands went far beyond economic sovereignty to include Bashkir control of the republic government and the preferential development of Bashkir culture. More likely, the referendum result was a vote in favor of decentralization and local control over local resources, and against the often high-handed treatment of the regions by the central government (Safin 1997, 148–50).

In December 1993, the citizens of Bashkortostan simultaneously voted in four elections. In addition to voting on the proposed Russian constitution and electing representatives to both houses of the Duma, voters in Bashkortostan also elected a republic president. Only two candidates, Murtaza Rakhimov, the chairman of the republic's Supreme Soviet, and Rafis Kadyrov, a prominent banker, were able to collect the 100,000 signatures and to pass the Bashkir-language test required for registration. As it did in the run-up to the April referendum, the Bashkir nationalist movement supported the *nomenklatura*, endorsing Rakhimov. Rakhimov was also supported by all of the major media outlets in the region, as well as by prominent industrial leaders and even by the leader of the local Russian nationalist movement. In this context, Rakhimov's owed his easy victory (64% of the vote) mostly to the government's ability to mobilize its resources and the popularity of

---

[17] Partial results were printed in *Sovetskaia Bashkiria*, 12 March, 22 March, and 25 April, 1990. Complete results were compiled by the author from local newspapers.

its policies on economic self-rule, rather than to the nationalist movement's support (Hale 1998, 608).

Support for the local government was also evident in the results of the referendum on the proposed Russian constitution and the voting for the Federation Council. The strong pressure to support the constitution from the Moscow media was counterbalanced by the local media, in which several members of the Rakhimov government vehemently expressed their opposition to its adoption. As a result, almost 58% of voters in Bashkortostan voted against its adoption, the eighth highest percentage among Russia's regions (Hale 1998, 623–5). The power of the governing elite was further demonstrated in elections to the Federation Council, in which Supreme Soviet Chairman Rakhimov and Prime Minister Kopsov, campaigning on a single ticket, easily defeated four challengers. The nationalist movement did not explicitly endorse any candidates in this race, although its support for Rakhimov in the presidential contest carried over to the Federation Council race as well.

The nationalist movement was also relatively passive in the campaign for the lower house of parliament. A nationalist candidate joined the race in only one of the six Duma districts. The Baimak district was 43% ethnic Bashkir and included areas that were considered strongholds of the Bashkir nationalist movement. Nevertheless, the nationalist candidate, a prominent Bashkir writer, received only 10% of the vote, finishing fourth in a five-candidate field. The seat was won by an ethnic Bashkir local state farm chairman, showing that economic concerns outweighed cultural needs among the district's voters. All but one of the other five districts were won by candidates representing the governing elite. One district was won by a representative of the Russian national movement, who was helped by a tactical alliance with Rakhimov's team. Overall, the elections to the lower house confirm the results from the other 1993 races – the governing elite and its allies won all of the seats being contested (Hale 1999).

After a mediocre performance in the 1990 elections, the nationalist movement had learned that it could not compete with the governing elite in Bashkortostan. Starting in that year, the movement redoubled its efforts to increase its indirect influence in the corridors of power, rather than attempting to win elections. Because of its resultant close association with the Rakhimov government, the movement could not subsequently portray itself as an opposition force and gradually became more and more dependent on the governing elite.

Electoral Support in Chuvashia

From early in its development, the Chuvash nationalist movement focused its efforts on electoral politics. As we saw in the previous section, Chuvash nationalists rarely held public protests. Instead, they applied their energies to recruiting candidates and running campaigns. Their performance in early elections shows that this effort was not wasted.

At the time of the 1989 elections to the Soviet Congress of People's Deputies, Chuvash nationalists had not yet formed a political organization. Nevertheless, several candidates called for greater cultural autonomy and political rights. Candidates sympathetic to the nationalist agenda ran in five of the fourteen electoral districts and won in four districts.[18] Nikolai Fedorov, the future president of the republic, was the most radical of these candidates, calling for making Chuvashia a union republic. Supported by both nationalists and democrats, he won easily, taking 75% of the vote in his district. Other winning candidates advocated the expansion of native-language schooling, greater self-government for the ethnic republics, and a greater focus on ethno-cultural development. Although nationalists ran in less than half of Chuvashia's electoral districts in 1989, their convincing victories showed that they were a strong presence on the region's political scene.

By the time of the 1990 local and Russian legislative elections, Chuvash nationalists were better organized, having formed a pro-democracy political organization called Democratic Alternative and the Chuvash Public Cultural Center, which during this period focused primarily on cultural development, with only occasional forays into politics. With local and Russian legislative elections occurring simultaneously, nationalist activists had some difficulty finding enough candidates to run in both elections. Nationalists ran in five of twelve districts in the Russian election, primarily in the capital city and in southeastern rural districts. Unlike the previous year's election, this election saw the Chuvash nationalists shut out of the Russian Federation's legislative body. Altogether, nationalists averaged 18% support in the five districts in which they ran, a relatively high number considering that they had between five and eight opponents in each district. In fact, in only one district did a nationalist candidate fail to finish in one of the top three spots in the first round. In two districts, total nationalist support was split between two or three candidates, preventing any of them from making it into the second round. The two candidates who did make it into the second round both lost in close races, each receiving approximately 48% of the votes cast. Both of these contests took place in rural regions that included several majority-Russian areas that were traditionally hostile to Chuvash nationalism.[19]

The nationalists' failure to win any seats in the Russian Federation Congress can be attributed primarily to poor tactics, rather than to any lack of popular support. Unable to run candidates in all districts, they chose

---

[18] Results were published in *Sovetskaia Chuvashia*, 28 March, 1 April, 16 May, and 22 May 1989.
[19] Results were published in *Sovetskaia Chuvashia*, 8 March 1990 and 17 March 1990. District boundaries were discussed in *Sovetskaia Chuvashia*, 14 November 1989.

the two rural districts with the largest non-Chuvash populations. Similarly, by running multiple candidates in two urban districts, they split their supporters and prevented any nationalist candidates from reaching the second round of voting. In only one district did the nationalist seem to be genuinely unpopular, finishing in fourth place out of six candidates with 13% of the vote. Thus, although they failed to win any seats in the Russian Congress of People's Deputies, the nationalists showed that they could rely on the support of about 18% of the electorate in a crowded field.

The popularity of Chuvash nationalist candidates in early 1990 is confirmed by their performance in the elections to the republic Supreme Soviet, held simultaneously with the elections to the Russian Congress. With 200 seats being contested, once again the main problem was finding candidates to run in as many districts as possible. In the end, nationalists ran in 37 districts, including a quarter of the urban districts. They performed particularly well in the capital city, where nationalist candidates ran in 16 of the 62 districts. Nationalists won nine seats in Cheboksary and reached the runoff in an additional four races.[20] They had a hard time finding candidates to run in rural areas, entering only 12 of the 99 races in the countryside. In those areas where they did run, they were relatively successful, winning five contests and losing seven. Nationalist candidates did least well in urban areas outside the capital. Recognizing that several of these cities were predominantly non-Chuvash, they ran in only 9 of the 39 districts, winning 3 and reaching the runoff in 2 more.[21] Altogether, nationalists won 17 seats in the Supreme Soviet, winning an impressive 46% of the races in which they ran. The nationalists' electoral strength was recognized by the Supreme Soviet, which appointed Atner Khuzangai, their unofficial leader, as chairman of the parliamentary commission on culture and ethnic relations.

Electoral support for nationalism in Chuvashia reached its highest levels in the December 1991 presidential election. In this election, Khuzangai ran against three candidates, including Eduard Kubarev, the pro-democracy chairman of the republic Supreme Soviet, and Leonid Prokopev, a representative of the old Communist *nomenklatura*.[22] All of the candidates were ethnic Chuvash. This situation allows us to clearly distinguish both between supporters and opponents of democratic reforms and between supporters and opponents of nationalism among the supporters of democratic reform. In this race, Khuzangai finished in second place with 20% of the vote, behind

---

[20] *Sovetskaia Chuvashia*, 8 March 1990.
[21] Results for these races were published only in local district and city newspapers, appearing primarily in the 6, 8, and 17 March 1990 issues. Specific citations are available from the author. Results of the April 1990 repeat elections were published in *Sovetskaia Chuvashia*, 20 April 1990 and 29 April 1990.
[22] The fourth candidate, who was a representative of rural interests, finished with 13 percent of the vote.

Prokopev (who received 28%) but well ahead of Kubarev (who received 14%). Prokopev led in both rural and urban areas, finishing stronger in rural areas. Kubarev outpolled Khuzangai in the cities but was well behind him in the countryside. Because of his strong credentials as a democratic reformer, Khuzangai expected to pick up Kubarev's votes in the second round and thereby to overcome Prokopev's initial lead. As it turned out, Khuzangai received more votes than Prokopev but was defeated by the electoral law. The second-round results gave 46% of the votes to Khuzangai and 43% to Prokopev. Khuzangai won all of the Chuvash-majority rural districts and held his own in the cities. In fact, he received over 50% of the vote in the republic if the four Russian-majority districts were excluded. However, the electoral law stated that if neither candidate received over 50% of the total votes, the election would be declared invalid and rerun. For this reason, the Chuvash nationalist candidate failed to win the presidency of the republic despite receiving the most votes in the election. As it turned out, this election represented the peak of the nationalists' popularity among the electorate (Filippov 1994).

Because of the nationwide moratorium on elections declared by President Yeltsin in 1992, a repeat of the Chuvash presidential election was not held until two years later. Khuzangai ran again, facing six other candidates. Once again, all of the candidates were ethnic Chuvash. Although Kubarev also ran again, the leading democrat was now Nikolai Fedorov, the former minister of justice of the Russian Federation. Although he had run on a nationalist platform in 1989, by 1993 Fedorov had rejected nationalism, portraying himself instead as a political and economic reformer. The Communist Party supported Lev Kurakov, the rector of the state university, while the "party of power" supported Valerian Viktorov, the chairman of the Council of Ministers. The results showed the decline in support for nationalist candidates over the previous two years. Khuzangai received only 6% of the vote, finishing fifth. After the first round, Kurakov led in the rural areas, while Fedorov controlled the cities. In the second round, support for Fedorov in the rural areas increased significantly, allowing him to score a convincing victory with over 55% of the total vote (Voskhodov and Komarova 1995, 102).

A similar decline in support for nationalist candidates is seen in the results of the elections to the Russian Federation's State Duma, held at the same time as the 1993 election of the Chuvash president. For the purpose of this election, the republic was divided into two districts. The northern district was dominated by the urban population of Cheboksary and Novocheboksarsk, which comprised 82% of the electorate. The southern district was predominantly rural. An additional two representatives were elected from the republic at large to the Council of the Federation, the Duma's upper chamber. Having learned its lesson from the 1990 legislative elections, the CRP and the Chuvash National Congress united behind a single candidate in each race. The nationalist candidates received similar levels of support in all three races. In the southern Duma district, Gennady Volkov, the official candidate of the nationalist movement, finished fourth with 8% of the vote. An additional 9% of the vote went to the well-known writer Mikhail Iukhma, the leader of the CPCC, a rival branch of the nationalist movement. The race was won by a Communist-supported candidate who received nearly half of the total vote in a seven-candidate race. In the north, L. Fedorov, the nationalist candidate, finished third with 10% of the vote. This race was won by a female candidate who was supported by Women of Russia and who defeated the Communist candidate by only 0.4% of the vote. The nationalist candidate for the Council of the Federation also received 10% of the vote. The two seats were taken by unsuccessful presidential contenders Valerian Viktorov, supported by the "party of power," and Lev Kurakov, supported by the Communist Party. As these results show, at the end of 1993 nationalists had lost half of their supporters from two years earlier and could count on slightly less than 10% of the electorate (Voskhodov and Komarova 1995).

Voters in the December 1993 election also voted on whether to approve the new constitution of the Russian Federation. In Chuvashia, the constitution was opposed by all of the most important political players, including the Communist Party and the democrats, as well as by the nationalist movement. It is therefore not surprising that the majority (58%) of Chuvash voters rejected the constitution. In fact, only six regions of the Russian Federation registered less support for the constitution than Chuvashia. However, the nationalist movement could not have played more than a small role in this outcome.

Altogether, the Chuvash nationalists' strategy of influencing events through electoral participation rather than public protest can be judged to have been moderately successful. Between 1989 and 1991, over 20% of the electorate expressed strong support for nationalist candidates, with a total of just under 50% being willing to support nationalists in runoffs. This allowed nationalist candidates to win a significant number of seats in the USSR Congress of People's Deputies and the republic Supreme Soviet, as well as to come close to winning the republic presidency. By 1993, however, support for nationalist candidates had declined to less than 10%, leading to losses in the December elections and a precipitous decline in nationalists' influence on political life in the republic.

Electoral Support in Khakassia

The Khakass nationalist movement focused on electoral politics only during a brief period between 1990 and 1991. The movement actively participated in the 1990 elections to the Russian Congress and the 1990 and 1991 elections to the regional legislature. During this period, its close alliance with the pro-democracy movement gave its leaders hope of winning a significant number of seats despite the low share of Khakass in the total population. After the

Institutions Matter 145

collapse of this alliance, the Khakass nationalist movement turned away from electoral politics, focusing instead on increasing its influence among the region's governing elites.

At the time of the 1989 election to the USSR Congress of People's Deputies, the Khakass nationalist movement had not yet been organized. In six of the seven districts, none of the candidates expressed any position on issues related to the cultural development or political status of the Khakass ethnic group. Curiously, the district with the smallest Khakass population[23] became the one area in which the candidates focused on these issues. This situation may be attributable to the candidates' ethnicities, as this was the only district in which both Russian and Khakass candidates were running. Both candidates argued that they would seek to raise the political status of the region and seek to increase funding for Khakass schooling and publications. The ethnic Khakass candidate went further, tying the survival of the Khakass nation to the state of the region's ecology. It seemed this would be a particularly effective strategy considering that his opponent was the director of a local coal mine. However, despite his support for democracy, ecology, and national rights, the Khakass candidate could not overcome the greater resources and name recognition of the coal mine director, losing with 33% of the total vote.[24]

By the time of the 1990 elections, the Khakass nationalist movement was at the peak of its popularity. It supported candidates in all five Congress districts in the region. These candidates called for increasing Khakassia's administrative status from an autonomous province to an autonomous republic and called for the local government to take measures to revive Khakass culture. Two of the five were also supported by the region's pro-democracy movement, which was generally sympathetic to the nationalist agenda at the time. The nationalist candidates won in two districts and finished second in the others. Their average first-round showing was 26% of the vote. The issue of Khakassia's future political status had a broader appeal, with several Russian candidates also calling for creating a Khakass autonomous republic separate from Krasnoyarsk *krai*. These candidates differed from the nationalist movement's candidates in their lack of attention to Khakass cultural demands. They received an average of 24% of the votes in the five districts.[25] Perhaps the best indicator of the strength of support for the nationalist movement in this election was the performance of its leader, Alexander Kostiakov, in a rural district. His opponent in this race was Galina Troshkina, an ethnic Khakass and member of the region's Communist Party

---

[23] Four percent of the total district population.
[24] For details on these candidates' programs, see *Sovetskaia Khakassia*, 1 March 1989 and 12 March 1989. For election results, see *Sovetskaia Khakassia*, 28 March, 17 May, and 20 May 1989.
[25] *Sovetskaia Khakassia*, 7 March 1990 and 20 March 1990.

obkom. Kostiakov received 35% of the vote to Troshkina's 42%, with another 23% voting against both. Since neither candidate received over 50% of the vote, the election was rerun a month later with different candidates. Although he did not win the seat, Kostiakov's strong showing reflected the relative popularity of the Khakass nationalist movement at the time, even among ethnic Russians who were attracted by its strong pro-democracy stand.

Nationalists also won a large number of seats in the coincident elections to the provincial legislature. Nationalist candidates ran in 25 of the 149 districts, winning 10 and losing in the runoff in another 4. Ethnic Russian pro-democracy candidates who supported the nationalist movement ran in another nine districts, winning in six of them. Most of these districts were located in the capital city, where nationalists capitalized on their ties to the democrats to win votes from ethnic Russians. Nationalists also won several seats in the predominantly Khakass rural districts, where the most radical nationalists, including Tun cofounder Valeri Ivandaev, ran. After gaining a seat in the legislature, Ivandaev was given the chairmanship of the commission on culture and ethnic relations, indicating the strength of the nationalist bloc in the legislature at this time. Although members of the *nomenklatura* and industrial elite won 69 seats, they lost many more.[26] These losses, combined with the success of the nationalists' and democrats' campaigns, significantly weakened the *nomenklatura*'s position and allowed their opponents to gain a significant amount of influence in the new legislature.

The legislature elected in 1990 existed for a little over a year, being replaced by a 100-seat Supreme Soviet after Khakassia became an autonomous republic in 1991. The elections to this body, held in December 1991, showed the ephemeral nature of support for nationalism in Khakassia. Despite an even stronger alliance between nationalists and democrats, both groups were defeated by candidates representing the region's old political and industrial elite. Tun nominated a total of eight candidates, all in rural districts populated by ethnic Khakass. All of these candidates lost in the first round, with none receiving more than 23% of the vote. The Khakass Cultural Center, which was closely connected to the nationalist movement, nominated candidates to run in an additional fifteen districts, both in Abakan and in rural areas. Only one of this set of candidates won. Supporters of the nationalist movement who were not officially nominated by either of the nationalist organizations ran in another eighteen districts, winning in two. Finally, fifteen candidates nominated by Democratic Russia were considered supporters of the Khakass nationalist movement; three of them won seats. Although Tun and Democratic Russia were careful to avoid nominating candidates in the same districts, the other organizations were not so disciplined.

[26] Results are printed in *Sovetskaia Khakassia*, 8, 10, 12, 13, 14, and 22 March 1990.

Multiple nationalist candidates ran in fifteen districts. Altogether, nationalist candidates were nominated in 42 districts but won only 6 seats. Nationalist candidates lost runoff elections in another ten districts. Democratic Russia as a whole did not do much better, winning 9 seats out of 49 districts. By comparison, representatives of the government and the industrial elite won a total of 58 seats, taking control of the new legislature.[27] In the aftermath of their electoral defeat, the nationalist/democrat alliance collapsed, and the nationalist movement changed its focus from gaining public support to influencing government policies directly.

The Khakass nationalist movement did not actively participate in the 1993 Russian Duma elections. The two seats on the Federation Council were won by an ethnic Russian industrial director and an ethnic Khakass politician, neither of whom focused on the nationalist agenda in his campaign. The single Duma seat was won by Mikhail Mitiukov, one of the leaders of the republic's branch of Democratic Russia. Mitiukov had been strongly supportive of the nationalist movement prior to 1992, but he had just as vehemently turned against the movement after the collapse of their alliance, arguing that the nationalist movement had become too radical and was seeking to institute discriminatory measures against the republic's Russian population. The new constitution was popular in the republic, with 58% of the voters calling for its approval, a higher approval percentage than in all but three of Russia's ethnic republics.

Although the Khakass nationalist movement achieved significant electoral support in the 1990 legislative elections, this support proved to be short-lived. The 1991 elections showed that the majority of the population, even in majority-Khakass districts, rejected the nationalist movement in favor of traditional political leaders from the Soviet administrative and industrial hierarchy. Following this loss, the Khakass nationalist movement withdrew from electoral politics. Beginning in 1992, the movement sought to achieve its agenda primarily by increasing its influence in the corridors of power.

Electoral Support for Nationalist Movements

Electoral support for nationalist movements varied greatly among the regions and within each region over time. Their greatest electoral victories came between 1989 and 1991, which coincided with the peak period of protest activity. In some regions, nationalist movements were not yet sufficiently organized to have much success in the 1989 elections to the USSR Congress of People's Deputies. Beginning in 1992, as economic difficulties began to dominate other issues among the public, the nationalists' performance in electoral contests declined significantly. By the 1993 elections, support for

---

[27] For results, see *Sovetskaia Khakassia*, 27 December 1991, 28 December 1991, and 10 January 1992.

the nationalist movements had dropped to the point where their influence on electoral outcomes was minimal.

During the peak of mobilization, the greatest electoral support was achieved by party-based and grassroots nationalist movements that dedicated themselves to winning election campaigns and could credibly portray themselves as opponents of the *nomenklatura*. Thus, nationalists in Chuvashia received as much electoral support as nationalists in Tatarstan, although they lagged behind the Tatars on other indicators of popular support. Similarly, the initially party-based Khakass nationalist movement overcame demographic obstacles in the 1990 elections by establishing an alliance with ethnic Russian pro-democracy activists, while the Bashkir nationalist movement found itself isolated and did poorly. Altogether, the highest levels of electoral support for nationalism were found in Tatarstan and Chuvashia, with Khakassia and Bashkortostan lagging far behind.

SUPPORT FOR NATIONALISTS IN PUBLIC OPINION POLLS

While election results have the advantage of capturing the expressed preferences of a majority of the population, problems with their interpretation and their relative infrequency create limits on their use for determining the extent of popular support for nationalism. Public opinion surveys supplement the election results by providing data on support among the population for particular aspects of the nationalist agenda. In this way, support for nationalism can be disaggregated into its cultural and political dimensions. Differences in support for moderate and radical demands on each dimension can also be established. In the post-Soviet context, a moderate nationalist program is one that advocates increased autonomy for the region without calling for full independence and supports the adoption of a language law that includes both Russian and the titular language as official state languages. Radical nationalism, on the other hand, includes the demand for full independence for the ethnic region and the adoption of a language law that treats the titular language as the sole state language.

Of course, the measurement of support for nationalism on the basis of public opinion surveys also carries some level of uncertainty. Published survey results often do not describe the representativeness of the data or the quality of the methodologies used. Nevertheless, they can give a partial sense of the extent of popular support for nationalism, particularly when multiple surveys conducted during a narrow time span return relatively similar results.

The amount of public opinion polling varied significantly by region. Polling was most extensive in Bashkortostan and Tatarstan. Only a few polls were conducted in Chuvashia and Khakassia, which lacked the academic resources of the larger and wealthier republics. In all four regions, the polls focused primarily on two dimensions of the nationalist agenda. Cultural

Institutions Matter

demands were represented by questions about the status of the titular language, while political demands were represented by the related questions of whether the region should have higher status in the federal hierarchy and whether the region should withdraw from the Russian Federation (or from the Krasnoyarsk *krai*, in the case of Khakassia). Occasionally, more direct questions were asked about the political preferences of respondents, including whether they supported nationalist organizations and what sovereignty meant to them.

Public Opinion in Tatarstan

Because the republic had a well-developed academic system and its nationalist movement served as an example for other regions, support for nationalism and the nationalist movement in Tatarstan was frequently measured by public opinion polls. Unlike the situation in some of the other republics, most of the attention in Tatarstan was focused on the political dimension of nationalism, with few questions asked about popular support for cultural development. The earliest surveys focused on whether the public supported the transformation of Tatarstan into a union republic. Later surveys asked about independence and withdrawal from the Russian Federation. Finally, respondents were often asked about their support for various political figures and organizations.

Surveys show that raising Tatarstan's status to that of a union republic was popular among the republic's population. Throughout 1990 and prior to the August coup in 1991, over 70% of the Tatar population and a quarter of the republic's Russian population expressed support for union republic status (Figure 5.3). Altogether, almost 50% of the respondents expressed support for transforming Tatarstan into a constituent republic of the Soviet Union,

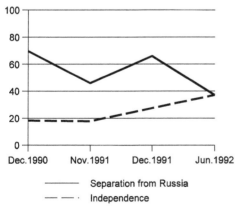

FIGURE 5.3. Support for Tatar separatism (percentage of total respondents).

separate from the Russian Federation.[28] As the Soviet Union began to collapse in the wake of the August coup, support for union republic status began to decline among the population as a whole. By the end of 1991, only 35% of the total population supported Tatarstan's separation from the Russian Federation.[29] The coup affected Russian and Tatar support for sovereignty in very different ways. While Tatars perceived the sovereignty declaration as a means of defending regional autonomy in the wake of the USSR's collapse, Russians feared that Tatarstan might follow the union republics in becoming an independent country. As a result, support for sovereignty among Tatars increased after the coup, while support among Russians dropped dramatically. Whereas in December 1990, 74% of Tatars and 51% of Russians surveyed expressed support for sovereignty, a year later Tatar support had increased to 84%, while Russian support had dropped to 23%.[30]

Although the Tatar nationalist movement did not begin to call for full independence for Tatarstan until after the August coup, a sizeable group of Tatars supported independence as early as the end of 1990. In three surveys conducted between December 1990 and November 1991, about 20% of the Tatars surveyed expressed support for independence. While many Russians wanted Tatarstan to become a union republic, support for independence among Russians was virtually nonexistent.[31] By the summer of 1992, the weakness of the Commonwealth of Independent States had made clear that withdrawal from the Russian Federation was tantamount to a declaration of independence. Nevertheless, support for withdrawal had increased among the Tatar population. A survey in June 1992 showed that 37% of Tatars advocated withdrawal, while 47% believed that Tatarstan could be sovereign within the Russian Federation (Isaev and Komlev 1992, 16). Radical Tatar nationalism was particularly strong in Naberezhnye Chelny, the second-largest city in the republic. In Chelny, 61% of Tatars expressed support for independence, while only 12% supported sovereignty within Russia (Gibadullin 1993, 60). Support for independence among Russians continued to be negligible. This data makes clear that many Tatars perceived the Soviet government as a balancing force against Russia and were willing to eschew independence as long as the possibility of union republic status within the Soviet Union but separate from Russia remained. When the breakup of the union made this option unrealizable, a majority of the moderate nationalist

[28] "Mezhnatsionalnye otnosheniia: Chto o nikh dumaiut Chelnintsy?," *Panorama*, no. 6 (1990); unpublished results of December 1990 VTSIOM survey; Leonid Tolchinskii, "Tatarstan: Uzly problem i perspektivy dvizheniia," *Vecherniia Kazan*, 27 February, 1991.
[29] "O sostoianii obshchestvenno-politicheskoi situatsii," *Sovetskaia Tatariia*, 30 November 1991; "Iazykom tsifr," *Kazanskie Vedomosti*, 29 April 1992.
[30] "Iazykom tsifr," *Kazanskie Vedomosti*, 29 April 1992.
[31] Unpublished results of December 1990 VTSIOM survey; Leonid Tolchinskii, "Tartarstan: Uzly problem i perspektivy dvizheniia," *Vecherniia Kazan*, 27 February 1990; "O sostoianii obshchestvenno-politicheskoi situatsii," *Sovetskaia Tatariia*, 30 November 1991.

Institutions Matter

TABLE 5.1. *Support for Tatar nationalist organizations among Tatars expressing a political preference, by survey date*

	Feb. 1991	Aug. 1991	Oct. 1991	Jun. 1992	Nov. 1992	Nov. 1994
Level of support	45%	33%	35%	39%	45%	31%

Sources: Calculated from Mukhametshin et al. 1993, 47; *Vecherniia Kazan*, February 27, 1991; Isaev and Fatykhov 1994, 30.

supporters accepted the status quo. Still, a sizeable number joined with the radical supporters of full independence. Russian supporters of union republic status, on the other hand, universally accepted the status quo over the possibility of independence. As a result, what began as a multi-ethnic movement for enhanced regional status became a mono-ethnic ethno-nationalist movement, strongly opposed by almost all Russians among the population.

Two polling organizations in Tatarstan asked respondents which political organizations they supported. Unfortunately, there is no data on this question prior to February 1991, a time when trust in political organizations was already beginning to decline. The data from these surveys show that support for nationalist organizations among Tatars gradually declined, from 32% of the respondents in February 1991, to 15% in November 1992, to less than 10% in November 1994. However, this decline in support is chiefly attributable to an increase in the public's alienation from politics altogether, rather than to a switch of allegiance to other political organizations. Support for Tatar nationalist organizations among respondents who did not express disenchantment with all political organizations declined significantly during the first half of 1991, then increased gradually until about the end of 1992, and finally dropped again by the end of 1994 (Table 5.1). As with support for independence, support for the nationalist movement was stronger in Naberezhnye Chelny than in the rest of the region, with 54% of the Tatar respondents describing themselves as TPC supporters in 1992. In all of these surveys with the exception of the 1994 survey, the Tatar Public Center received about two-thirds of the total support for Tatar nationalist organizations, with the more radical Ittifaq and Milli Mejlis receiving the rest. By 1994, internal conflict had adversely affected the TPC's popularity, and most of the public support for nationalist organizations had gone to the radicals.[32] Thus, during the movement's peak, a large segment of the republic's politically active Tatars considered themselves supporters of one of the several Tatar nationalist organizations.

As shown by these surveys, a moderate version of the Tatar nationalist movement's political program was initially supported by more than

---

[32] Mukhametshin et al. (1991, 47); Leonid Tolchinskii, "Tartarstan: Uzly problem i perspektivy dvizheniia," *Vecherniia Kazan*, 27 February 1991; Isaev and Fatykhov (1994, 30).

two-thirds of the Tatar population and over a quarter of the Russian population. Over time, political preferences became polarized along ethnic lines as more and more Tatars began to support sovereignty even as the Russians withdrew their support because of their fear of living outside the Russian Federation. At the same time, radical Tatar nationalism, as expressed by support for full independence, remained relatively constant at about 20% of the Tatar population. Clearly, the nationalist movement had struck a chord with the Tatar population.

Public Opinion in Bashkortostan

Numerous public opinion surveys were conducted in Bashkortostan between 1989 and 1994. Many of these surveys asked respondents about their views on ethnic relations and on both the cultural and political aspects of the nationalist agenda. The results of seventeen surveys were published in the local press. Some of them interviewed respondents from across the republic, while others focused on particular cities or districts. Some reported only aggregate results, while others grouped responses according to the respondents' ethnicity. Together, these surveys provide a picture of the extent of public support for the key nationalist goals of sovereignty and making Bashkir an official state language.

The adoption of an official state language had significant support among the republic's population, irrespective of nationality. Several surveys showed that approximately one-half of the population supported such a law. Even in Ufa, a primarily non-Bashkir city, it had the support of 40% of Russians and 47% of Tatars.[33] However, significant differences existed among the ethnic groups as to which combination of languages should be recognized as official. The Bashkir nationalist movement at first called for the recognition of Bashkir as the sole state language in the republic. In later years, movement leaders increasingly conceded that Russian could also be given official status, while remaining resolutely opposed to giving such status to Tatar. The Tatar nationalists, on the other hand, argued vehemently that all three languages should receive official status. Russian groups sought to ensure that Russian was included among the official languages but did not take a stand on the status of Tatar. Among Bashkirs, support for Bashkir as the sole state language reached 66% in the republic as a whole, although it was somewhat lower (46%) among residents of Ufa. Surprisingly, over one-third of Tatars in the republic also supported a Bashkir-only state language law. Russians registered negligible support for such a law.[34] Among the population as a whole, support for a Bashkir-only language law decreased from

---

[33] "Da ili net," *Sovetskaia Bashkiriia*, 3 November 1990.
[34] Ibid.; R. Baianov, "Iazyk vo vsekh aspektakh," *Vecherniia Ufa*, 9 January 1990.

Institutions Matter

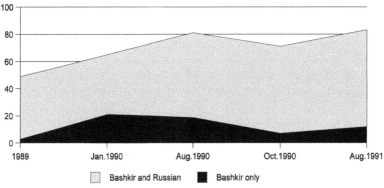

FIGURE 5.4. Support for state language in Bashkortostan (percentage of total respondents).

approximately 20% in 1990 to 12% in 1991.[35] Declaring both Russian and Bashkir official languages was the most popular alternative throughout this period, receiving the support of about 46% of those who supported a language law, while the three-languages proposal received the support of 25% to 30% of those respondents.[36] This data shows that support for including Bashkir among the official state languages was overwhelming (over 80%) among all ethnic groups, while a majority among the Bashkirs supported the establishment of Bashkir as the sole official language (Figure 5.4). Evidently, the nationalist movement's call for a linguistic revival had gained significant popularity among the population, with members of all ethnic groups supporting a moderate nationalist program, while a majority of Bashkirs supported radical nationalism.

Bashkir nationalists called for raising Bashkortostan's administrative status by turning it into a union republic, which would separate it from the RSFSR and place it under the direct authority of the Soviet government. Surveys show that during the early period of mobilization, a substantial number of respondents from all ethnic groups supported turning Bashkortostan into a union republic, while support for separation from Russia was confined to no more than a quarter of the ethnic Bashkir population. Until the fall of 1989, respondents were simply asked whether they supported giving Bashkortostan the status of a union republic. Levels of support for such an initiative varied between 60% and 75% of all respondents. Among

---

[35] Ibid.; "Vashe mnenie,"*Leninets*, 16 January 1990; R. Ianborisov, "Natsionalnye otnosheniia v Bashkirii," *Sovetskaia Bashkiriia*, 23 June 1990; "Suverenitet i my," *Vecherniia Ufa*, 27 December 1990; Vener Samigullin, "Kakoi byt konstitutsii suverennogo Bashkortostana," *Izvestiia Bashkortostana*, 8 August 1991.

[36] "Vashe mnenie," *Leninets*, 16 January 1990; "Suverenitet i my," *Vecherniia Ufa*, 27 December 1990; Vener Samigullin, "Kakoi byt konstitutsii suverennogo Bashkortostana," *Izvestiia Bashkortostana*, 8 August 1991.

Bashkirs, support for union republic status reached 87% as early as 1989. Beginning in the fall of 1990, pollsters began to ask more nuanced questions that reflected the different conceptions of union republic status among the population. An October mail-in survey of newspaper readers showed that only 31% of respondents supported union republic status, while another 44% supported an autonomous republic with all of the rights of a union republic. At the same time, less than 15% supported withdrawal from the Russian Federation. Support for a radical nationalist program was greater among ethnic Bashkir respondents, approximately 20% to 25% of whom supported withdrawal. Similar numbers supported the formation of an independent armed force and a separate currency for the republic.[37]

As the consequences of separation became more apparent, support for union republic status decreased somewhat, while support for independence remained steady. In June 1991, only 54% of a representative sample of the republic's population believed that Bashkortostan should sign the new Union Treaty separately from Russia, although three-quarters of Bashkir respondents favored such a move. At the same time, 22% of the respondents, including 41% of Bashkir respondents, believed that the republic should withdraw from the Russian Federation.[38] As the Soviet Union began to collapse, many non-Bashkirs who had previously supported moderate nationalism turned against the nationalist movement, fearing the spread of ethnic conflict and their country's further disintegration. After 1991, a majority of the population opposed any change in status beyond greater autonomy. Only a core group of radicals continued to support independence, with 14% of respondents calling for withdrawal from Russia in a March 1992 survey.[39] Even as late as 1993, 8% of respondents in Ufa called for full independence, while another 25% called for Bashkortostan to maintain independence in domestic affairs while delegating control over foreign policy to the Russian government.[40] Ethnic Bashkirs, on the other hand, increasingly came to view radical nationalism, including independence, as the best way to protect the position of their ethnic group. Even in early 1994, over 40% of the Bashkir population still argued in favor of independence.[41]

Three surveys asked specifically about whether the respondents supported the Bashkir National Center. On the eve of the republic Supreme Soviet's vote on sovereignty, 6% of the respondents declared that they supported the BNC's draft sovereignty declaration over alternatives drafted by the Supreme

---

[37] D. Giliazetdinov, "Chitateli VU o proektakh deklaratsii," *Vecherniia Ufa*, 1 October 1990.
[38] I. Akhmetov, V. Karabaev, and N. Stukalova, "Vashe mnenie," *Sovetskaia Bashkiriia*, 4 June 1991.
[39] F. Latypova, "Vybory prezidenta: informatsiia k razmyshleniiu," *Sovetskaia Bashkiriia*, 10 March 1992.
[40] R. Islamov, S. Li, A. Kurlov, and A. Selivanov, "My i nasha respublika," *Sovetskaia Bashkiriia*, 8 July 1993.
[41] A. Kuzmin and E. Alferova, "Kak zhivesh, selo S.?," *Ekonomika i My*, 26 February 1994.

Institutions Matter

Soviet, the Council of Ministers, and a group of lawyers. There was virtually no support for the BNC draft among Tatar and Russian respondents, while 20% of Bashkirs favored it over the others.[42] In 1991, 10% of the respondents stated that they would support a nationalist candidate in a possible presidential election.[43] Finally, in a 1995 survey of potential voting behavior, the BNC received the support of 12% of the total respondents.[44] Assuming that the vast majority of BNC supporters were ethnic Bashkirs, who made up only 22% of the total population in the republic, these results indicate that well over one-third of the Bashkir population supported the BNC, and that this support remained fairly steady even after the peak of the mobilization cycle.

Overall, the surveys show that approximately 80% of Bashkirs supported the nationalist movement's agenda during the mobilization period. The survey results also show that 20% to 25% of Tatars supported the Bashkir nationalist agenda, with respondents showing significant support both for independence and for declaring Bashkir the sole official language. Not surprisingly, these goals found the fewest adherents among the republic's Russian population. Overall, 15% to 20% of the total population were supporters of radical Bashkir nationalism during the initial period of mobilization, with another 40% willing to support a more moderate nationalist agenda. Over time, support for the radical agenda increased among the ethnic Bashkir population, while the moderates melted away. This change in the preferences of supporters may explain the gradual radicalization of the Bashkir nationalist movement.

Public Opinion in Chuvashia

Public opinion polling was much less developed in Chuvashia during this period. The most useful poll was a survey of newspaper readers jointly conducted by several newspapers in October 1989.[45] This survey asked respondents to state their attitudes about republic self-government and the status of the Chuvash language. Unfortunately, the survey did not include a question about whether Chuvashia should become a union republic. Instead, respondents were asked whether they supported the establishment of self-financing (*khozraschet*) in Chuvashia as a means of acquiring greater economic independence for the republic. Only 64% of the respondents expressed support for self-financing, including 72% of the Chuvash population. Many

---

[42] D. Giliazetdinov, "Chitateli VU o proektakh deklaratsii," *Vecherniia Ufa*, 1 October 1990.
[43] Latypova, "Vybory prezidenta: informatsiia k razmyshleniiu," *Sovetskaia Bashkiriia*, 10 March 1992.
[44] *Izvestiia Bashkortostana*, 3 August 1995.
[45] Note that this was a poll of newspaper readers and not a write-in survey. N. Galkin and G. Tafaev, "Itogi ne okonchatelnye, no ...," *Sovetskaia Chuvashia*, 14 October 1989.

respondents expressed doubts about the ability of the republic to become financially self-sufficient. Support for self-government was substantially weaker in Chuvashia than in Tatarstan and Bashkortostan.

Similarly, respondents were relatively reluctant to support promotion of the Chuvash language. Only 44% of the respondents (54% of Chuvash respondents) supported the adoption of an official language, and only 32% believed that Chuvash should become one of the official languages. Even among Chuvash respondents, support for official-language status for Chuvash was indicated by only 40% of respondents. A similar percentage believed that all people in positions of authority should know Chuvash. Although 1989 marked only the beginning of Chuvash nationalist mobilization, support for nationalist goals was significantly weaker in the republic than in neighboring Tatarstan and Bashkortostan at this time.

Public Opinion in Khakassia

Without a university to provide logistical and financial support, very few polls were conducted in Khakassia during the transition period. In fact, other than the survey conducted by a Moscow-based sociology institute that is discussed in the next section, only one public opinion poll was published in the republic. This poll was conducted in the city of Chernogorsk and several rural districts in the spring of 1990. As shown by the election data, this was the period of maximum public support for the nationalist movement and its goals. The survey focused only on the political dimension of the nationalist agenda, asking respondents how they envisioned Khakassia's future political status. Only 32% of those surveyed called for transforming the region into an autonomous republic within the Russian Federation, while 48% called for separation from Krasnoyarsk *krai* without a change in administrative status, and 17% preferred to maintain the status quo. Although exact figures are not provided, the writers mention that the change in status was preferred by most of the Khakass respondents and rural inhabitants generally. Supporters of separation from Krasnoyarsk included most respondents who worked for locally controlled enterprises, while supporters of the status quo tended to work for enterprises directly controlled by the central government in Moscow.[46] While the results of a single poll leave room for doubt, it seems clear that at least initially the Khakass nationalist movement's relatively moderate political agenda attracted the support of both Russians and Khakass. Unfortunately, we lack data on whether this multi-ethnic support base survived the collapse of the Soviet Union or divided at the time of the split between Tun and Democratic Russia.

---

[46] K. Sokolova, "Poisk putei obreteniia samostoiatelnosti," *Sovetskaia Khakassia*, 4 April 1990.

The Colton/Hough and ISPR RAS Surveys

One of the chief problems with using polling data to measure support for nationalism is the difficulty in comparing poll results from different regions, which may use different methodologies and ask slightly different questions. Fortunately, this problem can be partially solved by the use of multiregional social science surveys, which use identical methodologies and standardized questions in order to ensure cross-regional comparability. The Colton/Hough 1993 preelection survey was conducted in the sixteen former autonomous republics of the Russian Federation in November and December 1993.[47] It asked a broad set of questions about electoral preferences, attitudes toward economic reform, and ethnic politics. The results of this survey can be used to compare directly the extent of support for nationalism in Tatarstan, Bashkortostan, and Chuvashia. Since Khakassia was not an autonomous republic under Soviet rule, it was not included in the Colton/Hough survey. Fortunately, a similar survey was conducted in that region in January 1994 by the Moscow-based Institute for Socio-Political Research (ISPR) of the Russian Academy of Sciences (RAS).[48] Although not identical to the Colton/Hough survey, similarities in timing and question design make these surveys highly comparable.

The Colton/Hough survey was conducted in late 1993, a time when nationalist movements in all of the regions were already in decline to a greater or lesser extent. At the same time, the movements had had several years to affect the respondents' attitudes through protest activities and propaganda. The survey measured, among other things, attitudes toward sovereignty and nationhood, language status, control of local institutions, and the extent of individual identification with the region. For each measure, we can distinguish between radical and moderate nationalist answers.

While the extent of identification with the region does not necessarily reflect support for the nationalist movement, it does show the extent to which members of the titular ethnic group perceived themselves as belonging to a distinct nation with its own territory. Respondents were asked two questions about their identification with their region. When asked, "Which do you consider your homeland (*rodina*) – the former Soviet Union, Russia, or the republic in which you live?," 75% of Tatars and Bashkirs and only 35% of

---

[47] The survey interviewed 1,000 randomly selected respondents in each region, covering both urban and rural areas. Principal investigators included Timothy Colton of Harvard University, Jerry Hough of Duke University, Susan Lehmann of Columbia University, and Mikhail Guboglo of the Institute of Ethnology and Anthropology of the Russian Academy of Sciences.

[48] Principal investigators for this survey included Vilen Ivanov, Irina Ladodo, and Anatoly Kotov of ISPR and Gavriil Kotozhekov and Larisa Anzhiganova of the Khakass State University. The sample included 600 respondents from both urban and rural areas, evenly divided into Russian and Khakass samples. Because of the sampling method, results are representative only within each ethnic group and not for the sample as a whole.

Chuvash respondents answered "my republic."[49] A second question aimed at determining the extent of individual loyalty to the homeland asked to what extent respondents considered themselves representatives of their republic versus representatives of Russia as a whole. As Table 5.2 shows, a sense of belonging to their republic was strongest among Tatars and weakest among Chuvash, with Bashkirs occupying an intermediate position. Unfortunately, the Khakass survey did not ask about this topic. Interestingly, in all three republics a significant segment of the Russian population identified with the republic more closely than with Russia as a whole. Overall, the sense of connection with the region on the part of the respondents was relatively high.

The Colton/Hough survey also measured the extent to which respondents were aware of the existence and activity of the nationalist movement. Awareness of movement activity was strongly correlated with the amount of public protest in the region. As shown in Table 5.3, Tatarstan's nationalist movement had the highest profile, with over 60% of the population knowing about its existence. Awareness of movement activity was lower in Chuvashia and Bashkortostan. The adoption of sovereignty declarations by local Supreme Soviets was one of the key accomplishments of the regional nationalist movements. The number of people who had read these declarations may be taken as an indicator of the number of people strongly concerned with the activities of nationalist organizations. In every region, fewer people had read the declaration than were aware of the nationalist movement's existence. Also, while awareness of the movement did not vary according to ethnicity, members of the titular ethnic group were more likely to be familiar with the sovereignty declaration than were Russians. Chuvash respondents were particularly unlikely to have read the declaration, which parallels their lower levels of identification with Chuvashia as a homeland and shows that nationalism was less relevant there than in Tatarstan and Bashkortostan.

The extent of popular support for the nationalist movement's cultural agenda was measured by three questions about attitudes toward titular-language status. Respondents were asked whether the titular language should be the sole official language in the ethnic republics, whether all inhabitants of an ethnic republic should be required to know the titular language, and whether study of the titular language should be compulsory in all schools. The data show that, regardless of ethnicity, more respondents supported requiring study and knowledge of the titular language than supported granting it sole official status. During this period, the declaration of an official language had acquired symbolic importance as a statement of the government's intentions toward the non-titular population on its territory. The inclusion of Russian as an official language was seen as indicative of a policy of

---

[49] Unless otherwise noted, all proportions refer to the titular group in "its" ethnic region.

TABLE 5.2. *Sense of belonging to an ethnic region*

	Tatar in Tatarstan	Chuvash in Chuvashia	Bashkir in Bashkortostan	Russian in Tatarstan	Russian in Chuvashia	Russian in Bashkortostan	Tatar in Bashkortostan
Sees republic as homeland	75%	35%	75%	36%	19%	29%	60%
Identifies with region only	34%	14%	25%	7%	2%	5%	20%
Identifies with region more than with Russia	20%	9%	19%	7%	2%	6%	14%
Identifies with Russia at least as much as with region*	36%	69%	53%	77%	93%	86%	61%
No opinion	11%	8%	4%	8%	3%	4%	5%

*Includes "identifies with Russia as much as with region," "identifies with Russia more than with region," and "identifies with Russia only."

TABLE 5.3. *Awareness of nationalist activity*

	Tatar in Tatarstan	Chuvash in Chuvashia	Bashkir in Bashkortostan	Russian in Tatarstan	Russian in Chuvashia	Russian in Bashkortostan	Tatar in Bashkortostan
Aware of titular nationalist movement	61%	35%	37%	60%	30%	33%	30%
Have read sovereignty declaration	44%	16%	43%	36%	9%	27%	37%

inclusion. If the titular language were declared the sole official language, this was seen as tantamount to a declaration that non-titulars would be treated as second-class citizens. For this reason, in most regions a relatively small proportion even of the titular population supported sole official-language status, while support for such a move among Russians was virtually nonexistent (Table 5.4). Note, however, that among Bashkirs, support for Bashkir as the sole official language reached 41%, compared to 29% among Tatars and 20% among Chuvash. Support among Bashkirs was so high in part because Bashkirs were worried about the possibility of assimilation by the Tatars, especially as a quarter of Bashkirs already claimed Tatar as their native language.

A larger percentage of people believed that all inhabitants of an ethnic republic should make an effort to know the language of the titular ethnic group. More supported requiring all schoolchildren to learn the titular language than supported mandating that the entire population know the language (see Tables 5.5 and 5.6). The Khakass survey asked respondents to choose whether all inhabitants of the republic should be required to know both Russian and Khakass (35% support among Khakass), only Khakass (13%), only Russian (10%), or should not be required to know any language (39%). I considered anyone choosing either of the first two responses to support mandatory knowledge of Khakass, thus arriving at a figure of 48%. Note that although this figure is higher than figures from the other republics, this is an artifact of the high number of "no response" answers to this question in the Colton/Hough survey. If "no response" answers were excluded from both surveys, support for mandatory language knowledge would be higher among Bashkirs and Tatars than among Khakass. The data show that support for the nationalists' cultural agenda was highest among the Bashkirs and Tatars and lowest among the Chuvash, with the Khakass occupying an intermediate position.

The Colton/Hough survey included three indicators of the level of support for political nationalism in the ethnic republics, including measures of support for sovereignty declarations, support for the right to secede, and support for transferring control of law-and-order functions to the republic authorities. As shown in Table 5.7, support for sovereignty was high in Tatarstan and Bashkortostan. Well over half of the titular population, and even a quarter of the Russians, supported sovereignty in these regions. In Khakassia, 58% of the Khakass population responded positively to a similar question, which asked whether every nation living on the territory of the Russian Federation had the right to its own statehood. This view, however, found support among only 19% of Khakassia's Russian population. Support for political nationalism among the Chuvash was no greater than their support for cultural nationalism, with only 22% of Chuvash and 12% of Russians expressing support for sovereignty.

TABLE 5.4. *Should the titular language be the sole official language in ethnic republics?*

	Tatar in Tatarstan	Chuvash in Chuvashia	Bashkir in Bashkortostan	Russian in Tatarstan	Russian in Chuvashia	Russian in Bashkortostan	Tatar in Bashkortostan
Completely or partially agree	29%	20%	40%	3%	2%	4%	18%
No opinion	13%	22%	12%	5%	7%	5%	9%
Completely or partially disagree	59%	58%	48%	92%	91%	91%	73%

TABLE 5.5. *Should all inhabitants of an ethnic republic know the titular language of that republic?*

	Tatar in Tatarstan	Chuvash in Chuvashia	Khakass in Khakassia	Bashkir in Bashkortostan	Russian in Tatarstan	Russian in Chuvashia	Russian in Khakassia	Russian in Bashkortostan	Tatar in Bashkortostan
Agree	44%	35%	48%	43%	22%	10%	20%	15%	26%
No opinion	24%	27%	0%	17%	22%	15%	0%	13%	11%
Disagree	32%	38%	49%	40%	57%	75%	77%	72%	63%

Note: "No opinion" was not available as an option for the Khakassia survey.

TABLE 5.6. Should titular-language study be compulsory in all schools in ethnic republics?

	Tatar in Tatarstan	Chuvash in Chuvashia	Bashkir in Bashkortostan	Russian in Tatarstan	Russian in Chuvashia	Russian in Bashkortostan	Tatar in Bashkortostan
Completely agree	66%	44%	51%	38%	6%	11%	19%
Only if majority in region	14%	24%	22%	25%	23%	28%	24%
No opinion	10%	14%	10%	12%	17%	8%	12%
Completely disagree	10%	18%	17%	25%	54%	53%	46%

TABLE 5.7. How do you feel about the declarations of sovereignty by the former autonomous republics of the Russian Federation?

	Tatar in Tatarstan	Chuvash in Chuvashia	Bashkir in Bashkortostan	Russian in Tatarstan	Russian in Chuvashia	Russian in Bashkortostan	Tatar in Bashkortostan
Completely or partially support	56%	22%	67%	28%	12%	27%	53%
No opinion	39%	60%	27%	39%	41%	38%	32%
Completely or partially oppose	5%	18%	7%	34%	47%	35%	16%

Radicals within the nationalist movements in Tatarstan, Chuvashia, and Bashkortostan considered sovereignty insufficient and supported independence for their republics.[50] Although the Colton/Hough survey did not directly measure support for independence in these republics, it did ask respondents whether they believed that ethnic republics should have the right to secede from the Russian Federation. As Table 5.8 shows, in all three republics the right of secession was supported by approximately one-half as many people as supported sovereignty.

Radical nationalists also called for the transfer of control over military and law-and-order functions from the central to the republic government. Particularly important in this context were conflicts over the right to appoint the chief prosecutor of the republic in Tatarstan and Bashkortostan and the attempt to form a Tatarstan national guard, separate from the Russian army. Tatars in Tatarstan were particularly supportive of such a transfer; even among Russians there, 20% of the respondents were supportive. Bashkirs were somewhat less likely to support a transfer, possibly because it was not as salient an issue in local politics there. As with the other measures of support for nationalism, the Chuvash were least likely to call for a transfer (Table 5.9).

Support for nationalism in public opinion surveys: The results of public opinion surveys show that support for nationalism was highest in Bashkortostan and Tatarstan, where 70% to 80% of the titular population supported the moderate nationalist program. Even in 1993, when the nationalist movements were already in decline, a substantial majority among the titular ethnic groups expressed support for republic sovereignty. Furthermore, in Bashkortostan 30% to 40% of Bashkirs supported what I have termed the radical nationalist program. Support for radical nationalism was lower in Tatarstan (20% to 30%), although in some regions, and particularly in Naberezhnye Chelny, radical views were held by more than half of the Tatar population. It appears that support for nationalism was lower in Chuvashia and Khakassia, although the dearth of poll results makes the reliability of the results less certain. In Chuvashia, support for sovereignty declined significantly over time. In 1990, perhaps half of the Chuvash population could be considered supporters of the moderate nationalist agenda. At that time, the titular population was significantly more supportive of sovereignty than of language issues. By 1993, less than a quarter of the population supported sovereignty. The numbers were somewhat higher for language issues. Radical nationalism had the support of only a small minority (10%) of the Chuvash population. Finally, in Khakassia, moderate nationalism was supported by about 30% of the total population, including a majority among the ethnic Khakass. Separation from Russia was not advocated by the nationalist movement and seems to have had virtually no support in the region.

---

[50] Such demands were not publicly made by any nationalist activist in Khakassia.

TABLE 5.8. *Should all republics have the right of self-determination, including the right of withdrawal from the Russian Federation?*

	Tatar in Tatarstan	Chuvash in Chuvashia	Bashkir in Bashkortostan	Russian in Tatarstan	Russian in Chuvashia	Russian in Bashkortostan	Tatar in Bashkortostan
All republics	26%	13%	30%	14%	10%	13%	29%
Some republics*	27%	12%	25%	20%	14%	25%	23%
No opinion	39%	50%	23%	33%	34%	24%	29%
None	8%	25%	22%	34%	43%	38%	19%

*Includes "only large republics," "only republics on Russia's borders," and "only republics where the titular ethnic group comprises the majority of the population."

TABLE 5.9. *Should control of the army, police, and security forces be transferred to the jurisdiction of the sovereign republics of the Russian Federation?*

	Tatar in Tatarstan	Chuvash in Chuvashia	Bashkir in Bashkortostan	Russian in Tatarstan	Russian in Chuvashia	Russian in Bashkortostan	Tatar in Bashkortostan
Completely or partially support	42%	10%	32%	18%	4%	18%	22%
No opinion	40%	56%	31%	38%	38%	29%	37%
Completely or partially oppose	19%	34%	37%	44%	57%	53%	41%

CONCLUSIONS

In this chapter, I have examined the extent to which nationalist movements were able to attract the support of their potential constituents. The nationalist movements focused on different forms of mobilization. While for some movements success in mobilizing their constituents was represented by the ability to turn out large numbers of protesters, for others success could be measured in terms of electoral performance. Regardless of the forms of activity and types of organization, all nationalist movements sought to convince potential supporters of the validity and importance of their goals.

The movements' success varied dramatically across regions and over time. In all regions, the nationalists' ability to win elections and stage large protests peaked during the 1990–91 period. By 1993, protests had become very rare and attracted only small bands of dedicated activists, rarely exceeding 100 participants. Similarly, nationalists fared poorly in the 1993 elections, where they either lost outright or failed to nominate candidates. Poll and survey results show a similar picture, with support for nationalist ideas and leaders peaking in 1990 and 1991 and beginning to decline in all of the regions in 1992. The data thus clearly show that the wave of nationalist mobilization in these regions began in 1988 or 1989, peaked in 1991, and had began to decline by late 1992. By the first months of 1994, nationalist movements had largely lost popular support, retaining only a few hard-core activists and either fading from the political scene or becoming dependent on the governing elite for their continued existence.

The nationalist movements were strongest in Tatarstan and Bashkortostan. These were the regions where the largest number of protests occurred. Nationalist candidates also did reasonably well in local elections in these regions. Public opinion surveys show that in each region, a majority of the titular ethnic group supported the nationalist movement's agenda, while a significant minority believed in independence and other radical nationalist goals. Although support for nationalism in Chuvashia was significantly weaker, Chuvash nationalists performed very well in local legislative and presidential elections in 1990 and 1991. At the same time, they rarely organized protest actions, and polls showed that less than half of the Chuvash population supported their agenda. Finally, in Khakassia, while approximately half of the titular population expressed support for the nationalist agenda in surveys, the nationalists were not able to persuade significant numbers either to participate in public protests or to vote for nationalist candidates in local elections.

These results reinforce the institutionalist explanation of ethnic mobilization while contradicting the economic explanation, which argues that the extent of ethnic mobilization depends on the level of economic development of the region (Treisman 1997). Ethnic mobilization does not correlate with economic development in the regions analyzed in this study. Tatarstan and Bashkortostan have the highest levels of both economic and institutional development among the four regions examined here, so the key regions for distinguishing between the institutionalist and economic explanations are Chuvashia and Khakassia. Of these two regions, as discussed in Chapter 2, Chuvashia had the more highly developed ethnic institutions, whereas Khakassia had a better developed economy. As the evidence presented in this chapter clearly shows, the nationalist movements were far more successful in mobilizing the population in Chuvashia than they were in Khakassia, thus confirming the institutionalist explanation.

This explanation argues that regions that occupied higher positions in the Soviet administrative hierarchy had the most extensive and best developed systems of ethnic institutions. These ethnic institutions promoted the development of a strong sense of collective ethnic identity among the population and established social networks among potential activists and between the activists and their supporters. Because of these factors, regions with strong ethnic institutions had the highest levels of support for nationalism among the titular population.

6

Intragroup Variation in Support for Nationalism
Not All Ethnics Are the Same

Responses to the nationalist message varied not only by region but also by social group. The strongest support for the nationalist message came from social groups whose members felt that they could benefit from the nationalist movement's success. Although political and economic benefits played some role in determining support for nationalism, supporters responded most strongly to the psychological benefits of higher group status inherent in a successful cultural revival or an increase in regional autonomy. The extent to which individuals responded to these psychological benefits depended primarily on the extent of their exposure to the culture, traditions, and language of their ethnic group; such exposure was greatest among people who grew up in the largely mono-ethnic rural areas and/or received an education in the ethnic group's native language.

Scholars of nationalism have paid little attention to which social groups within an ethnic group are more likely to support nationalism and why they do so. The one major exception has been Miroslav Hroch's study on *The Social Preconditions of National Revival in Europe* (2000). Examining the development of nationalist movements among small European ethnic groups during the nineteenth century, Hroch showed that the strongest support for nationalism invariably came from the intelligentsia and students. Members of the elite, including the ruling classes and the industrial bourgeoisie, tended to assimilate to the majority group and therefore were not much involved in the movement. State officials and members of the petty bourgeoisie, on the other hand, supported nationalism in virtually every case, although they did not play a leading role. Teachers and members of the clergy helped to spread nationalist ideas to the countryside, although the latter group dropped out as the nationalist movements turned from cultural to political goals. The peasants came to support nationalism late, if at all, but were critical in determining whether or not the nationalist movement received mass support.

The relevance of these findings to post-Communist nationalist movements at the end of the twentieth century varies by social class. While ruling classes in the nineteenth-century meaning of the term were destroyed in the 1917 revolution, and the clergy were stripped of their role in society by the Communist regime, intellectuals and students largely maintained their positions in society, and teachers continued to play a key role in transmitting ideas from the urban intellectual centers to the countryside. In the following pages, I adapt and modify Hroch's findings on the extent of support for nationalism among various social groups and apply them to modern minority nationalist movements in the former Soviet Union.

In the first section of the chapter, I discuss why members of some social groups are more likely to support nationalism and the nationalist movement. I then describe the survey data and variables used to test the validity of this theory. The main part of the chapter is devoted to showing which groups supported nationalism in the four regions examined in this study. The connections between support for nationalism and ethnic institutions such as native language education are most clearly indicated in the survey data described here. The findings demonstrate that ethnic institutions play a crucial role not only in deciding the overall amount of support for nationalism in a particular region, but also in determining which parts of the population within the region are most likely to express such support.

SOURCES OF SUPPORT FOR NATIONALISM

A social group's likelihood of supporting nationalist goals depends strongly on how connected its members feel to the rest of their ethnic group. For example, the nationalist agenda is more likely to appeal to individuals who feel that they share a common identity with the rest of their ethnic community. Furthermore, the spread of the nationalist movement is particularly rapid among population groups who have dense intragroup social networks and who have close connections with the intellectual and academic community within which nationalist movements originate. While both shared ethnic identity and social networks exist independent of institutional arrangements, institutions can play a key role in determining the depth of the sense of common identity and the exact nature of the social networks among the minority population. The establishment of new institutions may fundamentally transform the identities and social networks of a particular society, especially in cases where the new institutions are imposed without regard to the traditional patterns of social interaction and/or government structure.[1] The construction of ethnic institutions by the Soviet government during the 1920s is a particularly clear example of a situation in which institutions were imposed on a society according to scholarly and political considerations that did not take existing social networks and identities into account.

---

[1] For a discussion of this argument in the context of the effect of electoral systems on party systems regardless of preexisting social cleavages, see Cox (1997).

During this period, ethnic homelands were almost always established based on political considerations or the beliefs of Russian social scientists about minority ethnic identities (Martin 2001). In the Soviet case, the transformation of social networks and ethnic identities brought about by the imposition of new ethnic institutions was particularly evident. Although many of the explanatory variables discussed in this chapter are influenced by both cultural and institutional factors, an institutionalist explanation is more useful in explaining the reasons for variation in support for nationalism among different population groups, because the institutional factors are, in this case, prior to the cultural factors.

Instilling a strong sense of ethnic community in individuals requires exposing them early and frequently to information about their ethnic identity. In the context of Soviet nationalities policy, this exposure came primarily through the educational system. By establishing separate systems of native-language education for most of the minority ethnic groups that had their own ethno-territorial administrative units, the Soviet government in effect created an institution dedicated to instilling a common and separate identity among the students. The school system fosters the development of a separate identity by physically separating students who belong to the titular ethnic group from their ethnic Russian counterparts. The identity is further reinforced in the classroom, where titular students are taught the culture and history of their ancestors, who are portrayed as having a direct genetic link to the members of the modern ethnic group. Other aspects of the institutionalization of ethnicity, such as museums of local history and titular-language periodicals dedicated to the spread of knowledge about the ethnic group's history, serve to further cement the importance of the shared ethnic identity among those educated in the native language. Because of the importance of ethnic identity in determining attitudes toward nationalism, social groups that are more likely to be exposed to native-language education are more likely to support the nationalist movement. Such groups include the older population, inhabitants of rural areas, and people who migrate to the city after growing up in the countryside.

A higher level of education – ethnic or secular – can also be linked to a stronger sense of common ethnic identity. Highly educated people, regardless of the language in which they have received this education, are more likely to be interested in history and culture generally, leading to greater exposure to information about the ethnic group and its history. In many cases, this exposure can lead to a sense of community with other members of the ethnic group that is similar to that imparted by being educated in the native language. Individuals with a more extensive education are also more likely to closely follow current political events, leading to more knowledge of the local nationalist movement's activities. For these reasons, support for nationalism should correlate positively with educational level, although the effect may not be as significant as that of native-language education.

Cultural theories would predict that in a predominantly antireligious country, religion would foster a sense of distinct ethnic identity that would lead to support for nationalism. In the Soviet case, this could be particularly true for those ethnic groups whose traditional religion was substantially different from Russian Orthodoxy. Islam, a religion whose adherents for centuries were treated as Russia's main enemies, might be particularly conducive to strengthening a sense of common ethnic identity distinct from the majority population. Muslims would thus be more likely than others to support the nationalist movement.[2] On the other hand, an institutionalist argument such as the one being made here would be more skeptical of the mobilizing potential of religious difference absent institutions that could channel religious differences into ethnic claims. The relationship between religion and support for nationalism is likely to depend on the extent to which religion was used as a proxy for nationalist claims during the Soviet period, and thus on the extent to which it was directly linked to ethnicity in the minds of members of each ethnic group.

The spread of support for any political movement depends largely on the spread of knowledge about the movement's existence and activities. Mass media typically provide some exposure, but for opposition groups in societies with semi-free media, this coverage is a mixed blessing, since most of the press coverage they receive is negative. In this setting, social networks become particularly important for spreading the message and for attracting new supporters. Because they increase the speed of information exchange and the degree of intragroup trust, dense networks of intragroup social ties make the spread of movement activism within a group far more rapid. In the Soviet Union, the formation of close ties within particular social groups was encouraged by state-run organizations such as academic institutes, Communist Party cells, youth organizations, factories, and collective farms. The density of social ties is also closely linked to the strength of collective identity. Members of a social group who also share a sense of common ethnic identity are that much more likely to trust each other and therefore to be willing to join causes supported by other members of their cohort.

In the same way that dense social networks facilitate the recruitment process within a social group, connections between members of different groups allow support for the movement to spread from one group to another. In urban areas, such connections between members of different groups may occur through contact at the workplace or at educational institutions. After a critical number of members of a new social group have been recruited by outsiders, the significantly more rapid process of intragroup recruitment begins.

In the Soviet Union, the initial formation of nationalist movements took place among ethnic intellectuals closely linked to each other through the

---

[2] See Huntington (1996) for an argument along these lines.

academic institutions where they worked and where they had received their training. Because their work was focused on the history and culture of the ethnic group, these intellectuals had a clear sense of the importance of ethnic community. This sense of ethnic identity led them to organize an ethnic revival movement, a project that was made more feasible because of their close-knit community.

Many of these intellectuals taught classes at the state universities and pedagogical institutes, where their ideas had a strong influence on the student population. Students maintained close ties with each other through youth organizations, which also served to build connections among students from different universities. After the collapse of the Communist Youth League (Komsomol), many unassimilated students joined ethnically based youth organizations such as the Union of Bashkir Youth and Azatlyk, which gradually took on the role of the nationalist movements' youth wings. Because of their strong organizational links and their ties to movement organizers, these students were particularly likely to support nationalist movements.

Students were also instrumental in spreading the nationalist message to regions outside the capital cities where the movements were founded. Students from rural areas recruited sympathizers in their home regions during university vacations. Furthermore, members of the teaching staffs of the local teachers' colleges found throughout the ethnic republics were often graduates of the academic institutes, and most rural schoolteachers had degrees either from those colleges or from the history and philology departments of republic universities. These schoolteachers, in turn, were the dominant figures of the rural intelligentsia and were instrumental in persuading the rural population to support the nationalist cause. Urban and rural communities were also connected through the many urban migrants who maintained close contact with their home villages. Students and migrants thus provided channels for the movement to spread from its initial stronghold among the intellectual elite to rural villagers.

Inhabitants of rural areas were sympathetic to the nationalist movement because of their strong belief in tradition, much of which was based on their ethnic identity. Whereas native-language education was almost nonexistent in the cities, a majority of the rural population attended schools where they were taught in their native language, further strengthening their ethnic identity. Finally, social ties among villagers were particularly dense, with most inhabitants of a community knowing the other members of that community quite well. In this population, levels of trust were rather high, allowing new ideas to spread rapidly after their introduction. At the same time, the spread of nationalism among this population was sometimes hindered by the local administration. If important local officials, such as the collective farm chairman or the chairman of the local council, declared themselves opposed to the nationalist movement, the high density of social ties meant that dissenters could easily be discovered and punished. In this environment, the likelihood that villagers would join the nationalist movement depended in large part on the position taken by the local governing elite.

Migrants from rural areas, on the other hand, were similar to the rural population in terms of their sense of ethnic identity and dense networks of social ties, but they lived in the cities, where they were less constrained by the potential for punishment by local leaders. For this reason, migrants were among the strongest and earliest supporters of nationalist movements in ethnic regions.

Urban industrial workers were similar to rural inhabitants in the density of their social networks and their high levels of intragroup trust. However, they were much less likely to have had exposure to native-language education, had a weaker sense of their ethnic identity, and did not have strong links with the intellectuals who founded the movement. Their reaction to the nationalist movements was therefore likely to be mixed and highly path-dependent. In areas where nationalist ideas gained early support among at least a few workers, these workers were quite likely to persuade other workers to join as well. In regions where nationalism did not penetrate the worker community early on, they were far more likely to become hostile to the movement.

The potential reaction of various social groups to the emerging nationalist movement depended largely on the extent to which they had been socialized to perceive ethnicity as an important component of their identity. Their group cohesiveness, as measured by the density of social ties and degree of mutual trust among the members of the group, and the presence of links between them and other social groups determined the extent to which potential supporters were actually mobilized in support of the nationalist movement.

DATA AND METHODS

In order to test this theory of ethnic mobilization, I use data from two surveys of the population in the ethnic regions of Russia. Most of the data comes from the Colton/Hough preelection survey described in the previous chapter. Because this survey does not include measures of the language in which respondents received their education, it is supplemented by the Language and Nationality in the Former Soviet Union survey designed by David Laitin and Jerry Hough and conducted by the same team of investigators as the Colton/Hough survey.[3] The latter survey, which includes a detailed set of questions on language knowledge and learning, was conducted in Bashkortostan and Tatarstan in 1993. It includes approximately 3,000 respondents from urban areas, divided equally among the major ethnic groups in each region and randomly selected on the basis of voting lists. Because it includes only urban respondents, the survey provides only a partial picture

---

[3] For the sake of brevity, this survey is hereinafter referred to as the Laitin/Hough survey. For more information on the survey and its results, see Laitin (1998).

of the sources of ethnic mobilization in these regions. By using data from the two surveys in combination, I show which social groups were particularly supportive of the nationalist movements in their regions and thus demonstrate the extent to which the data supports the institutional political process theory of ethnic mobilization. I use ordinary least-squares (OLS) multivariate regression to isolate the effect on support for nationalism of belonging to each of the various social groups. The OLS method has the advantage of producing easily interpretable coefficients and may be used when the dependent variable is continuous. Because I am interested in the spread of support for the nationalist movement among the titular ethnic group, I restrict the sample to include only those respondents who, according to their survey responses, consider themselves to be members of the titular ethnic group.[4]

Explanatory and Control Variables

Most of the explanatory and control variables used in this study are measured directly by questions in the Colton/Hough survey. In addition to variables that measure belonging to the social groups described by the theory,[5] I include several social groups that are likely to be opposed to nationalist mobilization, including former and current members of the Communist Party and people holding leadership positions in government and industry. Finally, I include gender as a demographic control variable. The variables thus include all of the social groups discussed in the theory except those who received a native-language education. The variables used are not meant to represent a complete breakdown of society into either occupational or status categories. Since the purpose of the analysis is to determine the accuracy of the hypotheses about which groups may support the nationalist movement's agenda, only groups that are relevant to the theory and groups that are necessary as control variables are included in the analysis.

The effect of native-language education is measured by using three composite indexes from the Laitin/Hough survey. All three indexes range in value from 0 to 1. The native-language education index is a composite of four questions that determine whether the respondent studied in Russian or in the native language in kindergarten, primary school, secondary school, and at the university. The greater the extent of native-language schooling,

---

[4] The Laitin/Hough survey shows that ethnic self-identification is virtually always identical to the ethnic identity listed on the respondent's passport. This correlation ensures that the study is not excluding people who could support nationalism but instead have decided not even to identify with "their" ethnic group any longer. I am grateful to an anonymous reviewer for bringing this issue to my attention.

[5] These include intellectuals, students, migrants from rural areas, industrial workers, agricultural workers, and Muslims. I also include variables that measure the respondent's education level, religiosity, and age. For an explanation of how these variables were created, see Appendix.

the higher the value of this index. The index of language-use homogeneity is designed to reflect the extent to which respondents speak their native language with family members, at work, and with friends. The higher the index value, the more homogeneous the respondent's language use. Finally, the index of language fluency reflects how well respondents know their native language. It includes questions on which language the respondent learned to speak first, in which language the respondent thinks, reads, writes letters, and watches television. The higher the value of the fluency index, the greater the respondent's facility with his or her native language and the greater the range of activities for which it is used.[6]

Most of the social group indicators used in regressions with the Colton/Hough data are also used with the Laitin/Hough survey data. Because the latter survey was conducted only in urban areas, the variables "community size" and "agricultural worker" are omitted. Also, since the Laitin/Hough survey did not ask respondents about their religion or whether they belonged to the Communist Party, these variables are also excluded from the analysis.

Dependent Variables

The survey data includes a series of questions about respondents' attitudes toward nationalist demands. These questions may be grouped into two indicators, each of which measures a particular aspect of nationalist mobilization. Both of the indicators are scaled from 0 to 1, with higher values indicating greater support for nationalism. The language-status index represents attitudes toward the establishment of a privileged status for the titular language. In the Colton/Hough data set, this index is based on two questions that measure the respondent's support for proposals to make the titular language the sole official language of the region and to make it a required subject for the republic's schoolchildren irrespective of their ethnicity, and a third question that asks whether the respondent agrees that all inhabitants of an ethnic republic should speak the titular language. Although the Laitin/Hough data set is specifically focused on language politics and therefore includes a wide variety of measures of attitudes toward language status, in the interest of ensuring maximum comparability across surveys, the only questions used for constructing the language-status index for this survey are questions that correspond exactly to the ones used in the Colton/Hough

---

[6] Factor analysis was used to confirm that these indexes are in fact measuring a single underlying tendency. One factor was detected for the indexes of native-language education and the language-knowledge index. For the language-use index, in addition to the dominant factor that describes language knowledge, two additional factors were detected. These factors group the partners in the communication according to their status relative to the respondent. The second factor includes elder relatives; the third factor includes nonrelatives. The exact wording of the questions, the factor loadings, and other technical information may be found in Appendix.

survey. A comparison of regression results for this index with a broader index of ethnic exclusivism, which includes both questions on language issues and other ethno-political questions, shows virtually identical results. Attitudes toward the status of the titular language can therefore be viewed as indicators of attitudes toward ethnic exclusiveness more generally.[7]

The other indicator of support for nationalism, the index of regional separatism, represents attitudes toward an increase in republic sovereignty. In the Colton/Hough data set, this index includes questions on whether respondents support the ethnic republics' declarations of sovereignty; whether they support the transfer of control over the army, police, and security forces to the ethnic republics; and whether they believe that ethnic republics should have the right of self-determination, up to and including secession from the Russian Federation. In the Laitin/Hough data set, the index includes questions on whether respondents support the establishment of an independent Volga-Ural confederation that would include their republic and whether they support the transfer of control over the army, police, and security forces to their republic. The third question asks respondents about their attitudes toward separatism in the neighboring region. The Tatarstan survey asks respondents whether they support the sovereignty of Bashkortostan, while the Bashkortostan survey asks respondents whether they support the independence of Tatarstan.

These two indexes measure two distinct aspects of support for nationalist mobilization. Tables 6.1 and 6.2 show that the six questions used to construct these indexes represent two underlying factors that are largely uncorrelated in both surveys. This statistical finding makes sense theoretically. Support for ethnic exclusiveness and privileged status for the titular language does not necessarily correlate with support for increasing the status and power of the ethnic republic. The first corresponds to a purely ethnic vision of nationalism that seeks to increase the status of a particular ethnic group, while the second corresponds to a civic nationalism that seeks to gain benefits for all inhabitants of a particular region irrespective of their ethnicity. While supporters of the first type of nationalism focus primarily on cultural issues that are important for preserving the status of their ethnic group, supporters of the second type focus more on power politics as they seek to change the balance of power between their region and the central government in Moscow. In some cases, social groups that are strongly predisposed toward supporting one of these types of nationalism are hostile toward the other.

Before using these indexes to show which social groups supported nationalism, we need to establish the baseline level of this support in each of the regions. Table 6.3 shows the means and standard deviations of each of the indexes for each region. These data reconfirm that support for

---

[7] For the specific wording of the questions used in the language-status index, see Appendix.

TABLE 6.1. *Factor matrix for indexes of support for nationalism: Colton/Hough survey, by survey question*

	Sole State Language	Language Required in School	All Must Know Titular Language	Support Sovereignty	Local Control of Army	Support Secession
Tatarstan						
Language status	.596	.813	.783	.160	.053	.095
Regional separatism	.311	−.069	.156	.703	.744	.749
Bashkortostan						
Language status	.578	.741	.874	.243	.140	.038
Regional separatism	.535	.263	−.009	.578	.827	.810
Chuvashia						
Language status	.710	.798	.630	.397	.357	−.106
Regional separatism	.107	.049	.221	.713	.468	.875
Three republics combined						
Language status	.634	.800	.769	.280	.190	.045
Regional separatism	.259	.107	.115	.724	.753	.805

TABLE 6.2. *Factor matrix for indexes of support for nationalism: Laitin/Hough survey, by survey question*

	Sole State Language	Language Required in School	All Must Know Titular Language	Support Neighbor's Sovereignty	Local Control of Army	Support Independent Ural-Volga Confederation
Tatarstan						
Language status	.592	.777	.786	.054	.247	.236
Regional separatism	.311	−.069	.156	.703	.744	.717
Bashkortostan						
Language status	.659	.754	.794	.157	.287	.052
Regional separatism	.300	.223	.008	.743	.657	.714

Note: The construction of the Laitin/Hough surveys makes a combined factor analysis for the two regions impossible.

TABLE 6.3. *Mean values of ethnic mobilization indexes*

	Colton/Hough Survey			Laitin/Hough Survey	
	Tatarstan	Bashkortostan	Chuvashia	Tatarstan	Bashkortostan
Language status	.465 (.314)	.454 (.332)	.353 (.287)	.451 (.308)	.352 (.326)
Regional separatism	.388 (.324)	.399 (.307)	.142 (.218)	.348 (.287)	.312 (.272)

Note: Range of possible values for each index is 0–1. The value of one standard deviation is listed in parentheses. Values are comparable only across regions for a single index, not across indexes.

nationalism was stronger in Tatarstan and Bashkortostan than in Chuvashia. Furthermore, they show that this gap was narrower on the language-status index than on the regional separatism index, implying that the Chuvash were relatively more supportive of cultural nationalism than of regional separatism.[8] Keeping in mind these relative levels of support, we can now examine which population groups were more likely to include supporters of the nationalism movement.

SUPPORTERS OF ETHNIC MOBILIZATION IN THE REGIONS

Tatarstan

In Tatarstan, the regression results show that the strongest supporters of nationalism included Muslims, intellectuals, migrants, and inhabitants of rural areas. Support for nationalism also increased with greater use of and fluency in the Tatar language. At the same time, women, industrial workers, and agricultural laborers were less likely to support nationalism. Among the people who identified themselves as Muslims, support for nationalism varied inversely with religiosity.

Table 6.4 shows that the standard socioeconomic variables cannot account for a large part of the variation in support for nationalism. As shown by the adjusted R^2 indicator, the model explains between 5% and 11% of the variation. This finding does not mean that the exercise is fruitless, however. While many factors other than the socioeconomic ones discussed here play a role in persuading individuals to support the nationalist agenda, the results show that a great deal can be learned from examining the effect of social group on preferences for nationalism.

---

[8] Note that variation in support for nationalism across regions is explored in detail in Chapter 5, which includes analysis of cross-regional variation in responses to the questions that make up the indexes used in this chapter. Because this chapter focuses on variation in support for nationalism within each region, the brief description and summary table here are intended primarily as a reminder of the findings discussed in Chapter 5.

TABLE 6.4. *Ethnic mobilization in Tatarstan (OLS coefficients, standard errors in parentheses)*

	Language-Status Index		Regional Separatism Index	
	Colton Data	Laitin Data	Colton Data	Laitin Data
Occupational groups				
Intellectual[a]	.055 (.036)	.052 (.020)***	.059 (.037)*	.062 (.019)***
Student[a]	-.010 (.053)	.012 (.028)	-.031 (.053)	.051 (.026)**
Leader[a]	.044 (.045)	.030 (.034)	-.063 (.046)	.070 (.032)**
Industrial worker[a]	-.108 (.040)***	-.037 (.025)	-.098 (.040)**	-.016 (.024)
Agricultural worker[a]	-.185 (.061)***	—	-.109 (.062)*	—
Social characteristics				
Migrant[a]	.072 (.037)**	.129 (.018)***	.082 (.038)**	.093 (.017)***
Community size[b]	.035 (.015)**	—	.022 (.015)	—
Education[c]	-.009 (.017)	.007 (.009)	.022 (.017)	.019 (.009)**
Sex (1 = female)	-.076 (.031)**	-.011 (.018)	-.165 (.031)***	-.032 (.017)*
Age[d]	.166 (.117)	.104 (.063)*	-.002 (.118)	.043 (.059)
Beliefs				
Muslim[a]	.166 (.052)***	—	.176 (.052)***	—
Religious[c]	-.032 (.017)**	—	-.034 (.017)**	—
Communist[a]	-.009 (.047)	—	.061 (.048)	—
Constant	.521 (.130)***	.324 (.052)***	.561 (.131)***	.205 (.049)***
Adjusted R²	.070	.054	.111	.047
N	478	1259	478	1259

*** $p < .01$
** $p < .05$
* $p < .10$
[a] Variable is dichotomous and equals 1 when respondent belongs to the group.
[b] A proxy variable for "rural." Value inversely related to community size and measured on a four-point scale.
[c] Measured on a six-point scale.
[d] Variable scaled to measure from 0 to 1.

Unsurprisingly, this analysis shows that the strongest across-the-board support for nationalist demands in Tatarstan is found among migrants. Migrants are between 7.2% and 12.9% more likely to support cultural nationalism and between 8.2% and 9.3% more likely to support regional separatism than nonmigrants. Both of the surveys found that intellectuals are also likely to support both linguistic and separatist demands, with the size of the positive effect at about 5.5% for the former and 6% for the latter. The Muslim and religious variables are highly significant in part because of their offsetting nature. Being a Muslim increases the likelihood of support for cultural nationalism by 16.6% and for regional separatism by 17.6%, while a unit increase in the six-step measure of religiosity decreases the likelihood of support for cultural nationalism by 3.2% and for regional separatism by 3.4%. Thus, strong believers are actually less likely to support nationalism than respondents who do not identify themselves as Muslims at all. The significance of this finding will be discussed later. Although educational level does not significantly affect the likelihood of support for cultural nationalism, each step in the eight-step educational measure increases a respondent's likelihood of supporting regional separatism by about 2%. On the other hand, older respondents strongly support measures to promote the Tatar language but are more ambivalent regarding regional separatism. Each unit change in the age of the respondent increases support for language status by between 0.10% and 0.17%. Similarly, rural inhabitants are more likely than city dwellers to support cultural nationalism but are more ambivalent about regional separatism. Agricultural and industrial workers are the strongest opponents of nationalism in Tatarstan, although women are also highly opposed to separatism. Finally, several groups, including students, members of the political elite, and former Communists, do not show a clear tendency either to support or to oppose nationalism when compared to the average Tatar.

Overall, it appears that being an intellectual, being male, identifying as Muslim without being devoutly religious, and either living in a rural area or having migrated from a rural area to the city are the most important factors in predicting support for nationalism. At the same time, being an agricultural or industrial worker is correlated with a lower likelihood of support for nationalism.

Before addressing the extent to which these results corroborate the institutional political process model, we need to examine the role of language knowledge and use in predicting support for nationalism. Regressions of the three language-use indexes on the language-status and regional separatism indexes are presented in Table 6.5. Comparing the adjusted R^2 for the regressions in Tables 6.4 and 6.5 shows that the three language indexes together do a better job of explaining variation in support for cultural nationalism than occupation, social characteristics, and beliefs, and that they are almost as good in explaining support for regional

TABLE 6.5. *Effect of language-use variables on support for nationalism in Tatarstan – Laitin data (OLS coefficients, standard errors in parentheses)*

	Language-Status Index	Regional Separatism Index
Native-language education[a]	.086 (.036)**	.068 (.035)**
Language-use homogeneity[a]	.139 (.051)***	.143 (.050)***
Language fluency[a]	.257 (.057)***	.038 (.055)
Constant	.238 (.021)***	.257 (.021)***
Adjusted R^2	.122	.037
N	1259	1259

*** $p < .01$
** $p < .05$
[a] Variable scaled to measure from 0 to 1.

separatism. All three variables are highly significant and have a strong positive relationship with support for both increased language status and regional separatism, except for language fluency in the regional separatism regression.

In Table 6.6, I add the language factors to the model. Comparing the results with and without the language variables, three differences become apparent. Most importantly, whereas migrant status is the most significant factor in the initial model, it becomes much less significant when language factors are added. In effect, these results show that the apparent propensity of migrants to support nationalism is actually mostly the result of migrants' higher propensity to know and use the Tatar language. Second, when language factors are added to the model, educational level becomes highly correlated with support for nationalism at a high level of significance. For each unit increase in level of education, the likelihood of support for cultural nationalism increases by 2.8%, and the likelihood of support for regional separatism increases by 3.1%. This occurs because the language factors are negatively correlated with educational level. Because they are not included in the initial model, respondents who score high on the language factors but low on educational level mask the overall positive effect of education on support for nationalism. A similar process is responsible for the third difference between the two models, the increase in the likelihood of registering support for nationalism among students. In this model, students are 5.2% more likely to support increases in language status and 7.1% more likely to support regional separatism than otherwise similar nonstudents.

The three language factors are not independent of each other. In fact, receiving a native-language education is the best predictor of both language-use homogeneity and language fluency. This factor alone explains over 30% of

TABLE 6.6. *Effect of language-use variables in Tatarstan – Laitin data (multivariate analysis; OLS coefficients, standard errors in parentheses)*

	Language-Status Index		Regional Separatism Index	
	Without Language	With Language	Without Language	With Language
Occupational groups				
Intellectual[a]	.052 (.020)***	.047 (.019)**	.062 (.019)***	.058 (.019)***
Student[a]	.012 (.028)	.052 (.027)*	.051 (.026)**	.071 (.026)***
Leader[a]	.030 (.034)	.020 (.033)	.070 (.032)**	.065 (.032)**
Industrial worker[a]	−.037 (.025)	−.024 (.024)	−.016 (.024)	−.009 (.023)
Social characteristics				
Migrant[a]	.129 (.018)***	.019 (.021)	.093 (.017)***	.039 (.020)**
Education[b]	.007 (.009)	.028 (.009)***	.019 (.009)**	.031 (.009)***
Sex (1 = female)	−.011 (.018)	−.017 (.018)	−.032 (.017)*	−.035 (.017)**
Age[c]	.104 (.063)*	.004 (.061)	.043 (.059)	−.004 (.056)
Language factors				
Native-language education[c]	—	.059 (.038)	—	.020 (.037)
Language-use homogeneity[c]	—	.144 (.051)***	—	.149 (.049)***
Language fluency[c]	—	.303 (.058)***	—	.090 (.056)
Constant	.324 (.052)***	.085 (.055)	.205 (.049)***	.089 (.053)*
Adjusted R^2	.054	.140	.047	.073
N	1259	1259	1259	1259

*** $p < .01$
** $p < .05$
* $p < .10$
[a] Variable is dichotomous and equals 1 when respondent belongs to the group.
[b] Measured on a six-point scale.
[c] Variable scaled to measure from 0 to 1.

the variation in each of the other two indexes.⁹ For this reason, even though the positive correlation between the index of native-language education and support for nationalism is not significant in the combined model (Table 6.6), native-language education nevertheless plays a dominant role in determining the extent of popular support for nationalism.

Although these statistical results do not directly identify the manner in which support for the nationalist movement spread through the Tatar population, they do help to shed light on this process. If we assume that those groups that expressed greater support for the nationalist movement in 1993 were the ones that were most deeply committed to the nationalist movement at its peak, we can determine how well the Tatar case fits the theory of how nationalist movements spread.

After its founding by Tatar intellectuals based at the Institute of Language, Literature, and History and at Kazan State University, the movement focused its initial recruitment efforts on the urban population, particularly those living in Kazan and Naberezhnye Chelny, the two cities where most of the organizers lived. They were particularly successful among two segments of this population. Members of the educated elite joined the movement because they believed that Tatar culture was in decline and that this decline could be reversed through political action. Many of these intellectuals believed that the decline of Tatar culture and language would inevitably result in the gradual extinction of the Tatars as a separate nation (Giuliano 2000, 305). Intellectuals comprised over half of the delegates to the first two TPC congresses. Other than academics, these intellectuals included members of the creative intelligentsia, teachers, and doctors (Iskhakov 1992, 7–9).

Migrants to urban areas also joined in large numbers because of their greater exposure to Tatar culture. Migrants, in effect, were the ideal converts to the nationalist cause, because they combined a strong belief that Tatar culture needed to be preserved with the experience of their children's assimilation into a Russian-dominated urban environment. The most radical supporters of Tatar nationalism came largely from the ranks of recent migrants from rural areas. The high proportion of such migrants in Naberezhnye Chelny helps to explain the strength and radical views of the nationalist movement there (Gibadullin 1993).

Support in the villages was strongest among the rural intelligentsia, particularly among village teachers and doctors. The teachers were frequently former students of the TPC leaders and represented the primary means by which the movement's message was spread to rural areas. The importance of these groups for the spread of nationalism to rural areas is shown by the

---

⁹ Other important factors that contribute to language use and fluency include the age of the respondent and growing up in a rural area. Education level and being a student are correlated negatively with these variables.

growth of their participation in TPC congresses between 1989 and 1991. While members of these groups comprised 7% of the delegates at the 1989 congress, two years later 22% of the delegates were teachers and doctors (Iskhakov 1992, 7–9). Their ties to movement leaders in Kazan encouraged these members of the rural intelligentsia to support the nationalist movement.

Teachers and doctors sought to spread the nationalist movement's message to the rest of the rural population because of their position as the rural areas' intellectual elite. As such, they commanded respect and wielded a great deal of influence among the less-educated rural inhabitants. In fact, only through teachers and doctors could ideas that were not supported by the district administrators and collective farm chairmen reach the rural population.[10] However, their efforts were not very successful. Villagers who worked directly in agriculture had no more than an average likelihood of supporting the nationalist movement's agenda. Among *kolzhoz* workers, traditionalism and fear of reprisals by *kolkhoz* chairmen led to a reluctance to support nationalism. Even those rural inhabitants who supported nationalist views largely remained passive supporters and did not take part in political activity in support of these views. Tatar activists recognized their weakness in these areas and did not focus much of their recruitment effort in rural areas.

Although the statistical analysis shows that belonging to the Muslim religion is highly correlated with support for the nationalist movement, this result is tempered by the strong negative correlation between religiosity and support for nationalism. People who identify themselves as Muslims are strongly supportive of nationalism when compared to non-Muslim Tatars. At the same time, among the Muslim Tatars this support decreases as the level of religiosity increases, with highly religious Muslim Tatars being even less likely to support nationalism than non-Muslim Tatars. In effect, the data show that support for nationalism is high among those Tatars who consider themselves Muslims but do not actively practice their religion. Although the factors leading to such a result are not totally clear, it seems likely that nonreligious Tatars who declare themselves to be Muslims perceive belonging to Islam to be part of their political, rather than their religious, identity. As a result, identifying as a Muslim for nonreligious Tatars may be not a cause of increased support for nationalism but simply a statement of such support. The contradiction in support for nationalism between nonreligious and religious Muslims may thus reflect the existence of two separate subcategories within the Muslim population.

The statistical data confirms the importance of native-language education and facility in speaking Tatar for determining the extent of support

---

[10] On the lack of support for Tatar nationalism among the rural administration, see Giuliano (1997). Elsewhere, Giuliano argues that rural Tatars responded weakly to nationalist appeals because urban Tatars' concerns simply did not resonate with the rural Tatars (Giuliano 2000, 306).

for nationalism. Higher levels of these language-use variables explain the greater propensity of migrants and the older population to support nationalist demands. As expected, extensive native-language use encourages the development of a strong sense of national identity. Those who know Tatar and have studied it in school are more likely to believe that the Tatar nation is threatened by assimilation and thus are more likely to advocate political action to ameliorate this threat.

The data show that not all groups who might be expected to support nationalism do so. In particular, students and members of the governing elite are largely neutral with regard to the nationalist movement's agenda. Although some of the Tatar student population were among the most enthusiastic and radical supporters of the Tatar nationalist movement, their effect was offset by those students who had essentially become Russified, with little sense of a Tatar collective identity and few links to the part of the Tatar ethnic group that had a strong sense of ethnic identity. This latter group was primarily urban, educated in Russian-language schools, and living in an almost completely Russian-language environment. For many of these students, interaction with Tatar culture came only during summer visits to their grandparents in the village and during school field trips to the local history museum. On the other hand, the students who supported the nationalist movement had grown up primarily in rural areas. Although most were attending university programs taught in the Russian language, they had received their previous education in Tatar. Even those students who attended rural Russian-language high schools were more closely connected to their Tatar identity simply by virtue of having lived in the village, where they were surrounded by Tatar culture and where Tatar was the primary spoken language. This analysis is confirmed by the combined model in Table 6.6, which shows that students had a higher-than-average likelihood of supporting nationalism once language factors are controlled for.

The governing elite had an ambivalent attitude toward the nationalist movement. On the one hand, members of this elite had extensive interaction with members of other ethnic groups and functioned in an almost completely Russophone setting. On the other hand, some members of this elite recognized that the nationalist agenda could be used to secure their positions in the context of the collapse of Soviet rule and even to increase their power vis-à-vis the central government. This explains the leaders' propensity to support regional separatism while remaining reluctant to embrace the drive for improvements in the status of the Tatar language. Despite this ambivalence, some members of the governing elite attended the TPC founding congress, where they made up 9% of the total number of delegates (Iskhakov 1993, 7). The leaders of the nationalist movement returned the elite's ambivalence. On the one hand, they blamed the elite for implementing policies that had led to the decline of Tatar culture and the collapse of Tatar schooling. On the other hand, they recognized that members of this elite could be particularly helpful in implementing the nationalist agenda. For this reason, some of the movement's leaders eventually joined the Communist Party *obkom* and became deeply involved in plans to establish a separate Tatarstan Communist Party – plans that were thwarted by the August 1991 coup.[11]

In Tatarstan, the nationalist movement first formed among the intellectual elite and then spread primarily to migrants, nonobservant Muslims, and a segment of the student population. The Tatar movement received little help from the governing elite. By contrast, in other regions members of governing elites were often supportive of nationalist movements.

Bashkortostan

Although support for nationalism was as strong in Bashkortostan as in Tatarstan, its social bases are substantially different. The strongest support comes from students and the governing elite, with intellectuals and migrants also being supportive. In addition, native-language education has a particularly large impact on support for nationalism. Because Bashkirs make up only 22% of the republic's population, they are represented by a relatively small sample ($N = 211$) in the Colton/Hough survey. This increases the size of the coefficients' standard errors, decreasing the likelihood that an existing relationship will be deemed significant by the regression model. While some of the coefficients have relationships that are strong enough to be significant even with the larger standard errors, other probable relationships between belonging to a particular social group and support for Bashkir nationalism are not shown to be significant by the results displayed in the Colton columns in Table 6.7.

Analysis of support for nationalism in Bashkortostan shows that support for linguistic preferences is only partially congruent with support for regional separatism. As shown in Table 6.7, the age of the respondent is the single strongest predictor of a high score on the language-status index, although migrants, agricultural workers, and members of the political and industrial elite also have high positive coefficients (albeit generally below the .10 level of significance). Migrants are 4.1% more likely than the average respondent to support cultural nationalism, while agricultural workers are 13.2% more likely to do so. Finally, for every additional level of education, there is a 3% decrease in likelihood of support for cultural nationalism. For the regional separatism index, the social groups with the greatest propensity to support separatism again include migrants (20% above average) and members of the political elite (23% above average). Students are 15% more likely than the average respondent to support separatism according to the Colton/Hough data, although the Laitin/Hough data shows no statistically significant correlation. Agricultural workers are also more likely to support

[11] Interview with Damir Iskhakov, November 1995.

TABLE 6.7. *Ethnic mobilization in Bashkortostan (OLS coefficients, standard errors in parentheses)*

	Language-Status Index		Regional Separatism Index	
	Colton Data	Laitin Data	Colton Data	Laitin Data
Occupational groups				
Intellectual[a]	.011 (.077)	.022 (.030)	.096 (.068)	.016 (.025)
Student[a]	.089 (.085)	−.065 (.045)	.146 (.075)**	−.061 (.038)
Leader[a]	.146 (.105)	.006 (.038)	.231 (.092)**	.004 (.032)
Industrial worker[a]	.073 (.062)	−.045 (.028)*	.084 (.055)	−.025 (.023)
Agricultural worker[a]	.132 (.087)	–	.153 (.077)**	–
Social characteristics				
Migrant[a]	.084 (.068)	.041 (.023)*	.198 (.060)***	.028 (.019)
Community size[b]	.010 (.024)	–	.040 (.021)*	–
Education[c]	.020 (.023)	−.032 (.012)***	.042 (.020)**	−.014 (.010)
Sex (1 = female)	−.021 (.053)	−.024 (.023)	−.023 (.046)	−.059 (.019)***
Age[d]	.576 (.210)***	.250 (.091)***	.020 (.185)	−.080 (.076)
Beliefs				
Muslim[a]	.048 (.092)	–	.023 (.080)	–
Religious[c]	−.033 (.031)	–	−.028 (.027)	–
Communist[a]	−.097 (.081)	–	−.065 (.072)	–
Constant	.180 (.236)	.408 (.082)***	.102 (.207)	.371 (.069)***
Adjusted R^2	.016	.032	.109	.012
N	211	905	211	905

*** $p < .01$
** $p < .05$
* $p < .10$

[a] Variable is dichotomous and equals 1 when respondent belongs to the group.
[b] A proxy variable for "rural." Value inversely related to community size and measured on a four-point scale.
[c] Measured on a six-point scale.
[d] Variable scaled to measure from 0 to 1.

TABLE 6.8. *Effect of language-use variables on support for nationalism in Bashkortostan – Laitin data (OLS coefficients, standard errors in parentheses)*

	Language-Status Index	Regional Separatism Index
Native-language education[a]	.037 (.037)	.056 (.033)*
Language-use homogeneity[a]	.200 (.067)***	.046 (.059)
Language fluency[a]	.322 (.071)***	.011 (.063)
Constant	.110 (.030)***	.278 (.026)***
Adjusted R^2	.113	.007
N	905	905

*** $p < .01$
** $p < .05$
* $p < .10$
[a] Variable scaled to measure from 0 to 1.

separatism (15% above average), as are rural inhabitants generally. As in the other regions, support for separatism is highly correlated with level of education, and intellectuals are 9.6% more likely than the average respondent to support greater autonomy (although this correlation is not statistically significant in the Colton/Hough data and is altogether nonexistent in the Laitin/Hough data). Unlike the situation in Tatarstan, Bashkir Muslims and religious respondents are not any more likely to support nationalism of any kind, probably because the positive influence of being a Muslim is not sufficient to offset the strong respect for tradition that seems to come with high levels of religiosity. Finally, according to the Laitin/Hough data, regional separatism finds little support among women, who are 5.9% less likely than men to support it.

Language-use variables by themselves are less significant in Bashkortostan than in Tatarstan, particularly for regional separatism (Table 6.8). For language status, native-language education is not significant, while for regional separatism, neither language-use homogeneity nor language fluency are significant. When the language variables are combined with the occupational and social characteristic variables (Table 6.9), we find, as in Tatarstan, that several social characteristic variables that are significant in the initial model are actually acting as proxies for the language variables. Of the initial model for the language-status index, only the negative correlation between being an industrial worker and support for language preferences remains significant in the new model. The effects of age, low education, and being a migrant disappear when language is added. The low explanatory power of the initial model for regional separatism means that these three variables are already insignificant. Nevertheless, their coefficients all change in the same direction as the coefficients for language status, while the coefficients of the other variables in the model remain relatively

TABLE 6.9. *Effect of language-use variables in Bashkortostan – Laitin data (multivariate analysis; OLS coefficients, standard errors in parentheses)*

	Language-Status Index		Regional Separatism Index	
	Without Language	With Language	Without Language	With Language
Occupational groups				
Intellectual[a]	.022 (.030)	.019 (.028)	.016 (.025)	.013 (.025)
Student[a]	-.065 (.045)	-.019 (.043)	-.061 (.038)	-.048 (.038)
Leader[a]	.006 (.038)	.014 (.037)	.004 (.032)	.006 (.032)
Industrial worker[a]	-.045 (.028)*	-.060 (.027)**	-.025 (.023)	-.030 (.023)
Social characteristics				
Migrant[a]	.041 (.023)*	-.027 (.024)	.028 (.019)	-.001 (.021)
Education[b]	-.032 (.012)***	-.014 (.012)	-.014 (.010)	.021 (.011)**
Sex (1 = female)	-.024 (.023)	-.015 (.022)	-.059 (.019)***	-.056 (.019)***
Age[c]	.250 (.091)***	.078 (.089)	-.080 (.076)	-.127 (.078)
Language factors				
Native-language education[c]	—	.051 (.039)	—	.075 (.034)**
Language-use homogeneity[c]	—	.179 (.068)***	—	.070 (.060)
Language fluency[c]	—	.332 (.074)***	—	.027 (.065)
Constant	.408 (.082)***	.184 (.083)**	.371 (.069)***	.320 (.073)***
Adjusted R²	.032	.116	.012	.023
N	905	905	905	905

*** $p < .01$
** $p < .05$
* $p < .10$
[a] Variable is dichotomous and equals 1 when respondent belongs to the group.
[b] Measured on a six-point scale
[c] Variable scaled to measure from 0 to 1.

unchanged, thus adding further evidence that these variables are acting as proxies for the language-use variables for both indexes. In the regional separatism regression, the addition of the language variables leaves only level of education and being male as positively correlated with regional separatism. The explanatory power of the combined model is significantly better than that of the model without language-use variables for both dependent variables.

As in Tatarstan, language fluency has the strongest effect on support for both language preferences and separatism. Unlike the results in Tatarstan, native-language education is significant only in predicting support for regional separatism and not for cultural nationalism. Again, however, native-language education is the strongest predictor of the other language variables, explaining 25% of the variation in language-use homogeneity and over 50% of the variation in language fluency.[12] Once again, native-language education proves to be crucial in predicting the extent of support for both language preferences and regional separatism.

By comparison to nationalists in Chuvashia and Tatarstan, the nationalist movement in Bashkortostan was distinguished by the close ties between the intellectuals who led the movement and the governing elite that sanctioned it. The Bashkir case also differed from the others in the strength of support for nationalism among students and the rural population and the lack of support from Muslims.

Knowledge of the Bashkir language was the most significant element in determining whether Bashkirs supported the nationalist movement. Those who were educated in Bashkir and/or used it as their primary language of communication were substantially more likely to support both Bashkir cultural revival and republic sovereignty. The Bashkir language not only was important for maintaining a sense of collective identity among the population, but also served to divide the Bashkir ethnic group into two subgroups with very different political interests. The approximately 20% of Bashkirs who considered Tatar to be their native language were far less interested in both Bashkir cultural revival, which focused on increasing the status of the Bashkir language, and regional separatism, which they feared would give the local authorities free rein to discriminate against the Tatar-speaking population. This linguistic divide further increased the role of Bashkir-language use in determining the extent of support for Bashkir nationalism.

The social groups that supported Bashkir nationalism were precisely those groups that had the greatest exposure to native-language education and were

---

[12] Other factors that positively influence the level of language-use homogeneity and language fluency include age, being a migrant, being a student, and being an intellectual (language-use homogeneity only). Furthermore, educational level is negatively correlated with language-use homogeneity.

most fluent in the native language. The older population, particularly those who had gone to school before the 1960 education reform had produced a decline in native-language education, were one such group. As in other regions, rural inhabitants and migrants from rural areas stood out as the strongest supporters of nationalism. Because the nationalist movement operated with the approval of the local government, rural inhabitants did not need to fear the consequences of supporting the nationalists. In fact, Bashkir intellectuals recognized that the small size and large-scale assimilation of the Bashkir population in Ufa meant that they could not rely on recruiting in the capital city. If their movement were to succeed, they would need to gain the support of rural Bashkirs. Unlike nationalists in Tatarstan and Chuvashia, they focused their recruitment campaigns on rural areas, even basing the nationalist newspaper in the Bashkir village of Maloiaz rather than in Ufa. This recruitment drive was highly successful, and nationalist leaders frequently boasted that they had the support of a majority of the population in several Bashkir-populated districts in the southern and northeastern regions of Bashkortostan.

Students were the other major social group that came out in support of the nationalist movement. Unlike students in other regions, who were divided into two groups, the vast majority of Bashkir students came from rural areas. Until quite recently, few Bashkirs lived in the republic's major cities, and therefore there were relatively few assimilated children of urban Bashkirs to balance out the students from rural areas. These students, closely identifying with their ethnic group, became some of the most radical and dedicated activists in the Bashkir nationalist movement.

Although Bashkirs are a Muslim ethnic group, being Muslim had little effect on respondents' feelings about national identity or their support for the nationalist movement. As many observers have noted, Islam is not nearly as important to the Bashkirs' conception of their ethnic identity as it is for the Tatars. In fact, most of the Muslim clergy in Bashkortostan come from the ethnic Tatar population. A few Bashkirs have even advocated a return to a pre-Islamic Bashkir religion that is often equated with paganism (Filatov 1997). Because Islam does not play an important role in Bashkir ethnic identity, declaring oneself Muslim could not reflect support for nationalism among nonreligious Bashkirs in the same way that it did among nonreligious Tatars. For this reason, Bashkirs who considered themselves Muslim were not significantly more likely than others to support the nationalist movement.

Chuvashia

Support for nationalism in Chuvashia was much weaker than in Tatarstan or Bashkortostan among all segments of the population. Compared to other Chuvash, however, intellectuals, agricultural laborers, and members of the governing elite stand out as strong supporters of the nationalist agenda.

TABLE 6.10. *Ethnic mobilization in Chuvashia (OLS coefficients, standard errors in parentheses)*

	Language-Status Index (Colton Data)	Regional Separatism Index (Colton Data)
Occupational groups		
Intellectual[a]	.068 (.041)*	.074 (.030)**
Student[a]	.010 (.041)	.046 (.030)
Leader[a]	.032 (.042)	.088 (.031)***
Industrial worker[a]	.014 (.032)	.053 (.023)**
Agricultural worker[a]	.096 (.040)**	.054 (.030)*
Social characteristics		
Migrant[a]	.061 (.032)*	−.009 (.023)
Community Size[b]	.022 (.012)*	−.024 (.009)***
Education[c]	.009 (.012)	.015 (.008)*
Sex (1 = female)	.007 (.024)	−.022 (.017)
Age[d]	−.044 (.093)	−.080 (.068)
Beliefs		
Muslim[a]	N/A	N/A
Religious[c]	0 (.008)	.009 (.006)
Communist[a]	−.044 (.041)	.085 (.030)***
Constant	.213 (.099)**	.122 (.072)*
Adjusted R^2	.006	.076
N	688	688

*** $p < .01$
** $p < .05$
* $p < .10$
[a] Variable is dichotomous and equals 1 when respondent belongs to the group.
[b] A proxy variable for "rural." Value inversely related to community size and measured on a four-point scale.
[c] Measured on a six-point scale
[d] Variable scaled to measure from 0 to 1.

In Chuvashia, unlike Tatarstan, support for ethnic exclusiveness and regional separatism come from different segments of the population, with some groups showing diametrically opposed tendencies on the two indicators.

Perhaps because of their limited sense of identification with Chuvashia, Chuvash respondents are more likely to support preferential status for the Chuvash language than regional separatism. Linguistic preferences find their greatest levels of support in rural areas, as shown by the strong positive relationship of the community size and agricultural worker variables with the language-status index. Villagers are 6.6% more likely than inhabitants of the capital city to support cultural nationalism (Table 6.10). Linguistic preferences are also supported by intellectuals and migrants from rural to urban areas. Each of these two groups are slightly more than 6% more likely than the average respondent to support cultural nationalism. The strong support for linguistic preferences among respondents with ties to rural areas results from the relative lack of Russification there.

The low explanatory power of the multivariate model (adjusted $R^2 = .006$) suggests that in Chuvashia, as in the other republics, support for preferential treatment for the native language may be largely a function of whether the respondent is comfortable in using it and has been educated in it. In Tatarstan and Bashkortostan, adding language-use indicators to the model greatly increases the model's explanatory power. Although data on native-language education, language use, and language fluency are not available for Chuvashia, it seems likely that inclusion of such variables would have a similar effect in this case.

Support for regional separatism is particularly low in Chuvashia. Many respondents who strongly support preferential status for the Chuvash language and its speakers reject any possibility of increasing the region's sovereignty and powers at the expense of the central government. Only intellectuals and agricultural workers support both preferential language rights and regional separatism. The support of agricultural workers is mostly offset by opposition from people living in rural areas. Villagers are 7.2% less likely than residents of the capital city to support separatism. At the same time, greater-than-average support for separatism is found among governing elites, former Communists, and industrial workers, despite these groups' ambivalence about cultural issues. Members of the government are 8.8% more likely than the average respondent to support separatism, former Communists 8.5% more likely, and industrial workers 5.3% more likely. The likelihood of support for separatism increases by about 1.5% for each additional level of education of the respondent (see Table 6.10). In marked contrast to the findings for the language-status index, members of the intellectual, political, and industrial elites, including former Communists, are the groups most supportive of regional separatism. This stance may be explained in part by the realization among the republic's leadership that greater autonomy for their region would increase their power and/or economic well-being.

The Chuvash nationalist movement developed in a manner largely parallel to the Tatar movement's development. The key differences between the two included the greater role played in the Chuvash movement's development by the newly elected nationalist members of the governing elite after the 1990 elections to the local parliament, and the absence of religious identity as a strong nationalist force in the region.

The Chuvash nationalist movement was founded by a group of intellectuals based at the local social science institute and at Chuvash State University. Unlike movement leaders in Tatarstan, these intellectuals were able to take influential positions in the republic government in the wake of a strong performance in the 1990 elections. Once in government, they built alliances with other members of the governing elite, encouraging them to support the nationalist agenda. However, the governing elite and the intellectuals were divided on the main goals of nationalism. The intellectuals and their followers tended to focus on cultural goals, while those who followed the governing elite expressed ambivalence about the program of cultural revival but supported greater sovereignty.

As in Tatarstan, migrants from rural areas were an important source of recruits for the nationalist movement in Chuvashia. These migrants used their links to their home villages to spread the nationalist message throughout the countryside. Rural inhabitants tended to be highly supportive of the nationalists' cultural program but strongly opposed to sovereignty and separatism. This attitude showed that while villagers were concerned about the extent of Russification in the republic, they continued to view the Russians as "elder brothers." Most villagers believed that the Chuvash nation should heed the final testament of the Chuvash spiritual leader, Ivan Iakovlev, by striving to develop their culture without breaking their close relationship with the Russian people. All villagers, including *kolkhoz* workers, supported cultural revival. Because Chuvashia had gone further than Tatarstan in implementing political and economic reform, peasants were less subject to reprisals from *kolkhoz* and village council chairmen. Furthermore, many village leaders supported the Chuvash Peasants' Union, which was the most popular political organization in the countryside and a prominent ally of the urban nationalists.

The governing elites had close links to the Communist Party rank and file and through them to workers in the large urban factories. These groups were persuaded to support a decidedly different form of nationalism – one that was likely to bring them greater wealth and power. As happened in many regions, the Chuvash Communist Party recognized that it needed to find a new ideology in order to maintain its legitimacy and its hold on power. By advocating greater regional autonomy, it could not only retain control in the region but actually increase its power by improving its bargaining position with the central government. The governing elite was also able to convince a large number of industrial workers that their economic well-being depended on increasing local control over major industrial enterprises, something that could occur only if the republic achieved sovereignty. For this reason, workers also came out in support of regional separatism, without necessarily developing close ties with the cultural elite–led nationalist movement.

While students in Chuvashia were split between two opposing groups in much the same manner as students in Tatarstan, the effect of religion on support for nationalism in the two regions proved to be very different. The leaders of the Chuvash diocese of the Russian Orthodox Church, which was the spiritual center of the Chuvash population, were highly critical of the Chuvash nationalist movement. Archbishop Varnava did not allow Chuvash clergy to cooperate with the movement (Filatov and Shchipkov 1995, 241). Thus, unlike the situation in Tatarstan, Chuvashia's dominant religious organization could not provide an organizational focus for anti-Russian ethnic mobilization. This difference was one of the reasons for the Chuvash movement's relative weakness vis-à-vis the nationalist movements in Tatarstan and Bashkortostan.

Like the other movements, the Chuvash nationalist movement was founded by intellectuals, who were able to enter the government as a result of political reforms. Although the movement advocated both cultural revival policies and regional separatism, its supporters were sharply divided over the two sets of demands. Social groups with links to the intellectuals, including migrants and rural inhabitants, supported cultural revival without regional separatism. On the other hand, industrial workers and Communists, because of their ties to the republic's political leadership, supported regional separatism while remaining ambivalent about cultural revival.

Khakassia

Unfortunately, the available survey data on support for nationalism in Khakassia does not include breakdowns by age or social group. For this reason, in the following description of the patterns of recruitment and support for the Khakass nationalist movement, I rely primarily on nonstatistical sources, including newspaper accounts and interviews with movement leaders and local scholars.

Unlike nationalist movements in the other three regions, the Khakass movement was founded not by intellectuals but by students, although the Khakass intellectual elite quickly joined the movement and soon assumed many of the leadership positions. The movement's founders were predominantly graduates of Khakass schools and especially of the elite Khakass boarding school for rural schoolchildren, which was designed to train future cultural leaders (Kostiakov 1990). Even though Khakass schools taught the Khakass language only as a subject, they did emphasize Khakass culture and history. In addition, Khakass who grew up in rural areas were raised in a Khakass-speaking environment where they were constantly exposed to Khakass culture. On the other hand, the minority of Khakass students who came from urban areas received no instruction in the language or culture of their people, were therefore largely Russified, and did not play a role in the nationalist movement. The intellectuals and students who initially led the movement focused primarily on Khakass cultural revival, believing that increasing the region's autonomy was not as important as ensuring that the Khakass ethnic group survived as a distinct cultural entity.

However, the movement soon expanded its agenda to include regional autonomy. This change of emphasis came about largely as a result of close cooperation between the movement and the governing elite, whose members were more concerned with increasing their authority than with preserving Khakass culture. Although a large segment of the region's governing elite was ethnically Russian, Russian leaders joined the Khakass in calling for improving the region's administrative status. This interethnic alliance persisted until Khakassia became a republic in 1991.[13] By the beginning of 1992, support for nationalism among the governing elite had begun to follow the Bashkortostan pattern, with Khakass leaders seeking to maintain a privileged political status for the Khakass ethnic group and to foster a Khakass cultural revival, while Russian leaders called for the end of special privileges in the name of human rights and full equality for all individuals regardless of ethnicity.

Outside of the elites, support for Khakass nationalism came primarily from the rural areas, where the bulk of the Khakass population lived. Because most of the intellectuals, students, and political leaders who had organized the nationalist movement were first-generation urban residents, they were able to recruit relatives and friends from their home villages. As was the case in Chuvashia, rural Khakass were primarily concerned with cultural revival rather than with regional separatism.

Religion has played a unifying role among the Khakass people. Although the Khakass are nominally considered to belong to the Russian Orthodox Church, Christianity has only a superficial presence among them. Most Khakass continue to follow the traditional Khakass shamanist religion, despite the persecution of its followers during the Soviet period. Since one of the national movement's key goals was the revival of shamanism, many of the more religious Khakass were among the movement's strongest supporters.[14]

The Khakass movement, which at its peak included an alliance of convenience between its intellectual and student founders and the governing elites, drew many of its supporters from some of the same core groups that supported nationalist movements in other regions, particularly migrants and rural inhabitants. After the collapse of the alliance with the governing elites, these groups continued to support the movement's efforts to promote a Khakass cultural revival, although they remained ambivalent about further increases in the region's autonomy.

CROSS-REGIONAL PATTERNS OF ETHNIC MOBILIZATION

The strongest support for preferential status for the titular ethnic group's language came from social groups that had greater exposure to native-language education and whose members came from environments where the native language was used. These groups included older respondents, intellectuals, rural inhabitants, and migrants from rural areas. Evidence from Tatarstan and Bashkortostan lends support to the importance of exposure to the native language as the prime source of support for language preferences. In these

---

[13] Interview with Alexander Kostiakov, founder of Tun, June 1996.
[14] Interview with Viktor Butanaev, June 1996.

regions, while factors such as age, level of education, and being a migrant are positively correlated with support for language preferences, this relationship disappears when language-use variables are added to the model. Other than native-language education, factors that affect support for language preferences include being a worker and religion. In two of the three republics (not including Chuvashia), workers were less likely than members of other groups to express support for language preferences. Religion played an important role in Tatarstan – where Muslim identity was strongly linked with ethnic identity, and where a declaration of Muslim identity could thus be interpreted as a marker of support for nationalism – and in Khakassia, where the revival of shamanism likewise served as a unifying force for the ethnic group. In Bashkortostan, Islam was associated with the local Tatar population, which precluded its use as a statement of support for nationalism among Bashkirs. In Chuvashia, Orthodoxy united Chuvash and Russians, similarly precluding the use of religion as a tool for nationalist mobilization.

While in Bashkortostan and Tatarstan similar groups supported both regional separatism and language preferences, in Chuvashia and Khakassia the two aspects of the nationalist agenda drew support from different parts of the population. In the first two regions, support for regional separatism came from familiar groups, including intellectuals, migrants, and the rural population. Like the strongest supporters of language preferences, supporters of regional separatism came from groups with the strongest connection to the native language. Furthermore, Muslims in Tatarstan and students in Bashkortostan supported regional separatism out of their strong sense of local identity. In Chuvashia, on the other hand, of all the groups that supported language preferences, only intellectuals also supported regional separatism. In fact, the strongest support for separatism in Chuvashia came from groups with a weak sense of regional identity, including agricultural workers, industrial workers, and even members of the Communist Party. Industrial and agricultural workers also supported separatism in Bashkortostan, while those groups strongly opposed separatism in Tatarstan.

Why did these groups support nationalism in some regions while opposing it in others? The direction taken by *kolkhoz* workers depended primarily on whether they were likely to suffer reprisals for expressing support for nationalism. In reformist regions, such as Chuvashia, and in regions where their superiors also supported nationalism, such as Bashkortostan, *kolkhoz* workers expressed support for the nationalist program. In Tatarstan, where the leadership was ambivalent about the nationalist movement and the danger of reprisals was high, *kolkhoz* workers stated their opposition to the nationalist agenda despite the contrary views expressed by the rest of the rural population.

As noted in the introduction to this chapter, workers had dense internal social networks without necessarily having strong links to the founders of the nationalist movements. In this situation, the key role in determining whether workers in each region supported or opposed the nationalist movement was played by members of the governing elite, who were closely linked to both the intellectuals who founded the nationalist movement and to worker groups. In Bashkortostan, where leaders fully supported the nationalist agenda, workers and peasants also came out in support of both regional separatism and language preferences. In Chuvashia, where leaders formed an alliance with the nationalist movement but expressed support for regional separatism without language preferences, workers expressed similar preferences. We would expect a similar result in Khakassia, although we do not have specific evidence to prove or disprove such a conclusion. Finally, in Tatarstan, where governing elites did not support the nationalist movement, workers came out against the movement.

Thus, the reasons for supporting or opposing regional separatism varied depending on the group, although exposure to the native language and the existence of strong ties between the group and movement activists increased support for the nationalist agenda in all of the regions.

ETHNIC INSTITUTIONS AND SUPPORT FOR NATIONALISM

The evidence presented in this chapter further confirms the institutionalist model of ethnic mobilization outlined in Chapter 1. Support for the nationalist movement and its agenda was strongest among those social groups that had maintained the strongest connections to their ethnic group's cultural traditions and native language. In urban areas, these groups included intellectuals, many of whom worked in cultural fields that reinforced their sense of ethnic identity, and migrants from rural areas, many of whom had received a native-language education and/or had been brought up in an environment where the titular language was commonly used. University students who received a native-language education were also likely to support nationalism, while students educated in Russian-language schools usually avoided the movement. All of these groups were linked together through the republic's academic institutions, which provided a home base for the intellectuals who founded the movement. These institutes and universities employed many migrants, giving the nationalist movements access to a tightly interconnected social group that provided many of their recruits. Since many of the movement founders were university professors, the recruitment of students also occurred in the academic setting. Both students and migrants spread the nationalist message beyond the urban environment by using their strong ties with the villages where they had grown up. The spread of nationalism to rural areas was also facilitated by members of the rural intelligentsia, and particularly by teachers with ties to the urban academic institutions. Because of these links, rural inhabitants who were not employed by collective farms were likely to be supportive of the nationalist agenda. Although support among collective farm workers depended on the extent to which collective farm chairmen retained control over village life, the native-language education system, which had been best preserved in rural areas, made their support more likely.

The strength of connections between social groups and the extent to which an ethnic group's language and culture were preserved among the population depended largely on the region's ethnic institutions. Without exception, these institutions had been established by the Soviet state, which also had complete control over the extent to which they were allowed to develop. In regions where native-language education was confined to a few rural schools and where only the primary grades were taught in the native language, or where the native language was taught only as a subject, the sense of ethnic collective identity was relatively weak even among a movement's core constituencies: migrants, rural inhabitants and intellectuals. On the other hand, some regions had a complete system of primary and secondary education, with all teaching done in the native language from first to tenth grade. These were the regions that were most likely to become hotbeds of nationalist sentiment. Similarly, in areas where the study of ethnic culture was limited to a single institute, the small number of intellectuals dedicated to maintaining the culture and status of their ethnic group was correspondingly low, leading to a smaller pool of potential movement leaders. In such regions, nationalist movements tended to appear later and were likely to lack the dynamic leaders necessary to attract a large number of supporters to the movement's cause.

7

Outcomes

Did Regional Governments Adopt the Nationalist Agenda?

How successful were the nationalist movements in persuading regional political elites to implement their programs? In this chapter, I examine the extent to which the nationalist platform was adopted by republic governments. Implementation of the nationalist agenda was divided into two phases. First, governments seeking to implement nationalist policies had to create an institutional and symbolic framework that would legitimize such policies in the eyes of the population. Among the ethnic republics of the Russian Federation, the creation of this framework began with declarations of sovereignty and eventually came to include republic constitutions, language laws, and state symbols. Second, once the framework was in place, republic governments designed and implemented programs that would spur an ethnic revival. Ethnic revival programs in the republics focused on developing titular languages and cultures, increasing titular-language education, and taking steps to ensure that political power would remain in the hands of the titular ethnic group.

The extent to which nationalist demands were taken into account in designing the institutional and symbolic framework of sovereignty in each republic was only partially and indirectly a function of the extent to which ethnicity was institutionalized in the republic. The implementation of the nationalist agenda depended partially on the strength of the nationalist movement, which in turn depended on the institutionalization of ethnicity. But it also depended on the demographic balance between titulars and Russians in the republic, a factor not related to the ethnic institutions argument. A stronger nationalist movement and a larger titular percentage of the total population allowed for the creation of an institutional framework that acknowledged the special status of the titular ethnic group and accommodated nationalist demands for separatism. The extent to which the institutional framework legitimated special treatment of the titular ethnic group in turn played an important role in determining the extent to which republic governments were able to implement ethnic revival policies. The implementation of ethnic revival also depended on the extent to which titular elites had exercised political power prior to the start of political reform.

LAWS AND SYMBOLS: A CIVIC NATION OR AN ETHNIC NATION?

The adoption of sovereignty declarations and other laws was one of the first signs that nationalist movements were having an impact on regional government policies. In most regions, the influence of nationalist movements made government leaders reconsider their initial hostility to sovereignty. In all of the regions, although to varying degrees, nationalist discourse found its way into the content of these declarations and into the language laws and republic constitutions whose adoption followed the declarations of sovereignty.

Sovereignty Declarations

Both republic governments and nationalist movements saw sovereignty declarations as the first step toward a drastic change in relations between the regions and the central government in Moscow. While most government leaders sought sovereignty in order to increase their political authority in their region and to enhance their control of the region's economy, nationalist leaders saw the declarations as an affirmation of their ethnic group's right to statehood and self-determination and as a potential tool in their efforts to initiate cultural revival programs. The extent to which the nationalists were able to include their conception of sovereignty in the text of the declaration varied from region to region (Table 7.1).

In Tatarstan, through an organized campaign of protests and demonstrations, the nationalist movement was successful in forcing the republic government to renounce a draft declaration that stated that the newly established Tatar union republic would remain within the Russian federal republic (*Vecherniia Kazan*,' 15 August 1990). Instead, the adopted declaration stated that Tatarstan would independently participate in negotiations over a new union treaty and would establish relations with Russia on the basis of that treaty. Furthermore, the ethnic character of the emerging sovereign republic was made clear in the preamble to the declaration, which stated that sovereignty was being declared in order to "realize the inalienable right of the Tatar nation, and all of the people of the republic, to self-determination" (Mukhametshin 1995, 144). At the same time, the inclusion of the clause "and all of the people of the republic" was a defeat for the nationalists, who argued that sovereignty emanated exclusively from the Tatar nation's right to self-determination and its centuries-long struggle for independence. Nationalist leaders were also unsuccessful in having their demand to reserve for the

TABLE 7.1. *Regional sovereignty declarations*

Title	
Tatarstan	Declaration of State Sovereignty of the Tatar Soviet Socialist Republic
Bashkortostan	Declaration of State Sovereignty of the Bashkir Soviet Socialist Republic
Chuvashia	Declaration of State Sovereignty of the Chuvash Soviet Socialist Republic
Khakassia	Declaration on the Main Rights, Powers and Responsibilities of the Khakass Republic as a Member of the Russian Federation
Date of adoption	
Tatarstan	August 30, 1990
Bashkortostan	October 11, 1990
Chuvashia	October 24, 1990
Khakassia	March 6, 1992
Sovereignty declared in the name of:	
Tatarstan	Tatar nation and entire people of the republic
Bashkortostan	Bashkir nation, guaranteeing equal rights for all nations
Chuvashia	People of the republic, including citizens of all nationalities
Khakassia	No mention of sovereignty; republic established by Khakass nation and the society that had formed on this territory
Sovereignty belongs to:	
Tatarstan	Tatar nation and entire people of the republic
Bashkortostan	Multinational people of the republic
Chuvashia	People of the republic; republic is sole state of the Chuvash nation
Khakassia	The people of Khakassia as the source of state power
Status of titular culture	
Tatarstan	No mention
Bashkortostan	Republic assists Bashkir cultural development outside the republic
Chuvashia	Republic responsible for Chuvash cultural development
Khakassia	Republic assists Khakass cultural development outside the republic

republic the right to secede from the Soviet Union included in the final text of the declaration.[1] On other aspects of the text, including the supremacy of republic laws on its territory and the right of the republic to control all of its land and natural resources, the government and the nationalists were in agreement.

---

[1] R. Safin et al., "Za gosudarstvennyi suverenitet Tatarstana," *Vecherniia Kazan'*, 2 August 1990. See also the nationalists' draft text of the declaration in the same issue.

In adopting Chuvashia's declaration of sovereignty, the republic Supreme Soviet accepted most of the Chuvash nationalist movement's proposals dealing with the ethnic character of the newly sovereign republic. Although the text begins by stating that it is expressing the interests of all citizens of the republic regardless of ethnicity, the sovereignty declaration quickly goes on to state that it is "taking responsibility for the fate of the Chuvash nation" and "proceeding from the necessity of preserving and developing the culture, language, traditions, and way of life of the Chuvash nation." It declares that the Chuvash republic is, among other things, "the sole national state of the Chuvash nation," founded on the basis of the "Chuvash nation's inalienable right to self-determination," and that this state will "assure the free cultural development of the Chuvash nation." With the exception of the statement on preserving Chuvash culture and traditions in the preamble, all of these statements had been absent from the initial government draft and were added from the nationalists' draft.[2] All of the drafts agreed that sovereignty should belong to all of the republic's inhabitants regardless of their ethnicity.

At the same time, the Chuvash nationalist movement was less successful than its Tatar counterpart in having its political proposals included in the declaration text. The nationalists' draft declared that the republic would be self-governing with the exception of powers explicitly delegated to the Soviet Union or to Russia. Russian and Soviet laws would function in the republic only after their ratification by the Chuvash parliament. The adopted declaration, on the other hand, stated that Soviet and Russian laws would function in Chuvashia automatically unless they contradicted Chuvashia's Constitution. Thus, unlike the Tatar legislature, the Chuvash Supreme Soviet declared the republic's sovereignty primarily in the name of and for the sake of the titular nation, while declaring its intention to retain close relations with Russia.

The sovereignty declaration proposed by the Bashkir nationalist movement was significantly more radical than analogous proposals by nationalist movements in the other republics. It stated that the Bashkir republic was formed on the basis of the Bashkir nation's natural and inalienable right to self-determination and national sovereignty. Bashkortostan would assume responsibility for the fate of the Bashkir nation and would seek to foster Bashkir cultural development both inside and outside the republic. In discussing the republic's political status, the BNC called for replacing the Soviet Union with a confederation and giving the republic the right to secede from this new union. Furthermore, the BNC argued that the republic should have the right to seek the return of territories formerly belonging to Bashkortostan that had been transferred to other regions during the Stalinist

---

[2] Compare the nationalists' draft declaration in *MK*, 23 August 1990, with the government's draft in *Sovetskaia Chuvashia*, 20 October 1990, and the final text (in author's possession).

era. Finally, the BNC sought the establishment of a separate national bank and armed forces for the republic. In sum, the proposals contained in the BNC draft sovereignty declaration envisioned a virtually independent state, respecting the rights of all ethnic groups but dedicated to the development of the Bashkir nation (Guboglo 1992a, 126–8).

The government proposed two substantially different draft declarations. The Supreme Soviet's version included some nationalist proposals, while the Council of Ministers submitted a declaration that resembled the initial government proposals in the other republics. Both the Council of Ministers and the Supreme Soviet based their declarations on the right of the Bashkir nation to self-determination, although sovereignty was to belong to the entire "multinational people" of the republic. But while the Council of Ministers sought to establish Bashkortostan as a sovereign republic within both Russia and the Soviet Union, the Supreme Soviet's draft argued for affiliation solely with the Soviet Union. Like the BNC, the Supreme Soviet sought to make the republic responsible for the development of Bashkir culture in the diaspora (Guboglo 1992a, 112–19). After these drafts received a mixed reaction from the public, the government suspended discussion on the declaration, emerging a month later with a new proposal that was adopted after two weeks of debate.

Like all of the previous official drafts, the adopted declaration stated that sovereignty was based on the "realization of the inalienable right of the Bashkir nation to self-determination," adding that this right would not violate "the guarantee of equal rights for all nations in Bashkortostan." Also like all of the previous government drafts, it declared that sovereignty belonged to the entire multinational people. The final version followed the Council of Ministers in agreeing to treaty-based relations with both Russia and the Soviet Union (Guboglo 1992a, 141–3). In comparing the various texts, it becomes clear that the Bashkir nationalists lost their battle to influence the content of the sovereignty declaration. Whereas in Chuvashia and Tatarstan the final version of the declaration was more focused on the rights of the titular ethnic group than earlier government drafts had been, in Bashkortostan the final version remained unchanged on the role of the Bashkir nation and was less radical than even one of the initial government drafts on the future relationship between the republic and the federation.

In the fall of 1990, while Russia's other ethnic regions were adopting sovereignty declarations, the Khakass nationalist movement and the regional government were fighting to assert their independence from Krasnoyarsk. As a result, efforts to have parliament adopt a sovereignty declaration did not begin until after the establishment of the Khakass republic in July 1991. During the fall 1991 electoral campaign for the newly established republic Supreme Soviet, Tun called for the adoption of a sovereignty declaration that would assert the right of the Khakass nation to self-determination. Nationalist leaders hoped that such a declaration would make it possible for the new legislature to enact policies aimed at Khakass cultural revival and would serve to ensure that Khakass politicians played a leading role in governing the new republic.[3] Their defeat in the December elections and the subsequent collapse of the Khakass nationalist–Russian democrat alliance ended any chance that a sovereignty declaration would be adopted. Although ethnic Khakass deputies tried to convince them that sovereignty meant simply the recognition of Khakass self-determination and statehood, Russian deputies expressed fear that the adoption of a sovereignty declaration would lead to Khakassia's separation from Russia.[4]

In the end, the legislators compromised by adopting a sovereignty declaration–like document entitled "The Declaration on the Main Rights, Powers and Responsibilities of the Khakass Republic as a Member of the Russian Federation."[5] Having prevented the concepts of sovereignty and statehood from appearing in the document, the parliamentary majority was willing to declare that the republic was based on the "right of the Khakass nation and the society that had formed on this territory to self-determination." In another concession to the Khakass legislators, the declaration also stated that the republic was responsible for the cultural development of ethnic Khakass living outside the republic. The rest of the declaration's 40 articles were devoted to spelling out the powers and jurisdictions of the various branches of government, in effect making the declaration a limited constitution for the interim period before the adoption of a full constitution.

The strength of the local nationalist movement and the demographic balance in the region were the most important factors in determining the nature of sovereignty declarations in Russia's ethnic regions. The strength of the nationalist movement influenced the extent to which nationalist goals were included in initial government drafts of the declarations. The most radical initial drafts were offered in Bashkortostan and Tatarstan, the two republics with the most powerful nationalist movements. However, after the publication of these drafts, the nature of the final draft depended more on the demographic balance between the titular and Russian populations than on the strength of the nationalist movement. In Bashkortostan and Khakassia, the republics where titulars made up a minority of the population, initial drafts were revised to reduce the degree of republic independence from Moscow and the role of the titular ethnic group in state formation. By contrast, in Tatarstan and Chuvashia the adopted declaration texts increased the role of the titular ethic group and revised the center-region balance of power in favor of the region.

---

[3] For example, see G. Kotozhekov, "Vyrazhaem nedoveriie," *Sovetskaia Khakassia*, 5 December 1991.

[4] A. Borisova, "Parad suverenitetov. Komu on nuzhen?," *Sovetskaia Khakassia*, 18 February 1992.

[5] *Khakassia*, 14 March 1992.

TABLE 7.2. *Regional constitutions*

Date of adoption	
Tatarstan	November 7, 1992
Bashkortostan	December 24, 1993
Chuvashia	Proposed (April 1995 draft)
Khakassia	May 25, 1995
Based on the will of:	
Tatarstan	Multinational people of the republic
Bashkortostan	Multinational people of the republic, realizing right of Bashkir nation to self-determination
Chuvashia	Multinational people of the republic
Khakassia	Multinational people of the republic
Relations with Russia	
Tatarstan	None at first, later changed to treaty-based association
Bashkortostan	Independent subject of the Federation based on treaty
Chuvashia	Democratic state which is part of the Russian Federation
Khakassia	Subject of Russian Federation
Status of titular culture	
Tatarstan	No mention
Bashkortostan	Republic responsible for cultural development of Bashkirs and other peoples living in the republic
Chuvashia	Republic responsible for Chuvash cultural development and assists cultural development of all peoples of the republic
Khakassia	Republic assists in cultural development of all ethnic communities living on its territory
Required languages for president	
Tatarstan	State languages of the republic
Bashkortostan	Bashkir and Russian
Chuvashia	State languages of the republic
Khakassia	No language requirement

Constitutions

Without exception, the constitutions of the ethnic republics were adopted after nationalist movements had entered a period of decline. The constitutions' texts reflect this lack of nationalist influence. In each of the four republics, the constitution is less focused on the republic's ethnic character than on that republic's sovereignty declaration. Each constitution portrays the republic as a civic state based on the will of the republic's multinational people. However, the constitutions differ on how they see the relationship between the republic and the Russian Federation, and on the extent to which they recognize the priority of the titular ethnic group's culture and language (Table 7.2).

In Tatarstan, the nationalist movement's decline during the months between the publication of the draft constitution in January 1992 and its adoption in November of that year allowed the government to remove from the preamble text recognizing the right of the Tatar nation to self-determination.[6] Realizing the controversial nature of enshrining a single ethnic group's right to statehood in the constitution, the Tatarstan Supreme Soviet changed the final text to state that the republic's sovereignty emanated from the "whole multinational people of the republic" (Dmitriev and Malakhova 1995, 284). Khakassia's Constitution and Chuvashia's draft constitution also based sovereignty on the will of each republic's multinational population.[7] Similarly, the Bashkortostan Constitution claimed that the republic's sovereignty expressed the "will and interests of the entire multinational people of the republic." However, unlike the other republic constitutions, Bashkortostan's Constitution retained an article stating that the republic owed its existence to the Bashkir nation's exercise of its right to self-determination (Dmitriev and Malakhova 1995, 30, 44).

The most significant difference between the four constitutions was found in the type of relationship that the republics sought to have with the Russian Federation. On this question, Tatarstan was the most separatist of the republics. As initially adopted, its Constitution declared the republic fully independent and did not envision any sort of special relationship with the Russian Federation. After the successful negotiation of a bilateral treaty with Russia in 1994, the Constitution was amended to include an article that declared Tatarstan to be "a sovereign state, a subject of international law, associated with the Russian Federation on the basis of a treaty on the mutual delegation of power and areas of competence" (Dmitriev and Malakhova 1995, 293). With the exception of this single article, the Tatarstan Constitution reads as the constitution of an independent state. Bashkortostan's Constitution was somewhat more circumspect, declaring the republic to be an independent (*samostoiatelnyi*) subject of the Russian Federation. Mutual relations between the two were to be based on a treaty of intergovernmental relations, and the republic recognized the authority of Russian laws on its territory with regard to questions that fell under Russian jurisdiction according to the treaty. By comparison, the constitutions of Chuvashia and Khakassia were unequivocal in their recognition of the Russian government's authority. In both cases, the first article of the Constitution affirmed that these republics considered themselves part of the Russian Federation. However, status differences between the two republics were demonstrated in the phrasing of these articles. Whereas Khakassia's Constitution simply stated that the republic was a subject of the Russian Federation, Chuvashia's draft constitution called

---

[6] Draft constitution, published in *Vecherniia Kazan*, 8 January 1992.
[7] Constitution of the Republic of Khakassia, published in *Khakassia*, 22 June 1995; draft constitution of the Republic of Chuvashia, published in *Sovetskaia Chuvashia*, 12 April 1995.

the republic a democratic state within the federation. Both constitutions made repeated reference to the Constitution of the Russian Federation, references that were entirely missing in the Tatarstan and Bashkortostan constitutions. In Khakassia, the adopted formulation was a clear defeat for the nationalist movement, which had sought to have Khakassia declared a state within the Russian Federation.[8] These differences in each republic's relations with Russia were tied to the strength of the nationalist movement in each region, as well as these movements' attitudes toward relations with Russia.

The actual differences in the republics' relationships with the Russian Federation paralleled the republic constitutions. The government of Tatarstan refused to recognize the authority of the Russian government on its territory until 1994. Between the declaration of republic sovereignty in 1990 and the signing of a bilateral treaty between the governments of Tatarstan and Russia in February 1994, the republic government refused to sign the 1992 Federation Treaty, encouraged boycotts of several Russian elections and referenda in the republic, and repeatedly failed to transfer tax revenue to the central government. During this period, the Tatarstan government engaged in lengthy negotiations with the Russian government to establish the parameters of association between the republic and the federation. Only after the signing of the bilateral treaty did relations between Tatarstan and Moscow stabilize (Walker 1996). The government of Bashkortostan was more circumspect in its effort to establish a special status for the republic within Russia. Consistent with this aim, the republic leadership participated in signing the Federation Treaty, but only after receiving assurances that the republic's status would be recognized in a special addendum to the treaty. Eventually, Bashkortostani leaders signed a bilateral treaty with Moscow that in many ways paralleled the earlier treaty negotiated by Tatarstan. As the constitutions of the other two republics made clear, separatism was not really on the agenda in either Chuvashia or Khakassia. Both signed the Federation Treaty with no special provisions and did not become involved in negotiating bilateral treaties until the practice had become ubiquitous throughout the Russian Federation.

The republic constitutions also differed on the role they envisioned for the republic government in cultural development. Tatarstan's Constitution made no mention of the government's responsibility for the cultural development of any ethnic group. Khakassia's Constitution required the government to assist in the cultural and linguistic development of all ethnic groups living in the republic. Chuvashia and Bashkortostan, on the other hand, both sought to enshrine the government's responsibility for the preservation and development of the titular ethnic group's culture. In both cases, support for

---

[8] Albina Borisova, "Khakassia – ne gosudarstvo v gosudarstve, tak reshili deputaty," *Khakassia*, 27 January 1995.

the cultures of other ethnic groups living in the republic was considered secondary to the development of titular culture (see Table 7.2).

Finally, the republics differed in their requirements for language knowledge by the president or head of government. All three of the former autonomous republics required the head of state to know both Russian and the titular language. Chuvashia and Tatarstan expressed this requirement in terms of knowing the republic's official state languages. Since Bashkortostan had not adopted a language law that would regulate the status of languages, its Constitution simply stated that the president was required to know the Bashkir and Russian languages. Khakassia, the former autonomous province, placed no linguistic requirements on the republic's head of administration.

Unlike the sovereignty declarations, republic constitutions were written by government leaders to symbolize the multi-ethnic nature of the republics. In all four cases, the titular ethnic group's right of self-determination was either entirely absent from the text or downplayed in favor of the conception of the state's population as a civic nation. Nationalist leaders either did not contest the multiethnic character of the state or were ignored by the government leaders who wrote the constitutions. However, the movements' impact on the framing of government policy was felt in the inclusion of language requirements for heads of state in three of the regions and in articles giving priority to titular cultural development in Bashkortostan and Chuvashia.

The nationalist movements' most significant impact was on the nature of the relationship between the republic and the Russian Federation. In Tatarstan, the region with the strongest movement, independence from the Federation was part of the government agenda between 1991 and 1994. The republic Constitution reflected this policy in its silence on ties with Russia. Even after government policy changed, the relationship between the two states according to the Constitution was minimal. By comparison, nationalists in Bashkortostan were less insistent on full independence from Russia, calling instead for broad autonomy. This sentiment was reflected in the republic Constitution, which recognized Russian authority but sought to negotiate a treaty to determine the extent of ties between the republic and Moscow. In the other two republics, nationalists did not support independence, and the constitutions fully recognized Russian authority with no caveats. At the same time, differences in the extent of nationalist influence in each republic matched the description of each republic's relationship with Russia. The influence of Chuvash nationalists on government attitudes toward autonomy led to the statement that Chuvashia was a state within the Federation, whereas the weak Khakass movement failed to persuade parliament to declare Khakassia a state. Although none of the nationalist movements were able to affect the multiethnic character of their republic constitutions, they did influence the type of relationship between the region and the center enshrined in each document.

Language Laws

Language revival was the most important issue for nationalist movements throughout the entire Soviet Union, and one of the most contentious (Laitin 1998, 368). The republics of the Russian Federation were no exception. Nationalist movements in the former autonomous republics sought to copy newly adopted union republic language laws that declared the titular language to be the sole official language of the republic. In Khakassia, nationalists sought simply to ensure that Khakass and Russian were given equal status. Although parliaments in all four republics eventually chose to give official status to Russian in addition to the titular language, the nationalists were successful in persuading the legislatures to expand titular-language use in education, government, and the media (Table 7.3).

Chuvashia was the first of Russia's ethnic republics to adopt a language law. The importance attached to linguistic revival by the nationalist movement persuaded the republic's Supreme Soviet to link the language law to sovereignty. As a result, the language law was approved by the legislature a mere three days after the republic's declaration of sovereignty. The initial draft of the law declared Chuvash to be the only official state language, with Russian receiving the status of the language of interethnic communication and recognition as the state language of the Soviet Union.[9] However, this proposal received only thirteen votes during parliamentary debate and was changed in favor of equal official-language status for both Chuvash and Russian.[10]

Despite the defeat on language status, nationalists were able to persuade legislators to support several significant initiatives to increase the role of the Chuvash language in public use. The law made the republic government responsible for preserving and developing the Chuvash language. It required government workers dealing with the public to know both state languages, allowing for a ten-year transition period during which translators would be required to be present in all government agencies. It also called for unspecified financial bonuses to be given to those workers who were able to communicate in both languages. Government meetings and court proceedings were to be conducted in both languages, except in rural areas with an overwhelmingly Chuvash population, where they could be conducted entirely in Chuvash. The law gave priority to publishing Chuvash-language periodicals and books and guaranteed the development of Chuvash culture. Finally, Chuvash children were guaranteed the right to receive a Chuvash-language education, while all students regardless of ethnicity were to be required to study Chuvash as a subject.[11] These provisions made Chuvashia's language

---

[9] Draft language law, published in *Sovetskaia Chuvashia*, 17 August 1990.
[10] Chuvash State Archive, f. 1041, op. 6, d. 1899 and 1899a.
[11] Chuvash Republic Language Law, published in *Sovetskaia Chuvashia*, 27 October 1990.

Outcomes

TABLE 7.3. *Regional language laws*

Date of adoption	
Tatarstan	July 8, 1992
Bashkortostan	January 21, 1999
Chuvashia	October 27, 1990
Khakassia	October 20, 1992
Role of Russian	
Tatarstan	State language
Bashkortostan	State language
Chuvashia	State language
Khakassia	State language and language of interethnic communication
Language of laws	
Tatarstan	Laws are adopted and published in Tatar and Russian
Bashkortostan	Laws are adopted in Bashkir and Russian and published in Bashkir, Russian, and Tatar
Chuvashia	Laws are adopted and published in Chuvash and Russian
Khakassia	Laws are published in Russian and Khakass
Language requirements for employers	
Tatarstan	At least some bilingual employees within ten years
Bashkortostan	None
Chuvashia	At least some bilingual employees within ten years, bonuses for bilingualism among government employees
Khakassia	None
Language of instruction	
Tatarstan	Tatar and Russian required for all students
Bashkortostan	Bashkir and Russian required for all students
Chuvashia	Chuvash required for all students
Khakassia	Russian required for all students, Khakass required only for ethnic Khakass students
Language development programs	
Tatarstan	All languages, with special emphasis on Tatar
Bashkortostan	Government has special responsibility for Bashkir language
Chuvashia	Special emphasis on promotion of Chuvash throughout text of law
Khakassia	All languages

law the most favorable toward the titular language of all of the adopted language laws.

In Tatarstan, nationalist leaders also sought to make Tatar the only official state language. After heated debate in the press and in the Supreme Soviet, legislators rejected this idea, instead giving Tatar and Russian equal status. Nonetheless, the law significantly increased the status of the Tatar language, requiring that the government conduct its business and publish its laws in Tatar as well as in Russian. As in the other republics, signs and place names were to be displayed in both languages. The courts, media, industrial enterprises, public transport, and scientific and cultural institutions were also required to use both languages in conducting their affairs and in interacting with the public. However, unlike Chuvashia, Tatarstan did not mandate financial bonuses for state workers who displayed knowledge of both languages. The law did require schools to devote equal time to the study of both languages, irrespective of the dominant ethnicity of the schoolchildren attending the school. The law also mandated the development of a program for the preservation and development of the Tatar language, including provisions for broadening Tatar-language education and expanding Tatar publishing and television and radio broadcasting.[12] While legally enshrining linguistic equality between the two dominant ethnic groups, the republic's language law also established legal authority for the government to pursue a broad agenda of Tatar cultural revival.

By comparison, Khakassia's language law was more limited in its scope. Like the other republics, Khakassia declared both Russian and Khakass to be state languages with equal rights. However, in Khakassia not even the nationalist movement openly advocated the establishment of Khakass as the sole official language. Instead, nationalists focused on ensuring that ethnic Khakass students had access to Khakass-language education and on mandating equal status for the Khakass language in government activity and in the publication of laws. In addition, the law established the usual requirements for bilingual street signs and the presence of translators at government meetings.[13] However, unlike the language laws in the other republics, schoolchildren from all ethnic groups were not required to study both official languages, nor did the law make special provision for the development of the Khakass language. The Khakass language law was thus the least supportive of the nationalist agenda of cultural revival.

In Bashkortostan, the proposed language law quickly became the most controversial piece of legislation in the republic. A 1992 draft, based on a BNC proposal and the language laws of several union republics, called for Bashkir to be declared the sole state language so that the Bashkir people and their culture could be preserved. Russian was relegated to the status of the language of interethnic communication, while other minority languages would have official status in regions populated by those groups (Guboglo 1992a, 235–43). This proposal was widely criticized by non-Bashkir groups, both for making Bashkir the only official state language and for ignoring the status of Tatar entirely. Tatars were also angered by articles stating that book publishing and television broadcasting in the republic would be in Bashkir

---

[12] "Zakon o Iazykakh," *Vedomosti Verkhovnogo Soveta Tatarstana*, no. 6 (1992): 3–10.
[13] Khakass Language Law, text in author's possession.

and Russian and that state theaters would stage performances in Bashkir and Russian, while Tatar performances would be staged by "concert brigades." Because the establishment of a state Tatar theater and the expansion of book publishing and television broadcasting in Tatar were among the most prominent demands of the republic's Tatar nationalist movement, these articles were seen as a deliberate insult to the Tatar nation. An article declaring it a duty for all individuals to know their native language and to teach it to their children became a source of conflict with the Tatar-speaking Bashkir population, who feared that it would be used to force members of their community to switch to the Bashkir language. Finally, both Russian- and Tatar-speakers opposed the proposal that the study of Bashkir be required for all students regardless of nationality.

In later versions of the draft language law, Bashkir nationalists and government officials sought to create a partial compromise by according Bashkir and Russian equal status. However, continued conflict over the status of the Tatar language eventually led to the suspension of efforts to pass a language law. These efforts were renewed in the wake of a 1998 Russian Constitutional Court decision that the government could not exclude non-Bashkir speakers from seeking to be elected republic president unless Bashkir were made an official language of the republic. The new language law that was passed in January 1999 declared only Bashkir and Russian to be official state languages. The exclusion of Tatar from the list of official languages led to widespread protest and an increase in interethnic tension in the republic.[14]

A comparison of the four republics' experience with adopting language laws shows that the strength of nationalist movements was imperfectly correlated with the adoption of laws that supported titular cultural revival. Instead, a language law's strength largely reflected the region's demographic balance. Despite the relative weakness of its nationalist movement when compared to that of Tatarstan, the most radical language law was adopted in Chuvashia, the one republic with a sizeable titular majority. Although Tatarstan had a very strong nationalist movement, its population was evenly divided between titulars and Russians, and its language law was somewhat less radical than that of Chuvashia. Finally, Khakassia and Bashkortostan, the two republics where the titular ethnic group made up a minority of the total population, initially adopted, respectively, a weak language law and no language law at all. While strong nationalist movements were able to push regional governments into drafting radical language laws, such laws were adopted only in republics where the titular ethnic group made up a substantial proportion of the population.

---

[14] "Zakon 'O iazykakh narodov respubliki Bashkortostan' vstupil v deistvie," *Izvestiia Bashkortostana*, 16 April 1999; "Tatars Protest Bashkortostan Language Law," *RFE/RL Newsline*, 21 January 1999.

Symbols[15]

Nationalist movements recognized the role played by state symbols in sending a message to both citizens and outsiders about the type of state that had been created and whom it claimed to represent. In all of the republics, nationalists pressed the government to adopt state flags, seals, and hymns that represented the traditions and symbols of the titular ethnic group. Republics in which titulars represented a minority of the population adopted more universal symbols that sought to represent the entire population of the republic, whereas republics where titulars were a majority were less concerned about offending the non-titular population.[16] Thus, Chuvashia adopted the most clearly ethnic Chuvash symbols, while Bashkortostan adopted symbols that struck a balance between the ethnic and civic versions of the nation. Tatarstan was somewhere in between, while Khakassia had not yet begun to discuss state symbols at the time this research was completed.

In Tatarstan, nationalist leaders were mostly successful in enshrining ethnic Tatar symbols as the symbols of the newly sovereign republic, although not without significant conflict and a few setbacks. The nationalists sought to ensure that the symbols reflected "the people who gave the republic its name" and their "one thousand year tradition of ... statehood."[17] While some nationalists called for the flag to bear a crescent moon, in the end the flag avoided such blatant Islamic symbolism. The adopted design consisted of two large fields of green and red, with a small white line separating them and no central symbol (Dmitriev and Malakhova 1995, 319). Although the crescent was absent, the green color was intended to emphasize the Tatar connection to the rest of the Turkic and Muslim world. The new state seal had stronger ethnic Tatar associations, including a winged white leopard in the center, the leopard having been a symbol of the Tatar state since the fifteenth century.[18] In addition, the surrounding border was described as consisting of a "Tatar national ornamental design." The state hymn was written by a prominent ethnic Tatar composer. The government of Tatarstan thus sought to adopt state symbols that subtly accentuated the idea of Tatarstan as a Tatar state, without alienating the relatively numerous non-Tatar population.

In Bashkortostan, the nationalist movement had mixed success in persuading the government to adopt ethnic Bashkir symbols. Although all sides agreed that the republic flag should include the colors of the flag used by the Bashkir nationalist movement during the Russian Civil War, official descriptions of the flag noted that the colors represented more innocuous, nonethnic

---

[15] In this section, and particularly when discussing Tatarstan and Bashkortostan, I rely on the discussion of state symbols in Graney (1998).
[16] At the time of my research, no state symbols had been adopted in Khakassia.
[17] *Sovetskaia Tataria*, 18 November 1990, quoted in Graney (1998, 14).
[18] According to one commentator on the parliamentary debate, the wings were added as a compromise with an alternative proposal to have a dragon as the symbol (Allyn n.d.).

ideas. Thus, the entry for "state flag" in the *Bashkortostan Encyclopedia* reads, "The blue color represents the sky, clarity, good deeds, and the honest thoughts of the republic's peoples; white – the air, peace, openness and readiness to work together; and green – the earth, freedom, wisdom, and eternal life" (Shakurov 1996, 611). In the flag's center was placed a symbolic *kurai*, a native plant whose seven leaves were said to represent the friendship and unity of the seven ancient Bashkir tribes. Although the *kurai* was a traditional Bashkir symbol, it was described in official publications primarily as a symbol of friendship and unity, deemphasizing its ethnic nature. Similarly, the state seal included a representation of the eighteenth-century Bashkir national hero Salavat Iulaev. Although Iulaev was the leader of an anti-Russian rebellion, he was seen as a safe choice because of his status as a national hero during the Soviet period, when his rebellion was portrayed as part of a multiethnic struggle against tsarist oppression. The representation of Iulaev was chosen over a white wolf symbol, which represented an ancient Bashkir totem (Graney 1998, 38). By selecting symbols that possessed dual meaning as both ethnic Bashkir and multiethnic symbols, the leaders of Bashkortostan struck a balance between adopting symbols that represented Bashkir statehood and reflecting the republic's multiethnic population.

In Chuvashia, the parliamentary commission that was charged with developing state symbols for the newly sovereign republic was controlled by the nationalist movement. The commission sought to adopt symbols that embodied the history of the Chuvash people and its right to self-determination.[19] The state seal and flag that it approved strongly emphasized Chuvash symbology. The Chuvash state seal and flag are purple and yellow, both traditional Chuvash colors. Purple represents "the eternal striving of the nation for freedom, which allowed it to preserve its traditions and unique character (*samobytnost'*)," while yellow is considered the most beautiful color in Chuvash mythology. Both the seal and flag use the "tree of life," which symbolizes the long historical path of the Chuvash nation. The flag also includes the ancient Chuvash "three suns" emblem. The republic's national anthem uses the traditional Chuvash melody "Tavan Sershyv," with words written by a prominent Chuvash poet.[20] Because the vast majority of the republic's population is ethnically Chuvash, the government did not view the adoption of ethnic Chuvash symbols as a politically dangerous act.

In selecting its state symbols, each newly sovereign republic faced a choice between symbols that represented the titular ethnic group and symbols with a more universal meaning that could represent the entire population. This

---

[19] "Plan for National State Symbols of the Chuvash Republic," *Sovetskaia Chuvashia*, 26 December 1990.
[20] See *Express Inform*, 14 January 1992, and *Chavash En – Express Vypusk*, 3 June 1992, for representations and descriptions of these symbols. See also ⟨http://www.cap.ru/cap/PORTRET/simvol.htm⟩.

choice was an important one, as these symbols would tell the outside world whether the state should be perceived as primarily an ethnic homeland of the titular population or as a multiethnic, territorially based republic. The choice depended primarily on the proportion of the total population made up by the titular group. A higher titular percentage made the public representation of the republic as an ethnic homeland politically more acceptable, allowing the adoption of ethnically based state symbols.

Nationalist Movements and the Creation of an Institutional Framework for Ethnic Revival

Nationalist movements played an important role in setting the agenda for local debates on the creation of the new republic institutions associated with sovereignty. Strong nationalist movements were able to enshrine a special role for the titular ethnic group in the republic's political life and to maximize the region's independence from the central government in initial drafts of republic sovereignty declarations, constitutions, and language laws. However, the strength of the nationalist movement was not a good predictor of the government's ability to *enact* radical laws. In several cases, the initial drafts underwent extensive revision, with the final versions limiting both the republic's independence and the special role of the titular ethnic group. The extent to which nationalist demands were retained in the final versions of these laws depended on the demographic balance between titulars and nontitulars. Governments in republics where the titular population represented at least a plurality of the population were more willing to go along with nationalist demands, particularly in institutionalizing a special role for the titular ethnic group.

IMPLEMENTING THE NATIONALIST AGENDA

Although the nationalist movements had mixed success in creating a legal and symbolic framework for ethnic revival, they were able to gain government support for implementing ethnic revival programs. All four republics adopted policies and programs based on portions of the nationalist agenda, although both their goals and their abilities to implement the programs varied. This government-sponsored drive for ethnic revival included efforts to promote titular language and culture, to expand titular-language education, and to give preferential treatment to members of the titular group in education, government employment, and economic development (Table 7.4). Taken together, these policies contradicted the constitutional emphasis in each republic on the construction of territorially based civic nations with equal rights for all ethnic groups. As the extent of these policies demonstrates, although nationalists failed to take power in any of these regions, they succeeded in making their agenda the agenda of the political elites.

TABLE 7.4. *Regional ethnic revival policies*

Revival program	
Tatarstan	Program for implementation of language law
Bashkortostan	Bashkir cultural development program
Chuvashia	Program for implementation of language law
Khakassia	Program for linguistic development and program for cultural development in the republic
Date of adoption	
Tatarstan	July 1994
Bashkortostan	June 1996
Chuvashia	May 1993
Khakassia	October 1994 (language) and December 1995 (culture)
Language and culture	
Tatarstan	Salary bonus for language knowledge; list of professions requiring language knowledge; Tatar publishing; Tatar university
Bashkortostan	Quotas for Bashkirs in education and employment; economic development of Bashkir-populated districts
Chuvashia	List of professions requiring language knowledge; quotas for university admission; Chuvash publishing
Khakassia	Educational stipends for ethnic Khakass; Khakass publishing
Titular education	
Tatarstan	All Tatars study in Tatar; Tatar language required subject in all schools
Bashkortostan	Bashkirs increasingly study in Bashkir; attempt to make Bashkir language required subject in all schools failed
Chuvashia	Chuvash study in Chuvash or take language as subject; Chuvash language required subject in all schools
Khakassia	Khakass study Khakass language as subject; no effort at mandatory language requirement until summer 1998
Indigenous preferences	
Tatarstan	Medium – only in government
Bashkortostan	Extensive – in government, education, and industry
Chuvashia	Low – in government and in education
Khakassia	None

Cultural Development

All four republics adopted at least one program for the development of the culture and/or language of the titular ethnic group. Khakassia adopted three such programs. These programs introduced concrete measures to spur the revival of the titular culture and language, most prominently through increasing spending on titular-language publications and media, mandating titular-language use in government activity and, in some cases, making bilingualism a requirement for certain job categories. The extent to which these programs were implemented varied among the republics, with some focusing primarily on the most publicly visible aspects of cultural revival, while others sought to ensure that the titular language was used broadly.

Tatarstan's leaders took several concrete steps to spur the revival of Tatar culture and language. While the effect of the government's efforts to promote Tatar cultural development was largely limited to members of the titular ethnic group, the promotion of the Tatar language could be felt by all inhabitants, including the Russian population.

After the republic language law was adopted in 1992, the government focused its initial implementation efforts on increasing the use of Tatar in printed matter and on public signs, as well as taking steps to allow Tatar-language study for nonspeakers. In its March 1993 decree on initial measures for the implementation of the language law, the government required the replacement of all Russian-language public signs with signs printed in both Tatar and Russian, sought an increase in the publication of Tatar-language books – singling out in particular language textbooks and dictionaries – and declared that libraries must expand their Tatar-language collections. To promote Tatar-language instruction, it required television and radio stations to conduct language study programs. Russian and Tatar newspapers were also required to print materials on Tatar-language study. Local governments were required to organize Tatar-language courses for Russian speakers, while the Ministry of Education was to develop measures for introducing the study of Tatar into school curricula. Universities were required to open new programs for training Tatar-language teachers and to allow all students to take their entrance exams in Tatar. At the same time, the decree was largely silent on efforts to require Tatar use in government offices and commercial activity (Guboglo 1994, 308–12).

In general, the provisions dealing with publishing and signs were more likely to be implemented than the provisions dealing with language learning. All public signs and official announcements on public transport quickly became bilingual. Tatar grammar lessons appeared on television and in newspapers. A wide variety of Tatar-language publications began to appear in bookstores. At the same time, financial problems and a lack of qualified specialists ensured that few adult Tatar-language classes were organized, that most universities continued to hold Russian-language entrance exams for departments where instruction was in Russian, and that Russian continued to be the predominant language in offices and on the street.

Nonetheless, a June 1993 report on the law's implementation in Naberezhnye Chelny, Tatarstan's second-largest city, found that the city government was conducting its business in both languages, taking measures to expand Tatar-language education, and increasing access to Tatar-language materials in city libraries. The picture of language revival in Chelny was far less rosy outside the government sphere. Most industrial and commercial enterprises, the report found, had made no effort to conform to the language law and were continuing to conduct their affairs exclusively in Russian.[21]

To speed up implementation, in the summer of 1994 the Supreme Soviet adopted the "state program for the preservation, study, and development of the languages of the peoples of the Tatarstan Republic." Despite its name, this program was almost entirely devoted to the preservation, study, and development of a single language, Tatar. Of the program's 126 sections, 67 were devoted explicitly to Tatar. Another 26 did not mention Tatar explicitly but, in light of existing conditions, could be assumed to have addressed it primarily. Only 33 sections addressed all of the languages spoken in Tatarstan equally, and none addressed Russian exclusively.

This program was much broader than the initial implementation decree. Some of its more important specific recommendations included the creation of a list of professions that required knowledge of both state languages, the authorization of a 15 percent salary bonus for workers in those professions who knew both languages, and the establishment of a Tatar national state university.[22]

This program led to a rapid increase in the use of Tatar in public life. Participation in Tatar-language classes for adults increased, and the ethnic Russian vice-president of the republic was the most visible student. Synchronous translation became available for parliamentary debates. Several new Tatar-language journals and newspapers became available, including children's periodicals.[23] Radio and television broadcasting in Tatar increased by several hours per week (Malik 1994, 30). Traditional Tatar place names replaced Russian and Soviet ones throughout the republic (Garipova 1993, 214). Most significantly, this campaign for Tatar revival resulted in an increase in Tatar usage outside the home – on the street, at school, and in the workplace (Sharypova 1993, 194).

Direct promotion of Tatar culture had less impact on non-Tatars than did language policy. Tatars, on the other hand, were subjected to an unceasing bombardment of Tatar culture. By 1995, 1,645 Tatar clubs, over 100 folklore ensembles, and 1,063 Tatar libraries had been established throughout the republic. The government created a state center for the collection and dissemination of Tatar folklore, conducted several conferences on Tatar culture, and initiated many ethnic festivals, contests, and holiday celebrations. A newly opened Center for Tatar Culture actively promoted national music,

---

[21] "O khode realizatsii Zakona Respubliki Tatarstan 'O iazykakh narodov Respubliki Tatarstan' Naberezhno-Chelninskim gorodskim Sovetom narodnykh deputatov i gorodskoi administratsiei," *Vedomosti Verkhovnogo Soveta Tatarstana*, no. 6–7 (1993): 46–8.
[22] *Vedomosti Verkhovnogo Soveta Tatarstana*, no. 8–9 (1994): 3–19.
[23] Interviews and personal observation during research trips in November 1995, April 1996, and March 1998.

arts, and crafts. Over 240 mosques were opened (Abdullin et al. 1993). The media also played a prominent role in the promotion of Tatar culture. Articles describing Tatar history, art, and music appeared constantly in Tatar- and Russian-language newspapers. Television and radio were filled with cultural programming. In three years, the Tatar cultural revival had become a major component of government policy.

The Chuvash government did not delay in implementing its language law, setting up a commission for this purpose in April 1991.[24] In 1992, concerned about lagging implementation efforts, the government decided to expand the publication of Chuvash-language textbooks, to increase the number of students in the Chuvash philology departments at the Chuvash State University and the Chuvash State Teachers' Institute, to create a fund for the revival of Chuvash schools, and to declare April 25 Chuvash Language Day as a means of popularizing Chuvash-language study (Khuzangai and Kirillov 1993, 40–1). In May 1993, the government adopted a full-scale implementation program for the language law. Like the Tatar program, and despite its neutral name, this was essentially a program for the development of the Chuvash language, with 80 percent of its sections devoted exclusively to Chuvash (Khuzangai and Kirillov 1993, 58–73). It included a list of professions and positions that would require Chuvash-language knowledge, created short Chuvash courses for people who would need to use the language on the job, and established a Chuvash radio program. In the educational sphere, the law required the introduction of the Chuvash language as a subject in all republic schools and universities, the opening of new Chuvash teachers' training institutes and an institute of Chuvash culture, and the establishment of quotas for Chuvash applicants to arts and music departments of major universities. Because it included provisions for mandatory knowledge of Chuvash as a condition for holding particular jobs, and because it explicitly supported quotas for Chuvash applicants in higher education, this program was much more radical in its support of Chuvash cultural revival than the corresponding program in Tatarstan.

Implementation of the program's provisions was an entirely different matter. While most of the proposals that affected the public status of the Chuvash language were put into effect, proposals that affected the private linguistic behavior of individuals, including language requirements for employment and ethnic quotas at universities, were for the most part ignored. Thus, most government offices continued to use Russian in their work, but all official documents were translated into Chuvash for publication. Russian schoolchildren were required to study the Chuvash language but did not

---

[24] "Polozhenie o Komissii Prezidiuma Verkhovnogo Soveta Chuvashskoi Respubliki po realizatsii zakona 'O iazykakh v Chuvashskoi Respublike,'" 18 April 1991, in Khuzangai and Kirillov (1993, 32).

have occasion to use it outside of class. The promised classes for adults failed to materialize altogether. At the same time, an increase in the number of Chuvash-language publications and an expansion of Chuvash-language programming on radio and television ensured that the Chuvash language became more visible in public life.[25] For similar reasons, the government attached a great deal of significance to making street signs bilingual. The government appeared to recognize that balancing the use of the Chuvash and Russian languages would take a long time and that attempts to force people to learn and speak Chuvash could backfire. Raising the language's visibility and public status were thus seen as initial steps on the long path toward acceptance of bilingualism by the population.

After a cautious start, Bashkir leaders began to pursue an increasingly broad program of Bashkir ethnic revival. Once they firmly controlled the government, these leaders began to make increasingly ambitious plans for promoting Bashkir interests throughout the republic. The most ambitious plan was the state program for the rebirth and development of the Bashkir people, adopted in November 1996 (Uraksin and Valiakhmetov 1995).[26] Unlike the ostensibly multiethnic language law implementation programs in Tatarstan and Chuvashia, this program was dedicated explicitly to the development of Bashkir culture.[27] It called for establishing quotas and separate programs for Bashkirs applying to universities and enacting mandatory quotas for Bashkirs in all spheres of employment within five years. Financing for this program, which also included the standard articles on expanding publishing and promoting culture, was to come from a special fund dedicated to Bashkir cultural development.

Because of its late start, Bashkir cultural revival had only begun to have an impact on language use in the republic at the time fieldwork for this study was completed. Although bilingual signs had appeared on all government buildings, Russian remained the language of choice inside those buildings. While Bashkir-language publishing and television broadcasting had increased somewhat, the quotas for Bashkirs in education and employment had not yet been implemented. However, the adoption of the state program for Bashkir rebirth and development in 1996 promised a new effort on the part of the authorities to ensure the dominant role of Bashkir culture and language in the republic. Some steps in this direction soon followed. By 1997

[25] S. Iu., "Chuvashia," *Politicheskii Monitor*, May 1993: 72.
[26] The description of this program is based on the published draft, which was submitted for parliamentary approval and adopted without major substantive changes.
[27] The program is admittedly part of a larger project whose end result will be the promulgation of similar development programs for all of the republic's major ethnic groups, as well as a composite state program for all of the peoples of Bashkortostan. However, it is telling that this program was completed long before the other ones. For a discussion of the composite program, see Kuzeev (1997).

there had been a renewed emphasis on Bashkir-language education, an increase in the percentage of Bashkirs admitted to universities, and an increase in the number of Bashkirs in top government positions (Guboglo et al. 1997).

The Khakass government adopted separate programs for language development, cultural development, and the development of the Khakass ethnic group. These programs included measures to develop Khakass education in schools and universities, to conduct Khakass festivals and holiday celebrations, to support traditional arts and crafts, to publish books in Khakass and about Khakassia, to improve the health of the indigenous population, to give stipends to gifted Khakass children, to establish several new institutes and programs for Khakass study, to preserve historical and archeological monuments, to establish local Khakass newspapers, to establish Khakass-language courses for Khakass adults, and to expand Khakass cultural establishments such as theaters, musical ensembles, and libraries.[28]

The republic government quickly began to carry out many of these provisions. Khakass publishing increased over the next several years; a program for the revitalization of the State Language and Literature Institute was developed; state-sponsored ethnic festivals were thriving; and a center for traditional arts and handicrafts was established. At the same time, progress was limited by a lack of funds and by the precedence given to more general needs such as social programs and economic restructuring. Khakass-language signs in public places remained rare, and costly projects such as building a new home for the Khakass theater were delayed.

Khakass leaders also failed to implement those aspects of their revival programs that dealt with the state bureaucracy. Provisions that were not implemented included the introduction of Khakass-language use in government, the creation of a fund for Khakass ethnic development, and an increase in the number of government workers dealing with ethnic issues. The possibility of teaching Khakass language or history to non-Khakass students had not even been raised by 1996.[29]

In the years after sovereignty was declared, all four republics took steps to foster titular cultural revival. All four adopted extensive programs designed to ensure the continued development of the titular language and culture. However, the extent to which the adoption of these programs translated into action varied. Cultural revival went furthest in Tatarstan, the region that combined strong nationalist feelings with an institutional framework of language laws and constitutional articles that legitimated special measures

---

[28] State program for the preservation and development of the languages of the peoples of the Khakass republic, in Abakan (1994); program for the rebirth and spiritual development of the Khakass ethnos, published in *Vestnik Khakassii*, no. 51 (1995); and Republic of Khakassia cultural development program, in Abakan (1996).

[29] These observations come from fieldwork carried out in Khakassia in June 1996.

for the development of the titular language and culture. In regions where nationalist feeling was weaker, such as Chuvashia and Khakassia, revival programs were only partially implemented. Finally, in Bashkortostan, the lack of a language law delayed and complicated the start of an ethnic revival program despite the strength of nationalist feeling and the desire of the relevant government ministries to implement such a revival.

Education

All of the republics focused on expanding the system of titular-language education. Whereas before 1990, titular-language education was largely confined to remote rural areas, during the 1990s the republic governments focused on introducing titular-language education into the cities. In the process, they sought to transform schools where students studied the titular language as a subject into schools where all subjects were taught in the titular language. Two of the republics went further, introducing mandatory instruction in the titular language for the non-titular population. Finally, all four republics added classes on the history and culture of the titular ethnic group to the required curriculum.

Other than the expansion of the official functions of the Tatar language, the most significant aspect of the Tatar ethnic revival was the expansion of Tatar-language education. This expansion included both an increase in Tatar-language education for Tatar children and the introduction of the Tatar language and Tatar history as required subjects for non-Tatar schoolchildren. A Tatar education plan was approved by the Education Ministry in 1991. Its basic principles stated that the educational process must be based on the idea of Tatar national rebirth, that education should be provided in the child's native language, and that a Tatar environment needs to be fostered in all Tatar schools. The plan called for a special state fund for the development of Tatar schools that would receive priority in government funding. It also called for mandatory Tatar-language instruction for Russian children.[30] This last provision was later included in the language and education laws, which required that equal instruction in Russian and Tatar be provided in all schools and kindergartens in Tatarstan.[31]

The growth of Tatar-language education since the adoption of the sovereignty declaration has been unprecedented. Between 1991 and 1995, the proportion of ethnic Tatar students who study all subjects in their native language increased from 28% to 43%. It has continued to rise since then. The increase in urban areas, from 4% in 1991 to 28% in 1995, is particularly

---

[30] "Plan for the Development of Tatar Education," *Panorama*, no. 8 (1991): 15–30.
[31] Republic of Tatarstan Language Law, published in *Vedomosti Verkhovnogo Soveta Tatarstana*, June 1992; Republic of Tatarstan Education Law, published in *Vedomosti Verkhovnogo Soveta Tatarstana*, October 1993.

noteworthy.[32] Whereas before sovereignty, virtually no non-Tatar schoolchildren studied the Tatar language, in 1993 Tatar became a required subject in all of the republic's schools. Beginning in that year, Ministry of Education study plans called for four to five hours per week of Tatar-language instruction in each grade in all Russian-language schools. Tatar-language schools were to devote seven hours per week to Tatar in early grades, and four hours per week in high school. All schoolchildren in the republic were required to spend one hour per week in grades five, eight, and nine studying the history of Tatarstan and its people.[33] At the same time, language instruction outside the regular school system also increased. The number of Sunday Tatar-language schools increased from eight to twenty in one year. Universities expanded Tatar-language departments, creating new ones where they previously had not existed and conducting optional Tatar-language classes for interested students (Gaifullin 1996). Over a five-year period, exposure to Tatar-language instruction thus became ubiquitous for both ethnic Tatar and ethnic Russian students.

A similar expansion of titular-language education took place in Chuvashia. As early as February 1992 the number of hours devoted to Chuvash-language study was increased, as were the number of schools and kindergartens where the language was taught.[34] Within another year, several specialized Chuvash schools had been opened, and Chuvash language and history textbooks were being published with the assistance of George Soros's Cultural Initiative Foundation (Maliutin 1994, 15). Newly developed school lesson plans devoted four to six hours per week to Chuvash-language study in Chuvash schools, and three hours per week in multi-ethnic schools. In addition, one hour per week in grades ten and eleven in Russian ethnic schools was devoted to Chuvash literature.[35] Unlike officials in Tatarstan and Bashkortostan, Chuvash officials emphasized study of the Chuvash language over the teaching of all subjects in the Chuvash language.[36] Correspondingly, between 1990 and 1995 the number of students studying Chuvash as a subject rose from 45,000 to 80,000. The number of students studying all subjects in Chuvash rose much more slowly at first, increasing by only 700 students between 1990 and 1993, although the increase thereafter was quite rapid: the number of students in Chuvash-language classes had doubled (from 32,000 to 64,000) by 1995.[37] The expansion of Chuvash-language use thus included both an

---

[32] Republic of Tatarstan Ministry of Education data. See also Gaifullin, "Shkola Zavtrashnego Onia," *Tatarstan*, no. 7–8 (1995): 15.
[33] *Vestnik Ministerstva Narodnogo Obrazovaniia Respubliki Tatarstan*, August 1993: 10, 51–5.
[34] "Na Kontrole – Zakon o Iazykakh," *Narodnaia Shkola*, no. 2 (1992).
[35] Lesson plans, published in *Narodnaia Shkola*, no. 5 (1994).
[36] Interview with Minister of Culture Vitalii Ivanov, February 1996.
[37] The 1990 and 1993 numbers are from Goskomstat Rossii (1995, 92); the 1995 numbers are from the Chuvash Ministry of Education.

increase in its role in the education of ethnic Chuvash and an increase in the overall number of potential speakers of the language in the republic.

Bashkir-language education was long considered vital to Bashkir ethnic consolidation because of the large number of ethnic Bashkirs who spoke Tatar and their tendency over time to reidentify as ethnic Tatars (Gorenburg 1999). Attempts to convert Tatar-language schools in these areas into Bashkir-language schools were made intermittently starting in the 1970s (Khalim 1991). The current government has largely ended this practice, concentrating instead on converting Russian-language schools with predominantly Bashkir students into Bashkir-language schools. This practice has been justified by reference to the republic's education law, which gave all citizens the right to receive a native-language education and stated that ethnic schools were responsible for developing ethnic consciousness, culture, and traditions through teaching in the native language.[38]

As a result of this expansion of Bashkir-language schooling, the Ministry of Education has reported a 6% increase (20,000 students) in the number of students receiving a Bashkir-language education between 1988 and 1995. Overall, 39% of Bashkir schoolchildren studied in their own language in 1995, while another 32% studied Bashkir as a subject. If we consider that only 75% of all Bashkirs consider Bashkir to be their native language, it appears that by 1995 most Bashkir-speaking schoolchildren were studying their native language.[39] An additional 100 schools were planning to introduce Bashkir-language instruction by 1997, as schools increasingly began to shift from teaching Bashkir as a subject to full instruction in Bashkir.

Following the example of Tatarstan, Bashkortostan's Ministry of Education decided to require all non-Tatar schoolchildren in the republic to study Bashkir for two hours per week starting in the 1994 school year. In addition, one hour per week in four grades was to be spent studying the republic's history and geography.[40] After protests from local Russian organizations, this plan was suspended, and Bashkir-language instruction was made available on a voluntary basis beginning in 1994.[41] This voluntary initiative proved to be quite successful, with the number of non-Bashkirs studying Bashkir doubling to over 50,000 between 1992 and 1995.[42] However, the inability of the Bashkir government to enforce Bashkir-language study for

---

[38] *Zakony Respubliki Bashkortostan*, Vol. V.
[39] The 1988 data is in Safin (1997, 176–7); the 1995 data is from the Bashkortostan Ministry of Education; the data through 1994 has been published in Murzabulatov (1995).
[40] Tatars were exempt because it was recognized that the Tatar and Bashkir languages are mutually intelligible. Bashkortostan Ministry of Education, "Radi garmonizatsii mezhnatsionalnykh otnoshenii," *Vecherniaia Ufa*, 2 July 1993.
[41] Razif Abdullin, "Strasti po Iazyku," *Ekonomika i My*, no. 26 (1993); A. Shakirov, "V uchebnye plany vneseny korrektivy," *Vecherniaia Ufa*, 14 October 1993.
[42] Ministry of Education data for the 1992–3 and 1995–6 school years.

all students shows that despite Bashkir control of government institutions, the Bashkir ethnic group's weak demographic position in the republic has set limits on their ability to enact those aspects of the ethnic revival program that directly affect members of non-titular ethnic groups.

By comparison to the rapid expansion of titular-language education in the other three republics, the status of Khakass-language education presents a mixed picture. On the one hand, between 1989 and 1995, 28 new ethnic schools were established. On the other hand, although 70% of Khakass children studied their native language in school in 1995, this figure represented only a 2% increase since 1989. Furthermore, only 7% of Khakass children were studying in Khakass-language schools. The lack of Khakass-language education prompted nationalist leaders to argue that a few hours a day of language instruction was insufficient to counter the assimilative power of the Russian-language milieu that surrounded Khakass children.[43] As of 1996, Khakass leaders had failed to establish a Khakass school in the capital city or to expand Khakass-language schooling beyond one elite boarding school and a few village schools in the mostly mono-ethnic southern regions of the republic. Up to that time, there had been no discussion of introducing instruction in the Khakass language for the non-titular population. However, in July 1998 the republic's Ministry of Education approved a plan that would make Khakass language and history a required subject in all of the republic's schools.[44] If this plan is successfully implemented, it would mark a radical change in the role of the Khakass language in the republic, one that could not have been imagined even by the Khakass nationalist movement at its peak.

The expansion of titular-language education was supported by governments in all four republics. It was the focus and the extent of the expansion that varied somewhat. All four governments made it their first priority to ensure that all members of the titular ethnic group learned the group's language. In Bashkortostan and Tatarstan, where an extensive native-language education system continued to function in rural areas through the end of the Soviet period, this meant extending native-language education to the cities. In Chuvashia and Khakassia, where native-language education had been largely replaced by Russian-language education, with the titular language taught as a subject in some schools, the first priority was to ensure that all titular students attended classes where the titular language was taught. Only

---

[43] Data provided by the Khakass Ministry of Education; nationalist attitudes toward native language education are based on an interview with Valerii Ivandaev, chairman of the Khakass People's Congress, June 1996.
[44] "Khakassian Language to Become Required Subject in Republic," *RFE/RL Newsline*, 30 July 1998.

after this task had been accomplished did the republic administration begin to focus on transforming Russian-language schools in predominantly titular areas into titular-language schools.

The expansion of titular-language education also affected the non-titular population. Republics where the titular population made up 50% or more of the total population made the study of the titular language mandatory for all students. Republics where the titulars represented a minority of the total population either did not try to force non-titulars to learn the titular language (Khakassia) or were forced to renounce efforts to do so after strong popular protest (Bashkortostan).

Expanding Opportunities

The third aspect of ethnic revival implemented by republic governments involved the expansion of job opportunities for members of the titular population. In each republic, this expansion consisted of some combination of titular domination of top positions in government, an expansion of the number of jobs requiring knowledge of the titular language, and an increase in funding for economic development in areas with high titular concentrations. Where enacted successfully, these policies ensured that members of the titular group would maintain control of political life in the republic while gaining a disproportionate share of the economic benefits of sovereignty.

In Tatarstan, the ethnic Tatar governing elite moved quickly to ensure that ethnic Tatars would retain control of the republic government. The republic Constitution required the president of Tatarstan to know both Tatar and Russian, virtually ensuring that only Tatars would hold that office for the foreseeable future. The privileged position of Tatars in government, however, went beyond the top job. After the adoption of sovereignty legislation, the leadership of the republic became much more Tatar-dominated than it had ever been. One analyst argues that between 1990 and 1995, the elite structure changed from rough parity between Tatars and Russians to an 80/20 dominance in favor of Tatars (Spirin 1995, 87). Other data confirm this trend, showing that in 1995 Tatars made up 77% of the republic's political elite, up from 56.2% in 1990. Tatar representation in parliament also increased during this period, from 58% in 1990 to 73.3% in 1995 (Kaiser 1997, 20). While most sources argue that this political dominance is counterbalanced by Russian dominance in local industry, one Moscow observer believes that the economic elite has also undergone Tatarization.[45] Overall, it seems unquestionable that Tatars have a greater role in running the republic than they did in 1990, although whether this change extends beyond the political realm is difficult to document.

---

[45] Alexander Kasimov, "Tatarstan," *Politicheskii Monitor*, May 1993: 78.

This increase in titular representation in the executive and legislative branches of government occurred as a result of deliberate policy initiatives on the part of the ethnic Tatar ruling elite. Parliamentary overrepresentation was assured through the establishment of a territorial districting scheme that increased representation from less densely populated and predominantly Tatar rural districts at the expense of the denser urban districts where most of the Russian population resided. In the executive branch, the president had the power to select both members of the republic government and city and district heads of administration. He used this power to appoint personal supporters from his home area. Since the president was an ethnic Tatar, these supporters were also Tatars (Kaiser 1997, 12). Together, these actions by the governing elite ensured that Tatars would retain political authority in the republic.

The economic benefits of ethnic revival in Tatarstan were not limited to the political elite. The expansion of cultural programs in the republic increased the demand for employees who spoke Tatar. The newly established centers and programs required workers to staff and implement them. In the educational sphere alone, the Ministry of Education expanded its ethnic schools department; each county and city education department was required to hire an assistant department head in charge of ethnic education; and there was a vast increase in the number of openings for Tatar-language teachers in both cities and rural areas (Gaifullin 1996). The expansion of opportunities extended beyond the educational sphere into the private sector. According to the language law, each enterprise needed a Tatar-speaker to deal with Tatar-speaking customers. Although this provision was not enforced initially, in the long run it would serve to significantly improve job prospects for Tatar-speakers. Since almost no Russian had sufficient facility in Tatar to qualify for such a job, this provision of the language law would benefit ethnic Tatars almost exclusively.

While Tatar ethnic revival policies have significantly increased prospects for ethnic Tatars in the spheres of politics and employment, there is no evidence that the government of Tatarstan has sought to institute affirmative action programs for Tatars in university admissions or to redirect funds for economic development to predominantly Tatar districts. Higher education in Tatarstan continues to function according to an informal division wherein certain universities and institutes are known as predominantly Tatar, while others are known as predominantly Russian.[46] Similarly, funding allocated for new economic development in rural districts was not correlated with the ethnic balance in the districts (Goskomstat Tatarstana 1995, 124). Nonetheless, the ethnic revival policies that were implemented assured that Tatars would enjoy significant economic and political advantages in the republic.

---

[46] Based on discussions with Tatar university students, March 1998.

Bashkortostan has perhaps gone the furthest in favoring members of the titular ethnic group for top government positions. Like elites in the other republics, Bashkir political elites sought to ensure their continued control of the republic by requiring presidential candidates to know the Bashkir language. During the period following sovereignization, most top government positions were given to ethnic Bashkirs. Whereas in 1989 Bashkirs made up 27.7% of the republic's political elite, by 1996 they made up 67.5% of the Cabinet of Ministers and 58.5% of the district and city heads of administration. In the legislature, the percentage of Bashkirs increased from 34.0% in 1990 to 43.9% in 1995 (Kaiser 1997, 20–1; Galliamov 1997, 152–3). Perhaps most significantly, government officials themselves did not deny that Bashkirization was occurring. Sergei Kabashov, assistant director of the sociological department of the Bashkortostan Cabinet of Ministers, argued that Bashkirization is acceptable because it is natural for a leader to want to have supporters from his own group.[47] Similarly, Ildar Iulbarisov, the head of the department of international and ethnic issues in the presidential administration, noted that the president believes in setting ethnic quotas for top government positions.[48] According to one study, Bashkirization has gone beyond the heads of ministries to include "appointing Bashkirs to all even slightly powerful positions" (Filatov and Shchipkov 1996, 99). The means used by government officials to promote Bashkirization in government have been identical to those used in Tatarstan, with cronyism and rural overrepresentation commonplace.

One unique aspect of Bashkortostan's ethnic revival has been the concentration of economic development in predominantly Bashkir regions. The southeastern regions of the republic, where the Bashkir population is concentrated, have received development credits, and the bulk of foreign investment projects have been located there.[49] Several universities have opened branches in Sibai, the largest city in this region. The state program for the rebirth and development of the Bashkir people explicitly called for locating new industrial plants in the southeast and for expanding that region's socioeconomic infrastructure in general. Cultural and educational facilities in this region were also to be expanded; this was to include the creation of Bashkir theaters in southeastern cities, the opening of an art institute in Sibai, and the establishment of a Bashkir national university in Sibai by the end of 1996.[50] Some opposition figures believe that Bashkir leaders are preparing for the possibility of shifting the republic's capital to Sibai if they feel they

---

[47] Interview, December 1995.
[48] Ibid.
[49] "O polozhenii Tatar v Bashkirii," Bashkortostan Tatar Public Center report (1994): 1.
[50] "State Program for the Rebirth and Development of the Bashkir People (Ufa, 1995): 33, 53, 71.

can no longer control political life in the republic from largely non-Bashkir Ufa.[51]

The Chuvash nativization program appeared to be less extensive than its Tatar and Bashkir counterparts. This was partially because there was less need for such a program, and partially because the steps that were taken were less noticeable. Since 67 percent of the republic's population was Chuvash, it seemed quite normal for the majority of government officials to be Chuvash. At the same time, the demographic balance reduced the Chuvash elite's fears of Russian dominance, allowing them to react more easily to having some non-Chuvash in positions of power. This does not mean that Chuvash were not given certain privileges. As in the other two republics, the Constitution required that the president speak both government languages. In a context of partial linguistic assimilation, this meant that even ethnic Chuvash candidates for president were forced to take language exams in order to be registered by the republic's electoral commission (Voskhodov and Komarova 1995, 89). After 1990, Russians were partially squeezed out of top administrative posts, especially in the areas of cultural, educational, and media administration (Filippov 1994, 5). Even Nikolai Fedorov's administration, despite its public rejection of ethnic revival, included only two non-Chuvash in its thirteen-person Cabinet of Ministers.[52] This nativization occurred largely because of the same tendency toward appointing loyal allies that we observed in Tatarstan and Bashkortostan. However, Chuvashia was the only republic where local officials were elected, decreasing not only the republic government's control there but also the extent of nativization of local government. Furthermore, legislative districts were based on population rather than on territory, eliminating rural overrepresentation and thus minimizing titular overrepresentation. Although 76 percent of the deputies elected to the republic's Supreme Soviet in 1994 were ethnic Chuvash, this overrepresentation occurred because low turnout prevented the election of deputies in several urban districts. The proportion of Chuvash deputies in parliament was roughly equal to the Chuvash proportion of the population, excluding districts where new elections had been called (Voskhodov and Komarova 1995, 105). Despite these limitations, the combination of partial preferences in the republic administration and the creation of new positions for ethnic Chuvash in the fields of education and culture led to a substantial increase in employment opportunities in the governmental sphere for ethnic Chuvash.

Of the four republics examined in this study, Khakassia proved to be the only case where efforts to ensure titular control of political life in the republic

---

[51] Interview with Kaderle Imametdinov, editor of the Tatar newspaper *Idel-Ural*, November 1995.
[52] S. Iu., "Chuvashia," *Politicheskii Monitor*, January 1994: 91.

failed. The election of a non-titular head of the republic, Aleksei Lebed, who appointed members of his own circle of supporters to top positions, ensured that members of the titular ethnic elite would also be relatively absent at lower levels of the political hierarchy. The 100-member republic Supreme Soviet elected in 1991 included 13 titular deputies, a representation only slightly higher than the Khakass proportion of the republic's population and not enough to have a significant impact on legislation. Attempts to increase Khakass representation in the next parliament also failed. Of the four proposed versions of the Law on Parliament, three contained measures designed to guarantee a level of Khakass representation higher than their proportion of the population. Possible measures included gerrymandering to create minority-majority districts, adjusting representation levels to create smaller districts in Khakass areas, and basing electoral districts on administrative districts in order to overrepresent rural areas, where the majority of the ethnic Khakass population lived.[53] The law that was actually adopted rejected all such measures for boosting ethnic Khakass representation.[54]

Because the government was not controlled by members of the Khakass ethnic group, there were fewer opportunities for the titular ethnic group to have a dominant role at lower levels of the administrative hierarchy. At the same time, the steps taken to promote Khakass culture and language led to an increase in the demand for teachers, writers, and editors fluent in Khakass. Although these opportunities were not as extensive as in the republics where titular-language education was declared mandatory, they did signify a relative increase in the marketability of knowledge of the titular language and placed members of the titular ethnic group at an advantage in competing for an admittedly small share of jobs.

The expansion of job opportunities in the republics thus depended largely on the extent to which titular elites controlled the government of the republic prior to the beginning of the sovereignty drive and on the demographic balance between the titular and Russian ethnic groups. Titular elites sought to enact policies of ethnic preference to the extent necessary to ensure that they maintained control of the republic despite democratization. The most extensive program of preferences for titulars was implemented in Bashkortostan, the republic where the demographic balance among ethnic groups placed the titular elite in the greatest danger of losing control of the republic. The necessity of the policy thus depended on whether or not the titular ethnic group comprised a majority of the population. The extent of the policy depended on the difference between the actual size of the titular population and 50 percent. However, in regions such as Khakassia, where the titular political elite did not control the administration

---

[53] Draft laws on the Supreme Soviet, published in *Khakassia*, 23 November 1993.
[54] Law on the Supreme Soviet, adopted 20 October 1994, published in *Khakassia*, 11 November 1994.

prior to democratization, there was no opportunity to implement such a policy.

NATIONALIST INFLUENCE ON GOVERNMENT POLICY AND THE FUTURE OF NATIONALISM IN THE REPUBLICS

Nationalist movements played an important role in determining the political agendas of regional governments in all four regions. The policies of greater regional self-government and ethnic revival promoted by the movements, and initially opposed by the regional governments, gradually came to be accepted by local political elites. This change occurred in part because of political pressure by the nationalists, and in part because political elites recognized that these policies could be politically beneficial to them. Sovereignty would bring an increase in regional self-government and would thereby increase these elites' power vis-à-vis the central government, while ethnic revival would help to ensure that the elites, mostly composed of members of the titular ethnic group, would have an easier time retaining political control in the region. However, once these policies became part of the political agenda in the republics, the extent to which they were implemented had little relation to the strength of the nationalist movement. Instead, the demographic balance between titulars and non-titulars and the extent to which members of the titular political elite controlled the republic's political institutions were the critical factors in determining the scope of ethnic revival and sovereignization policies and the extent to which the adopted ethnic revival measures were actually implemented.

Although the actual impact of nationalist movements on the adoption of specific laws and programs was often minimal, their role was critical in setting the political agenda in the ethnic republics. While this agenda was later taken over by the governing elite, which sought to take full credit for these policies by minimizing the role of nationalist movements in their initial formulation, without pressure from the nationalist movements during the early period of political transformation, it is unlikely that political elites would have supported sovereignty and ethnic revival.

Despite their role in persuading republic governments to adopt policies of sovereignty and ethnic revival during the immediate post-Soviet period, nationalist movements in all four regions were unable to gain significant and lasting political influence. Nationalist leaders who had been elected to republic legislatures in 1990 and 1991 lost their seats in the next round of legislative elections, which took place in the mid-1990s. By adopting moderate versions of the nationalist agenda and portraying the nationalists as dangerous radicals, entrenched political elites in the republics were able to eliminate the nationalists as a viable political alternative. At the same time, these elites gradually consolidated control over the regions, eliminating the political opportunities that had made nationalist protest possible during the period of regime instability. By 1996, the nationalist movement organizations had lost most of their active supporters. In some republics, only a few dedicated activists remained in leadership positions. In others, the nationalist organizations were effectively moribund and existed only in name, the movement leaders having returned to full-time employment in other spheres.

Because regional political elites are now firmly entrenched in power and are pursuing moderate nationalist policies, it is unlikely that nationalist mobilization will reemerge as a strong political force in Russia's ethnic republics in the short or medium term.[55] It is possible that if the central government becomes stronger and seeks to curtail the political power of regional leaders and to reverse regional ethnic revival policies in the regions, powerful politicians in ethnic regions would mobilize the population against the central government. However, as long as the current generation of regional political leaders remains firmly in control, popular nationalist mobilization will not occur, and the nationalist opposition will continue to have its ideas co-opted by the government.

In the long run, however, a new round of nationalist activism is quite likely to occur. The ethnic revival policies enacted by the current regional governments have set the stage for a new cycle of ethnic mobilization in ten or twenty years. The strengthening of existing ethnic institutions and the establishment of new ethnic institutions will encourage a stronger sense of ethnic identity among members of the titular ethnic groups. In particular, the advent of universal titular-language education will slow the rate of Russification among the titular population. Considering the strong correlation between titular-language knowledge and support for nationalism described in the previous chapter, the titular-language education program is likely to result in stronger support for ethnic revival and regional separatism among the generations who will be educated in these newly titular schools. A new round of popular nationalist mobilization is therefore likely to take place after the current generation of political and cultural leaders passes from the scene, to be replaced by a new generation of leaders educated in a post–ethnic revival environment. This cohort will seek a more extensive role for the titular ethnic group in regional politics, further extension of the role of titular language and culture in the republics, and greater republic independence in political decision making. If at that time the central or regional governments show signs of weakness, cultural elites will again adopt the role of saviors of the national culture and mobilize the population in support of nationalism.

---

[55] These conclusions are based on analysis of the four cases but may be applied to all ethnic regions in the Russian Federation outside of the North Caucasus, where the political situation has been transformed by the violent conflict in Chechnya. In this region, nationalism is likely to remain a potent political force for the foreseeable future.

8

The Larger Picture

Support for Nationalism in Russia's Other Republics

To this point, I have developed the institutionalist explanation of ethnic mobilization on the basis of four ethnic regions of the Russian Federation: Bashkortostan, Chuvashia, Khakassia, and Tatarstan. In this chapter, I seek to test the validity of the theory by applying it to another fifteen ethnic groups in fourteen republics of the Russian Federation. The findings of this chapter further strengthen the ethnic institutions argument by showing that it applies not just to the selected republics, but to all of the major ethnic regions of the Russian Federation.

The rest of the chapter proceeds as follows: First, I discuss the measures of support for nationalism and examine the extent of support for nationalism in the selected cases. Then I use statistical analysis to determine which social groups are more likely to support nationalist ideas. Finally, I discuss the extent to which these data confirm the theory developed in the earlier chapters.

DATA AND EXPLANATORY VARIABLES

This chapter relies exclusively on the Colton/Hough survey described in Chapter 5. In addition to being conducted in Bashkortostan, Chuvashia, and Tatarstan, this survey was carried out in all of the former autonomous republics of the Russian Federation. We thus have an additional fifteen cases in fourteen republics.[1] Unfortunately, the Laitin/Hough survey used to supplement my results in Chapter 6 was not conducted in any of Russia's ethnic republics other than Bashkortostan and Tatarstan. For this reason, its findings on the effect of native-language education and use on ethnic mobilization cannot be confirmed in the larger sample. As in Chapter 6, I use

---

[1] I treat the Kabardin and Balkars of Kabardino-Balkaria as two separate cases. For ease of comparison, I repeat some of the information for Bashkortostan, Chuvashia, and Tatarstan that was presented in Chapters 5 and 6.

least-squares (OLS) regression to isolate the effects of belonging to each of the various social groups on support for nationalism. I also use the same explanatory and dependent variables. Because I am primarily interested in the spread of support for nationalism among the titular ethnic group, I restrict the sample to include only those respondents who, according to their survey responses, considered themselves to be members of the titular ethnic group.

I use only multivariate regression in the analysis. While bivariate regression shows the relationship between a particular social characteristic and support for nationalism independent of the respondent's other social characteristics, it may be that the relationship is entirely the product of a high correlation between the explanatory variable and some third variable. For this reason, multivariate analysis is used to show the relationship between a particular social characteristic and support for nationalism, while controlling for all other social characteristics used in the analysis. This analysis is done separately for each ethnic region. The analysis shows the social structure of support for nationalism in each republic. After the specific sources of support for nationalism in each region are identified, the analysis is performed on pooled data from all regions, both with and without dummy variables for each region. Results from these regressions identify the average tendency of particular social groups to support nationalism, independent of the specifics of each region.

MEASURES OF SUPPORT FOR NATIONALISM IN THE ETHNIC REPUBLICS

The extent of popular support for cultural nationalism is measured by the language-status index, which is based on the same three questions about attitudes toward titular-language status that were discussed in Chapter 6. To review, respondents were asked whether the titular language should be the sole official language in the ethnic republics, whether all inhabitants of an ethnic republic should be required to know the titular language, and whether study of the titular language should be compulsory in all schools. The data show that among most of the titular ethnic groups, a majority of the respondents opposed making the titular language the sole official language in the republic. Only 41% of the respondents who belonged to the titular ethnic group supported a single official language for their republic, while 48% opposed it, although the level of support varied a great deal from region to region. As shown in Table 8.1, making the titular language the sole official language in the republic had the support of a majority of the respondents among only four ethnic groups – the Tyvans, Chechens, Kalmyks, and Sakha. Among five other groups, such a policy had the support of between 29% and 40% of the respondents. Finally, the least support for such a policy was found among the non-Muslim groups of the Russian heartland. Among Karelians, Komi, Udmurts, Chuvash, Mari, and Mordovians, the

TABLE 8.1. Should the titular language be the sole official language in ethnic republics? (percent)

	Bashkortostan	Buriatia	Dagestan	Ingushetia	Kabardino-Balkaria (Kabardin)	Kabardino-Balkaria (Balkar)	Kalmykia	Karelia	Komi
Completely or partially agree	40	35	N/A	37	40	12	66	13	26
No opinion	12	11	N/A	1	14	11	5	15	14
Completely or partially disagree	48	54	N/A	63	46	78	29	72	60

	Mari El	Mordovia	Osetia	Sakha	Tatarstan	Tyva	Udmurtia	Chechnya	Chuvashia	Total
Completely or partially agree	23	26	34	53	29	80	18	69	20	41
No opinion	15	15	9	10	13	3	12	9	22	11
Completely or partially disagree	62	59	57	38	59	17	70	22	58	48

one-language policy was supported only by between 13% and 26% of the respondents.[2] During this period, the declaration of official languages had acquired symbolic importance as a statement of a government's intentions toward the non-titular population on its territory. The inclusion of Russian as an official language was seen as indicative of a policy of inclusion. If the titular language were declared the sole official language, this was seen as tantamount to a declaration that non-titulars would be treated as second-class citizens. For this reason, in most regions a relatively small proportion even of the titular population supported giving sole official language status to the titular language.

A larger percentage of titulars (49%) believed that all inhabitants of an ethnic republic, regardless of their ethnicity, should make an effort to know the language of the titular ethnic group. Only 16% opposed such a goal (see Table 8.2). Tyva was the only region in which more respondents supported a sole official language than believed that all inhabitants should know the titular language. A majority agreed with this statement in six republics, with the highest levels of support found among the Ingush, Chechens, Tyvans, and Sakha. Four other ethnic groups had levels of support that ranged from 41% to 49%. Finally, the groups that had the lowest levels of support for sole official language status also had the lowest levels of support for universal titular-language knowledge, except that here over 30% of the population believed that all inhabitants should know the titular language.

Compulsory study of the titular language in republic schools was the most moderate of the three cultural demands discussed in the survey and received the broadest support among Russia's ethnic minorities (see Table 8.3). A full 65% of the titular respondents believed that all inhabitants of an ethnic region should study that region's titular language in school, regardless of the titular group's proportion of the total population. A further 17% supported this demand as long as the titular group comprised a majority of the region's population. Only 12% opposed such a move. A majority of respondents among twelve ethnic groups supported mandatory titular-language study. Only among Mordvins and Udmurts did fewer than 40% of the respondents express full support for such a policy, while over 70% of Buriats, Ingush, Kabardins, Kalmyks, Osetians, Sakha, Tyvans, and Chechens unconditionally supported universal study of the titular language.

Support for political nationalism is measured by the regional separatism index, which is based on attitudes toward republic declarations of sovereignty, toward the right of ethnic republics to secede from the Russian Federation, and toward whether control over law and order should be transferred to republic authorities. The highest levels of support were registered

---

[2] The lowest level of support was registered among the Balkars, who may have been voicing concern that such a policy would make Kabardin the sole official language in their joint republic.

TABLE 8.2. *Should all inhabitants of an ethnic republic know the titular language of that republic?* (percent)

	Bashkortostan	Buriatia	Dagestan	Ingushetia	Tatarstan	Kabardino-Balkaria (Kabardin)	Kabardino-Balkaria (Balkar)	Tyva	Udmurtia	Chechnya	Kalmykia	Chuvashia	Karelia	Komi
Agree	43	49	33	92	44	41	35	73	36	78	62	35	34	34
No opinion	17	17	28	0	24	16	7	10	17	5	6	27	13	14
Disagree	40	34	39	8	32	43	58	17	47	17	33	38	53	52

	Mari El	Mordovia	Osetia	Sakha	Total
Agree	31	31	56	69	49
No opinion	19	14	11	13	35
Disagree	50	55	33	18	16

TABLE 8.3. *Should titular-language study be compulsory in all schools in ethnic republics?* (percent)

	Bashkortostan	Buriatia	Dagestan	Ingushetia	Tatarstan	Kabardino-Balkaria (Kabardin)	Kabardino-Balkaria (Balkar)	Tyva	Udmurtia	Chechnya	Kalmykia	Chuvashia	Karelia	Komi
Completely agree	51	71	N/A	72	66	77	59	74	36	94	83	44	52	43
Only if majority in region	22	19	N/A	26	14	12	18	20	30	4	11	24	17	22
No opinion	10	3	N/A	0	10	7	9	3	10	0	2	14	7	12
Completely disagree	17	7	N/A	2	10	4	14	3	24	2	4	18	24	24

	Mari El	Mordovia	Osetia	Sakha	Total
Completely agree	42	37	79	73	65
Only if majority in region	17	24	10	17	17
No opinion	12	11	4	5	7
Completely disagree	30	28	7	5	12

for the most moderate of these three demands: the declaration of sovereignty by ethnic republics. Forty-seven percent of the titular respondents supported the right of these regions to declare sovereignty, while only 16% opposed it. Majorities among eight ethnic groups supported sovereignty, with the highest levels of support found among Ingush, Chechens, and Sakha (see Table 8.4). At the other end of the spectrum, fewer than 30% of titulars in Mari El, Mordovia, Chuvashia, Karelia, and Dagestan supported sovereignty.

Radical nationalists in the ethnic republics considered sovereignty insufficient and advocated the right of secession for their republics. As shown in Table 8.5, such demands found support among a majority of Tyvans, Sakha, Chechens, and Ingush. At the same time, fewer than 20% of Mari, Mordvins, Udmurts, and Chuvash supported the right of secession. Among titular respondents overall, 36% believed that all republics should have the right of secession, while another 14% thought that only republics that fit various criteria of size, demographic balance, and location should have such a right.

Radical nationalists in some republics also sought to increase the authority of republic governments by giving them control of local army units and the police and security apparatus of the region. Such demands were supported by one-third of the titular respondents. In most republics, respondents were not enthusiastic about such demands, which received the support of less than 20% of the titular population in six regions and majority support in only two – Chechnya and Ingushetia (Table 8.6).

These measures of support for cultural preferences and regional separatism are summarized by two composite measures, the language-status index and the regional separatism index. These two indexes measure two distinct aspects of support for nationalist mobilization. Table 8.7 shows that the six questions used to construct these indexes represent two underlying factors that are as uncorrelated for all seventeen cases as they are for Bashkortostan, Chuvashia, and Tatarstan.[3] Based on the mean values of the indexes, shown in Table 8.8, the surveyed republics can be divided into three categories.[4] The groups with the highest levels of support for both forms of nationalism include the Ingush, Chechens, Tyvans, and Sakha. These groups have mean values above 0.6 on the language-status index and above 0.5 on the regional separatism index. The middle category includes ethnic groups scoring between 0.4 and 0.6 on language status and between 0.3 and 0.5 on regional separatism. The ethnic groups in this category include the Buriats, Kabardins, Bashkirs, Tatars, and Osetins. The groups with the lowest levels of support for both kinds of nationalism include the Mordovians, Mari, Chuvash, Udmurts, Karelians, Komi, Balkars, and the titular inhabitants

---

[3] See Table 6.1 in Chapter 6.
[4] Note that the means of the two indexes are not directly comparable and *cannot* be interpreted to show that there is greater support for cultural nationalism than for regional separatism in most regions.

TABLE 8.4. *How do you feel about the declarations of sovereignty by the former autonomous republics of the Russian Federation?* (percent)

	Bashkortostan	Buriatia	Dagestan	Ingushetia	Tatarstan	Kabardino-Balkaria (Kabardin)	Kabardino-Balkaria (Balkar)	Kalmykia	Karelia	Komi
Completely or partially support	67	54	22	94	56	44	36	61	25	33
No opinion	27	36	54	0	39	41	29	24	50	49
Completely or partially oppose	7	10	24	6	5	16	36	16	25	18

	Mari El	Mordovia	Osetia	Sakha	Tyva	Udmurtia	Chechnya	Chuvashia	Total
Completely or partially support	22	10	37	87	71	39	85	22	47
No opinion	53	45	35	12	24	44	10	60	37
Completely or partially oppose	25	46	27	1	5	17	5	18	16

TABLE 8.5. *Should all republics have the right of self-determination, including the right of withdrawal from the Russian Federation?* (percent)

	Bashkortostan	Buriatia	Dagestan	Sakha	Ingushetia	Kabardino-Balkaria (Kabardin)	Kabardino-Balkaria (Balkar)	Tyva	Udmurtia	Chechnya	Kalmykia	Karelia	Komi
All republics	30	33	22	60	91	42	29	68	17	79	46	21	20
Some republics*	25	22	10	15	7	5	12	14	13	12	14	11	12
No opinion	23	33	51	21	0	35	22	15	43	5	17	41	42
None	22	12	17	4	2	18	37	3	28	3	23	27	26

	Mari El	Mordovia	Osetia	Tatarstan	Chuvashia	Total
All republics	9	9	27	26	13	36
Some republics*	11	16	12	27	12	14
No opinion	45	32	32	39	50	32
None	35	43	29	8	25	18

* Includes "only large republics," "only republics on Russia's borders," and "only republics where the titular ethnic group comprises the majority of the population."

TABLE 8.6. *Should control of the army, police, and security forces be transferred to the jurisdiction of the sovereign republics of the Russian Federation?* (percent)

	Bashkortostan	Buriatia	Dagestan	Ingushetia	Kabardino-Balkaria (Kabardin)	Kabardino-Balkaria (Balkar)	Kalmykia	Karelia	Komi
Completely or partially support	32	37	20	80	28	21	43	20	27
No opinion	31	32	51	7	43	21	19	33	38
Completely or partially oppose	37	31	29	13	29	58	38	48	35

	Mari El	Mordovia	Osetia	Sakha	Tatarstan	Tyva	Udmurtia	Chechnya	Chuvashia	Total
Completely or partially support	13	16	35	49	42	46	18	70	10	33
No opinion	39	36	27	36	40	35	35	18	56	36
Completely or partially oppose	48	48	37	16	19	19	47	12	34	31

TABLE 8.7. *Factor matrix for indexes of support for nationalism: Colton/Hough survey, by survey question*

	Sole State Language	Language Required in School	All Must Know Titular Language	Support Sovereignty	Local Control of Army	Support Secession
Language status	.691	.778	.752	.271	.262	.135
Regional separatism	.310	.142	.204	.771	.725	.820

of Dagestan.[5] This third category has mean values on the language-status index below 0.4 and on the regional separatism index below 0.3. Finally, the Kalmyks, who are among the strongest supporters of cultural nationalism, do not support regional separatism as strongly.

This quick overview of the sixteen former autonomous republics of the Russian Federation shows that support for nationalism varies greatly among the ethnic groups. Some of the findings are somewhat surprising. While the groups with the lowest levels of support for nationalism include the relatively Russified Finno-Ugric groups of the north that are usually considered to have a weak sense of nationalism, they also include the Balkars and the inhabitants of Dagestan, from the usually highly nationalistic Caucasus. Members of these groups are probably reluctant to support nationalism because they live in multi-ethnic republics and fear that they would be dominated by other groups within the republic should the status quo change. In addition, one might not expect to find the Sakha and Tyvans in the same highly nationalist category as the Chechens and Ingush. The extent of support for nationalism among these groups, as well as among the moderately nationalist Buriats, indicates that Siberian ethnic groups have as strong a sense of nationalism as Muslim and Caucasian groups that are usually seen as the most nationalistic in Russia. In the next section, I show that despite the wide variation in levels of support for nationalism across ethnic groups, data from the sixteen republics largely confirms the institutionalist explanation of the spread of support for nationalism within each group.

WHO SUPPORTS MINORITY NATIONALISM?

Cultural Nationalism

The multivariate regression results for the language-status index are shown in Table 8.9. While there is significant variation among the republics, some

---

[5] Titular inhabitants of Dagestan include Avars, Dargins, Kumyks, Lezgins, Laks, Tabasarans, and people listed as "other peoples of Dagestan."

TABLE 8.8. *Mean values of ethnic mobilization indexes, by region*

	Bashkortostan	Buriatia	Dagestan	Ingushetia	Kabardino-Balkaria (Kabardin)	Kabardino-Balkaria (Balkar)	**Kalmykia**	Karelia	Komi
Language status	.454 (.332)	.518 (.278)	N/A	.757 (.284)	.519 (.299)	.372 (.249)	**.678 (.298)**	.352 (.282)	.360 (.321)
Regional separatism	.399 (.307)	.365 (.296)	.199 (.272)	.782 (.208)	.335 (.349)	.265 (.290)	.443 (.296)	.205 (.260)	.246 (.274)

	Mari El	Mordovia	*Osetia*	Sakha	Tatarstan	Tyva	Udmurtia	**Chechnya**	Chuvashia
Language status	.331 (.326)	.329 (.313)	.549 (.280)	**.651 (.298)**	.465 (.314)	**.737 (.260)**	.333 (.292)	**.780 (.261)**	.353 (.287)
Regional separatism	.137 (.220)	.118 (.175)	.298 (.304)	.618 (.301)	.388 (.324)	.565 (.311)	.213 (.220)	**.757 (.284)**	.142 (.218)

Note: Range of possible values for each index is 0–1. The value of one standard deviation is listed in parentheses. Values are comparable only across regions for a single index, not across indexes.

Bold: Category 1, *Italics: Category 2*, Normal: Category 3.

TABLE 8.9. *Support for increase in language status, by region*

	Bashkortostan	Buriatia	Ingushetia	Kabardino-Balkaria (Kabardin)	Kabardino-Balkaria (Balkar)	Kalmykia	Karelia	Komi
Occupational groups								
Intellectual[a]	.011 (.077)	.082 (.045)*	.006 (.057)	−.024 (.046)	.054 (.070)	.057 (.037)	.013 (.062)	−.028 (.057)
Student[a]	.089 (.085)	−.050 (.055)	−.030 (.047)	−.066 (.049)	−.105 (.091)	−.051 (.047)	.026 (.096)	−.124 (.088)
Leader[a]	.146 (.105)	.060 (.075)	−.086 (.059)	−.031 (.061)	−.137 (.103)	.043 (.056)	−.026 (.062)	−.017 (.077)
Industrial worker[a]	.073 (.062)	.035 (.049)	.019 (.052)	−.025 (.035)	−.068 (.065)	−.027 (.035)	−.084 (.048)*	−.076 (.052)
Agricultural worker[a]	.132 (.087)	.125 (.069)*	.066 (.073)	.008 (.065)	.074 (.115)	.048 (.068)	−.489 (.282)*	−.084 (.079)
Social characteristics								
Migrant[a]	.084 (.068)	.058 (.060)	.080 (.059)	−.008 (.048)	−.020 (.073)	.039 (.049)	−.021 (.057)	.148 (.060)**
Community size[b]	.010 (.024)	.008 (.017)	.040 (.019)**	−.004 (.014)	−.035 (.030)	.018 (.012)	.020 (.025)	.058 (.021)***
Education[c]	.020 (.023)	−.021 (.015)	.031 (.015)*	.014 (.012)	−.008 (.021)	−.031 (.011)***	0 (.016)	−.012 (.018)
Sex (1 = female)	−.021 (.053)	.094 (.038)**	−.052 (.040)	−.046 (.031)	−.045 (.054)	−.026 (.029)	−.006 (.044)	.026 (.045)
Age[d]	.576 (.210)***	.087 (.124)	.368 (.176)**	−.037 (.124)	−.013 (.195)	.096 (.106)	.051 (.161)	−.137 (.156)
Beliefs								
Muslim[a]	.048 (.092)	N/A	−.011 (.094)	.046 (.054)	.114 (.177)	N/A	N/A	N/A
Buddhist[a]	N/A	.141 (.062)**	N/A	N/A	N/A	.120 (.058)**	N/A	N/A
Religious[c]	−.033 (.031)	−.042 (.020)**	−.016 (.035)	.007 (.022)	−.037 (.056)	−.019 (.018)	.040 (.015)***	.010 (.015)
Communist[a]	−.097 (.081)	−.012 (.052)	−.259 (.078)***	−.016 (.045)	−.054 (.068)	−.001 (.044)	−.116 (.057)**	−.004 (.066)
Constant	.180 (.236)	.483 (.142)***	.462 (.231)**	.499 (.132)***	.698 (.260)***	.784 (.113)***	.204 (.149)	.249 (.185)
Adjusted R^2	.016	.075	.113	−.009	−.053	.040	.064	.013
N	211	248	104	478	112	502	204	273

	Mari El	Mordovia	North Osetia	Tatarstan	Tyva	Udmurtia	Chechnya	Chuvashia	Sakha
Occupational groups									
Intellectual[a]	.051 (.045)	−.048 (.054)	.030 (.034)	.056 (.036)	−.034 (.026)	.065 (.041)	.117 (.030)***	.068 (.041)*	−.075 (.037)**
Student[a]	.041 (.071)	−.085 (.084)	−.055 (.046)	−.010 (.052)	.037 (.037)	.031 (.066)	.014 (.040)	.010 (.041)	−.027 (.054)
Leader[a]	−.047 (.072)	−.050 (.103)	.093 (.059)	.044 (.045)	.032 (.033)	−.009 (.057)	−.087 (.047)*	.032 (.042)	−.094 (.050)*
Industrial worker[a]	.044 (.044)	.049 (.047)	.017 (.032)	−.110 (.040)***	.009 (.026)	.023 (.045)	.008 (.026)	.014 (.032)	−.032 (.055)
Agricultural worker[a]	.045 (.061)	−.047 (.056)	.079 (.081)	−.186 (.061)***	−.085 (.056)	.102 (.060)*	.059 (.037)	.096 (.040)**	−.125 (.077)
Social characteristics									
Migrant[a]	.038 (.060)	.109 (.067)	.084 (.031)***	.072 (.037)**	−.001 (.037)	.104 (.051)**	.041 (.042)	.061 (.032)*	.050 (.049)
Community size[b]	.062 (.019)***	.019 (.021)	.006 (.011)	.034 (.015)**	.035 (.011)***	.061 (.018)***	.024 (.011)**	.022 (.012)*	.024 (.015)
Education[c]	.015 (.014)	.006 (.017)	−.010 (.010)	−.009 (.013)	−.019 (.009)**	.003 (.014)	−.005 (.009)	.009 (.012)	.006 (.013)
Sex (1 = female)	−.081 (.039)**	−.067 (.041)	.001 (.027)	−.077 (.031)**	.016 (.022)	−.054 (.036)	−.068 (.022)***	.007 (.024)	−.052 (.033)
Age[d]	−.032 (.130)	.014 (.134)	−.012 (.091)	.165 (.115)	.027 (.091)	.060 (.121)	−.066 (.078)	−.044 (.093)	.134 (.136)
Beliefs									
Muslim[a]	N/A	N/A	−.102 (.065)	.165 (.052)***	N/A	N/A	−.274 (.255)	N/A	N/A
Buddhist[a]	N/A	N/A	N/A	N/A	.029 (.037)	N/A	N/A	N/A	N/A
Religious[c]	.045 (.014)***	.033 (.014)**	.034 (.008)***	−.032 (.017)**	−.007 (.012)	.049 (.013)***	.135 (.024)***	0 (.008)	.008 (.013)
Communist[a]	.023 (.062)	−.097 (.049)**	−.020 (.041)	−.008 (.047)	.016 (.031)	−.015 (.046)	−.142 (.046)***	−.044 (.041)	−.037 (.049)
Constant	−.026 (.138)	.210 (.161)	.419 (.100)***	.533 (.129)***	.697 (.088)***	−.027 (.147)	.334 (.268)	.213 (.099)**	.607 (.134)***
Adjusted R²	.057	.024	.045	.071	.029	.087	.116	.006	.010
N	354	312	524	478	653	315	588	688	378

*** $p < .01$, ** $p < .05$, * $p < .10$.

[a] Variable is dichotomous and equals 1 when respondent belongs to the group.
[b] A proxy variable for "rural." Value inversely related to community size and measured on a four-point scale.
[c] Measured on a six-point scale.
[d] Variable scaled to measure from 0 to 1.

important tendencies can be seen. First of all, intellectuals in seven republics support cultural nationalism, while opposition is registered in only two. Likewise, migrants from rural to urban areas support cultural nationalism in nine regions and oppose it in none. In more than half of the regions, rural inhabitants are more likely than the average respondent to support cultural nationalism. Similarly, in six regions agricultural workers exhibit strong support for increasing language status. Only in Tatarstan is support for cultural nationalism negatively correlated with working at a collective farm. Support for cultural nationalism also tends to increase with the age of the respondent, although in only two regions at a statistically significant level. Finally, the respondent's religious identity increases support for nationalism in many regions. In particular, identifying as a Buddhist in the Buddhist republics of Buriatia and Kalmykia has a strong correlation with cultural nationalist feelings. In Tyva, the third Buddhist republic, the correlation, although not statistically significant, is also positive. A strong sense of religious belief is highly correlated with support for nationalism in six republics, which include ethnic groups that belong to all three major religious traditions of Russia's titular minorities. Groups that are more likely than others to oppose cultural nationalism include women, who are less likely than men to support cultural nationalism in eight republics, and former members of the Communist Party. In several republics, students have a pronounced tendency to oppose cultural nationalism, although this negative relationship is not significant in any of the regions. Finally, educational level does not exhibit a strong correlation with cultural nationalism in either direction.

Regional Separatism

Support for regional separatism is shown in Table 8.10. The results show a strong tendency among intellectuals and students in most republics to support regional separatism. There is an extremely strong correlation between level of education and support for separatism, with higher education predicting greater separatist tendencies in thirteen of the eighteen cases. Migrants from rural to urban areas show a tendency to support separatism in four regions and to oppose it in two. There is also a clear correlation between affiliation with Buddhism and support for separatism in the same two Buddhist regions that showed such a link for cultural nationalism. Other religious factors, including religiosity and affiliation with Islam, showed no correlation with regional separatism in either direction. Opposition to separatism is strongest among women (in twelve regions) and industrial workers (in four regions). The results also show that in most regions support for separatism increases with the age of the respondent. When controlling for other factors, living in a rural area and working in agriculture have no effect on support for separatism. For both variables, an equal number of cases show significant negative and positive correlations with support for separatism.

Similarly, neither belonging to the political elite nor having once belonged to the Communist Party has a clear positive effect on separatist attitudes.

Pooled Results

Pooling the data from all of the regions into a single data set allows us to examine general tendencies in determining who supports nationalism, independent of the specifics of each region and ethnic group. At the same time, the larger size of the data set shrinks the standard errors, increasing our confidence that the statistical results are correct and significant.[6] The pooled data are analyzed both with and without dummy variables representing each ethnic group. While excluding dummy variables allows us to focus purely on the key factors driving the theoretical explanation, it is likely that at least some of the social group variables that appear significant in this analysis are actually proxies for the effect of belonging to a particular ethnic group or living in a particular region. Both sets of regression results are presented in Table 8.11, although, unless otherwise noted, all of the examples presented here use the results of the analysis that controls for ethnicity.

These results show that support for cultural nationalism is most pronounced among intellectuals, rural inhabitants, and migrants from rural to urban areas. Being an intellectual increases a respondent's language-status index score by 2.3%, while being a migrant increases it by 8.8%. Women and Communists are particularly likely to express opposition to cultural nationalism. Everything else being equal, women are 1.7% lower on the language-status index than men; having belonged to the Communist Party lowers one's support for cultural nationalism by 2.7%. When ethnicity is controlled for, support for cultural nationalism increases with the respondent's age and religiosity. Support for language status increases by 1.5% for each step on the six-point religiosity measure, so that fully practicing believers score 9% higher on the language-status index than militant atheists. For every year of age, the respondent's support for language status increases by .07%. Without the ethnicity control variables, neither of these variables has a statistically significant effect on support for cultural nationalism. When ethnicity is controlled for, being a student or a Muslim has a negative effect on support for cultural nationalism. In this case, support for cultural nationalism also decreases as educational level increases. Two factors that are significant without ethnic control variables lose their significance when these variables are

---

[6] The results presented here are based on all sixteen republics so as to present the most generalizable findings available. Because the theory was originally based on three of these sixteen regions (Bashkortostan, Chuvashia, and Tatarstan), in order to make sure that data from these regions was not causing bias I also performed the analysis on pooled data from the other thirteen republics only. The results were virtually identical to the results from all sixteen republics.

TABLE 8.10. *Support for regional separatism, by region*

	Bashkortostan	Buriatia	Dagestan	Ingushetia	Kabardino-Balkaria (Kabardin)	Kabardino-Balkaria (Balkar)	Kalmykia	Karelia	Komi
Occupational groups									
Intellectual[a]	.096 (.068)	.014 (.050)	−.056 (.031)*	−.033 (.067)	.067 (.050)	−.091 (.075)	.032 (.037)	.014 (.057)	.001 (.048)
Student[a]	.146 (.075)**	−.084 (.062)	.079 (.048)*	−.039 (.055)	−.075 (.053)	.117 (.096)	.019 (.047)	.148 (.088)*	−.022 (.075)
Leader[a]	.231 (.092)**	.081 (.083)	.066 (.034)*	−.009 (.070)	−.103 (.067)	−.219 (.110)**	.080 (.056)	−.003 (.056)	−.023 (.065)
Industrial worker[a]	.084 (.055)	.013 (.055)	.022 (.028)	.045 (.061)	−.067 (.039)*	.004 (.069)	.033 (.035)	.001 (.044)	−.074 (.044)*
Agricultural worker[a]	.153 (.077)**	.030 (.077)	−.039 (.030)	−.028 (.087)	−.067 (.072)	−.116 (.122)	.053 (.068)	.253 (.258)	−.157 (.067)**
Social characteristics									
Migrant[a]	.198 (.060)***	−.003 (.067)	.004 (.031)	.068 (.070)	.047 (.053)	−.099 (.077)	−.075 (.049)	.035 (.052)	.018 (.051)
Community size[b]	.040 (.021)*	−.026 (.018)	.022 (.010)**	.092 (.022)***	−.043 (.015)***	−.067 (.032)**	−.013 (.012)	.010 (.023)	.011 (.018)
Education[c]	.042 (.020)**	.001 (.017)	.029 (.008)***	.015 (.018)	.016 (.013)	.030 (.023)	.027 (.011)**	.032 (.015)**	.014 (.015)
Sex (1 = female)	−.023 (.046)	−.013 (.042)	−.019 (.020)	.023 (.047)	−.095 (.034)***	−.101 (.057)*	−.036 (.029)	.010 (.040)	−.043 (.038)
Age[d]	.020 (.185)	−.082 (.139)	−.228 (.070)***	−.161 (.208)	−.439 (.136)***	−.041 (.207)	−.106 (.106)	−.318 (.148)**	−.181 (.132)
Beliefs									
Muslim[a]	.023 (.080)	N/A	−.013 (.045)	−.131 (.111)	.083 (.059)	.104 (.188)	N/A	N/A	N/A
Buddhist[a]	N/A	.100 (.069)	N/A	N/A	N/A	N/A	.135 (.058)**	N/A	N/A
Religious[c]	−.028 (.027)	−.036 (.022)*	.023 (.014)	.087 (.042)**	−.018 (.024)	−.049 (.059)	−.035 (.018)**	.010 (.013)	.001 (.013)
Communist[a]	−.065 (.072)	.004 (.058)	.062 (.030)**	.105 (.092)	.030 (.050)	−.083 (.072)	−.079 (.044)*	−.058 (.052)	−.006 (.056)
Constant	.102 (.207)	.585 (.159)***	.004 (.092)	.079 (.274)	.729 (.145)***	.671 (.276)**	.508 (.113)***	.119 (.136)	.344 (.157)**
Adjusted R²	.109	−.013	.089	.177	.104	.123	.036	.081	.027
N	211	248	104	478	112	502	204	273	

	Mari El	Mordovia	North Osetia	Tatarstan	Tyva	Udmurtia	Chechnya	Chuvashia	Sakha
Occupational groups									
Intellectual[a]	−.003 (.030)	.032 (.030)	.030 (.037)	.059 (.037)*	−.006 (.032)	.017 (.031)	.083 (.034)**	.074 (.030)**	.061 (.036)*
Student[a]	.003 (.048)	.059 (.048)	−.058 (.050)	−.032 (.053)	.021 (.044)	.054 (.049)	−.011 (.045)	.046 (.030)	−.037 (.054)
Leader[a]	.016 (.049)	−.046 (.059)	.083 (.063)	−.063 (.046)	.024 (.040)	.008 (.043)	−.092 (.053)*	.088 (.031)***	.055 (.050)
Industrial worker[a]	.016 (.029)	.033 (.026)	.023 (.035)	−.099 (.041)**	.017 (.031)	−.109 (.034)***	−.014 (.029)	.053 (.023)**	−.033 (.054)
Agricultural worker[a]	.062 (.041)	.004 (.032)	.086 (.087)	−.113 (.062)*	−.129 (.068)*	−.078 (.045)*	.105 (.041)**	.054 (.030)*	−.101 (.076)
Social characteristics									
Migrant[a]	−.018 (.041)	.031 (.038)	.062 (.033)**	.081 (.037)**	−.035 (.045)	.030 (.038)	.069 (.048)	−.009 (.023)	.032 (.048)
Community size[b]	.006 (.013)	.018 (.012)	−.033 (.012)***	.022 (.015)	.013 (.014)	−.007 (.014)	.035 (.013)***	−.024 (.009)***	.014 (.015)
Education[c]	.017 (.010)*	.008 (.010)	.017 (.011)	.015 (.013)	.022 (.011)**	.015 (.011)	.006 (.010)	.015 (.008)*	.027 (.013)**
Sex (1 = female)	−.085 (.026)***	−.024 (.023)	−.050 (.029)*	−.165 (.031)***	−.014 (.026)	−.066 (.027)**	−.082 (.025)***	−.022 (.017)	−.092 (.033)***
Age[d]	−.095 (.088)	.003 (.076)	−.223 (.098)**	−.014 (.116)	.083 (.110)	−.059 (.091)	−.077 (.087)	−.080 (.068)	−.121 (.135)
Beliefs									
Muslim[a]	N/A	N/A	−.077 (.069)	.177 (.052)***	N/A	N/A	.254 (.287)	N/A	N/A
Buddhist[a]	N/A	N/A	N/A	N/A	.036 (.045)	N/A	N/A	N/A	N/A
Religious[c]	.008 (.009)	−.001 (.008)	.024 (.009)***	−.034 (.017)**	−.012 (.015)	.005 (.010)	.054 (.027)**	.009 (.006)	.004 (.013)
Communist[a]	−.046 (.042)	−.040 (.028)	.024 (.044)	.062 (.048)	.054 (.038)	−.023 (.034)	−.070 (.052)	.085 (.030)***	−.036 (.048)
Constant	.156 (.094)*	.053 (.091)	.317 (.108)***	.571 (.131)***	.486 (.106)***	.297 (.110)***	.185 (.301)	.122 (.072)*	.593 (.133)***
Adjusted R²	.042	−.002	.062	.110	.010	.088	.056	.076	.045
N	354	312	524	478	653	315	588	688	378

*** $p < .01$, ** $p < .05$, * $p < .10$.

[a] Variable is dichotomous and equals 1 when respondent belongs to the group.
[b] A proxy variable for "rural." Value inversely related to community size and measured on a four-point scale.
[c] Measured on a six-point scale.
[d] Variable scaled to measure from 0 to 1.

TABLE 8.11. *Pooled results*

	Language-Status Index		Regional Separatism Index	
	Without Ethnic Dummies	With Ethnic Dummies	Without Ethnic Dummies	With Ethnic Dummies
Occupational groups				
Intellectual[a]	.037 (.011)***	.023 (.010)**	.053 (.011)***	.030 (.009)***
Student[a]	−.003 (.015)	−.021 (.013)*	.011 (.015)	.001 (.012)
Leader[a]	.005 (.015)	.011 (.013)	.038 (.015)***	.031 (.012)**
Industrial worker[a]	−.011 (.011)	−.001 (.009)	−.012 (.010)	.001 (.009)
Agricultural worker[a]	−.082 (.016)***	−.006 (.013)	−.073 (.015)***	.001 (.013)
Social characteristics				
Migrant[a]	.025 (.013)**	.047 (.011)***	.013 (.012)	.022 (.010)**
Community size[b]	.029 (.004)***	.022 (.003)***	.015 (.004)***	.003 (.003)
Education[c]	−.004 (.003)	−.005 (.003)*	.019 (.003)***	.020 (.003)***
Sex (1 = female)	−.021 (.009)**	−.017 (.007)**	−.054 (.008)***	−.051 (.007)***
Age[d]	−.038 (.032)	.072 (.027)***	−.231 (.030)***	−.132 (.026)***
Beliefs				
Muslim[a]	.018 (.012)	−.117 (.015)***	.177 (.011)***	.015 (.016)
Buddhist[a]	.231 (.016)***	.006 (.017)	.201 (.015)***	.003 (.017)
Religious[c]	0 (.004)	.015 (.003)***	−.016 (.003)***	.006 (.003)*
Communist[a]	−.042 (.013)***	−.027 (.011)**	−.008 (.012)	.015 (.011)
Constant	.442 (.035)***	See Table 8.12	.388 (.033)***	See Table 8.12
Adjusted R^2	.054	.349	.099	.349
N	6951	6951	7215	7215

*** $p < .01$, ** $p < .05$, * $p < .10$.
[a] Variable is dichotomous and equals 1 when respondent belongs to the group.
[b] A proxy variable for "rural." Value inversely related to community size and measured on a four-point scale.
[c] Measured on a six-point scale.
[d] Variable scaled to measure from 0 to 1.

added. While Buddhist affiliation has an extremely strong positive effect on support for cultural nationalism (23.1%), religious members of traditionally Buddhist ethnic groups do not support cultural nationalism any more than nonreligious members of these groups. Similarly, while agricultural workers on average strongly oppose cultural nationalism, this effect simply reflects the lower levels of support for cultural nationalism among ethnic groups that have a higher-than-average proportion of agricultural workers. Finally, industrial workers and members of the political elite are consistently neutral in their attitudes toward cultural nationalism.

TABLE 8.12. *Intercepts for pooled results with ethnic dummies*

	Language-Status Index	Regional Separatism Index
Bashkortostan	.404	.386
Buriatia	.405	.338
Dagestan	N/A	.173
Ingushetia	.647	.755
Kabardin	.496	.305
Balkar	.362	.226
Kalmykia	.568	.427
Karelia	.045	.211
Komi	.252	.250
Mari El	.213	.124
Mordovia	.209	.122
North Osetia	.454	.280
Tatarstan	.421	.365
Tyva	.628	.541
Udmurtia	.227	.203
Chechnya	.755	.724
Chuvashia	.246	.139
Sakha	.557	.594

Regional separatism, like cultural nationalism, is strongly supported by intellectuals and migrants, although for migrants the results are only significant when ethnicity controls are included. Intellectuals are 3% more likely to support regional separatism than others, while migrants' scores are 2.2% higher than those of nonmigrants. Members of the political elite also strongly support regional separatism. Support for regional separatism is particularly pronounced among those with higher levels of education. For each additional level of education possessed by the respondent, his or her regional separatism index score increases by 2%. The overall increase, from illiterate to doctorate, equals 16.3%. Opposition to regional separatism is particularly strong among women and tends to increase with the age of the respondent. Several factors are significant without ethnicity controls but lose their significance when these controls are added. While inhabitants of rural areas, Muslims, and Buddhists are all predisposed toward supporting regional separatism, these factors simply reflect the characteristics of ethnic groups that are particularly supportive of regional separatism, rather than representing the characteristics of individuals within these ethnic groups. As is the case with cultural nationalism, agricultural workers are predisposed toward opposing regional separatism, reflecting the lack of support for separatism among ethnic groups with high proportions of agricultural workers. Religiosity is particularly complicated. Without ethnic controls, it is strongly negatively correlated with support for regional separatism. When ethnic controls are added, this correlation becomes positive. Finally, belonging to any of several other groups, including former Communists, students, and workers, on average does not affect attitudes toward regional separatism.

ANALYSIS

The institutionalist explanation of support for nationalism developed on the basis of research in Bashkortostan, Chuvashia, Khakassia, and Tatarstan is largely confirmed by investigation of survey data from Russia's other ethnic regions. As expected, some of the strongest and most consistent support for nationalism is found among the primarily urban intellectuals, who spearheaded the establishment of nationalist movements and who have largely been responsible for the cultural revival that accompanied political liberalization in most regions. Members of the political elite joined this push for nationalism later and, as the statistical results show, have primarily tended to support the regional separatist side of nationalism, while remaining neutral on questions of cultural revival. These findings suggest that local political leaders support nationalism primarily because they recognize that greater regional autonomy would increase their political power. Since cultural nationalism does not affect these leaders' power, they do not have a strong tendency to support it. Among students, support for both cultural revival and separatism is mixed, reflecting the division of this population into two groups: students from rural areas, who usually have received a native-language education and have a strong sense of ethnic identity, and students from urban areas, who are often highly assimilated into the majority-Russian population and do not have a strong sense of ethnic identity.

Groups with ties to rural areas are particularly likely to support nationalism, especially in its cultural form. Very strong support for cultural nationalism is found among inhabitants of rural areas and among people who have migrated from rural to urban areas. These people are particularly likely to have grown up in an environment where their sense of ethnic identity was reinforced, in part because of the maintenance of traditional ways of life, but primarily because of the widespread existence of native-language education. Migrants and rural inhabitants also support regional separatism, although this support is not as strong as their support for increasing their ethnic group's language status. Among rural inhabitants, agricultural workers are somewhat less likely than others to support nationalism. This finding is explained by the greater dependence of this group on traditional village structures as compared to village teachers, doctors, and other members of the rural intelligentsia. Support for cultural nationalism also increases with the age of the respondent. Again, this result is largely a function of education.

TABLE 8.13. *Highest grade in which national language serves as medium of instruction, by year*

	1958	1972		1958	1972
Bashkir	10	10	Komi	7	3
Buriat	7	6	Mari	7	3
Chechen	4	0	Mordovian	7	3
Chuvash	7	4	N. Osetian	4	0
Ingush	4	0	Dagestani	4	2
Kabardin	4	0	Tatar	10	10
Balkar	4	0	Tuvan	7	7
Kalmyk	4	0	Udmurt	7	3
Karel	0	0	Yakut	7	8

Source: Brian Silver, "The Status of National Minority Languages in Soviet Education: An Assessment of Recent Changes," *Soviet Studies* 26 (1974), pp. 28–40, at pp. 33–4.

Between 1958 and 1988, native-language education was eliminated in almost all urban areas and greatly reduced in most rural districts throughout Russia's ethnic regions (see Table 8.13). As a result, the likelihood of having received a native-language education increases with the age of the respondent and is reflected in the increase in support for cultural nationalism among older respondents. At the same time, support for separatism drops dramatically with age. The older population appears to be especially reluctant to support a change in federal relations within Russia. The reasons for this attitude are not completely clear, but may have to do with the trauma of the Soviet collapse.

Some factors not directly linked to ethnic institutions also influence support for nationalism. Level of education has a strong positive effect on support for regional separatism and a relatively weak but statistically significant negative effect on cultural nationalism. Many among the well-educated see regional separatism as a means for increasing local self-government. The relationship between religion and support for nationalism is particularly complicated. On the whole, religiosity tends to increase support for cultural revival. The relationship between religiosity and regional separatism depends on the particular region, with religious titulars tending to support separatism in some regions and to oppose it in others. Muslim and Buddhist minority groups tend to be more supportive of nationalism than Christian ones, although this relationship has more to do with differences among ethnic groups than with differences among individuals within each group.

These results largely correlate with the findings from Bashkortostan, Chuvashia, Khakassia, and Tatarstan presented in Chapter 6. While support for nationalism in each region has its own unique features, such as the opposition to separatism found among Bashkir Muslims and the support for separatism found among older Tatars, the overall pictures that emerge from the two samples are largely identical.

In this chapter, I have shown that support for nationalism is by no means consistent among members of particular ethnic groups. Members of social groups that have a stronger sense of national identity or that have links to nationalist movements are, perhaps unsurprisingly, more likely to support nationalist demands than other members of their ethnic group. Although lack of data on native-language education in the Colton/Hough survey prevents me from presenting conclusive proof, it appears almost certain that the strength of national identity and the extent of links to nationalist movements depend in large measure on the ethnic institutions of the state. Any future discussion of sources of support for nationalism among minorities needs to take into account variations in nationalism not only among various minority groups but also within the groups.

9

Institutions and Nationalism

This study began with two contrasting vignettes that illustrated the range of variation in the mobilizing power of minority nationalism in Russia's ethnic regions. I have shown that these differences are the product of variations in the development of ethnic institutions in these regions. I have also explained the mechanisms through which these institutions have affected the extent of ethnic mobilization. In this chapter, after a brief summary of the explanation, I examine its empirical and theoretical implications. Empirically, the interaction between mass-based nationalist movements and local political elites has important implications for the future of center-periphery relations in the Russian Federation, foreshadowing a time when the forces of civil society will be able to constrain the policy options available to the governing elite.

This study also has theoretical implications for three areas of scholarship. For students of ethnic mobilization, the study demonstrates the importance of institutions for structuring not just the extent and form of ethnic mobilization, but even the identity categories on which such mobilization is based. At the same time, the mass-based approach highlights the importance of actors outside the political elite in determining the course of ethnic mobilization. Ethnic mobilization may spiral into violence because of internal movement dynamics, rather than because of the characteristics of groups, ethnic security dilemmas, or particular sets of economic and political incentives.

While democratization theorists often argue that successful democracies are born from well-structured negotiations between the key actors involved in the transition, this study demonstrates that the institutional legacies of the ancien régime can be equally important in determining political outcomes during the transition process. Finally, this study shows that ethnonationalism can be seen through the prism of social movement theory as a form of popular mobilization. Furthermore, while social movement theorists often treat political opportunity structure (POS) as a country-level variable, this study shows that political opportunity structures can vary substantially across regions within a country as well as among different types of movement within a region.

Thus, while this study has focused on nationalist mobilization in the ethnic republics of the Russian Federation, it has broad theoretical implications for students of ethno-nationalism, popular mobilization, and regime transition.

SUMMARY OF THE ARGUMENT

Explanations of ethnic mobilization differ on the reasons for the emergence of nationalism. Some scholars argue that ethnic mobilization occurs because of the cultural differences between groups inhabiting a common space or adjoining territories, while others tie ethnic mobilization to the goal of gaining material benefits for group members. This study shows that in the Soviet Union, nationalist movements developed as a consequence of the shaping of ethnic categories and the creation of incentives by the institutions of the state. The regions with the most extensive systems of ethnic institutions had the most-frequent and best-attended nationalist public protest actions, and nationalist candidates in these regions had the highest rates of election to local legislative bodies. These regions also displayed the highest levels of public support for nationalist demands in surveys of public opinion.

This study not only explains why ethnic mobilization occurs, but also describes the process through which ethnic institutions are able to promote ethno-nationalist mobilization. State institutions affect ethnic mobilization both directly, by creating constituencies that support nationalism and providing them with resources, and indirectly, by shaping collective identities and creating social networks that foster the spread of nationalism among the populace. The direct effects of ethnic institutions are particularly important in promoting the emergence of nationalist movements, while indirect effects are critical in determining which parts of the population support nationalism.

Soviet ethnic institutions, which included passport ethnic identification, territorial homelands for most ethnic groups, a four-tier ethno-federal territorial hierarchy, and titular control of administration in ethnic homelands, created conditions that promoted ethnic mobilization during periods of political liberalization. Nationalist movements were formed in the academic institutes and cultural organizations in each ethnic region and were run by members of the cultural elite of that region's titular ethnic group. Although these ethnocultural institutions existed in all of the ethnic regions, their size, number, and power depended on the position of the region in the ethno-federal territorial hierarchy. Since the capacity of nationalist movements to mobilize depended largely on resources provided by these organizations, a movement's strength varied with the level of the region in the hierarchy. Although there was significant variation in movement strength within each category, nationalist movements in union republics were stronger than movements in autonomous republics, which in turn were more powerful than movements in autonomous provinces and districts.

Not only were ethnic institutions responsible for the formation of nationalist movements in the regions, they also played a crucial role in determining which social groups within the titular ethnic group were supportive of nationalist mobilization. Soviet ethnic institutions influenced the sources of popular support for nationalism indirectly, by strengthening the sense of ethnic identity among some social groups and by creating social networks that assisted in the spread of nationalist ideas between groups. Soviet ethnic institutions, and particularly the census and passport identification, reified ethnic categories and forced individuals to choose a single identity. Other ethnic institutions, including ethnic homelands and preferential treatment of members of titular ethnic groups within these homelands, strengthened the sense of ethnic identity among members of the minority group living in the homeland. Over the decades of Soviet rule, ethnic identities replaced regional, religious, and linguistic identities as the primary form of group identification among the non-Russian population. These identities were particularly strong among members of the ethnic groups' cultural elites, who felt themselves responsible for ensuring the cultural development of their ethnic group and even its survival as a separate group. Because they felt a sense of responsibility for their ethnic group, ethnic intellectuals took a leading role in the formation of the nationalist movement.

At the same time, a contradictory policy of Russification, focused on urban areas in the homelands, ensured that the strength of ethnic identification among members of the titular ethnic group would vary. Members of the ethnic group who were educated in Russian-language schools, primarily the younger residents of urban areas, had a weaker sense of ethnic identity than individuals who were educated in titular-language schools, which were restricted to rural areas after the 1958 educational reform. The ethnic institution of titular-language education was thus largely responsible for the strength of collective identity among the titular population.

Just having a strong ethnic identity was not sufficient to cause individuals to support the nationalist movement. Because strong ethnic identities were found predominantly among the rural population, whereas the movements had been founded in cultural and academic centers located in urban areas, social networks were crucial in providing the link that allowed the nationalist ideology to spread. These social networks connected academics and cultural figures to the rural community through students and rural intellectuals, two groups with strong ties in both the urban and rural settings. While social networks always exist in society, the particular types of networks found in the Soviet Union were influenced by ethnic institutions, which brought ethnic academics and cultural figures into contact with students from rural areas. After graduating, many of the students returned to their villages to become teachers and doctors – the rural intelligentsia. In this way, the academic institutes were linked to the preservation of titular-language education in rural areas and were able to maintain ties to an important social group in the rural community – a group that became instrumental in spreading the nationalist message.

The form of the nationalist movements upon their emergence depended largely on the political conditions of the region. Nationalist movements in all four regions at first exhibited similar characteristics, beginning as cultural revival organizations at a time when other forms of nationalist organization were not yet permissible and then, as liberalization gained momentum, quickly transforming themselves into popular front organizations dedicated to both nationalism and democratization. However, the movements' subsequent organizational trajectories depended on the structure of available political opportunities during their early stages of development. In regions where nationalist leaders quickly gained influence in government, nationalist movements turned into interest group organizations dedicated to achieving their agendas through backroom politics. In regions where such access was not available but electoral competition was open, nationalist movements transformed themselves into political parties and dedicated themselves to attaining power through elections. Finally, where both access to policy makers and electoral competition were closed to opposition groups, nationalist movements turned to the people, establishing decentralized grassroots organizations and seeking to achieve their agendas by putting pressure on the government through public protest.

The impact of ethnic institutions extended beyond their effects on movement organization and support. Through their influence on commonly held norms and beliefs, ethnic institutions influenced the ways in which nationalist demands were framed by movement leaders. Thus, the establishment of ethnic homelands created the norm that members of a titular ethnic group had the right to control the republic government and to receive preferential treatment in education and government employment. Similarly, the creation of academic institutes dedicated to the study and preservation of the titular language and culture and the establishment of a system of titular-language education encouraged the widespread belief that the government was responsible for the cultural development of minority groups. Finally, the creation of an ethno-federal administrative hierarchy fostered a belief that territories at lower levels of the hierarchy were being exploited by Russia and the other union republics, leading to campaigns to raise the administrative status of these territories. The common themes found in minority nationalist movement agendas were based on these norms and beliefs.

In all four republics, nationalist pressure forced governing elites to support both ethnic revival and greater regional autonomy. However, the extent to which these policies were pursued by the governments depended only partially on the strength of the nationalist movements. Strong nationalist movements were able to pressure the executive branches of government in their regions into supporting radical nationalist proposals, including withdrawal of the region from the Russian Federation and strict language-knowledge requirements for important positions in government. At the same time, the adoption of these proposals by the republic legislatures depended less on the strength of the nationalist movements and more on the demographic balance among ethnic groups in the regions. In regions where the titular group comprised at least a plurality of the population, governments had more leeway to pass laws supportive of nationalist demands and to implement ethnic revival programs based on these laws. In regions where the titular ethnic group comprised a minority of the total population, the governments were usually forced to modify their initial proposals in order to make them less overtly nationalist.

BROAD COMPARISONS

While this study has focused on explaining the ethnic mobilization process in the ethnic regions of the Russian Federation, it has important implications for explaining ethnic mobilization in other parts of the world. The other constituent republics of the Soviet Union were based on virtually identical ethnic institutions and experienced very similar processes of ethnic mobilization. While their more highly developed ethnic institutions ensured that nationalist movements in union republics were more popular and more successful than nationalist movements in Russia's ethnic republics, the emergence, organizational structures, and demands of these movements mirrored those found in Tatarstan, Chuvashia, and the other Russian regions.[1] While nationalist movements in regions such as Estonia and Georgia received much more support than similar movements within Russia, they also originated at academic institutions and used virtually identical mobilizing frames (Hosking et al. 1992).

The theory may also be applied with minimal modification to ethnonationalist mobilization in other multi-ethnic former communist states, such as Yugoslavia, Bulgaria, and Czechoslovakia. While the specific ethnic institutions in these states differed from those found in the Soviet Union, they all shared a tendency to reify ethnic identities and to create institutions that maintained and strengthened a sense of common group identity and made mobilization along ethnic lines relatively easy. As Valerie Bunce shows, the ethnic institutions of these states played a crucial role not only in spurring nationalist mobilization but also in the disintegration of the states themselves (Bunce 1999). As Veljko Vujacic (1996, 782–3) shows, differences between Yugoslavia and the Soviet Union in the role of the dominant nation

---

[1] Numerous studies of ethnic mobilization in the former union republics are available. Some examples include Wilson (1996), Aves (1992), Hosking (1992), Taagepera (1993), as well as chapters in the edited volumes by Bremmer and Taras (1993) and Smith (1996).

in ethnic institutional arrangements were the most important factor in determining whether nationalists succeeded in overthrowing the Communist system (Soviet Union) or allied themselves with the Communists in order to preserve the system (Yugoslavia). In both cases, however, the crucial role in starting the mobilization process and encouraging mass support for nationalism was played by ethnic intellectuals.[2]

Most intriguing, however, is the possibility of applying this theory outside of the former Communist world. Nationalist mobilization is ubiquitous throughout Africa, Asia, and Latin America. And it appears quite likely that similar processes are at work in all of these areas. As Neuberger (1995) shows, the colonial powers in Africa created new ethnic identities by establishing internal administrative boundaries that placed related groups together in one region, and by providing the regions with native government systems run by a native ruler. "The very act of classifying and registering people according to ethnicity had a formative effect, and created bounded ethnic groups" (Neuberger 1995, 61). The creation of new written languages that were taught in the local schools produced "ethnic brokers" – teachers, lawyers, writers, and journalists who sought to create new and modern ethnic identities. This desire led them to create new cultural and political associations based on these new identities (Neuberger 1995, 62–3). While Neuberger does not relate these developments to the widespread political mobilization along ethnic lines throughout Africa, it seems quite likely that the processes that turned cultural identification into political mobilization among minorities in Russia played a similar role over the last several decades in Africa.

The role of social networks and voluntary associations in channeling nationalist mobilization is described in Hank Johnston's study of minority nationalism in Spain. Johnston shows that in Catalonia and the Basque region, as in the minority regions of Russia, "those who mobilize are not isolated individuals but rather tend to be enmeshed in a web of relationships that often have direct bearing on the nature and course of their participation [in nationalist movements]" (Johnston 1995, 232). Johnston finds that interpersonal networks are especially important during periods of authoritarian rule, when the danger involved in opposition activity is high and a great deal of mutual trust is required to ensure personal security among nationalist movement members. These findings mirror the initial development of nationalist movements in Russia at the beginning of the *perestroika* period, when opposition activity still carried great personal risk.

Recent research in Latin America likewise shows remarkable parallels between the mobilization process among indigenous ethnic groups in several countries and ethnic mobilization in the Russian Federation. While there are no direct parallels with Soviet ethnic institutions, the Latin American

---

[2] For Yugoslavia, see Devic (1998).

cases show that differences in the extent of mobilization there can also be explained by differences in the form of state institutions, the extent of political liberalization, and the density of social networks. Yashar shows that a context of gradual political liberalization created an environment that encouraged indigenous activists to organize political movements. At the same time, "[p]oliticized indigenous identity... has found organized expression as an indigenous movement only where communities have been able to draw upon preexisting network" (Yashar 1998, 24). In Latin America, these "transcommunity networks" were constructed in large part by the state and nongovernmental organizations, which "(unwittingly) provided institutional links that allowed the forging of translocal indigenous identities and movements" (Yashar 1998, 36). By establishing development agencies, Indian institutes, and schools, and by carrying out land reform, the state increased indigenous peasant independence and "enabled indigenous communities to strengthen and (re)construct local public spaces" (Yashar 1998, 33). These institutions thus created an environment that allowed indigenous groups to successfully mobilize their followers to challenge the very state that had provided them with the resources to mount the challenge.

On the basis of the examples provided in this section, it seems reasonable to suspect that state institutions, social networks, and common identities are crucial in determining the process by which nationalist leaders mobilize their followers throughout the world.

IMPLICATIONS FOR THE STUDY OF CENTER-PERIPHERY
RELATIONS IN RUSSIA

Discussion of center-periphery relations in the Russian Federation usually centers on interactions between Moscow and the governors or presidents of the federation subjects (provinces and republics). Several studies have examined changes in the political and economic balance of power between the center and the provinces during the recent period of regime transition (Solnick 1995; Stoner-Weiss 1999; Treisman 1996, 1998). Scholars who focus on the ethnic republics have noted that several of these republics have been able to retain significant economic and political advantages when compared to the nonethnic provinces, and they have argued that these advantages result from the political elites' use of nationalism as a tool to force the central government to grant concessions to their republics (Treisman 1996, 327).

This study shows that the process by which these elites gained economic and political advantages over the center is more complicated than the conventional wisdom suggests. Regional political elites were playing a two-level game, engaging in simultaneous negotiations with the central government and with nationalist opposition movements in their regions.[3] Negotiations

---

[3] On the concept of two-level games, see Putnam (1988).

with the central government were constrained by the demands of internal opposition forces in each region. Since the main topic of negotiations between the central and regional governments concerned the extent of regional autonomy, local governing elites had to take into account demands posed by strong nationalist movements that advocated regional separatism. This interaction between governing elites and opposition movements at the regional level complicated the negotiations between regional and central governing elites by limiting the regional elites' freedom of action. Tatarstan's nationalists, for example, were powerful enough to pressure the republic legislature to back the republic's withdrawal from the Russian Federation both in the sovereignty declaration and in post-coup resolutions on independence and on Tatarstan's accession to the Commonwealth of Independent States. When the nationalist movement was at its peak, Tatarstan's leaders could not compromise on the principle of separation from Russia. A settlement between the center and the region was made only after Tatarstan's political elite had defeated the nationalist opposition movement and could compromise with Moscow without fear of losing political control in the republic.

At the same time, the presence of a strong nationalist movement at home allowed regional leaders to ensure their political survival by pointing to the threat of political instability and even violence in the region if the central government were to be seen as interfering in republic affairs. Thus, in the aftermath of the 1991 coup, President Shaimiev of Tatarstan used the perceived danger of a nationalist takeover to avoid being removed from office for failing to support President Yeltsin. The nationalist threat was also used by regional leaders to increase their regions' power vis-à-vis the center. In March 1992, President Rakhimov of Bashkortostan argued that his government would be overthrown if he signed the Federation Treaty without any concessions. As a result, the central government agreed to sign an addendum to the treaty that gave Bashkortostan additional powers and competencies and was used to mollify Bashkir nationalists.

Viewing negotiations over the authority of regional governments as a two-level game provides an explanation for Treisman's (1996) finding that the regions that were most hostile to the central government were often the ones that were able to extract the most significant concessions from the government, while regions that remained quiescent were penalized for their stability. In many cases, the regions that made the strongest demands for autonomy were threatened with internal instability if concessions were not granted. This threat spurred local political elites to increase their demands and encouraged the central government to compromise.

The role of nationalist movements in this bargaining process reinforces the finding that these movements played an important role in shaping agendas among regional political elites. At the beginning of the political reform process, governing elites in ethnic regions universally opposed expressions of nationalism and sought to repress nationalist movements. After such repression proved to be impossible, these elites gradually adopted parts of the nationalist agenda, eventually enacting programs of ethnic revival and supporting regional separatism. Although this shift occurred in part for instrumental reasons – titular political elites recognized that they could use nationalism as a tool to ensure that power remained in their hands despite democratization – over time many of these leaders became genuinely supportive of nationalist ideas. Their support was demonstrated by their approval of ethnic revival policies that had no clear instrumental benefits for the political elite. Although the political systems of Russia's ethnic regions during this period were far from democratic, the example of the nationalist movements shows that popularly supported opposition forces did have an impact on the policies pursued by the regional administrations.

IMPLICATIONS FOR THEORIES OF DEMOCRATIZATION AND HISTORICAL INSTITUTIONALISM

This study has shown that when a country's political system undergoes fundamental change as a consequence of revolution or defeat in war, new institutions are not created from scratch. Because of their impact on the self-identities and interests both of members of the political elite and of the population as a whole, the institutions of the previous regime exert a strong influence on institutional design in the new political environment. This is the essence of the concept of path dependence, according to which initial choices limit future options. The literature on transitions to democracy has largely ignored the concept of path dependence, portraying the creation of new democratic institutions as the outcome of a bargaining game between rational actors in a context of high uncertainty (O'Donnell and Schmitter 1986, Przeworski 1991). The historical institutionalist perspective used in this study shows that explanations which assume that a stock set of actors is present in all transitions and that these actors' preferences are endogenous neglect the effects of prior structural and sociohistorical contexts on the democratization process.[4]

Historical institutionalism seeks to correct the transitions model by showing that the structural-historical context has a direct role in determining the form and function of the new institutions that are created during the transition. This study demonstrates that old regime institutions affect not just the design of new institutions by political actors involved in the transition process, but even the nature of the political actors who gain popular support during the transition period. Although ethnic institutions often played a purely formal role under Soviet rule, they were nonetheless critical in determining the identities and incentive structures of members of titular ethnic groups. The expectations and norms created by these institutions led

---

[4] For a similar critique, see Luong (2002).

to widespread resentment among non-Russians of their treatment by the state and encouraged the formation of nationalist popular movements as the strongest opposition to local political elites. These new political actors were able to co-opt existing ethnic institutions into serving their own agendas, persuading the governing elites to fill the ethnic forms of the Soviet state with ethnic content. Institutions previously regarded as serving no useful purpose thus became critical in shaping the nature of political competition during and after the transition period.

The legacy of the Soviet institutionalization of ethnicity thus outlives the Soviet state, shaping the nature of political competition and government ethnic policies during the post-Soviet period. The ability of these institutions to resist elimination and structural change shows that explanations of the paths of democratization cannot be based on a notion of institutional design through negotiated transitions that begin with a blank slate. Despite the intentions of dominant political actors, the institutions of the previous political regime limit the choices available to the negotiators and influence the ways in which these negotiators think about institutional design in the first place.

IMPLICATIONS FOR SOCIAL MOVEMENT THEORY

The political process theory of social movement development originated in an analysis of the civil rights movement in the United States (McAdam 1982) and has been used extensively since then in explaining labor protest, environmentalist and peace movements, student protest, and the Eastern European democratization movement (Kriesi et al. 1995; McAdam, McCarthy, and Zald 1996). This book has shown that the political process model can be used to explain the development of ethno-nationalist movements, an area previously unexplored by political process social movement theorists.[5] The emergence of these movements in the Soviet Union occurred as a result of the expansion of political opportunities under Gorbachev's rule. Although political liberalization affected the entire society, nationalist movements were more successful than other types of movements because they had better access to organizational resources that could be used to assist the mobilization efforts of movement leaders. Finally, Soviet nationalities policy had created beliefs and values among the movements' target audiences that made them receptive to nationalist mobilizing frames. Analyzing ethno-nationalist mobilization among minorities in the Russian Federation as a form of social movement allows the analyst to shift the emphasis away from the political elites to reveal the importance of the mass-based nature of this mobilization.

---

[5] But see Beissinger (2001) for a recent parallel effort to bring social movement theory to the study of nationalism.

This study not only applies the political process model to a new type of social movement, but also extends the model in two important ways. First, it shows that state institutions play a critical role in determining the ability of particular movements to exploit openings in the political opportunity structure. In the cases examined in this study, these institutions both provided the financial and organizational resources that enabled nationalist movements to create durable movement organizations and shaped the beliefs and values of members of the titular ethnic group in a way that made them receptive to the nationalist message. By comparison, the environmentalist and pro-democracy movements that emerged in these regions during the same period of liberalization were unable to create lasting organizations or to gain the support of a large part of the population for an extended period of time because they did not benefit from the institutional structure of the Soviet state. This study has shown that state institutions are an important factor in determining what types of movements are best positioned to take advantage of new political opportunities and what types of mobilizing frames best resonate with the target audience. Stated in the broadest terms, this finding shows that state institutions determine organizational structure and belief systems, which in turn determine the ability of an emerging social movement to mobilize followers.

Previous studies of social movement development have focused on cross-national differences in political opportunity structure as a source of differences in movement emergence and development. This study's second contribution to social movement theory is to show that political opportunity structure may vary as much within a single country as it does across different countries. Even in a state with highly centralized decision making such as the Soviet Union, local and regional governments are able to have a significant impact on the development of social movements because they are able to affect how quickly and to what extent central policies of liberalization are carried out in each region. In the cases examined in this study, some regional governments embraced the new political openness, quickly ending press censorship, embracing free and open electoral competition, and allowing protest demonstrations to occur without repression. Other regional governments maintained press censorship as long as possible, controlled the electoral process, and sent police to break up unauthorized protests. Also, regional governments frequently treated different types of movements in different ways. Thus in many regions, democratization movements were initially treated favorably in comparison to nationalist movements. Because political opportunity structure determines the timing of movement emergence and each movement's organizational structure, these cross-regional and within-region differences in political opportunities help to explain differences in the emergence and organizational development of nationalist movements in Russia's ethnic regions. As far as social movement theory as a whole is concerned, this finding shows the need for caution when discussing political opportunity structure in a specific country. Differences in POS within a single country may be as great as differences in POS between two different countries. Also, each region within a country may have a unique POS for each type of potential protest movement. Disaggregating the concept of political opportunity structure in this way should help to explain regional differences in movement development and support within a single country.

IMPLICATIONS FOR THEORIES OF ETHNIC MOBILIZATION

Most existing theories of ethnic mobilization are macro theories that focus on the factors that lead to the phenomenon of ethnic mobilization in particular places and at particular times. The conflicts between primordialist and instrumentalist theories are based on disagreements over macro issues, such as the nature of ethnicity and the types of factors that influence its politicization. The theory presented in this study attempts to adjust the focus of explanations of ethno-nationalism toward the micro processes of mobilization. Rather than joining the conflict over *why* ethnic mobilization occurs, I set out to create an explanation of *how* ethnic mobilization develops. In developing this explanation, I find that ethnic mobilization is often a mass-based phenomenon that is structured by the form of state institutions.

While most theories of ethnic mobilization focus on structural or cultural factors that predispose certain ethnic groups toward ethnic conflict, a few explanations have focused on the micro processes that lead to such conflict.[6] However, these explanations tend to explain the phenomenon of ethnic mobilization through the actions of political elites, ignoring the role of rank-and-file members of the ethnic group by assuming either that the masses are easily manipulable by ethnic entrepreneurs or that they act strictly in accordance with a particular theoretical logic. By contrast, this study demonstrates the importance of popular action in determining the course of ethnic mobilization. Ethno-nationalist movements may emerge even in situations where political elites are hostile to nationalism and seek to suppress it. The elite-based explanations are correct in arguing that ethnic mobilization, like any kind of mass movement, can occur only when there are leaders who are willing to organize a popular movement and have the resources to carry off such a mobilization. However, such leaders do not have to come from the political elite. In the case of the Soviet Union, for example, these leaders came from the cultural elite, whose links to the population were closer than those of the political leadership. These ties were established through the medium of Soviet ethnic institutions.

---

[6] These explanations are mostly instrumentalist or based on the security dilemma model imported from international relations theory (Gagnon 1994/95, Posen 1993)

The effects of state institutions were crucial in creating the mechanisms through which ethnic mobilization developed in Russia's ethnic regions. These institutions not only shaped the available resources and opportunity structures for ethnic movements, but also created the ethnic categories on which mobilization was based and determined the strength of ethnic identity among the non-Russian population. Previous research has shown that the Soviet state reified ethnic identities by creating official nationality lists and by establishing territorial homelands for most recognized minority ethnic groups (Hirsch 1998, Slezkine 1994a). This study shows how these policies, designed to ameliorate ethno-nationalism in the short term, inadvertently promoted ethno-nationalism in the long term by creating resources and expectations that made ethnic mobilization possible and popular during the Gorbachev period of liberalization. Without the reification of ethnic identities and the creation of ethnic homelands during the 1920s and 1930s, assimilation would have proceeded much further, shrinking the potential constituency for ethnic mobilization efforts by narrowing the extent of titular-language use and weakening individuals' sense of ethnic identity, the two biggest factors in determining support for nationalist mobilization. Furthermore, without these ethnic institutions, emerging nationalist movements would have been hard-pressed to find organizational resources and to establish social networks, which were vital for movement emergence and the recruitment of new members.

While Soviet nationalities policy made the impact of institutions on ethnic mobilization particularly visible, the impact of institutions on ethnic mobilization may be generalized to other regions. Every multi-ethnic country institutes policies to deal with minority populations. The nature and longevity of these policies are critical in determining the viability of popular ethno-nationalist movements among these groups. If a government refuses to create special institutions relating to minority groups and pursues an assimilationist policy for an extended period of time, and particularly if these policies are implemented in a repressive environment, the potential of such minorities for mobilization will be weakened as the sense of collective ethnic identity gradually dissolves, and potential ethnic entrepreneurs will lack the resources to mobilize protest actions against these policies.[7] Governments that create ethnic institutions and allow minority groups to have substantive political power and cultural rights will experience a split within the minority population, with part of the group seeking ever-greater concessions and possibly independence, while the rest accept the status quo.[8] As events in the Soviet Union and other multi-ethnic countries in the Soviet bloc have shown, the most unstable situation is one in which the state creates ethnic institutions

---

[7] The assimilationist policies would require at least several decades to take effect.
[8] The position of Quebec in Canada is one example of this type of outcome (Lublin 1998, Meadwell 1998).

for minority groups but refuses to give these groups substantive autonomy or cultural rights. Such a political environment is particularly unstable if the state simultaneously pursues an assimilationist policy against its minorities. In this situation, the ethnic institutions hinder and even counteract assimilation, ensuring that a strong ethnic identity is retained, and they provide organizational resources that make the organization of a nationalist movement possible. At the same time, the government's assimilationist policies ensure that a sense of grievance against the state exists among a majority of the ethnic group's members. For this reason, ethnic mobilization is more likely to occur in countries in this category, and when it occurs, it is likely to include most members of the minority ethnic group.

The implicit argument of the preceding paragraph is that ethnic institutions determine the extent of assimilation. State institutions have the power to create new ethnic identities by creating officially recognized ethnic categories and then establishing economic or political incentives for people who describe themselves as belonging to these categories. Thus, after the Soviet state created the Khakass ethnic category during the 1920s and officially identified members of several related but distinct Turkic tribal groups as members of the same ethnic group, the people so labeled rapidly came to perceive themselves as Khakass, even though the ethnonym had been unknown to them prior to the 1917 revolution. Even as new ethnic identities were being created, old identities were disappearing. People dropped identities that were not included on the official lists of ethnic categories in favor of identities that were on these lists. Thus, Mishars and Teptiars reidentified as Tatars and/or Bashkirs, while the Viryals were entirely subsumed by the Chuvash. By creating lists of ethnic groups that were recognized by the Soviet state and establishing ethnic homelands for these groups, the Soviet government ensured that the non-Russian population of the state would have state-recognized identities that they could adopt. Had the Soviet state followed the Turkish route and refused to admit the existence of ethnic minorities within Russia, it is likely that its subsequent efforts at Russification would have been even more successful than they were.

Soviet nationalities policy also hindered assimilation directly, through the mechanism of passport ethnic identity. By requiring all citizens to list their ethnicity on their identity document, and by limiting their choice to the ethnicities listed on their parents' passports, the state prevented many culturally Russified members of minority ethnic groups from fully assuming a Russian identity. Many titulars who perceived themselves as Russian were nevertheless listed as Bashkir or Chuvash on their passports and were therefore obliged to declare themselves non-Russian in circumstances when their ethnic identity had to be revealed for some official purpose. The institution of passport ethnicity ensured that culturally Russified members of titular ethnic groups retained a sense of their ethnic identity even when they did not know the titular language or care about the titular culture. In doing so, passport ethnicity counteracted the assimilationist policies of the Soviet government.

In their efforts to ameliorate ethnic tensions in the short term, the creators of the Soviet state established institutions that countered their later efforts to create a single Soviet people based on the Russian language and culture. By reinforcing ethnic identities and creating networks and resources within each ethnic group, the institutions that were designed to eliminate ethnic movements ironically ended up creating conditions that encouraged nationalist mobilization in the long term. The Soviet experience provides an important lesson for contemporary efforts to eliminate ethnic conflict: the creation of institutions that foster separate ethnic identities within a single state may be a short-term solution to an otherwise intractable cycle of hostility, but it is a solution that is likely to lead to renewed conflict in the future.

Appendix

Construction of Variables and Indices

Creation of Explanatory Variables

With several important exceptions, the explanatory variables used in the statistical analysis are either indexes or dichotomous variables. The latter are used to identify respondents who belong to particular occupational groups or who share particular social characteristics or beliefs.

Occupational Groups

Intellectual: This category includes all respondents who identified themselves as working in the field of science, culture, or education.

Student: This category includes all respondents who identified themselves as either full-time or part-time students.

Industrial worker: This category includes all respondents who, when asked about the group to which they belonged, identified themselves as workers.

Agricultural worker: This category includes all respondents who, when asked about the group to which they belonged, identified themselves as workers at a collective farm (*kolkhoz*) or state farm (*sovkhoz*).

Leader: This category includes all respondents who, when asked about the group to which they belonged, identified themselves as managers or supervisors.

Social Characteristics

Community size: The value of this variable is based on the respondent's place of residence at the time of the interview. The values were initially arranged as follows:
1 = capital,
2 = city,
3 = town,
4 = village.

Migrant: This category includes all respondents who had spent the majority of their childhood in a rural area but were living in a city at the time that the survey was conducted.

Appendix

Education: This variable represents the respondent's level of education. The values were initially arranged as follows:
1 = illiterate or primary,
2 = incomplete secondary,
3 = secondary,
4 = specialized secondary,
5 = higher education,
6 = advanced degree.

Age: This variable represents the self-reported age of the respondent, divided by 100 for ease of comparison.

Gender: This variable is coded 0 if the respondent is male and 1 if the respondent is female.

Beliefs

Communist: This variable is coded 1 if the respondent stated that he or she had belonged to the Communist Party of the Soviet Union (CPSU), and 0 otherwise.

Muslim: This variable is coded 1 if the respondent self-identified as belonging to the Muslim religion, and 0 otherwise.

Religious: This variable represents the respondent's attitude toward religion. The values were initially arranged as follows:
1 = believer who performs religious rituals,
2 = believer who does not perform religious rituals,
3 = respondent is uncertain about the extent of his or her faith,
4 = agnostic,
5 = nonbeliever who respects the feelings of those who believe,
6 = I think that we need to fight religion.
These values were then inverted, so that the most religious respondents had the highest values.

Index Creation and Analysis[1]

To facilitate the analysis of survey results and to capture certain attributes and propensities of the respondents, several indexes were constructed from related survey questions. The indexes are scaled from 0 to 1, with 0 representing the minimum and 1 the maximum of the attribute being measured. The indexes are constructed by assigning points to various responses to the questions asked, adding together the points each respondent received, and dividing by the total possible points.

Regional Separatism Index

This index is designed to reflect the respondent's level of support for increasing the republic's autonomy from the Russian Federation. It is composed of somewhat

---

[1] The methods of index creation used in this study are based on the methods used by David Laitin in his study of identity formation in former Soviet republics. More information may be found in his methodological appendix (Laitin 1998, 380–90).

different questions on the two surveys. For the Colton/Hough survey, it is based on the following three questions:

1. How do you feel about the declaration of sovereignty by former autonomous republics of the Russian Federation?
2. How do you feel about the transfer of control over the army, police, and security forces to the sovereign republics of the Russian Federation?
3. Do you think that all republics in Russia should have the right of self-determination, up to and including secession from the Russian Federation?

The respondent's raw score increases by:
2 if the respondent completely approves of the policy mentioned in question 1.
1 if the respondent partially approves of the policy mentioned in question 1.
2 if the respondent completely approves of the policy mentioned in question 2.
1 if the respondent partially approves of the policy mentioned in question 2.
2 if the respondent agrees with question 3 for all republics.
1 if the respondent agrees with question 3, but only for large republics.
1 if the respondent agrees with question 3, but only for border republics.
1 if the respondent agrees with question 3, but only for republics where the titular nationality comprise a majority of the population.

For the Laitin/Hough survey, the regional separatism index is based on the following three questions:

1. Do you approve of the plans to create a Ural-Volga Confederation in the Volga region with the participation of Tatarstan (Bashkortostan) and separate from Russia?
2. How do you feel about the transfer of control over the army, police, and security forces to the jurisdiction of Tatarstan (Bashkortostan)?

For Tatarstan:
3. How do you feel about Bashkortostan's declaration of sovereignty?

For Bashkortostan:
3. How do you feel about Tatarstan's declaration of independence?

For each question, the respondent's raw score increases by:
2 if the respondent fully approves of the policy described in the question.
1 if the respondent partially approves of the policy described in the question.

Language-Status Index

This index is designed to reflect the respondent's level of support for increasing the status of the republic's titular language. For both the Colton/Hough and Laitin/Hough surveys, it is based on the following three questions:[2]

1. Do you agree that the language of the nation for which the republic is named should be considered the sole state language of the republic?
2. Do you agree that the language of the nation for which the republic is named should be taught in all of the republic's schools as a required subject?

---

[2] The wording of the questions reproduces the wording of the Colton/Hough survey. The Laitin/Hough survey replaces the generic terms 'republic' and 'state language' with the names of the republics and languages in question.

Appendix

3. Do you believe that all people who live in the republics of Russia (regardless of their ethnicity) must be fluent in the language of the nation for which the republic is named?

The respondent's raw score increases by:
2 if the respondent completely agrees with question 1.
1 if the respondent partially agrees with question 1.
2 if the respondent completely agrees with question 2.
1 if the respondent agrees with question 2 for cases where the titular inhabitants constitute a majority of the population [Colton/Hough survey only].
1 if the respondent partially agrees with question 2 [Laitin/Hough survey only].
2 if the respondent agrees with question 3.

Native-Language Education Index

This index measures the extent to which the respondent's education was conducted in his or her (self-reported) native language. It is used only with the Laitin/Hough data. It is constructed from the following five variables:
Respondent's self-reported native language.
Language of education in kindergarten.
Language of education in primary school.
Language of education in secondary school.
Language of education in higher education.

The respondent's raw score increases by 1 for each case in which the language of education matches the respondent's self-reported native language.

Language Fluency Index

This index reflects measures how well the respondent knows his or her native language. It is only used with the Laitin/Hough data. It is constructed from the following eight variables:
1. Respondent's self-reported native language.
2. How fluent the respondent considers himself or herself in Tatar [Bashkir].
3. Respondent's first spoken language.
4. Language in which the respondent is most fluent.
5. Language of last personal letter written by respondent.
6. Language in which the respondent reads newspapers.
7. Language in which the respondent watches television.
8. Language in which the respondent reads fiction.

The respondent's raw score increases by:
4 if the respondent thinks in Tatar [Bashkir] (variable 2).
3 if the respondent freely speaks Tatar [Bashkir] (variable 2).
2 if the respondent speaks Tatar [Bashkir] with difficulty (variable 2).
1 if the respondent speaks Tatar [Bashkir] with great difficulty (variable 2).
2 if the respondent answers Tatar [Bashkir] only for variables 3–8.
1 if the respondent answers mixed Tatar [Bashkir] and another language for variables 3–5.
1 if the respondent answers equally Tatar [Bashkir] and another language for variables 6–8.

TABLE A.1. *Factor matrix for native-language education index*

	Tatarstan	Bashkortostan
Kindergarten	.851	.819
Primary school	.925	.897
Secondary school	.893	.812
Higher education	.453	.359

Language-Use Homogeneity Index[3]

This index is designed to reflect the extent to which the respondent speaks his or her native language in various social environments. It is used only with the Laitin/Hough data. It is constructed from the following twelve variables:
Respondent's native language.
Language used at home with father.
Language used at home with mother.
Language used at home with paternal grandmother.
Language used with maternal grandmother.
Language used with spouse.
Language used with oldest child when he/she was in preschool.
Language used with oldest child at present.
Language used with closest friend.
Language used with colleagues at work.
Language used with immediate superior at work.
Language used at the market.

The respondent's raw score increases by 1 for each situation in which the respondent speaks his or her native language.

Index Consistency

Factor analysis was used to ensure that each of the indexes measured a single underlying tendency in the data. The factor matrix scores used in the tables represent the correlation between the responses to a particular survey question and the composite index. The principal components method is used in the factor analysis, and the factor matrix scores are derived through a varimax rotation.[4]

Because of its importance for the study, the factor analysis of the two indexes used as the primary dependent variables has already been discussed in Chapter 7. The factor matrices for the language indexes based on the Laitin/Hough data are presented below.

Native-Language Education Index (Table A.1)

One factor was detected for this index. Three of the variables had very high factor loadings. The slightly lower score for higher education reflects the small number of respondents who received their higher education in a language other than Russian.

---

[3] This index is adapted directly from Laitin (1998, 383).
[4] For more information on factor analysis techniques, see Kim and Mueller (1978a, 1978b).

Appendix

TABLE A.2. *Factor matrix for language fluency index*

	Tatarstan	Bashkortostan
Fluency in native language	.761	.679
First spoken language	.600	.592
Language in which most fluent	.858	.814
Language of last personal letter	.792	.712
Language of TV viewing	.564	.568
Language of newspaper reading	.797	.785
Language of fiction reading	.825	.800

TABLE A.3. *Factor matrix for language-use homogeneity index*

	Tatarstan Speaks Language With:			Bashkortostan Speaks Language With:		
	Elders	Family	In Public	Elders	Family	In Public
Father	.752	.361	.163	.696	.267	.174
Mother	.771	.321	.166	.811	.210	.116
Paternal grandmother	.800	.038	.059	.742	.024	.076
Maternal grandmother	.852	.046	.056	.807	.142	.012
Spouse	.328	.736	.258	.297	.710	.174
Preschool child	.151	.878	.164	.123	.855	.159
Oldest child	.081	.863	.230	.110	.846	.206
Best friend	.255	.493	.571	.191	.548	.429
Colleagues	.130	.248	.794	.062	.309	.783
Superior	.070	.161	.767	.017	.073	.814
At the market	.055	.098	.721	.171	.179	.526

Language Fluency Index (Table A.2)

One factor was detected for this index. All of the variables had high factor loadings.

Language-Use Homogeneity Index (Table A.3)

Although three factors were detected for this index, these factors are based on the category of persons with whom the language is used. Because of the homogeneity of the questions used in this index and their identical phrasing, it is clear that all three factors reflect the extent to which the native language is consistently spoken in various situations. At the same time, the presence of three factors indicates that language-use homogeneity varies substantially depending on the context. The variables are thus grouped into three factors: (1) older family members, (2) other family members, and (3) public situations. The factors are fairly distinct, with the exception of the best-friend variable, which overlaps factors 2 and 3.

References

Regional Newspapers

Bashkortostan

Ekonomika i My
Idel-Ural
Istoki
Izvestiia Bashkortostana
Leninets
Sovetskaia Bashkiria
Otechestvo
Vecherniia Ufa
Volga-Ural
Volia
Zamandash

Chuvashia

Atalanu
Avani
Chavash'en
Cheboksarskie Novosti
KLIP
MK/Molodoi Kommunist
Pravitelstvennyi Vestnik
Sovetskaia Chuvashia

Khakassia

Abakan
Iuzhno-Sibirskii Vestnik
Khakassia
Respublika

Sovetskaia Khakassia
Vestnik Khakassii

Tatarstan

Altyn Urda
Chelny
Izvestiia Tatarstana
Izvestiia TOTs
Kazanskie Vedomosti
Kazanskiy Telegraf
Molodezh Tatarstana
Nezavisimost'
Respublika
Respublika Tatarstan
Sovetskaia Tatariia
Suverenitet
Tatar Ile
Vecherniia Kazan
Vestnik NF

Interviews

Bashkortostan

Alexander Arinin, Russian State Duma deputy and head of the Russian national organization Rus.
Vasil Babenko, member of the Bashkortostan parliament staff.
Zufar Enikeev, deputy to the Bashkortostan parliament.
Ildar Gabdrafikov, deputy director of the Bashkortostan anthropological museum.
Altaf Gaifullin, deputy chairman of the Bashkir National Party.
Karim Iaushev, former head of the Tatar nationalist organization Idel-Ural.
Kaderle Imametdinov, editor of the Tatar nationalist newspaper *Idel-Ural*.
Ildar Iulbarisov, member of the nationalities department staff in the Bashkortostan government.
Bilal Iuldashbaev, historian.
Marat Kulsharipov, chairman of the Bashkir National Center, professor.
Niaz Mazhitov, leader of the Bashkir nationalist movement, professor.
Marat Ramazanov, leader of the Tatar nationalist movement in Bashkortostan, professor.
Damir Valeev, leader of the Bashkir nationalist movement, professor.

Chuvashia

Ivan Andreev, professor of language at Chuvash State University.
Ivan Boiko, deputy director of the Institute for the Study of Chuvash History, Culture, and Language.
Mikhail Iukhma, head of the Chuvash nationalist organization CHOKTS, writer.

Vitalii Ivanov, Chuvash minister of culture.
Atner Khuzangai, head of the Chuvash nationalist party CHAP, former deputy to the Chuvash parliament, professor.
Aleksei Leontiev, editor of the Chuvash language newspaper *Khypar*.

Khakassia

Viktor Butanaev, shaman, scholar of Khakass culture.
Valerii Ivandaev, chairman of Chon Chobi.
Maria Kabelkova, political scientist.
Alexander Kostiakov, head of the Khakass nationalist organization Tun, radio broadcaster.
Gavriil Kotozhekov, editor of the Khakass newspaper, scholar of Khakass history and nationalism.
Valentina Tuguzhekova, scholar of Khakass politics.

Tatarstan

Ildus Amirkhanov, chairman of the Tatar Public Center (radical wing).
Fauzia Bairamova, head of the radical nationalist Ittifaq Party.
Talgat Bareev, nationalist journalist.
Roman Beliakov, deputy director of the nationalities department in the Tatarstan government.
Elena Chernobrovkina, journalist at *Vecherniaia Gazeta*.
Damir Iskhakov, co-founder of the Tatar Public Center, deputy director of the Tatarstan Institute of History.
Rafael Khakimov, cofounder of the Tatar Public Center, political advisor to President Shaimiev, director of the Tatarstan Institute of History.
Amir Makhmutov, chairman of the Sovereignty Committee, writer.
Guzel Mansurova, political scientist at Kazan State University.
Rafael Mukhametdinov, Co-founder of Ittifaq, Chairman of Association of Turkic Peoples.
Rafik Mukhametshin, Scholar of Islam in Tatarstan.
Gennady Mukhanov, Director of Tatarstan State Museum, head of Slavic Cultural Society.
Marat Muliukov, Chairman of Tatar Public Center (moderate wing).
Aleksandr Salagaev, Chairman of the anti-sovereignty political group Citizens of the Russian Federation.
Ildus Sultanov, leader of Tatar Public Center (radical wing).
Rimzil Valeev, Director of organization for outreach to Tatar diaspora.

Books and Articles

Abdullin, Ia. G., et al., eds. 1993. *Mezhetnicheskie i Mezhkonfessionalnye Otnosheniia v Respublike Tatarstan*. Kazan: Office of the President.
Akhazov, T. A. 1977. "Natsionalno-gosudarstvennoe stroitelstvo i razreshenie natsionalnogo voprosa v Chuvashskoi ASSR." In *Voprosy istorii Chuvashii*. Cheboksary: Institute of Language, Literature, History, and Economics.

Akhazov, T. A. 1979. "O pervoi konstitutsii Chuvashskoi ASSR." In *Voprosy istorii sovetov, partiinykh i komsomolskikh organizatsii Chuvashskoi ASSR*. Cheboksary: Institute of Language, Literature, History, and Economics.

Akhmetov, R. 1993. "Islam i vybory." In *Vybory – 1989*, ed. Anatoly Papp and Vladimir Pribylovskii. Moscow: MBIO.

Allen, William Sheridan. 1984. *The Nazi Seizure of Power: The Experience of a Single German Town, 1922–1945*, rev. ed. New York: Franklin Watts.

Allyn, Bruce. n.d. "The Battle for the Hymn of the Republic." Unpublished manuscript.

Anderson, Barbara, and Brian Silver. 1990. "Some Factors in the Linguistic and Ethnic Russification of Soviet Nationalities: Is Everyone Becoming Russian?" In *The Nationalities Factor in Soviet Politics and Society*, ed. Lubomyr Hajda and Mark Beissinger. Boulder, CO: Westview Press.

Anderson, Benedict. 1991. *Imagined Communities*. New York: Verso.

Aves, Jonathan. 1992. "The Evolution of Independent Political Movements after 1988." In *The Road to Post-Communism: Independent Political Movements in the Former Soviet Union, 1985–1991*, ed. Geoffrey A. Hosking, Jonathan Aves, and Peter J. S. Duncan. New York: Pinter Publishers.

Bates, Robert. 1983. "Modernization, Ethnic Competition, and the Rationality of Politics in Contemporary Africa." In *State versus Ethnic Claims: African Policy Dilemmas*, ed. Donald Rothchild and Victor Olorunsola. Boulder, CO: Westview Press.

Batyev, S. G., and F. N. Fatkullin. 1982. *Istoriia natsionalnoi gosudarstvennosti v Tatarii*. Kazan: Kazan University Press.

Beissinger, Mark. 1998. "Nationalist Violence and the State: Political Authority and Contentious Repertoires in the Former USSR." *Comparative Politics* 30 (4): 401–22.

Beissinger, Mark. 2002. *Nationalist Mobilization and the Collapse of the Soviet State: A Tidal Approach to the Study of Nationalism*. New York: Cambridge University Press.

Brass, Paul. 1991. *Ethnicity and Nationalism*. Newbury Park, NJ: Sage.

Bremmer, Ian, and Ray Taras, eds. 1993. *Nations and Politics in the Soviet Successor States*. New York: Cambridge University Press.

Brubaker, Rogers. 1996. *Nationalism Reframed*. Cambridge: Cambridge University Press.

Brzezinski, Zbignew. 1989/90. "Post-Communist Nationalism." *Foreign Affairs* 68 (5): 1–25.

Bunce, Valerie. 1999. *Subversive Institutions*. New York: Cambridge University Press.

Carrere d'Encausse, Helene. 1979. *Decline of an Empire: The Soviet Socialist Republics in Revolt*. New York: Newsweek Books.

Chistanov, Igor. 1989. "Stalinskii genotsid po otnosheniiu k Khakasskomu narodu 1920–30gg." *Tos* (5): 30–4.

Connor, Walker. 1984. *The National Question in Marxist-Leninist Theory and Strategy*. Princeton, NJ: Princeton University Press.

Cox, Gary W. 1997. *Making Votes Count: Strategic Coordination in the World's Electoral Systems*. New York: Cambridge University Press.

Dawson, Jane. 1996. *Eco-Nationalism: Anti-Nuclear Activism and National Identity in Russia, Lithuania, and Ukraine*. Durham, NC: Duke University Press.

Devic, Ana. 1998. "Ethnonationalism, Politics, and the Intellectuals: The Case of Yugoslavia." *International Journal of Politics, Culture, and Society* 11 (3): 375–409.

Dmitriev, V. D. 1994. "Istoriia i natsionalnye problemy Chuvashskogo naroda." *Vestnik CHNA* 1 (2): 26–33.

Dmitriev, Iu. A., and E. L. Malakhova. 1995. *Konstitutsii Respublik v Sostave Rossiiskoi Federatsii*. Moscow: Manuscript Publishing Company.

Downs, Anthony. 1957. *An Economic Theory of Democracy*. New York: Harper and Row.

Eller, Jack David, and Reed M. Coughlin. 1993. "The Poverty of Primordialism: The Demystification of Ethnic Attachments." *Ethnic and Racial Studies* 16 (2): 183–201.

Fearon, James, and David Laitin. 1996. "Explaining Interethnic Cooperation." *American Political Science Review* 90 (4): 715–35.

Ferree, Myra Marx. 1992. "The Political Context of Rationality: Rational Choice Theory and Resource Mobilization." In *Frontiers in Social Movement Theory*, ed. Aldon D. Morris and Carol McClurg Mueller. New Haven, CT: Yale University Press.

Filatov, Sergei, and Aleksandr Shchipkov. 1996. "Bashkortostan: religiia i vlast." *Druzhba Narodov* (5): 98–107.

Filatov, Sergei, and Aleksandr Shchipkov. 1995. "Religious Developments among the Volga Nations as a Model for the Russian Federation." *Religion, State & Society* 23 (3): 233–48.

Filatov, Sergei. 1997. "Religion, Power and Nationhood in Sovereign Bashkortostan." *Religion, State & Society* 25 (3): 267–80.

Filippov, V. R. 1994. "Etnopoliticheskaia Situatsiia v Chuvashii." (Working Paper No. 59.) Moscow: Institute of Ethnology and Anthropology, Russian Academy of Sciences.

Fish, M. Steven. 1995. *Democracy from Scratch*. Princeton, NJ: Princeton University Press.

Fisher, Siobhan. 1993. "Appendix A: Chronology of Ethnic Unrest in the USSR, 1986–92." In *Nations and Politics in the Soviet Successor States*, ed. Ian Bremmer and Ray Taras. Cambridge: Cambridge University Press.

Friedman, Debra, and Doug McAdam. 1992. "Collective Identity and Activism: Networks, Choices, and the Life of a Social Movement." In *Frontiers in Social Movement Theory*, ed. Aldon D. Morris and Carol McClurg Mueller. New Haven, CT: Yale University Press.

Gagnon, V. P., Jr. 1994/95. "Ethnic Nationalism and International Conflict: The Case of Serbia." *International Security* 19 (3): 130–166.

Gaifullin, Vasil. 1996. "Natsionalnoe obrazovanie v respublike Tatarstan." Speech given at the UNESCO International Conference on National School Development, Kazan, 27–31 March 1996.

Galliamov, Rushan. 1997. "Natsionalnaia politika v sovremmenom Bashkortostane: Konstitutsionnyi i zakonodatelno pravovoi aspekty konfliktogennosti." In *Resursy Mobilizovannoi Etnichnosti*, ed. M. N. Guboglo. Moscow: Russian Academy of Sciences.

Garipova, F. G. 1993. "Toponyms." In *Mezhetnicheskie i Mezhkonfessionalnye Otnosheniia v Respublike Tatarstan*, ed. Ia. G. Abdullin et al. Kazan: Office of the President.

Geertz, Clifford. 1973. "The Integrative Revolution: Primordial Sentiments and Civil Politics in the New States." In his *The Interpretation of Cultures*. New York: Basic Books.

Gellner, Ernest. 1983. *Nations and Nationalism*. Ithaca, NY: Cornell University Press.

Gibadullin, Rustam. 1995. "Tatarskoe natsionalnoe dvizhenie v reshenii problemy gosudarstvennogo vozrozhdeniia Tatarstana." Doctoral dissertation, Kazan State University.

Gibadullin, R. M. 1993. *Tatarskoe Naselenie Naberezhnykh Chelnov v Tsifrakh Etnosotsiologii*. Naberezhnye Chelny: Magrifat.

Giliazetdinov, J. M. 1993. *Gosudarstvennaia programma Respubliki Bashkortostan po resheniiu natsionalnykh i mezhnatsionalnykh problem na sovremennom etape*, Part 2. Ufa: Bashkortostan Council of Ministers.

Giuliano, Elise. 1997. "Maintaining Russian Integrity: Nationalism and Social Transformation in Tatarstan." Paper presented at the annual meeting of the American Political Science Association, Washington, DC.

Giuliano, Elise. 2000. "Who Determines the Self in the Politics of Self-Determination? Identity and Preference Formation in Tatarstan's Nationalist Mobilization." *Comparative Politics* 32 (3): 295–316.

Gleason, Gregory. 1990. *Federalism and Nationalism*. Boulder, CO: Westview.

Gorenburg, Dmitry. 1997. "Organizing Nationalists in Russia's Republics: The Effect of Political Context." Paper presented at the annual meeting of the American Political Science Association, Washington, DC.

Gorenburg, Dmitry. 1999. "Identity Change in Bashkortostan: Tatars into Bashkirs and Back." *Ethnic and Racial Studies* 22 (3): 554–80.

Goskomstat Rossii. 1992. *Nekotorye pokazateli, kharakterizuiushchie natsionalnyi sostav naseleniia Rossiiskoi Federatsii*, Vol. 2. Moscow: Republic Information-Publishing Center.

Goskomstat Rossii. 1995. *Obrazovanie v Rossiiskoi Federatsii*. Moscow: State Statistics Committee.

Goskomstat Tatarstana. 1995. *Tri Goda Reform v Respublike Tatarstan (Ekonomicheskii Obzor)*. Kazan: State Statistics Committee. Respubliki Tatarstan.

Graney, Katherine. 1998. "Institutionalizing National Communities in Post-Soviet Russia: The Politics of State Symbols, Public Space, and Culture in Tatarstan and Bashkortostan." Paper presented at the annual meeting of the American Political Science Association, Boston, MA.

Guboglo, M. N., ed. 1992a. *Etnopoliticheskaia Mozaika Bashkortostana*, Vol. 1. Moscow: Russian Academy of Sciences.

Guboglo, M. N., ed. 1992b. *Etnopoliticheskaia Mozaika Bashkortostana*, Vol. 2. Moscow: Russian Academy of Sciences.

Guboglo, M. N., ed. 1993. *Etnopoliticheskaia Mozaika Bashkortostana*, Vol. 3. Moscow: Russian Academy of Sciences.

Guboglo, Mikhail. 1994. *Perelomnye Gody*, Vol. 2. Moscow: Russian Academy of Sciences.

Guboglo, M. N., R. G. Kuzeev, and G. Kh. Shakhnazarov, eds. 1997. *Resursy Mobilizovannoi Etnichnosti*. Moscow: Russian Academy of Sciences.

Hale, Henry E. 1998. "Bashkortostan: The Logic of Ethnic Machine Politics and Democratic Consolidation." In *Growing Pains: Russian Democracy and the Election of 1993*, ed. Timothy J. Colton and Jerry F. Hough. Washington, DC: Brookings Institution Press.

Hale, Henry E. 1999. "Machine Politics and Institutionalized Electorates: A Comparative Analysis of Six Duma Elections in Bashkortostan." *Journal of Communist Studies and Transition Politics* 15 (4): 70–110.

Hall, Peter, and Rosemary Taylor. 1996. "Political Science and the Three New Institutionalisms" *Political Studies* 44: 936–57.

Hardin, Russell. 1995. *One for All: The Logic of Group Conflict*. Princeton, NJ: Princeton University Press.

Hechter, Michael. 1992. "The Dynamics of Secession." *Acta Sociologica* 35: 267–83.

Hirsch, Francine. 1997. "The Soviet Union as a Work-in-Progress: Ethnographers and the Category *Nationality* in the 1926, 1937, and 1939 Censuses." *Slavic Review* 56 (2): 251–78.

Horowitz, Donald. 1985. *Ethnic Groups in Conflict*. Berkeley: University of California Press.

Horowitz, Donald. 1992. "How to Begin Thinking Comparatively about Soviet Ethnic Problems." In *Thinking Theoretically about Soviet Nationalities*, ed. Alexander J. Motyl. New York: Columbia University Press.

Hosking, Geoffrey A. 1992. "The Beginnings of Independent Political Activity." In *The Road to Post-Communism*, ed. Geoffrey A. Hosking, Jonathan Aves, and Peter Duncan. New York: Pinter Publishers.

Hosking, Geoffrey A., Jonathan Aves, and Peter Duncan, eds. 1992. *The Road to Post-Communism*. New York: Pinter Publishers.

Hroch, Miroslav. 2000. *Social Preconditions of National Revival in Europe*. New York: Columbia University Press.

Huntington, Samuel P. 1996. *The Clash of Civilizations and the Remaking of World Order*. New York: Simon and Schuster.

Huttenbach, Henry. 1990. "Sources of National Movements." *Nationalities Papers* 18 (1): 49–53.

Iakovlev, Ivan. 1992 [1921]. *Spiritual Testament to the Chuvash People*. Cheboksary: Chuvash National Academy.

Isaacs, Harold R. 1975. *Idols of the Tribe: Group Identity and Political Change*. Cambridge, MA: Harvard University Press.

Isaev, G., and R. Fatykhov. 1994. "Tatarstan v otsenkakh izbiratelei." *Kazan* (7–8): 30–1.

Isaev, G., and Iu. Komlev. 1992. "Nastroeniia, kak i pogoda, izmenchivy." *Tatarstan* (9–10): 13–17.

Iskhakov, Damir. 1992. "Neformalnye obedineniia v sovremennom Tatarskom obshchestve," In *Sovremennye natsionalnye protsessy v Respublike Tatarstan*, Vol. 1, ed. D. M. Iskhakov and R. N. Musina. Kazan: Russian Academy of Sciences.

Iskhakov, Damir. 1993. "Sovremennoe Tatarskoe natsionalnoe dvizhenie: pod'em i krizis." *Tatarstan* (8): 25–31.

Iskhakov, Damir. 1994. "Obshchestvennye formirovaniia v Respublike Tatarstan." *Idel* (3/4): 62–9.

Iskhakov, D. M., and R. N. Musina, eds. 1992. *Sovremennye natsionalnye protsessy v Respublike Tatarstan*. Kazan: Russian Academy of Science.

Ittifaq. 1995. *Resolutions, Declarations, and Statements*. Naberezhnye Chelny: no publisher.

Iuldashbaev, B. Kh. 1995a. *Noveishaia istoriia Bashkortostana*. Ufa: Kitap.

Iuldashbaev, B. Kh. 1995b. *Bashkiry i Bashkortostan: Etnostatistika*. Ufa: World Bashkir Congress.
Ivanov, V. P. 1992. *Rasselenie i chislennost Chuvashei*. Cheboksary: State Institute of Language, History and Economics Press.
Johnston, Hank. 1995. "The Trajectory of Nationalist Movements: Catalan and Basque Comparisons." *Journal of Political and Military Sociology* 23 (Winter): 231–49.
Kaiser, Robert J. 1997. "Homeland-Making in Russia's Republics." Paper presented at the annual conference of the American Association for the Advancement of Slavic Studies, Seattle, WA.
Kaplan, Robert. 1993. *Balkan Ghosts: A Journey through History*. New York: St. Martin's.
Karklins, Rasma. 1986. *Ethnic Relations in the USSR*. Boston: Allen and Unwin.
Kasimov, Aleksandr. n.d. "Respublika Khakassia: Neizvestnaia Teritoria." Unpublished manuscript.
Kasimov, S. F. 1991. "O narusheniiakh leninskoi natsionalnoi politiki v Bashkirskoi ASSR (20–30e gody)." In *Stranitsy istorii Bashkirskoi respubliki: Novye fakty, vzgliady, otsenky*. Ufa: Institute of History, Language, and Literature.
Khalim, Aidar. 1991. *Kniga Pechali*. Vilnius: Mosklas.
Khusainova, G. T. 1991. "Natsionalnye dvizheniia v Bashkirii v kontse 80-kh C nachale 90-kh godov." In *Stranitsy Istorii Bashkirskoi Respubliki*, ed. V. V. Boltushkin. Ufa: Russian Academy of Sciences.
Khuzangai A. P., and A. K. Kirillov. 1993. *Problemy Vozrozhdeniia i Razvitiia Chuvashskogo Iazyka*. Cheboksary: Chuvash Republic Supreme Soviet.
Kim, Jae-on, and Charles W. Mueller. 1978a. *Introduction to Factor Analysis: What It Is and How to Do It*. Beverly Hills, CA: Sage.
Kim, Jae-on, and Charles W. Mueller. 1978b. *Factor Analysis: Statistical Methods and Practical Issues*. Beverly Hills, CA: Sage.
Kitschelt, Herbert. 1995. "Formation of Party Cleavages in Post-Communist Democracies." *Party Politics* 1 (4): 447–72.
Komarova, G. A. 1994. *Khronika mezhnatsional'nykh konfliktov v Rossii: 1991 god*. Moscow: Institute of Ethnology and Anthropology.
Komarova, G. A. 1996. *Khronika zhizni natsional'nostei v SSSR: 1990 god*. Moscow: Institute of Ethnology and Anthropology.
Komarova, G. A. 1997. *Khronika zhizni natsionalnostei nakanune raspada SSSR: 1989 god*. Moscow: Institute of Ethnology and Anthropology.
Konstitutsiia (osnovnoi zakon) Chuvashskoi avtonomnoi sovetskoi sotsialisticheskoi respubliki. 1930. Cheboksary: Central Executive Committee.
Konstitutsiia (osnovnoi zakon) Chuvashskoi avtonomnoi sovetskoi sotsialisticheskoi respubliki. 1961. Cheboksary: Chuvash State Publishing.
Kostiakov, Alexander. 1990. "Tun Znachit Pervyi." *Tyyr* (1): 10–12.
Kowalewski, David. 1980. "Protest for National Rights in the USSR: Characteristics and Consequences." *Nationalities Papers* 8 (2): 179–94.
Krasner, Stephen. 1988. "Sovereignty: An Institutionalist Perspective." *Comparative Political Studies* 21(1): 66–94.
Kriesi, Hanspeter, Ruud Koopmans, Jan Willem Duyvendak, and Marco G. Giugni. 1995. *New Social Movements in Western Europe: A Comparative Analysis*. Minneapolis: University of Minnesota Press.

Kulchik, Iuri. 1992. *Etnopoliticheskie protsessy v Bashkortostane.* Moscow: Cultural Initiative Foundation.
Kulsharipov, Marat. 1992. *Z. Validov i Obrazovanie Bashkirskoi Avtonomnoi Respubliki.* Ufa: Bashkir Book Publishing.
Kuper, Leo. 1969. "Plural Societies: Perspectives and Problems." In *Pluralism in Africa*, ed. Leo Kuper and M. G. Smith. Berkeley: University of California Press.
Kuznetsov, I. D., ed. 1967. *Istoriia Chuvashskoi ASSR*, Vol. 2. Cheboksary: Chuvash State Publishing.
Laitin, David D. 1988. "Language Games." *Comparative Politics* 20: 289–302.
Laitin, David D. 1991. "The National Uprisings in the Soviet Union." *World Politics* 44 (1): 139–77
Laitin, David D. 1998. *Identity in Formation.* Ithaca, NY: Cornell University Press.
Lapidoth, Ruth Eschelbacher. 1997. *Autonomy: Flexible Solutions to Ethnic Conflicts.* Washington, DC: United States Institute of Peace Press.
Lofland, John. 1996. *Social Movement Organizations.* New York: Aldine de Gruyter.
Lublin, David. 1998. "Context and Francophone Support for Quebec Sovereignty." Paper presented at the annual meeting of the American Political Science Association, Boston, MA.
Luong, Pauline Jones. 1998. "Tatarstan: Elite Bargaining and Ethnic Separatism." In *Growing Pains: Russian Democracy and the Election of 1993*, ed. Timothy J. Colton and Jerry F. Hough. Washington, DC: Brookings Institution Press.
Luong, Pauline Jones. 2002. *Institutional Change and Continuity in Post-Soviet Central Asia: Power, Perceptions, and Pacts.* New York: Cambridge University Press.
Malik, Hafeez. 1994. "Tatarstan's Treaty with Russia." *Journal of South Asian and Middle Eastern Studies* 18 (2): 1–36.
Maliutin, S. 1994. "O programme vozrozhdeniia i razvitiia naroda," *Vestnik Chuvashskoi Natsionalnoi Akademii* (2) : 44–50.
Martin, Terry D. 2001. *An Affirmative Action Empire: Nations and Nationalism in the Soviet Union, 1923–1939.* Ithaca, NY: Cornell University Press.
Materialy Uchreditelnogo S'ezda. 1989. Kazan: Tatar Public Center.
McAdam, Doug. 1982. *Political Process and the Development of Black Insurgency, 1930–1970.* Chicago: University of Chicago Press.
McAdam, Doug. 1986. "Recruitment to High-Risk Activism: The Case of Freedom Summer." *American Journal of Sociology* 92: 64–90.
McAdam, Doug, and Ronnelle Paulsen. 1993. "Specifying the Relationship between Social Ties and Activism." *American Journal of Sociology* 99 (3): 640–67.
McAdam, Doug, John D. McCarthy, and Mayer N. Zald. 1996. "Introduction." In *Comparative Perspectives on Social Movements*, ed. Doug McAdam, John D. McCarthy, and Mayer N. Zald. New York: Cambridge University Press.
McAuley, Mary. 1997. *Russia's Politics of Uncertainty.* New York: Cambridge University Press.
Meadwell, Hudson. 1998. "Nations, States, Unions: Institutional Design and State-Breaking in the Developed West." Paper presented at the annual meeting of the American Political Science Association, Boston, MA.
Meshalkin, P. N., ed. 1963. *Ocherki istorii Khakassii sovetskogo perioda.* Abakan: Khakass Publishing.

Mitiukov, M. A. 1973. "Razvitie sovetskoi gosudarstvennosti Khakasskogo naroda." In *Torzhestvo Leninskoi natsionalnoi politiki*. Abakan: Khakass Institute of Language, Literature, and History.
Mukhametshin, Farid, ed. 1995. *Respublika Tatarstan: Ot Referenduma do Dogovora*. Kazan: Republic of Tatarstan Supreme Soviet.
Mukhametshin, F. Kh., A. P. Lozovoi, N. B. Bakirov, G. A. Isaev, Iu. Iu. Komlev, and R. S. Salakhova. 1993. *Tatarstan na Perekrestke Mnenii*. Kazan: Tatarstan Supreme Soviet.
Mukhametshin, R. 1993. *Tatary i Tatarstan*. Kazan: Kazan Book Publishing.
Murzabulatov, M. V. 1995. *Bashkortostan i Bashkiry v Zerkale Statistiki*. Ufa: Russian Academy of Sciences.
Nahaylo, Bohdan, and Victor Swoboda. 1990. *Soviet Disunion: A History of the Nationalities Problem in the USSR*. New York: Free Press.
Neuberger, Benyamin. 1995. "Colonialism and the Creation of Ethnicity in Africa." *Migration* 28: 55–65.
Offe, Claus. 1991. "Capitalism by Democratic Design? Democratic Theory Facing the Triple Transition in East Central Europe." *Social Research* 58 (4): 865–93.
Olcott, Martha Brill. 1997. "Kazakhstan: Pushing for Eurasia." In *New States, New Politics: Building the Post-Soviet Nations*, ed. Ian Bremmer and Ray Taras. New York: Cambridge University Press.
Olson, Mancur. 1965. *The Logic of Collective Action*. Cambridge, MA: Harvard University Press.
O'Donnell, Guillermo, and Philippe C. Schmitter. 1986. *Transitions from Authoritarian Rule: Tentative Conclusions about Uncertain Democracies*. Baltimore: Johns Hopkins University Press.
Pechat' Rossiiskoi Federatsii v 1991 godu. Moscow: all-Union Book Chamber.
Pimenov, V. V., and V. P. Ivanov. 1991. *Etnokulturnye protsessy v Povolzhie i Priuralie*. Cheboksary: State Institute of Language, History and Economics Press.
Pipes, Richard. 1964. *The Formation of the Soviet Union*, rev. ed. Cambridge, MA: Harvard University Press.
Posen, Barry R. 1993. "The Security Dilemma and Ethnic Conflict." *Survival* 35 (1): 27–47.
Pribylovskii, Vladimir. 1993. "Kazan." In *Vybory-1989*, ed. Anatolii Papp. Moscow: Panorama.
Prokopev, I. P., T. A. Akhazov, V. D. Dimitriev, S. M. Isliukov, and I. D. Kuznetsov. 1974. *Ocherki istorii Chuvashskoi oblastnoi organizatsii KPSS*. Cheboksary: Chuvash Publishing.
Przeworski, Adam. 1991. *Democracy and the Market: Political and Economic Reforms in Eastern Europe and Latin America*. New York: Cambridge University Press.
Putnam, Robert. 1988. "Diplomacy and Domestic Politics: The Logic of Two-Level Games." *International Organization* 42 (3): 427–60.
Putnam, Robert. 1993. *Making Democracy Work: Civic Traditions in Modern Italy*. Princeton. NJ: Princeton University Press.
Rabushka, Alvin, and Kenneth Shepsle. 1972. *Politics in Plural Societies: A Theory of Democratic Instability*. Columbus, OH: Charles E. Merrill.
Roeder, Philip. 1991. "Soviet Federalism and Ethnic Mobilization." *World Politics* 43: 196–232.

Rorlich, Azade-Ayse. 1986. *The Volga Tatars: A Profile in National Resilience*. Stanford, CA: Hoover Institution Press.

Rucht, Dieter. 1996. "The Impact of National Contexts on Social Movement Structures: A Cross-Movement and Cross-National Comparison." In *Comparative Perspectives on Social Movements: Political Opportunities, Mobilizing Structures, and Cultural Framings*, ed. Doug McAdam, John D. McCarthy, and Mayer N. Zald. New York: Cambridge University Press.

Rywkin, Michael. 1990. *Moscow's Muslim Challenge*. New York: M. E. Sharpe.

Safin, Fail'. 1997. *Printsipy Etnopoliticheskogo Razvitiia Bashkortostana*. Moscow: Russian Academy of Sciences.

Sattarova, Z. N. 1990. "Nekotoroye sotsialnye problemy migratsii v BASSR." In *Sotsiologiia sotsialno politicheskikh problem obnovleniia sotsialisma*. Ufa: Russian Academy of Sciences.

Schwartz, Lee. 1990. "Regional Population Redistribution and National Homelands in the USSR." In *Soviet Nationalities Policies: Ruling Ethnic Groups in the USSR*, ed. Henry R. Huttenbach. New York: Mansell Publishing.

Sergeev, T. S., and Ia. N. Zaitsev. 1995. *Istoriia i kultura Chuvashii: Vazhneishie sobytiia, daty*. Cheboksary: Chuvashia Press.

Shakurov, R. Z. 1996. *Bashkortostan: Kratkaia entsiklopedia*. Ufa: Bashkir Encyclopedia.

Sharypova, N. Kh. 1993. "Problema izucheniia Tatarskogo iazyka v respublike." In *Mezhetnicheskie i Mezhkonfessionalnye Otnosheniia v Respublike Tatarstan*, ed. Ia. G. Abdullin et al. Kazan: Office of the President.

Sheehy, Ann. 1991. "Ethnographic Developments and the Soviet Federal System." In *Soviet Federalism: Nationalism and Economic Decentralization*, ed. Alastair McAuley. New York: St. Martin's Press.

Shnirelman, Victor A. 1996. *Who Gets the Past? Competition for Ancestor among Non-Russian Intellectuals in Russia*. Washington, DC: Woodrow Wilson Center Press.

Silver, Brian. 1974. "The Status of National Minority Languages in Soviet Education: An Assessment of Recent Changes." *Soviet Studies* 26: 28–40.

Silver, Brian. 1978. "Language Policy and the Linguistic Russification of Soviet Nationalities." In *Soviet Nationality Policies and Practices*, ed. Jeremy R. Azrael. New York: Praeger.

Simon, Gerhard. 1991. *Nationalism and Policy toward the Nationalities in the Soviet Union*. Boulder, CO: Westview.

Slezkine, Yuri. 1994a. *Arctic Mirrors: Russia and the Small Peoples of the North*. Ithaca, NY: Cornell University Press.

Slezkine, Yuri. 1994b. "The USSR as a Communal Apartment, or How a Socialist State Promoted Ethnic Particularism." *Slavic Review* 53 (2): 413–52.

Slocum, John. 1997. "Homeopathic Nationalism: The Case of Tatarstan." Paper presented at the annual convention of the Association for the Study of Nationalities, New York City.

Smith, Graham, ed. 1996. *The Nationalities Question in the Post-Soviet States*, 2nd ed. New York: Longman.

Smith, M. G. 1974. *The Plural Society in the British West Indies*. Berkeley: University of California Press.

Snow, David A., Louis A. Zurcher, Jr., and Sheldon Ekland-Olson. 1980. "Social Networks and Social Movements: A Microstructural Approach to Differential Recruitment." *American Sociological Review* 45: 787–801.
Snow, David A., E. Burke Rochford, Jr., Steven Worden, and Robert Benford. 1986. "Frame Alignment Processes, Micromobilization, and Movement Participation." *American Sociological Review* 51: 464–81.
Snow, David A., and Robert Benford. 1992. "Master Frames and Cycles of Protest." In *Frontiers in Social Movement Theory*, ed. Aldon D. Morris and Carol McClurg Mueller. New Haven, CT: Yale University Press.
Solnick, Steven. 1995. "Federal Bargaining in Russia." *East European Constitutional Review* 4 (4): 52–8.
Sperling, Valerie. 1997. "Engendering Transition: The Women's Movement in Contemporary Russia." Ph.D. dissertation, University of California, Berkeley.
Spirin, I. A. 1995. "Etnokratiia v Tatarstane." In *Etnopolitika na poroge XXI veka*. Kazan: Office of the President.
Stalin, Josef. 1950 [1913]. *Marksism i Natsionalnyi Vopros*. Moscow: State Political Literature Publishing.
Stoner-Weiss, Kathryn. 1999. "Central Weakness and Provincial Autonomy: Observations on the Devolution Process in Russia." *Post-Soviet Affairs* 15 (1): 87–106.
Suny, Ronald. 1992. "State, Civil Society, and Ethnic Cultural Consolidation in the USSR – Roots of the National Question." In *From Union to Commonwealth*, ed. Gail Lapidus and Victor Zaslavsky, with Philip Goldman. New York: Cambridge University Press.
Suny, Ronald. 1993. *The Revenge of the Past*. Stanford, CA: Stanford University Press.
Taagepera, Rein. 1993. *Estonia: Return to Independence*. Boulder, CO: Westview Press.
Tafaev, Gennadii. 1991a. *Chuvashskaia SSR v Usloviakh Mnogopartiinosti*. Cheboksary: Chuvash State University Press.
Tafaev, Gennady, ed. 1991b. *Programmnye Documenty Politicheskikh Partii I Dvizhenii*. Cheboksary: Chuvash State University Press.
Tarrow, Sidney. 1992. "Mentalities, Political Cultures, and Collective Action Frames: Constructing Meanings through Action." In *Frontiers in Social Movement Theory*, ed. Aldon D. Morris and Carol McClurg Mueller. New Haven, CT: Yale University Press.
Tarrow, Sidney. 1994. *Power in Movement: Social Movements, Collective Action and Mass Politics in the Modern State*. Cambridge: Cambridge University Press.
Tarrow, Sidney. 1996. "States and Opportunities: The Political Structuring of Social Movements." In *Comparative Perspectives on Social Movements*, ed. Doug McAdam, John D. McCarthy, and Mayer N. Zald. New York: Cambridge University Press.
Tatar Public Centre. 1990. *Central Asian Survey* 9: 155–65.
Taylor, Verta, and Nancy E. Whittier. 1992. "Collective Identity in Social Movement Communities: Lesbian Feminist Mobilization." In *Frontiers in Social Movement Theory*, ed. Aldon D. Morris and Carol McClurg Mueller. New Haven, CT: Yale University Press.
Terentieva, I. V., and A. S. Alishev. 1993. *Mnogonatsionalnyi Tatarstan*. Kazan: Office of the President.
Thelen, Kathleen, and Sven Steinmo. 1992. "Historical Institutionalism in Comparative Politics." In *Structuring Politics: Historical Institutionalism in Comparative*

Analysis, ed. Sven Steinmo, Kathleen Thelen, and Frank Longstreth. New York: Cambridge University Press.

Tilly, Charles. 1992. "How to Detect, Describe, and Explain Repertoires of Contention." (Working Paper No. 150.) New York: Center for Studies of Social Change, New School for Social Research.

Treisman, Daniel. 1996. "The Politics of Intergovernmental Transfers in Post-Soviet Russia." *British Journal of Political Science* 26: 299–335.

Treisman, Daniel. 1997. "Russia's Ethnic Revival: The Separatist Activism of Regional Leaders in a Postcommunist Order." *World Politics* 49: 212–49.

Treisman, Daniel. 1998. "Fiscal Redistribution in a Fragile Federation: Moscow and the Regions in 1994." *British Journal of Political Science* 28: 185–222.

Tuguzhekova, V. N. 1993. "Iz istorii Khakassii. Sovetskii period. 1917–1991 gg." Abakan.

Uraksin, Z. G., and R. M. Valiakhmetov. 1995. "Gosudarstvennaia programma Vozrozhdenie i Razvitie Bashkirskogo Naroda." Ufa.

Urban, Michael. 1997. *The Rebirth of Politics in Russia*. New York: Cambridge University Press.

Voskhodov, I. I., and G. A. Komarova. 1994. "Predvybornaia Situatsiia v Chuvashskoi Respublike." (Working Paper No. 66.) Moscow: Institute of Ethnology and Anthropology, Russian Academy of Sciences.

Voskhodov, I. I., and G. A. Komarova. 1995. "Predvybornaia Situatsiia v Chuvashskoi Respublike." In *Razvivaiushchiisia Elektorat Rossii*, Vol. 2, ed. Mikhail Guboglo. Moscow: Russian Academy of Sciences.

Vujacic, Veljko. 1996. "Historical Legacies, Nationalist Mobilization, and Political Outcomes in Russia and Serbia: A Weberian View." *Theory and Society* 25 (4): 763–801.

Walker, Edward. 1996. "The Dog That Didn't Bark: Tatarstan and Asymmetrical Federalism in Russia." *Harriman Review* 9: 1–35.

Wallich, Christine I., ed. 1994. *Russia and the Challenge of Fiscal Federalism*. Washington, DC: World Bank.

Wilson, Andrew. 1996. *Ukrainian Nationalism in the 1990s*. New York: Cambridge University Press.

Yashar, Deborah. 1998. "Contesting Citizenship: Indigenous Movements and Democracy in Latin America." *Comparative Politics* 31 (1): 23–42.

Zakiev, M. Z. 1995. *Tatary: Problemy istorii i iazyka*. Kazan: Tatarstan Academy of Science.

Zaslavsky, Victor, and Yuri Luryi. 1979. "The Passport System in the USSR and Changes in Soviet Society." *Soviet Union* 6 (2): 137–53.

Zdravomyslova, Elena. 1996. "Opportunities and Framing in the Transition to Democracy: The Case of Russia." In *Comparative Perspectives on Social Movements*, ed. Doug McAdam, John D. McCarthy, and Mayer N. Zald. New York: Cambridge University Press.

Index

Abakan, 45, 65, 66–7, 130–1, 146
Abakan State Pedagogical Institute, 42, 66
Africa, 28, 262
Aidak, Arkadi, 63
Ak Tirme, 58–9
Almetevsk, 124–5
Armenia, 88
August 1991 coup, 55, 72, 89, 123, 130, 186
Azatlyk, 16, 171
Azerbaijan, 79

Baimak, 140
Bairamova, Fauzia, 1, 56, 92, 124, 135
Balkars, 234n1, 237n2, 240, 244
Baltic republics, 14, 56, 60–1
Bashkir clans, 59–60
Bashkir National Center "Ural," 59–60, 71, 99, 101, 129, 138, 154–5, 203–4, 212
Bashkir National Party (BNP), 96
Bashkir State University, 41, 59
Bashkortostan Academy of Sciences, 42, 100
Beissinger, Mark, 3, 18n17, 120–2, 266n5
boundaries, territorial, 12, 83, 85–6, 95, 102, 114, 115–16, 262
Brubaker, Rogers, 3, 5, 29n4, 31, 52, 83
Buddhism, 248, 252–3, 255
Bulgaria, 261
Bulgars, 20, 88, 103–4
Buriats, 237, 240, 244, 248

Central Asia, 88
Cheboksary, 45, 142–3
Chechnya, 92, 233n55
Chon Chobi, 74–5, 114n105
Chuvash National Congress, 104, 107, 143
Chuvash Public Cultural Center (CPCC), 62, 64, 107, 141, 144

Chuvash Rebirth Party (CRP), 61–4, 130, 143
Chuvash State University, 42, 61, 193, 220
collective identity, 17, 52–3, 57, 170, 185, 190, 199, 258, 259
definition of, 52
Colton, Tim, 18n18, 48n24, 157–60, 163, 172–5, 186, 188, 234, 256
Connor, Walker, 29n4, 31n11, 77, 90n25
Communist Party, 9n9, 40, 46, 48, 77, 120
in Bashkortostan, 8, 34, 46, 60, 71, 126
in Chuvashia, 35, 46, 61–2, 72–3, 129–30, 142–4, 193–5, 197
and elections, 130, 133–7, 142–6
in Khakassia, 35, 47, 64–7, 74, 145–6
membership in, and support for nationalism, 50, 51, 170, 173, 180, 193, 195, 197, 248–9, 254
in Tatarstan, 34, 54–7, 69–70, 134–7, 180, 186
Congress of People's Deputies of the Russian Federation, 132, 142
Congress of People's Deputies of the Soviet Union, 56, 63, 85, 91, 132, 134, 138, 141, 144–5, 147
Constitution of the Russian Federation, 35–6, 132, 136, 139–40, 144, 147, 208
Constitution of the Soviet Union, 106
Coordinating Center for Creative Youth (CCCY), 61–3
Czechoslovakia, 103, 261

Dagestan, 240, 244
Democratic Alternative, 61–2, 129, 141
Democratic Party of Russia, 125
Democratic Russia (Khakassia), 113, 146–7, 156

293

democracy movements, 50–3, 267
  in Bashkortostan, 60, 126–7
  in Chuvashia, 60–2, 72–3, 129–30, 141–4
  in Khakassia, 64–5, 67, 109–10, 120, 131, 144–7, 205
  in Tatarstan, 56, 123–5, 135, 136
democratization, 7, 8, 63, 69, 87, 98, 114, 120, 122, 138, 231, 257, 260, 265–6
demonstration effects, 14
demonstrations, *see* protest demonstrations

elections
  in Bashkortostan, 138–40
  boycotts of, 136–7
  in Chuvashia, 140–4
  in Khakassia, 144–7
  as show of support for nationalist movements, 133, 137–8, 147–8
  in Tatarstan, 133–8
environmental damage, as source of support for nationalism, 79–80, 89, 94, 101, 109, 111, 126–7, 267
Estonia, 50, 261
ethnic identity, 3, 4, 12, 15, 17–18, 28, 51, 92, 166, 168–72, 185, 191, 197, 198, 233, 259, 269–70
  definition of, 3
  and native-language education, 37, 111, 254
ethnic institutions, 2–3, 5–6, 12, 15, 18–20, 25, 28–9, 37–48, 49, 68, 76, 77, 84, 166, 168–9, 198–9, 233, 256, 257, 259–70
  in Bashkortostan, 34, 41–2
  in Chuvashia, 34–5, 42
  institutionalization of, 36, 82–3
  in Khakassia, 35–6, 42–3
  passport listing of, 13, 15, 17, 24, 28, 29–30, 32, 38, 86–7, 98, 102, 117, 173n4, 258–9, 270–1
  in Tatarstan, 33–4, 41
ethno-federalism
  effect on mobilization, 83–5, 168–9
  in the Soviet Union, 12, 25, 29, 30–3, 36, 43
  see also ethnic institutions
event analysis, 18n17, 24, 121–2

Federation Treaty, 128, 139, 208, 264
Fedorov, Nikolai, 141, 143, 230
frames
  cultural revival frame, 78–9, 80–1, 93–4, 98–100, 105–8, 110–12
  definition of, 11
  economic autonomy frame, 79–80, 94–5, 100–2, 112–13
  and ethnic institutions, 115–17
  role in nationalist mobilization, 12, 78, 95–6, 102, 108, 114

sovereignty frame, 81–2, 89–92, 103–4, 109–10

Georgia, 50, 79, 261
Giuliano, Elise, 183, 184n10
glasnost, 7, 14, 54–5, 103, 120
Gorbachev, Mikhail, 7, 28, 49, 50, 71, 120, 130, 266, 269
Graney, Katherine, 214–15

Hale, Henry, 140
Hirsch, Francine, 29–30, 269
Horowitz, Donald, 4n3, 12, 37
Hroch, Miroslav, 50, 167–8
hunger strikes, 1, 72, 118, 120–1, 124–5, 127, 128, 130
Huntington, Samuel, 4n3, 170n2

Iakovlev, Ivan, 61–2, 105, 107, 194
independence, demands for, 81–2, 89–90, 92, 97, 104–5, 150–1, 154
Ingush, 237, 240, 244
institutes of language and history, 32, 37, 39–41, 106
  in Bashkortostan, 42
  in Chuvashia, 42, 61–4, 193, 222
  and the creation of nationalist movements, 9–10, 51–3, 171, 198–9, 258–60
  in Khakassia, 42–3, 66
  in Tatarstan, 41, 54–5, 183
institutions, 3, 9, 27–8, 265–6, 269
  definition of, 3, 27
Iskhakov, Damir, 38n15, 54, 55n3, 56, 57, 79n5, 183–5, 186n11
Islam, 23
  among Bashkirs, 188, 190–1, 197, 256
  and support for nationalism, 170, 173n5, 197, 235, 244, 248–9, 253, 255
  among Tatars, 20, 33–4, 93, 178, 180, 184, 186, 197, 214
Ittifaq, 56–7, 70, 78, 89–90, 92–5, 124–5, 135, 151
Iukhma, Mikhail, 144
Ivandaev, Valerii, 66n40, 109, 113n101, 114n104, 146, 226n43

Kabardins, 234n1, 237, 240
Kadyrov, Rafis, 139
Kaiser, Robert J., 227–9
Kalmyks, 235, 237, 244, 248
Karelians, 235, 240
Kazakhstan, 62
Kazan, 1, 20, 22, 41, 55, 57, 88, 93, 124–5, 135, 183–4
Kazan State University, 10, 41, 54, 197
Khakass Congresses, 74, 110–14
Khakass Cultural Center, 146
Khakimov, Rafael, 55, 89, 93n32, 94n35

Index

Khuzangai, Atner, 61–3, 73n52, 104n71, 106n76, 142–3, 220
Komarova, Galina, 121–2, 143–4, 230
Komi, 235, 240
Komsomol, 16, 61, 63–4, 65, 171
korenizatsiia (indigenization), 46–8, 227–31
Kostiakov, Alexander, 64n34, 65, 67, 74n54, 110n90, 112n96, 113n98, 145–6, 195
Krasnoyarsk *krai*, 36, 65, 74, 109–10, 145, 149, 156, 204
Kubarev, Eduard, 142–3
Kulsharipov, Marat, 96, 97n43, 98n47, 101n65
Kurakov, Lev, 143–4
Kyrgyzstan, 88

Laitin, David, 4n4, 5, 6, 15, 18n18, 30n5, 65, 172–5, 186, 188, 210, 234, 273n1
land privatization, 95, 101, 112–13
language policy, 210–13
language revival, 12
  in Bashkortostan, 99–100, 152–3, 212–13, 221–2
  in Chuvashia, 106–7, 156, 210, 220–1
  in Khakassia, 111, 212, 222
  in Tatarstan, 93, 211–12, 218–20
Latin America, 262–3
Latvia, 50, 88, 116
Lenin, Vladimir, 33, 77, 90, 115
liberalization, 3, 5, 7–8, 11, 24, 31, 40, 49–50, 53, 54–5, 58–9, 75, 84, 120, 131, 254, 258, 260, 263, 266–9
linguistic assimilation, *see* Russification
Lithuania, 124
Luong, Pauline Jones, 28, 136n13, 137, 265n4

Mari, 235, 240
McAdam, Doug, 7, 9, 11, 52, 53, 266
McAuley, Mary, 55, 137n14
Milli Mejlis, 92, 165
Mitiukov, Mikhail, 35–6, 42n20, 47, 147
Mordva, 235, 237, 240
Moscow, 2, 6, 8, 18, 20, 22, 33, 34, 36, 56, 79–80, 100, 120, 122, 125, 127, 132, 136–7, 139–40, 156, 175, 201, 205, 208, 209, 227, 263, 264
Muliukov, Marat, 55, 57n9, 88n16, 134

Naberezhnye Chelny, 20, 41, 91, 124, 135, 150–1, 163, 183, 218
national symbols, 36, 104–5, 130, 214–16
nationalism
  cultural (primordialist) theories of, 4, 29, 77–8, 268
  instrumentalist theories of, 4–5, 17, 19–20, 268

nationalist mobilization
  causes of, 2–3, 269
  popular support for, 15, 165–6
  repression of, 7–8, 14, 24, 50, 118–20, 264, 267
nationalist movements
  and academic institutions, 9–10, 39–43, 51, 66, 198, 259–60
  in Bashkortostan, 58–60, 71–2, 96–103, 126–9, 138–40, 152–5, 186–91
  in Chuvashia, 60–4, 72–3, 103–8, 129–30, 140–4, 155–6, 191–5
  and the Communist Party, 55
  and the democracy movement, 56, 60–2
  and ethnic institutions, 2–3, 4–5, 10–11, 25, 28, 199, 257–60, 269–71
  formation of, 51, 54–5, 58–9, 60–2, 64–5
  and governing elites, 2, 5–6, 8, 60
  influence on government policy, 232–3, 264–5
  in Khakassia, 64–8, 73–5, 108–15, 130–1, 144–7, 156, 195–6
  and the media, 14
  recruitment, 9–10, 15–18, 183–4
  in Tatarstan, 54–8, 69–70, 87–96, 122–6, 133–8, 149–52, 178–86
nationalist violence, 1, 14, 48, 67, 89, 92, 120–1, 122, 125, 128, 131–2, 257, 264
native-language education, 15–17, 23, 31–2, 37–40, 48, 169, 171–2, 173–4, 181, 196–9, 225–7, 254–6, 259
  in Bashkortostan, 38, 186–91, 225–6
  in Chuvashia, 39, 224–5
  in Khakassia, 39, 226
  in Tatarstan, 38, 183–4, 223–4
native-language newspapers, 43–4, 218

Olson, Mancur 49
Osetians, 237, 240

perestroika, 3, 18, 29, 34, 40, 43, 47–8, 49, 59, 77, 86, 120, 262
political opportunity structure, 7–8, 50, 257–8, 267–8
  and the organization of nationalist movements, 68–75
popular front, 56, 61, 64, 75, 124, 260
  definition of, 49
Popular Front of Tataria, 56, 124
Prokopev, Leonid, 142–3
protest demonstrations, 1, 7, 14, 119–32
  in Bashkortostan, 126–9
  in Chuvashia, 129–30
  definition of, 120
  environmental, 7, 122, 126, 129
  in Khakassia, 130–1
  in Tatarstan, 122–6

public opinion surveys
    awareness of the nationalist movement, 158–9
    in Bashkortostan, 152–5, 186–91
    in Chuvashia, 155–6, 191–5
    in Khakassia, 156, 195–6
    and support for cultural revival, 158–60, 161–2, 174–8, 180–1, 186–8, 192–3, 197, 235–9, 240, 244, 248, 249, 252
    and support for nationalism, 16, 18, 119, 148–9, 163, 258
    and support for regional separatism, 160, 162–4, 175–8, 180–1, 186–8, 193, 197, 240–4, 248, 253–4
    in Tatarstan, 149–52, 178–86

Rakhimov, Murtaza, 60, 71, 128, 139–40, 278
referenda
    on Bashkortostan sovereignty, 97, 139
    on the preservation of the USSR, 124
    on the Russian constitution, 132, 136–7, 140
    on Tatarstan sovereignty, 1, 89, 128, 133, 135–7
republic constitutions, 31–6, 70, 104, 206–9, 216
    Bashkortostan, 34, 127
    Chuvashia, 35, 203, 230
    Khakassia, 74, 205
    Tatarstan, 33, 70, 222, 227
republic language laws, 62, 81, 99, 106, 148, 152–3, 209, 210–13, 216, 218–23, 228
Roeder, Philip, 4n4, 5, 48
Russian Orthodox Church, 23, 34, 105, 170, 194, 196–7
Russian Soviet Federated Socialist Republic (RSFSR), 31, 153
Russian State Duma, 132, 136–7, 139, 140, 143–4, 147
Russification, 10, 13, 32–3, 37–8, 65, 78–82, 85–7, 97–9, 102–3, 106, 108, 110–11, 117, 183–5, 191, 193–4, 230, 233, 259, 269–71

Sakha, 235, 237, 240, 244
Sakharov, Andrei, 13n12, 85, 95
self-determination, 13, 31, 77, 81, 90, 96–9, 106, 109–10, 116, 175, 201–9, 215
Shaimiev, Mintimer, 69, 70, 125, 134, 264
Sibai, 45, 229
Silver, Brian, 32, 37–8, 86, 255
Simon, Gerhard, 31, 46, 48
Slezkine, Yuri, 3, 28, 29n4, 30n8, 32, 37, 46, 269

social movement organizations, 49, 51–3, 75
social networks, 9, 15–18, 24, 26, 48, 49, 53, 54–9, 63, 66–7, 75–6, 166, 168–72, 197, 258–9, 262–3, 269
sovereignty
    declarations of, 1, 62, 89, 104, 113, 124, 127, 150, 154, 158–60, 175, 200, 201–5, 206, 208–9, 216, 223, 237, 240, 264
    economic, 13, 94–5, 100–2, 227
    political, 13, 31, 36, 83 88–94, 96–7, 103–7, 109–10, 116, 125–8, 150–2, 176–7, 190, 193–4, 207–8, 232
Sovereignty Committee, 57, 125
Spain, 262
Stalin, Joseph, 29–30, 109, 203–4
St. Petersburg (Leningrad), 56, 64–5, 67, 120, 130
Suny, Ronald, 3, 4n4, 29n4, 30
support for nationalist mobilization
    and age, 191, 254–5
    among Communists, 194
    among government officials, 185–6, 194, 195–6, 254
    among industrial workers, 172, 194, 197–8
    among intellectuals, 2, 9–10, 16, 40–1, 44, 52–3, 56–7, 65, 167, 170–1, 183, 193, 195, 254
    and level of education, 169, 255
    among migrants, 15, 17, 59, 172, 183, 191, 194, 254
    among Muslims, 184, 191
    and native-language knowledge, 180–3, 184–5, 188–90, 255
    and religion, 170, 194–5, 196, 197, 255
    among rural residents, 17, 59, 67, 171–2, 183–4, 191, 194, 196, 197, 254
    among students, 16, 59, 167, 171, 185, 191, 194, 195, 254
Supreme Soviet, 14, 32
    Bashkortostan, 46, 71, 127–8, 138–40, 154, 204
    Chuvashia, 62–3, 72, 106, 142, 144, 203, 210, 230
    Khakassia, 74–5, 112–13, 131, 146, 204, 231
    RSFSR, 33, 35–6, 106
    Tatarstan, 33, 46, 69–70, 92, 124–5, 133, 135, 137, 207, 211, 219
    USSR, 31n11, 33, 35–6

Tarrow, Sidney, 7n5, 11, 50, 78n1, 82
Tatar Public Center (TPC), 54–7, 70, 88–94, 124–5, 134–5, 151, 183–5
Tatar Public Center of Bashkortostan, 58
Tatar-speaking Bashkirs, 38, 97, 213
Tatarstan Academy of Sciences, 10, 41, 54, 93

Index

Treisman, Daniel, 6, 29n3, 36, 165, 263, 264
Troshkina, Galina, 145–6
Tun, 64–7, 74–5, 110–14, 131, 146, 156, 204
two-level games, 263–4
Tyvans, 235, 237, 240, 244, 248

Udmurts, 235, 237, 240
Ufa, 22, 33–4, 45, 86, 116, 126, 152, 154, 191, 230
Ukraine, 79, 86n10, 91
Union of Bashkir Youth, 16, 72, 128–9, 171

USSR Academy of Sciences, 40–2
Uzbekistan, 50, 79, 101

Volga-Ural Confederation, 34, 90, 175

writers' unions, 9, 44, 57, 61, 62, 64

Yashar, Deborah, 263
Yeltsin, Boris, 120, 127, 130, 139, 143, 264
Yugoslavia, 261–2

For EU product safety concerns, contact us at Calle de José Abascal, 56–1°, 28003 Madrid, Spain or eugpsr@cambridge.org.

www.ingramcontent.com/pod-product-compliance
Ingram Content Group UK Ltd.
Pitfield, Milton Keynes, MK11 3LW, UK
UKHW011322060825
461487UK00005B/269